Communities of Saint Martin

Communities of Saint Martin

LEGEND AND RITUAL IN MEDIEVAL TOURS

Sharon Farmer

Cornell University Press

ITHACA AND LONDON

First published 1991 by Cornell University Press.

International Standard Book Number 0-8014-2391-0
Library of Congress Catalog Card Number 90-43451
Printed in the United States of America
*Librarians: Library of Congress cataloging information
appears on the last page of the book.*

♾ The paper used in this book meets the minimum requirements of the American National Standard for Information Sciences—Permanence of Paper for Printed Library Materials, ANSI Z39.48–1984

Contents

Illustrations

Tables

Preface

This book concerns the relationship between group identities and cultural expression. Specifically, it examines three medieval communities—the town of Tours, the chapter of Saint-Martin in Tours, and the abbey of Marmoutier near Tours—and the ways in which they defined themselves, or were defined, through the cult of Saint Martin. Because the three communities drew on Martin's cult in different ways, my analysis serves to demonstrate, I hope, that culture is contested territory.

Sources from the early Middle Ages might lead us to believe that there was only one interpretation of Martin's cult. As I indicate in chapter 1, the bishops of fifth- and sixth-century Tours, who controlled the cult, created an idealized image of Tours as Martin's town, and of themselves—the heirs to Martin's see—as the rightful leaders of the community. By the late eleventh century, however, the canons of Saint-Martin and the monks of Marmoutier had gained control of Martin's cult, and they produced new legends and rituals that excluded the cathedral of Tours and its prelate from the symbolic urban community that Martin protected. The two houses also turned to Martin's cult in efforts to define their own corporations and to enhance the interests of their lay patrons. They were especially anxious to strengthen the internal cohesion of their communities, which social and political changes threatened to undermine.

Marmoutier and Saint-Martin used Martin's cult for similar reasons, but they differed in their internal structures and external ties and thus in the ways they elaborated and manipulated it. The cult of Saint Martin did not "mean" simply one thing. Rather, it leant itself to varying uses and interpretations.

By relating the manifold uses and meanings of a single saint's cult to its specific local contexts, I have attempted to elucidate how that cult served the practical, psychological, and spiritual needs of differ-

ent collective groups. Although my discussion focuses on the communities of Marmoutier and Saint-Martin, it also shows that Martin's
cult was associated with other groups as well—the comital lineages of
Blois and Anjou, the cathedral community of Tours, and the burghers of Tours. If this were an ideal world, I would have analyzed the
interpretations each of those groups gave to the cult. Unfortunately,
however, the sources speak with the voices of Marmoutier and Saint-
Martin alone.

Like many historians, I was drawn to my subject by personal
concerns and convictions, and in turn I found that my subject shaped
those concerns and convictions. As an undergraduate and graduate
student, I first took an interest in the study of religion because I was
both attracted to and disturbed by the propensity of Americans to
explain, confront, or escape social and political processes by refor-
mulating and reinterpreting their cultural and religious traditions. As
a woman who is also a professional academic, I have become increasingly aware that I myself and those whom I know, love, and
teach have been molded and affected by the cultural construction of
our feminine and masculine identities. Indeed, the more I think and
write about human society, the more I become convinced that we all
find meaning in, and are shaped by, the groups we belong to, either
voluntarily or involuntarily, and by the attitudes that we ourselves
and those around us hold concerning those groups. My own intellectual approach to knowledge and experience thus compels me to preface this work by acknowledging the people and groups who participated in its formation.

Three teachers especially contributed to my general attitude toward the past and enhanced my enthusiasm with their demand for
discipline. Lester Little, whose courses at Smith College first inspired
my interest in the relation between religion and society, has remained
a source of encouragement and advice and has provided enthusiastic
support for my work. Caroline W. Bynum, through her courses,
writings, and close readings of my earlier work and parts of this
book, has been a source of intellectual stimulation and emotional
courage. She has continually reminded me, moreover, that religion is
a matter of meaning and that language—my own, as well as that of
the people I study—is extremely important. Giles Constable patiently
advised me in the early stages. I am grateful for his meticulous readings and for the lesson that it takes enormous discipline, endeavor,
and caution to begin to make sense of the past.

Pierre Gasnault and Dom Guy Oury offered advice on the sources of the religious and institutional history of Touraine; Jacques Le Goff and Jean-Claude Schmitt helped with certain problems regarding miracle collections, exempla collections, and ghost stories; and Megan McLaughlin provided useful references on prayers for the dead. David Herlihy, Gabrielle Spiegel, Elizabeth Brown, Edward Muir, and Junius Martin were gracious in reading an early draft and generous in offering advice. Patrick Geary, Barbara Rosenwein, Bernard Bachrach, Geoffrey Koziol, Jeffrey Russell, Warren Hollister, Michael Burger, Barbara Abou-El-Haj, Ronald Sawyer, John Martin, Alan Kaplan, and Thomas Haskell read parts of the manuscript and made many useful comments. Caroline Bynum, Thomas Head, Geoffrey Koziol, Barbara Abou-El-Haj, and Quentin Skinner shared their unpublished work with me. John Ackerman at Cornell University Press has demonstrated tremendous faith in my work and provided support and encouragement when they were needed. I am grateful to them all.

For financial support, I owe a large debt to the Committee of General Scholarships and the Sheldon Fund at Harvard for providing me with a Sinclair Kennedy Traveling Fellowship; to Rice University and the Mellon Foundation for a two-year postdoctoral fellowship; and to the University of California at Santa Barbara for two Faculty Career Development Awards and financial support for ordering research materials, preparing art, and hiring research assistants. Those assistants included Miriam Davis, Michael Burger, and Richard Barton, whose careful help in preparing the manuscript saved me an enormous amount of time and energy.

The Interlibrary Loan department at SUNY Binghamton was especially resourceful in ferreting out books for me, and I am grateful to the library staffs at Rice University and UCSB as well. Madame Laurent, curator at the Bibliothèque Municipale of Tours, offered useful advice and was always cooperative in sending microfilms and photographs. I am also indebted to the photographic staff at the Bibliothèque Nationale, the research and photographic staffs at the Institut de Recherche et d'Histoire des Textes, and the staffs at the Bibliothèque Municipale of Charleville and the Archives d'Indre-et-Loire.

Portions of Chapter 4 appeared earlier in different form in my article "Persuasive Voices: Clerical Images of Medieval Wives," *Speculum* 61 (1986). Chapter 5 incorporates and augments material drawn from my article "Personal Perceptions, Collective Behavior: Twelfth-Century Suffrages for the Dead," published in *Persons in Groups: Social Behavior as Identity Formation in Medieval and Renaissance Europe,* edited by Richard C. Trexler. Medieval & Renaissance Texts & Studies 36. © Center for Medieval & Early Renaissance Studies, SUNY, Binghamton, 1985. I am grateful to the publishers for permission to reprint this material.

Finally, I thank my parents for their love and support and for the humane values that first shaped my approach to the world.

SHARON FARMER

Santa Barbara, California

Communities of Saint Martin

Introduction

In the past decade and a half historians have brought to light the various uses and interpretations that medieval men and women applied to the relics and cults of the saints. Early medieval bishops associated themselves with the supernatural power of saintly relics, thereby enhancing their own authority. Townspeople defended their communities from Germanic and Viking invaders by carrying the bodies of saints to the ramparts of decaying Roman towns. Monks recounted miracle stories in which their holy patrons wreaked vengeance upon knights who attacked their monasteries and threatened their possessions. The royal abbey of Saint-Denis legitimized royal power and helped to consolidate the collective identity of the French nation by associating the Capetian kings and their subjects with the cult of Saint Denis.[1]

The beliefs and rituals that medieval people focused upon the bones of holy dead persons illuminate a society in which perceptions of this world and the next were fundamentally different from our own. The relics of the saints were not inert bones, they *were* the saints, and those saints sometimes acted in ways that revealed specific and peculiar personalities. The relics of Saint Foy of Conques, for example, performed miracles that were consistent with the personality of a sometimes vain, sometimes playful little girl.[2]

Monks, peasants, kings, and burghers interacted with the bones of

---

1. Brown, *Cult of the Saints;* Van Dam, *Leadership and Community in Late Antique Gaul,* 119–40; Herrmann-Mascard, *Reliques des saints,* 217–21; Sigal, "Aspect du culte des saints: Le châtiment divin"; Head, "Andrew of Fleury and the Peace League of Bourges," 520–21; Spiegel, "Cult of St. Denis and Capetian Kingship"; Bournazel, "Suger and the Capetians"; Poly and Bournazel, "Couronne et mouvance: Institutions et représentations mentales." On bishops and saints and the uses of relics during the invasions, see below, chapter 1; on Saint Martin's role as patron saint of the kings of Francia, see chapters 1, 3, and 7.

2. Geary, *Furta Sacra;* Remensnyder, "Bernard of Angers and the *Liber Miraculorum Sancte Fidis*"; Ward, *Miracles and the Medieval Mind,* 36–42.

dead men and women just as they did with living persons. If a saint failed to deliver protection, a peasant might curse or beat that saint's reliquary, the inhabitants of a town might threaten abandonment and oblivion, or a community of monks or canons might "humiliate" the holy patron by placing the bones on the ground and surrounding them with thorns.[3]

In the chapters that follow I examine these kinds of beliefs and forms of behavior in a new way. Through a carefully contextualized local study of the cult of Saint Martin in Tours, I have sought to deepen our analytic understanding of two interrelated themes: the relation between cultural expression and group identity, and the "polysemic" nature of saints' cults and rituals.

The idea that symbols are "polysemic" is a concept anthropologists and historians borrowed from linguists. It suggests that the meaning of a cultural symbol or artifact is never predetermined. Symbols are open-ended; their significance is a matter of interpretation.[4] Thus, as Patrick Geary pointed out in his study of medieval narratives about stolen relics, the bones of dead persons have no intrinsic meaning. Rather, living communities interpret the bones, as well as the events and rituals associated with them.[5] It stands to reason, and indeed a number of historians have demonstrated, that the uses and interpretations of particular rituals and particular saints' cults changed over time.[6] Some historians have suggested, moreover, that different groups simultaneously interpreted the same relics and the same rituals in divergent ways.[7]

To date, however, studies of conflicting interpretations of saints' cults have emphasized that competing corporate groups used and manipulated relics and legends to enhance their claims to status and legitimacy. They have devoted less attention to how the specific inter-

---

3. Geary, "Humiliation of Saints"; Geary, "Coercion des saints dans la pratique religieuse médiévale." On townspeople threatening a saint with oblivion, see chapter 1 below.
4. Turner, *Forest of Symbols*, esp. 50–51; Bynum, "Introduction," *Gender and Religion*, 1–20.
5. Geary, *Furta Sacra*, 5 ff.
6. Koziol, "Pageants of Renewal: Translations of Saints in the Province of Reims"; Jones, *Saint Nicholas of Myra, Bari, and Manhattan*. Jacques Dubois's careful study of Saint Fiacre's cult in Brie reveals a number of significant changes over time, but his approach is more textual than interpretive: see *Sanctuaire monastique au Moyen Age*.
7. See, for example, Colette Beaune's discussion of resistance to Saint-Denis's claims concerning the royal saint, *Naissance de la nation France*, 83 ff.; and Geary on competing monastic communities, *Furta Sacra*, 68 ff. Some historians have evoked both popular and clerical points of view from individual texts that were written by clerics: see Remensnyder, "Bernard of Angers"; Schmitt, *Holy Greyhound*; and chapter 9 below.

nal structures and religious purposes of corporate groups affected their relations to the cult of saints, and they have tended to ignore questions of spirituality and psychological need. The culture of the group, as presented in these studies, is a matter of functional utility; polysemy is a matter of competing claims to status.

In much of this book, I too provide a functional analysis, focusing on the uses of Saint Martin's cult in an era of intense group competition—the eleventh century through the early thirteenth century. During that period, several competing communities and lineages in and around Tours appropriated or referred to Martin's cult in their attempts to enhance their status and prestige. Their texts and rituals represented Martin and his relation to the community in ways that were radically different from the representations that had been produced in the early Middle Ages.

As I show in chapter 1, the fifth- and sixth-century bishops of Tours created a powerful and pervasive image of an organic and harmonious civic community, united (or so they claimed) under the leadership of the dead bishop Martin and his living partner, the occupant of the episcopal see. Tours, as those bishops represented it, was Martin's town, and it was thus appropriate that Martin's successors—the bishops of Tours—should act as its leaders and protectors.

By the end of the eleventh century this cultic image of a unified secular and religious community no longer existed. Three competing religious institutions—the cathedral of Saint-Maurice, the Benedictine abbey of Marmoutier, and the canonical chapter of Saint-Martin—claimed roots that extended back to the saintly bishop. Moreover, the contentious burghers of the town also had a stake in the saint's cult. Indeed, on one level or another each of these competing collectivities defined itself, or was defined, by its relationship to Saint Martin. Only two of those communities, however, actively generated texts and rituals concerning Martin's cult: the abbey of Marmoutier, founded by Martin himself in the fourth century, and the chapter of canons at the basilica of Saint-Martin, which had possessed Martin's relics since the time of his death.

Community life was no more contentious in the eleventh and twelfth centuries than it had been in the fifth and sixth. Nevertheless, bishops in the earlier period held a monopoly over saints' cults; this was no longer true in the later period. And though violence remained a way of resolving disputes in the later period, church reformers and powerful rulers were interested in curbing uncontrolled force, assigning to the prince alone this means of keeping the peace and ensuring justice.[8] Ecclesiastical reformers and secular rulers—and town dwellers, too—thus encouraged the use of judicial procedures, in which verbal presentation and written documentation could help various claimants obtain their rights, property, and privileges. The eleventh-century conflict between the emperor and the pope, for example, was both a judicial conflict and, in Brian Tierney's words, a "war of propaganda."[9] This same expression characterizes the rhetorical disputes between Cistercians and Cluniacs in the twelfth century and among various proponents of the "true apostolic life." In this atmosphere of rationalized dispute, conflicting groups developed a heightened consciousness of their collective identities and of the need to lend written legitimacy to their claims to status, power, or independence. It was a time of fabricated customs and invented traditions.[10]

As I discuss in chapter 2, the monks of Marmoutier and the canons of Saint-Martin began to fabricate new customs and to invent new traditions in the late eleventh and twelfth centuries, when both were struggling to gain exemption from the jurisdiction of their archbishop. The monks and canons cooperated in creating rituals, feasts, and texts that effectively excluded the archbishop from those places and celebrations associated with Saint Martin and his sacred authority. In this way they shattered the unified image of their town that had been passed down to them from the early bishops of Tours. In their textual representations the canons and monks demonstrated that Saint Martin no longer belonged to the town as a whole, and he certainly did not belong to its archbishop. Rather, he was the patron and protector of Marmoutier and Saint-Martin, and in his capacity as protector he fended off evil enemies, including the archbishop of Tours. In their liturgical representations, the canons and monks transformed Tours from a unified ecclesiastical space, with the archbishop at its hub, into a divided space in which the most notable division served to

---

8. Dunbabin, *France in the Making*, 277 ff.

9. Tierney, *Crisis of Church and State*, 74. See also, on the propagandistic nature of many religious sources from this period, including the kinds examined in this book, Constable, "Papal, Imperial and Monastic Propaganda."

10. I have borrowed the concept of "invented traditions" from Hobsbawm and Ranger, *Invention of Tradition*. For discussions of various invented and legitimizing traditions of the eleventh century through the thirteenth century, see Duby, "French Genealogical Literature: The Eleventh and Twelfth Centuries," in Duby, *Chivalrous Society*, 134–57; Spiegel, *Chronicle Tradition of Saint Denis*, 4, 44–45; Chenu, "Monks, Canons and Laymen in Search of the Apostolic Life," in Chenu, *Nature, Man, and Society in the Twelfth Century*, 202–38; Benson, "Political *Renovatio*: Two Models from Roman Antiquity"; Southern, "Aspects of the European Tradition of Historical Writing: 4. The Sense of the Past"; Southern, *Western Society and the Church*, 101.

exclude the archbishop and his cathedral from the two sections of town dominated by Marmoutier and Saint-Martin.

On one level, it is not surprising that Marmoutier and Saint-Martin joined together to restrain the authority of the archbishop of Tours or that they drew on Martin's cult to do so. The two houses not only traced their origins to Martin himself, they also shared, at various times in the tenth century, the same institutional structure. But near the end of the tenth century Benedictine monks from the abbey of Cluny reformed Marmoutier, and as a result, Marmoutier and Saint-Martin evolved into radically different institutions with distinct social functions and spiritualities. They also formed different alliances with powerful noble and royal families.

To highlight the differences between Marmoutier and Saint-Martin in the eleventh, twelfth, and thirteenth centuries, and the consequent differences in their representations of Saint Martin and his cult, I have discussed the two institutions separately in parts 2 and 3. Part 2 addresses the cultural and cultic activities of the monks of Marmoutier, whose monastery was, in the eleventh and twelfth centuries, one of the most successful and prestigious Benedictine houses in western Europe. Its religious life was so respected that many of the leading noble families of western Francia called upon its monks to restore and reform other religious houses. Those nobles granted vast amounts of landed property to Saint Martin and his monks, who reciprocated with spiritual favors such as burial at the abbey and assistance for the souls of the dead.

The monks of Marmoutier rewarded some of their noble patrons not only with spiritual favors but also with literary works, including legends associating Martin with those patrons. Especially in the case of the comital family of Anjou, those legends enhanced the collective prestige and status of the lineage. Yet, while the monks of Marmoutier were willing to serve their noble patrons with legends about Saint Martin, they were even more interested in enhancing the legitimacy, cohesion, and spiritual needs of their own community. Those needs resulted, in the twelfth century, from two sets of changes. First, because nobles were becoming more cautious in giving away property, and because the concept of purgatory transformed the role monks could play in assisting the souls of the dead and dying, the reciprocal relationship between monks and their patrons took new forms. And second, the need to administer and organize a vast empire of landed property placed enormous strain on the cohesion of the monastic community. In chapters 4, 5, and 6 I describe the monks' cultural responses to these problems. In legends about Martin and his cult, they propagated new ideas about spiritual relations between monks and laypeople and about the relations among the monks themselves.

Part 3 analyzes the cultural and cultic activities of the canons of Saint-Martin. As I note in the introduction to that section, the chapter of secular canons at Saint-Martin differed from the monastery of Marmoutier in its institutional structure, its spiritual functions, and its political alliances. These differences led the canons to represent, perceive, and employ Martin's cult in ways that differed from those of the monks.

Unlike the monks, who renounced personal property and usually lived together in dormitories, the canons lived in private houses and managed their own private properties. Thus their personal conduct and business activities tended to blend with those of the secular men and women around them. The canons were also intimately linked to the realm of secular politics. One reason for this link was that their lay "abbot" was the king of France, who exercised considerable control over the internal governance of the chapter. In their literature about Saint Martin, the canons sometimes enhanced the legitimacy of their royal patron and abbot, but they also attempted to protect their corporate community from his interference.

A second factor linking the canons of Saint-Martin to the realm of secular politics was the canons' role as the seigneurial lords of an important section of Tours, known as Châteauneuf. The center of the most active commercial life in Tours, Châteauneuf was inhabited by a group of prosperous burghers who in the twelfth and thirteenth centuries attempted to overthrow the lordship of the canons. As I describe in chapter 9, the canons of Saint-Martin responded to the rebellious burghers with legends and miracle stories conveying the message that Saint Martin himself was the source of authority, justice, and prosperity in Châteauneuf.

The primary spiritual function of the chapter of canons was to care for Martin's tomb and to perform the elaborate liturgy in his church. That liturgy served in part to impress pilgrims and devotees, who gave gifts to Saint-Martin, just as noble patrons contributed to Marmoutier, because they believed the saint himself was the actual recipient and hoped he would reciprocate with supernatural favors. But whereas at Marmoutier Martin usually reciprocated with gifts that benefited the souls of lay benefactors, at Saint-Martin he tended to restore the bodily health of those who came to his tomb seeking cures.

The monks and canons drew on Martin's cult to promote their respective social and political interests and needs. More important, they turned to the cult, elaborated it, and expressed themselves through it in attempts to meet their deeper needs for meaning and order. Thus the polysemic meanings of Martin's cult arose not simply from different functional uses, but also from different spiritualities and psychological needs.

Differences in the spiritual styles and preoccupations of Marmoutier and Saint-Martin are readily apparent. At Marmoutier, almost all the texts dealing with Martin's cult address immaterial concerns—moral persuasion, conscience, sin, and salvation. Those from Saint-Martin, by contrast, reveal a corporation whose members were preoccupied with defending their collective position vis-à-vis kings, archbishops, and burghers. It appears, moreover, that the canons of Saint-Martin were more concerned with external behavior, gesture, and ritual than were the monks of Marmoutier. Nevertheless, through their ritualized forms of behavior the canons expressed pressing spiritual concerns; and despite their interest in conscience, the monks continued to assume that liturgy, ritual, and behavior were extremely important aspects of the Benedictine way of life.

By the twelfth and thirteenth centuries, Marmoutier and Saint-Martin were generating distinctive images of Saint Martin and using his cult to fulfill different needs. Nevertheless, the sources reveal that the two houses shared certain underlying psychological and spiritual concerns and that they drew on their relationship with Saint Martin to address those concerns.

One central psychological preoccupation entailed corporate cohesion. Through Martin's cult, both the monks and canons articulated, discovered, and elaborated the cultures of their institutions, and those cultures enabled the residents of each house to experience their membership in the group. At both Marmoutier and Saint-Martin the need to reinforce the cohesion of the community seemed especially urgent in the twelfth and thirteenth centuries. The growth of bureaucratic organization, the extension of centralized governments—such as those of the Angevins and Capetians—and the expansion of monastic and papal empires drew the monastery and the chapter of canons into widening circles of association and caused those institutions to become structurally extended in ways they had never been before. As I show in chapters 5 and 6, the monks of Marmoutier addressed the consequent problems of cohesion by writing histories that deepened their sense of connection to Saint Martin and by telling miracle stories that stimulated the monks' sense of brotherhood within the monastery. At Saint-Martin, as I argue in chapter 7, common rituals provided an antidote, however weakened, to the centrifugal forces that were stretching the boundaries of the corporate group.

For the monks of Marmoutier and the canons of Saint-Martin,

cultural expressions that centered on their patron saint involved both the legitimacy and the integrity of their communities. But those cultural expressions also involved a collective spirituality, one that focused, above all, on concern for the souls of the dead. The monks and canons worried about the cohesion of their religious communities because they believed in the efficacy of vicarious assistance for the dead and dying. Each monk and canon relied on the brothers within his community, and on Saint Martin as well, to help him in his quest for a relatively painless afterlife. An emphasis on such vicarious assistance was at the center of the monks' way of life, and it constituted an important part of the religious life at Saint-Martin as well.

Necessarily, this book presents both chronological narratives describing change over time and more static analyses of symbolic and cultural layers. The chronological approach is most apparent in the first part, which traces the evolution from unified to fragmented representations of Tours between the late fourth and early twelfth centuries. By contrast, parts 2 and 3 are not arranged in strict chronological order. Rather, each chapter deals with a particular set of functions or meanings of the cult. Nevertheless, virtually every chapter traces chronological developments. Indeed, one of my recurring arguments is that the monks and canons generated an impressive number of cultic innovations in the years between 1050 and 1250 because they were responding to the forces of change.

PART I

Martin's Town: From Unity to Duality

Introduction

In the early Middle Ages the primary "community of Saint Martin" was the city of Tours. Martin's cult gave physical shape to the medieval town, whose principal centers of settlement, religious cult, and commercial activity grew up around three churches associated with the saint. More important, however, fifth- and sixth-century bishops of Tours employed Martin's cult to create an ideal image of the civic community. Tours, the bishops suggested, was Martin's town, and it was united under the authority of its bishop, who guarded Martin's cult and inherited his position.

By the beginning of the twelfth century this "community of Saint Martin" no longer existed. Although a number of earlier events chipped away at this idealized civic community, it was above all the monastic exemption movement of the eleventh and twelfth centuries that caused its complete demise. The monks of the abbey of Marmoutier and the canons of the basilica of Saint-Martin succeeded in gaining exemption from the disciplinary and liturgical dominance of their archbishops. As a result, the archbishops' access to Martin's cult became severely limited. New legends and liturgical observances underscored this change: Tours became, in the symbolic representations that emanated from Marmoutier and Saint-Martin, two communities. On the one hand, there was the new "community of Saint Martin," consisting of Marmoutier, Saint-Martin, and the walled suburb of Châteauneuf. And on the other hand, there was the now isolated, and less vibrant, cathedral town.

gemma facerdotum·
Capła· In laudibȝ ꝛ ad horaſ uꞇ ſupꞃa·
·iiii· id nouenꝑ Tranſiꞇuſ bꞇ marꞇinı

PLATE I. Saint Martin's body returns to Tours. "But almighty God would not allow the town of Tours to be deprived of its patron." So claimed Gregory of Tours when he recounted how the men of Tours stole away from the parish of Candes with Saint Martin's body while the men of Poitiers, who thought *their* town had the better claim to the body of the saint, slept. For Gregory this story signified that Martin's power belonged, in a special way, to the town of Tours.

In the top half of this twelfth-century illumination for the feast of Martin's death (November 11), the men of Tours pass the saint's body through a window in Candes (while the Poitevins sleep); in the bottom half the men of Tours sail back to Tours with their prize. Like Gregory of Tours, the canons of Saint-Martin, who produced this illustration, wished to demonstrate that Martin and his power belonged to a particular community. As I argue in chapter 2 and in part 3, however, their definition of the community of Saint Martin differed from Gregory's. Tours, Bibliothèque Municipale, MS. 193 (late twelfth century), fol. 117. Photograph courtesy Tours, Bibliothèque Municipale.

1

Martinopolis (ca. 371–1050)

While the royal seat of Paris excels in military endeavors and command over nations, and the fertile Beauce enriches Chartres, and Orléans prevails with the privilege of natural qualities and of vines, Martinopolis is second to none of these. She is endowed with gifts that are not nature's least, and her land is not so much wide and spacious as it is fertile, useful, and accommodating.

("Commendation of the Province of Touraine" [twelfth century])[1]

Saint Martin and the Topography of Tours

It was customary in the Middle Ages for an urban commendation to commence by describing the setting of a town—the natural resources of its region, the rivers and lesser towns within its domain.[2] Topography, as the author of this twelfth-century text was well aware, can play an important role in the development and economy of a city. The region around Tours—with its fertile plains, vine-covered hills, forests, and rivers—provided abundant resources for the support of the town's inhabitants, and Tours's location on the Loire, the major east-west artery in France, promoted the commercial endeavors of local merchants.

But natural resources and geographical location alone do not go far in explaining the history of "Martinopolis." For this town was, from

1. "Cum enim regia sedes Parisius martio labore et nationum dominatu praeemineat, Carnotum Belgica fertilis opimet, Aurelianis ingeniorum et vinorum privilegio polleat; Martinopolis nulli istarum secunda, naturae non extremis ditata est bonis. Haec siquidem terra non tam lata et spatiosa quam fertilis, utilis et commoda" (*Narratio de commendatione Turonicae provinciae*, 292). For a discussion of the dates and authorship of this text, see Source Appendix, I-B.

2. For descriptions of the genre, see Baron, *Crisis of the Early Italian Renaissance*, 2:514–17 nn. 7, 8; Curtius, *European Literature and the Latin Middle Ages*, 157; and Hyde, "Medieval Descriptions of Cities." Despite its title, the *Narratio de commendatione Turonicae provinciae* is really an urban commendation.

its inception, a product of human artifice, institutions, and imagination. The Romans had defied geographical logic when in the first century they placed the new town of Caesarodunum on the south bank of the Loire, where several of their roads intersected, rather than on the higher, more defensible land of the north bank. Then in the fourth century they contributed to the survival of the town, which came to be known as Tours, by designating it the capital of the province of the Third Lyonnaise.[3]

But it was above all the Christian religion, and especially the cult of Saint Martin, that contributed to the survival, the importance, and even the shape of medieval Tours. Like other Roman cities, Tours outlived the empire and perpetuated its institutions because it had become an episcopal town. More important, Martin, who was venerated not only as a saint but also as the apostle to the Gauls, occupied the episcopal see there between about 371 and 397. His relics, which remained in the town, became the most prestigious in Frankish Gaul, attracting the attention of pilgrims and kings.[4]

A former Roman soldier who had relinquished his arms to meet the demands cf Christianity, Saint Martin remained a man of action throughout his life. Indeed, the landscape of medieval Francia was dotted with the consequences and commemorations of his deeds (see map 1). An oratory near one of the gates of Amiens marked the spot where, as an unbaptized soldier, Martin performed his most famous act of charity, dividing his cape in two and offering half to a beggar. At the northern gate of Paris (on the Ile de la Cité, where the rue Saint-Martin begins) another oratory marked a second act of charity, when Martin cured a leper by kissing him.[5]

Soon after he left the army Martin founded Ligugé, the first monastery in Gaul. Medieval pilgrims continued to seek cures at this abbey near Poitiers, in the cell where the saint had resuscitated a dead novice. By the twelfth century the monks of Ligugé maintained that the bell in their belfry was the one Martin had used to call his brothers to worship. People suffering from headaches or toothaches found

3. Boussard, "Etude sur la ville de Tours," 318; Mirot, *Manuel de géographie historique de la France*, 1:29–32.

4. On the role of bishoprics and saints' cults in the evolution of medieval towns, see Latouche, *Birth of Western Economy*, 103–6. For a general discussion of Martin, his dates, and his biographer, see Stancliffe, *St. Martin and His Hagiographer*, 116–19, and Fontaine, *Sulpice Sévère: Vie de Saint Martin*, 1:17–243. For a discussion of the various foundations and commemorations of Martin, see Vieillard-Troiekouroff, *Monuments religieux de la Gaule*. See also Ewig, "Culte de Saint Martin à l'époque franque."

5. Sulpicius Severus, *Vita Sancti Martini*, 3:1–2, 18:3–4, pp. 254–58, 292; Gregory of Tours, *De virtutibus beati Martini* 1:17, p. 598; Gregory of Tours, *Historia francorum*, 8:33, p. 349. Vieillard-Troiekouroff, *Monuments religieux*, 32–33, 203.

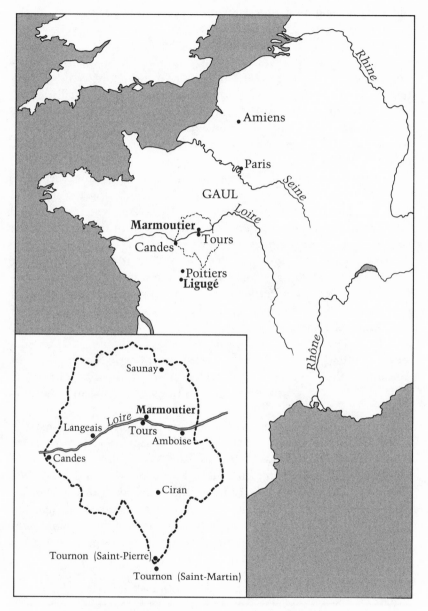

MAP 1. The footsteps of Saint Martin. *large map:* Gaul; *inset:* diocese of Tours (with parishes founded by Saint Martin, according to Gregory of Tours). Adapted from Fontaine, *Sulpice Sévère,* vol. 3, following p. 1424.

relief by rubbing their afflicted parts against the bell's rim; striking the bell would dispel lightning and storms.[6]

From Ligugé Martin was called to the bishopric of Tours, where he waged an active war against paganism. In the face of violent opposition, he earned his reputation as apostle to the Gauls by destroying temples and erecting churches throughout his diocese—at Langeais, Saunay, Tournon, Amboise, Ciran, and Candes. Martin died while he was making an episcopal visit to the parish of Candes, which thereby became another center for pilgrims and miracles. In the twelfth century the priests there even claimed to possess a grapevine sprouted from the dried twigs that had served as the dying saint's bedding. From that vine they produced a wine that they used at the altar and offered to the sick, whose ailments they claimed the wine could cure.[7]

Clearly, many parts of Francia could exult with the words of the sixth-century poet Fortunatus: "O happy region, to have known the footsteps, look, and touch of the saint!"[8] But it was in Tours that Martin resided the longest and had the greatest impact. Ultimately he and his cult even played a fundamental role in influencing the physical form of that town, through the three religious monuments associated with him—the basilica that housed his relics, the abbey he founded, and the cathedral where he served as bishop. According to the thirteenth-century version of the "Commendation of the Province of Touraine," these were the major institutions of Tours.[9] They now formed the nuclei of three distinct sections of the urban conglomerate.

Of course the role that Martin and his cult played in shaping the physical form of medieval Tours was affected by other factors. Both Roman creations and later Germanic and Viking disruptions helped influence where his three institutions were located and how they developed. For example, the cathedral, founded by Litorius, Martin's predecessor as bishop, was situated, like other cathedrals in Gaul, on the ramparts protecting the administrative center of the Roman town. Hastily erected after Germanic tribes invaded the region sometime

6. Sulpicius, *Vita*, 7, pp. 266–68; Gregory, *De virtutibus*, 4:30, p. 657; "De cultu Sancti Martini apud Turonenses extremo saeculo XII," 250. On the identification of Ligugé with Martin's first monastic foundation, see Stancliffe, *St. Martin*, 23–24, and Prinz, *Frühes Mönchtum im Frankenreich*, 22–46.

7. Sulpicius, *Vita*, 9:1, p. 270; Sulpicius Severus, *Epistolae*, 3:6–17, pp. 336–43; Sulpicius Severus, *Dialogi*, 3:8, 3:17, pp. 206, 216; Gregory, *Historia*, 10:31, p. 444; Gregory, *De virtutibus*, 3:22, 2:19–22, pp. 638, 615–16; "De cultu Sancti Martini," 256.

8. "O felix regio, sancti pede, lumine, tactu!" (Venantius Fortunatus, *Vita Sancti Martini*, 1:507, p. 312).

9. *Narratio de commendatione Turonicae provinciae*, 296–317.

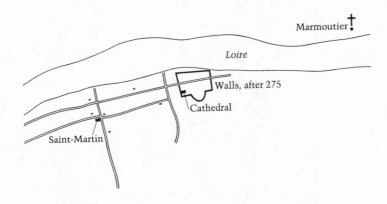

MAP 2. Tours, fourth century through sixth century. Adapted from Galinié and Randoin, *Archives du sol à Tours*, 21.

around 275, those walls—which continued to define the cathedral town until the twelfth century—reduced the area of Tours to one-quarter of its original size (see map 2).[10]

Roman institutions and later disruptions also influenced the location and development of Martin's basilica. This was at first a modest church, erected over Martin's burial place in a Christian cemetery one mile west of the cathedral. The construction of the basilica fit a general pattern: Christians everywhere in the West were building churches over the graves of their dead saints, who had been buried in cemeteries situated—in accordance with Roman prohibitions—outside city walls. Now, however, suburbs took shape around the holy tombs, and the Roman prohibition was abandoned.[11]

In Tours, the Viking invasions stimulated a further development around Martin's tomb. After the Vikings attacked the town in 903, the inhabitants of Martin's suburb decided to enclose their neighborhood with a defensive wall, which they completed in 918. Tours became a double town, and "new castle"—Châteauneuf—fell under the seigneurial jurisdiction of the basilica of Saint-Martin rather than

10. Boussard, "Etude sur la ville de Tours," 315, 317, 320–23; Boussard, "Essai sur le peuplement de la Touraine," 274–75; Gregory, *Historia*, 10:31, p. 443; Latouche, *Birth of Western Economy*, 112.

11. Gregory, *Historia*, 10:31, p. 444; Latouche, *Birth of Western Economy*, 110–11; Boussard, "Etude sur la ville le Tours," 321.

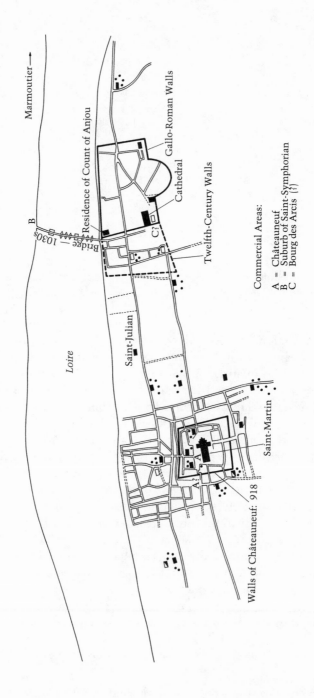

MAP 3. Tours in the twelfth century. Adapted from Galinié and Randoin, *Archives du sol à Tours*, 31.

Loire

Marmoutier →

Gallo-Roman Walls

Residence of Count of Anjou

Cathedral

Twelfth-Century Walls

Bridge — 1030s

B

C?

Saint-Julian

Saint-Martin

Walls of Châteauneuf: 918

A?

Commercial Areas:

A = Châteauneuf
B = Suburb of Saint-Symphorian
C = Bourg des Arcis (?)

that of the cathedral (see map 3).[12] In the tenth and eleventh centuries, while the cathedral town stagnated, Châteauneuf developed into a thriving commercial center whose artisans, money changers, wealthy merchants, innkeepers, and tavern owners provided services for the pilgrims to Martin's tomb. The eleven parish churches that had already been built in Châteauneuf by the end of the eleventh century indicate that it supported a thriving lay population. The cathedral town, by contrast, had only two parish churches.[13]

Even the abbey of Marmoutier, which Martin founded as an ascetic refuge soon after he became bishop, bore the marks of Romans, Germanic tribes, and Vikings. Martin's biographer, Sulpicius Severus, emphasized that the spot—two miles east of Tours on the opposite bank of the Loire—was "so sheltered and remote that it did not lack the solitude of the desert." But this was an exaggeration, contrived to highlight the similarities between Martin and the monks of Egypt. To be sure, Marmoutier was, as Sulpicius indicated, hemmed between the river and a cliff, and the original monks sought shelter in caves carved out of the soft chalk embankment, just as peasants of the region—the troglodytes—do today. But Martin was not the first to inhabit the site of Marmoutier, and indeed the ruins of first- and second-century Roman buildings may have attracted him to the spot.[14]

During the eras of both the Germanic and the Viking invasions, the religious life at Marmoutier declined. Ultimately, however, the disruptions of the ninth and tenth centuries may have helped to stimulate both the growth of the European economy and the flowering of monasticism, of which Marmoutier was a principal beneficiary. Reformed and restored at the end of the tenth century, Marmoutier became, in the eleventh, one of the most powerful Benedictine monasteries in western Francia. Indeed, the wealthy monastic complex

12. Giry, *Etablissements de Rouen*, 1:186. On the Vikings' role in the formation of other double cities, see Musset, *Invasions: Le second assaut*, 235.

13. On the prosperous residents of Châteauneuf, see below, chapter 9. On the number of parishes, the original growth of Châteauneuf in the ninth and tenth centuries, and the late and modest commercial development of the cathedral town, see Galinié and Randoin, *Archives du sol à Tours*, 26–33, and Chevalier, "Cité de Tours et Châteauneuf," 238–42. In the ninth, tenth, and eleventh centuries the inhabitants of the cathedral town included only clerics and lesser knights. After the 1030s, when Odo of Blois built a bridge joining the west side of the cathedral town to the north side of the Loire, a small commercial community grew up just outside the west wall of the cathedral town, but that community never included money changers and rich merchants, as was the case at Châteauneuf.

14. "Locus tam secretus et remotus erat, ut eremi solitudinem non desideraret" (Sulpicius, *Vita*, 10:4–5, p. 274). On the deliberate parallels with Egypt, see Fontaine, *Sulpice Sévère*, 1:49, 60 n. 2; 2:667. On the Roman buildings, see Stancliffe, *St. Martin*, 170 n. 31, and Lelong, "Etudes sur l'abbaye de Marmoutier," 279.

supported an active community of artisans and lesser merchants, who settled in the parish of Saint-Symphorian, across the river from the cathedral. After the 1030s, when Odo of Blois built a bridge joining the north side of the Loire to the cathedral town, Saint-Symphorian developed into an important suburb of Tours (see map 3). Marmoutier and its suburb lay outside the city itself, but they constituted an essential part of its economic, social, and symbolic fabric.[15]

Building on Roman foundations, Saint Martin and the promoters of his cult endowed Tours and its immediate vicinity with the physical legacy of two important churches in addition to the cathedral. Subsequent events caused those two churches to evolve into powerful nuclei, distinct from the episcopal seat. In the period after the Viking invasions those nuclei broke away from the cathedral with centrifugal force. As I explain in chapter 2, the ecclesiastical community of Tours was torn in the eleventh and twelfth centuries by the attempts of Saint-Martin and Marmoutier to free themselves from the dominance of the cathedral.

Civic Unity and Local Pride

If we look at the physical evidence alone, the rifts in the ecclesiastical community of eleventh- and twelfth-century Tours might seem a natural outgrowth of Martin's original legacy. Tours's inheritance from Martin and his early medieval cult, however, included not only physical vestiges, but also symbolic representations. Those representations, developed by the earliest promoters of Martin's cult, especially the bishops of Tours, helped to define the community and its status. They tied the nature and prestige of the city as a whole to its possession of the saint's relics.

The early medieval representations of the community of Tours emphasized three themes. First, Martin's presence enhanced local civic pride, enabling the bishops of Tours to draw favorable comparisons between their city and others. Second, the saint's relics tied Tours to the larger political community, because Martin was the pa-

---

15. On the destruction of the Viking invasions and the restoration of Marmoutier, see below, introduction to part 2, and chapter 6. On the economic prosperity of Marmoutier in the eleventh century, see Gantier, "Recherches sur les possessions et les prieurés de l'abbaye de Marmoutier." For the argument that the Viking invasions stimulated the European economy and monastic reform, see Duby, *Early Growth of the European Economy*, 118 ff.; Musset, "Renaissance urbaine des Xᵉ et XIᵉ siècles"; and Riché, "Consequences des invasions normandes sur la culture monastique," esp. 716–21. On Saint-Symphorian see Chevalier, "Cité de Tours et Châteauneuf," 238–42.

tron of the Frankish kings. And finally, the saint's benefits fell on the entire city, which was united in its devotion under the rule of the bishop, who was not only Martin's successor, but also the major guardian of his cult.

The themes of localism, royal patronage, and civic unity were not consciously articulated in the writings of Sulpicius Severus, the first to promote Martin's sainthood. Sulpicius, who published Martin's *Life* while the saint was still alive, was interested in the holiness of the man rather than the power of his relics. Moreover, Sulpicius resided not in Tours, but in southern Gaul, on the family estate that he, following the impulse of a number of his wealthy contemporaries, had converted into a monastery. For Sulpicius, whose *Life of Saint Martin* became the principal model for Western hagiographers, Martin represented both a spiritual patron—who guided his biographer and intimate devotee to salvation—and a model of the ascetic life that Sulpicius hoped to realize.[16]

Nevertheless, certain orientations in Sulpicius's writings had the potential to lend themselves to the local interests of later bishops of Tours.[17] First, Sulpicius promoted local Gallic pride by placing Martin and his region in direct competition with other holy men and their regions. He proclaimed that Martin, who was probably the first bishop in the region to show an interest in coverting the peasants, was the apostle for Gaul just as Saint Paul was for Greece. He argued further that Martin's asceticism was at least as praiseworthy as that of the hermits of the Egyptian desert.[18] In the fifth and sixth centuries, bishops of Tours would employ Martin's cult to develop their own sense of local pride, focusing it on the city of Tours rather than on Gaul. In the same period, Merovingian kings would transform Martin's special relationship with Gaul into a special relationship with the Frankish kings.

Sulpicius's discussion of Martin's simultaneous careers as bishop and as monk had a similar potential for supporting the idea that Tours was united under its bishop, as a city and as an ecclesiastical community. According to Sulpicius, Martin did not give up his monastic virtues when he became bishop of Tours. Rather, he became one of

16. On the date of the *Vita*, see Stancliffe, *St. Martin*, 71. On Sulpicius's asceticism, see Fontaine, *Sulpice Sévère*, 1:21–49. A good example of Sulpicius's personal relationship with Martin as mediator is Sulpicius, *Epistolae*, 2, pp. 324–34.

17. Raymond Van Dam made a similar distinction between Sulpicius's representation of Martin and the later uses of his cult. Martin, he argued, was an outsider who defied authority, but his cult came to bolster the power of those in positions of authority (*Leadership and Community in Late Antique Gaul*, 119–40).

18. Sulpicius, *Dialogi*, 3:17, 1:24–25, pp. 216, 176–78.

the first men to combine successfully ecclesiastical office and asceticism. Indeed, Bishop Martin's most loyal and consistent companions remained, through his final hours in Candes, the monks of
Marmoutier.[19] Martin, as Sulpicius described him, provided a model
for intimate relations between the bishop and the monasteries under
his jurisdiction. Such intimacy might be interpreted to promote the
authority of the bishop and the unity of Tours.

After Martin's death, the bishops of Tours showed more interest in
the saint's relics than in the model of his way of life. Martin's body
became a powerful possession, which could attract not only spiritual
but also earthly benefits to his town. And despite a slow start under
the saint's immediate successors, it was the bishop of Tours who,
from the beginning, took charge of the cult.

Brice, who was Martin's successor as bishop of Tours, constructed
only a tiny chapel over Martin's tomb, dedicating it, in all likelihood,
to Saint Peter and Saint Paul: only apostles and martyrs then qualified
for the honor of having a church dedicated to them.[20] Brice's successors did little to expand the cult of the saintly bishop, primarily
because they presided during the troubled age of Germanic invasions,
but Gregory of Tours (bishop of that town from 573 to 594) noted
that every bishop from Brice's time until his own—except two who
died in exile—was buried at Martin's basilica.[21]

It was largely owing to Perpetuus, who became bishop of Tours in
460, that Martin's cult first began to flower. Perpetuus built a magnif-
icent church over Martin's tomb, the first anywhere to be dedicated to
Martin himself. According to Gregory of Tours, Perpetuus built this
church because Martin's relics were performing numerous miracles
and because his people—the inhabitants of Tours—were ashamed of
their saint's modest tomb.[22]

Perpetuus expanded Martin's cult not only with a new church, but
also with new hagiographical texts and elaborations of the saint's feast
days. He asked Paulinus of Perigord and Sidonius Apollinaris, one of
the best-known poets of the fifth century, to compose inscriptions for

19. Sulpicius, *Vita*, 10, pp. 272–74; Sulpicius, *Epistolae*, 3:6–17, pp. 336–42; Stancliffe,
St. Martin, 260, 292–311.
20. On Brice and his successor Eustache, see Gregory, *Historia*, 2:1, 10:31, pp. 59–60,
444; Stancliffe, *St. Martin*, 360; Delehaye, "Saint Martin et Sulpice Sévère," 115–18; Ewig,
"Culte de Saint Martin à l'époque franque," 1–3; Pietri, *Ville de Tours du IVe au VIe siècle*,
103–18. On the revolts and invasions, see Werner, *Origines*, 267–80; Griffe, *Gaule chrétienne
à l'époque romaine*, 2:15–17, 53–62; Pietri, *Ville de Tours*, 91–103.
21. Gregory, *Historia*, 10:31, pp. 442–50.
22. On Perpetuus, Martin's two feasts, and Perpetuus's liturgical calendar, see Gregory,
Historia, 2:14, 10:31, pp. 81–82, 444–45; Gregory, *De virtutibus*, 1:6, pp. 591–92; Sidonius
Apollinaris, *Epistola*, 4:18, ed. Anderson, 2:132–34; Paulinus of Perigord, *De vita Sancti
Martini*, bk. 6, with indirect references to Perpetuus at lines 28 and 506, pp. 139, 159.

the new basilica, and he commissioned a poem from Paulinus describing Martin's life and posthumous miracles. Perpetuus also established vigils for the saint's two feasts, on November 11 and July 4. It is even possible that Perpetuus was the first to elevate the date associated with the saint's funeral (November 11) to the level of a feast day and that he invented the saint's second feast, that of July 4.[23]

Implicit in Perpetuus's innovations were the messages that Martin and the community of Tours were bound together, that they shared a special status, and that Tours was united under the bishop. That the saint was honored twice was a sign of his and Tours's importance. The feast of July 4 placed special emphasis on Martin's association with Tours—it celebrated his consecration as bishop of the city, the translation of his relics to Perpetuus's new basilica, and the dedication of that basilica. According to Gregory of Tours, a miracle confirmed the translation and dedication. After unsuccessfully attempting to move Martin's body on the first day of July, one of the men in charge of the translation remembered that Martin had been ordained on July 4, so he and the others decided to wait three days. When July 4 arrived, a mysterious old man came to help with the translation of the body and then disappeared. Apparently it was the saint himself, who wanted to make clear that the day of his translation to Perpetuus's basilica was to be a holy day.[24]

While the feast of July 4 called attention to Tours itself, Perpetuus's larger liturgical plan underscored the unity of the city and the authority of the bishop. In a religious calendar, he specified where the inhabitants and clergy of Tours were to keep vigils for the most important feasts of the year, and by assigning more vigils to Saint-Martin's basilica than to the cathedral, he indicated that the religious cycle of the community was to revolve around Martin's church, albeit under the direction of the bishop.[25]

23. Delehaye ("Saint Martin et Sulpice Sévère," 115–30) argued that the two feast days were commemorated all along, but neither he nor Duchesne (*Fastes épiscopaux de l'ancienne Gaule,* 2:302 n. 4) gave direct evidence for the feasts from the period before Perpetuus. As a bishop, Martin would have received at least a yearly commemoration of his death, but since there was resistance in the fourth century to assigning feast days to martyrs, it is probable that there was as much, or more, resistance to assigning feasts to confessors (those who had suffered for Christianity but were not martyrs), since confessors had not been recognized as saints before Martin's time: see Brown, *Cult of the Saints,* 32. Pietri (*Ville de Tours,* 474) offers evidence supporting the hypothesis that Perpetuus elevated the November feast to a new status: he changed the name from the more local *receptio* to the more solemn *depositio.*

24. Pietri, *Ville de Tours,* 480–81. Gregory, *De virtutibus,* 1:6, pp. 591–92; Gregory, *Historia,* 2:44. For a general discussion of translation narratives, their function of highlighting an important moment in the history of a community, and the topos of failed first efforts to make a translation, see Geary, *Furta Sacra,* 12–13, and Heinzelmann, *Translationsberichte.*

25. Gregory, *Historia,* 10:31, p. 445.

The role of Marmoutier in Perpetuus's liturgical plan is not clear. The fifth-century invasions may have disrupted the monastic life at Marmoutier, and in fact, though Gregory of Tours mentioned a monk and an abbot of Marmoutier, there are virtually no sources concerning the religious life there from the fourth century through the eighth. Nevertheless, the writings of Paulinus of Perigord suggest that the abbey—or its remains—was bound up in the religious life of the urban community as a whole. Paulinus described an annual Easter pilgrimage when all the inhabitants of Tours sailed across the Loire to Marmoutier to venerate the cell where Martin had fasted, prayed, and kept late-night vigils. One year when a boat capsized Martin sent a miraculous wind, thereby saving his devotees from drowning.[26]

Paulinus did not mention the bishop in this account of the annual pilgrimage, but his assertion that the entire city participated in the pious visit implied that the bishop was present. Besides, it was Perpetuus who had commissioned Paulinus's poem and who provided the poet with the primary material concerning Martin's miracles. Thus the poem suggests that in Perpetuus's day the bishop's orbit included Marmoutier.[27]

Bishop Perpetuus represents a major turning point in the history of Martin's cult. Not only did he help spread the fame and importance of Saint Martin, but he employed the saint's cult to enhance local pride and civic unity. Yet had it not been for the successes and inclinations of Clovis—who united the Franks under the Merovingian dynasty and extended his power over Northern Gaul—the innovations of Perpetuus might have been forgotten. In most of the forty years preceding Clovis's ascendency, Tours was held by Arian Visigoths. Indeed, the two Catholic bishops who succeeded Perpetuus were forced into exile because they were suspected of supporting the Franks.[28]

After winning a number of important victories and converting from paganism to Catholicism, possibly around 498, Clovis broke

26. Paulinus of Perigord, *Vita*, 6:351–460, pp. 153–57. On the silence concerning Marmoutier during the period immediately after Martin's death, see Delehaye, "Saint Martin et Sulpice Sévère," 100, and Stancliffe, *St. Martin*, 351. Gregory's reference to the monk and abbot of Marmoutier is in *De virtutibus*, 3:42, p. 642. On the general silence until the ninth century, see Lévêque, "Histoire de l'abbaye de Marmoutier," 94–95.

27. On Paulinus's relationship to Perpetuus, see above at note 21 and Van Dam, *Leadership and Community*, 235.

28. On the Visigoths and Tours, see Gregory, *Historia*, 10:31, p. 446; Boussard, "Essai sur le peuplement de la Touraine," 278; Mirot, *Manuel de géographie historique*, 45–46; Pietri, *Ville de Tours*, 129–60. On Clovis as a turning point for the spread of Martin's cult, see Prinz, *Frühes Mönchtum*, 27–33.

the power of the Visigoths in Aquitaine when he defeated Alaric II in 507. A wise politician, Clovis had turned for support to the Gallo-Roman bishops, the most powerful men in Gaul. He recognized that one pillar bolstering the power of those bishops was their relationship to the cult of saints. Before his decisive victory over Alaric, Gregory of Tours later claimed, Clovis sought and received a favorable sign from Saint Martin. According to Gregory, Clovis took care not to offend the saint or the living guardians of his property: as they passed through lands belonging to Tours, Clovis's soldiers were to requisition only fodder and water. When one soldier ignored this restriction, Clovis killed him on the spot, declaring, "We cannot expect to win this fight if we offend blessed Martin."[29] After his victory, Clovis went to Martin's basilica and placed a diadem on his own head. He then rode in a formal procession "all the way from the doorway of Saint Martin's church to the cathedral," showering the people with gold and silver coins as he went.[30]

It was Clovis, then, who established both the recognized status of the Frankish leaders and the relationship between the Frankish kings and the cult of Saint Martin. The interests of the old Gallo-Roman Catholic aristocracy and those of the Frankish leaders had merged in the ousting of the Arian Visigoths. Now Clovis's ceremony at Tours and his association with Martin and the bishops who watched over his cult symbolically integrated the two groups into a single community.[31] The victory procession also reflects the continued unity between Saint Martin's basilica and the cathedral of Tours.

Until the seventh century Martin remained the most important patron saint of the Merovingian dynasty. The relationship was beneficial to both Tours and the royal family. For Tours there were material rewards: Clovis showered Martin's basilica with gifts, King Lothar provided the church with a new tin roof in 558, several kings exempted the city from taxes, and King Dagobert (629–38) commissioned a sumptuous new reliquary for Martin. The kings, in turn,

---

29. "Et ubi erit spes victuriae, si beato Martino offendimus?" (Gregory, *Historia*, 2:37–38, pp. 99–102). All my translations of Gregory's *Historia* have drawn on Lewis Thorpe's translation. On the power of bishops and their relations with the Franks, see Bréhier and Aigrain, *Grégoire le Grand*, 368; Lot, *End of the Ancient World*, 385–88; Werner, *Origines*, 309. On Clovis's conversion, see Werner, *Origines*, 307. On bishops and saints' cults, see Brown, "Eastern and Western Christendom in Late Antiquity," 19; Brown, *Cult of the Saints*, 8–10, 93–95; Geary, *Before France and Germany*, 136–39.

30. "Tunc ascenso equite, aurum argentumque in itinere illo, quod inter portam atrii et ecclesiam civitatis est, praesentibus populis manu propria spargens, voluntate benignissima erogavit" (Gregory, *Historia*, 2:38, p. 102); Wallace-Hadrill, *Long-Haired Kings*, 175.

31. Brown, *Cult of the Saints*, 99, 167 n. 78.

looked to Martin's basilica as a major political asylum, and they invoked the saint's vengeance as a means of enforcing legal documents. Moreover, from 678 on they possessed the saint's cape, which protected the kings in battle and served as a divine guarantor of their solemn oaths. In fact Martin's cape was so important that the names for its custodian and for the place where it was kept became new words in the western European lexicon: "chaplain" and "chapel" are derived from *capella,* Martin's little cape.[32]

Perpetuus and Clovis made significant contributions to the growth of Martin's cult and to conceptions of the community of Tours. But Gregory of Tours probably did more than anyone else to promote the saint and shape the image of his town. The writings of Gregory, the most important hagiographer and historian of his age, provide most of our information concerning the roles that Perpetuus and Clovis played in developing Martin's cult.[33]

Like other bishops of his time, Gregory saw himself as a *defensor civitatis*—the guardian of his city against both spiritual and political aggression. His local pride was much more blatantly competitive than that of Perpetuus.[34] As far as Gregory was concerned, Tours possessed the relics of Saint Martin because the dead saint had chosen to reside there, and the saint's choice proved that the community was worthy of the possession.

This competitive localism was the central theme in Gregory's account of Martin's death. Gregory was not particularly interested in the saint's exemplary life. He made no allusion to Sulpicius Severus's moving descriptions of Martin's final struggle between his desire for Christ and his sympathy for the intimate companions he was leaving behind. Neither did Gregory describe the dying saint's persistent adherence to his ascetic ideals. For Gregory, as for the other bishops of Tours, Martin's life was almost an incidental prelude to the long career of his relics. He described the moment of Martin's death to record the miracles that proved his saintly power—a power that carried over into his relics.[35]

Since the spiritual potency of the relics revealed the status or merits

32. Ewig, "Culte de Saint Martin à l'époque franque," 8–9; Gregory, *Historia,* 2:37, 4:20, 9:30, pp. 102, 157, 384–85; Leclercq, "Chape de Saint Martin"; Van den Bosch, *Capa, basilica, monasterium.*

33. For general discussion of Gregory's writings, see Wallace-Hadrill, *Long-Haired Kings,* 49–70, and the beautiful discussion of Martin's cult in Van Dam, *Leadership and Community,* 179–300.

34. Bréhier and Aigrain, *Grégoire le Grand,* 368; Wallace-Hadrill, *Long-Haired Kings,* 69–70.

35. Sulpicius, *Epistolae,* 3:6–16, pp. 336–42; Gregory, *De virtutibus,* 1:3–5, pp. 589–91.

of the community possessing them, it was extremely important to Gregory to identify the precise group that was associated with Martin's body. And here he apparently considered inadequate Sulpicius's description of the saint's death and funeral. On the one hand, Sulpicius had identified no specific community at all: his Martin was everyone's saint. Not only the "whole city" of Tours but also the inhabitants of the countryside, the villages, and even other towns participated in the dead saint's return to Tours from Candes. On the other hand Sulpicius was too specific: he reported that the monks of Marmoutier, who had shared Martin's final and most intimate hours, were the saint's principal mourners.[36]

By eliminating both Sulpicius's emphasis on the monks of Marmoutier and his reference to the participation of surrounding villages and towns, Gregory made it clear that Martin belonged to *everyone* in Tours, but to *no one* else. And by adding an account of a dispute over Martin's body, he highlighted the unique distinction and privilege of the inhabitants of Tours, whose acquisition of the saint's relics was blessed with divine assistance.

According to Gregory the men of Poitiers, who had gathered around Saint Martin while he was dying in Candes, asserted that they had the right to claim the saint's body because he had become an abbot while living near their town, at Ligugé. The men from Tours answered that a bishop should be buried in the town where he was consecrated. The dispute continued into the evening, so the two parties stationed themselves on either side of the saint's corpse, which lay in the middle of a locked room. "But," Gregory asserted, "almighty God would not allow the town of Tours to be deprived of its patron." In the middle of the night the Poitevins fell asleep, allowing the men from Tours to seize the moment. After passing the saint through a window, they placed him in a boat and sailed up the Loire to Tours, "praising God and chanting psalms"[37] (see plate 1). Through divine intervention, Tours gained its prized possession, and Martin's continuing miracles proved, for Gregory, that the community still merited his favor.[38]

36. Sulpicius, *Epistolae*, 3:17–21, pp. 342–44.

37. "Sed Deus omnipotens noluit urbem Toronicam a proprio frustrari patrono. . . . cum Magnis laudibus psallentioque" (Gregory, *Historia*, 1:48, p. 56, trans. Thorpe, pp. 98–99).

38. In Gregory, *De virtutibus*, 2:25, pp. 617–18, a demoniac claims that Martin has left the people because of their sins, but a miracle proves his continued presence in the community. Brown ("Eastern and Western Christendom," 18) argues that meriting the saint's grace is also an individual and hierarchical matter, with the greatest favor directed toward bishops. For a similar discussion of the belief that the successful theft of a saint's relics indicated the saint's favor, see Geary, *Furta Sacra*, esp. 143–57.

Gregory's account of this dispute distinguished no individuals or groups within the community of Tours—he treated it as a single well-integrated body. His symbolic actions as bishop conveyed the same message: Tours was a single liturgical unit with the bishop at its head. Relations between the cathedral arfd the basilica were especially close. Gregory repaired Martin's basilica and recorded the saint's miracles in four books that became the principal model for later miracle collections. He decorated the cathedral with scenes from Martin's life, translated relics from the basilica to the cathedral, and celebrated Christmas vigils at both the cathedral and Saint-Martin.[39]

Gregory's image of the community of Tours was highly idealized. To be sure, he and the other bishops of his time did exercise tight control over religious institutions in their dioceses. But Gregory and his contemporaries were also intensely aware of the violent rivalries that constantly threatened their security and authority as bishops. One of Gregory's reasons for promoting the cult of Saint Martin was to anchor his own authority in a supernatural rallying point, one that had the potential to create consensus out of disorder.[40]

Civic pride and unity were Gregory's principal interests. Indeed, although he promoted the close association between the Merovingian kings and Saint Martin, he manipulated the image of that association to the advantage of the church and community of Tours. His accounts of earlier relations between Martin and the Merovingian kings provided models that might influence the behavior of his royal contemporaries. Clovis was rewarded for respecting Saint Martin's property; Charibert was punished for seizing it. Lothar, Charibert, and Sigibert never taxed Tours because they feared Martin; Childebert should do the same or face divine vengeance.[41] The Merovingian kings, Gregory maintained, were in a position of obligation toward Martin's city. They owed it both service and respect.

Perpetuus, Clovis, and Gregory created a set of associations between Martin's cult and the community of Tours that was preserved as a representational legacy into the eleventh century. Their images of community and their uses of the saint's cult were not unique in the late antique and early Frankish periods: bishops everywhere were taking the lead in developing the cult of relics to promote not only the

39. Gregory, *Historia*, 10:31, pp. 448–49; Fortunatus, *Carmina*, 1:10:6, pp. 234–38; Vieillard-Troiekouroff, *Monuments religieux*, 305; Gregory, *De virtutibus*, 2:25, p. 617.

40. See Brown, *Cult of the Saints*; Brown, "Relics and Social Status in the Age of Gregory of Tours"; Geary, *Before France and Germany*, 135–39.

41. Gregory, *Historia*, 2:37, pp. 99–102; Gregory, *De virtutibus*, 1:29, p. 602; Gregory, *Historia*, 9:30, pp. 384–85.

external prestige and internal unity of their cities, but also their own power as heads of those cities. Similarly, a number of saints became the patrons of secular rulers.[42]

What was unique about Martin's cult was the vigor and success of its promoters and the lasting importance of their writings. Not only did Martin become the most important saint in Gaul, at least until the seventh century, but the works concerning him continued to inspire and influence the literature about saints and their cults throughout the Middle Ages. Although relations within Tours never really matched the image the bishops created, and though those relations continued to change between the sixth century and the eleventh, the community of Tours inherited the record and memory of the rituals, symbols, and ideas that had represented and defined the city in the earlier period.

Change and Fragmentation

Perpetuus and Gregory employed Martin's cult in efforts to enhance the prestige of Tours, its ecclesiastical unity, and its relations with the Merovingian kings. Sources from the seventh century move beyond these idealized representations and reveal two new developments that began to undermine parts of Perpetuus's and Gregory's systems. First, the influence of Irish monasticism created cracks in the intimate relationship between the cathedral and the house of Saint-Martin. About 650 Saint-Martin became a reformed house, along the lines that had been introduced into Gaul by Saint Columbanus. Intrinsic to Columbanus's reform was the idea that monasteries should be exempt from episcopal interference in their internal affairs. That idea was implemented at Saint-Martin about 674.[43] The second seventh-century change involved the links between Martin's cult and the Frankish kings: about 680, Saint Denis superseded Martin as the favored royal patron saint.[44]

In the eighth and ninth centuries Carolingian reforms helped reestablish the authority of the bishop in his diocese, but those reforms

42. On other saints favored by the Frankish kings, see Ewig, "Culte de Saint Martin à l'époque franque," 9.

43. Privilege of Pope Adeodatus, 674, *PL* 87:1141; Prinz, *Frühes Mönchtum*, 293; Vaucelle, *Collégiale de Saint-Martin*, 35–36, 65–66; Gasnault, "Etude sur les chartes de Saint-Martin," 38–39. For a general discussion of exemption in this period, see Lemarignier, *Etude sur les privilèges d'exemption*, 1–7; for an analysis of the social implications of Columbanian monasticism, see Geary, *Before France and Germany*, 169–78.

44. Ewig, "Culte de Saint Martin à l'époque franque," 9–10.

also undermined the local pride and autonomy of Tours. Charlemagne appointed Alcuin abbot of Saint-Martin and expressed concern about the decline and ambiguous nature of the monastic life
there (a problem that was resolved about 815 when Saint-Martin
became a house of canons); Louis the Pious regulated the offerings of
pilgrims at Martin's shrine. Moreover, the sources from this period,
which often reflect the perspective of the Carolingian court, tend to
subordinate Martin's role as protector of his town to his role as national and royal symbol.[45] In this capacity, however, Martin was still
rivaled by Denis.

There were, then, in the late Merovingian and Carolingian periods,
both actual and representational divergences from Perpetuus's and
Gregory's perspectives on the nature and status of the community of
Tours and Martin's role in shaping it. Yet despite certain modifica-
tions, Martin's cult continued, through the time of the Viking invasions, to play a major role in defining the city's localism and unity.
Similarly, it continued to attract royal favor to Tours and to symbolize
royal and national dignity.

The continued importance of Martin's *cappa* at the Carolingian
court indicates that though Saint Denis may have attained preemi-
nence as the royal patron saint, Martin retained an important role as
well. Indeed, the Carolingian kings not only swore their oaths over
Martin's cappa, as had the Merovingians, they also carried it into
battle. At Eastertime in the year 800 Charlemagne paid his respects to
Saint Martin by visiting his tomb, and in the Carolingian *laudes regiae*—liturgical proclamations of the king—Martin and Denis were
invoked equally as patrons of the Frankish army.[46]

The example of Archbishop Theotolus (the see of Tours was elevated to an archbishopric sometime before 871) demonstrates that
despite Saint-Martin's privilege of exemption, close liturgical relations between the basilica and the cathedral were still possible in the
tenth century. Sometime before 940, Theotolus rebuilt and reformed
the monastery of Saint-Julian, which was halfway between the walls
of the cathedral town and those of Châteauneuf. Although monks
from the abbey of Cluny assisted in its reform, Saint-Julian remained
a dependency of the cathedral. Theotolus soon arranged for the

45. Chélini, "Alcuin, Charlemagne et Saint-Martin," 19, 28, 42; Gasnault, "Tombeau
de Saint Martin et les invasions normandes," 52; Alcuin, "De vita S. Martini Turonensis,"
PL 101:657–58; Alcuin, "Sermo de transitu S. Martini," PL 101:662; Kantorowicz, *Laudes
Regiae,* 15. On the transition at Saint-Martin from a house of monks to a house of secular
canons, see Semmler, "Benedictus II," 14–15.
46. Leclercq, "Chape de Saint Martin"; Vaucelle, *Collégiale de Saint-Martin,* 20; Kantorowicz, *Laudes Regiae,* 15.

monks of Saint-Julian to participate at Saint-Martin in the celebration of Martin's November feast, and for the chapter of Saint-Martin to give one of its prebends to Saint-Julian. The archbishop's actions reflect the continued possibility of symbolic unity between the cathedral and the community of Saint-Martin. The relationship, however, was not as close as it had been in the sixth century: Theotolus, who was buried at Saint-Julian, provides our first documented evidence that Saint-Martin was no longer the necropolis for the archbishops of Tours. In the High and later Middle Ages the archbishops of Tours would be buried at the cathedral or at monasteries of the archbishops' choice, but not at Saint-Martin.[47]

Local loyalties also survived into the tenth century. Although Charlemagne's centralizing policies temporarily undermined local autonomy and prestige, those policies were short-lived: the Viking and post-Viking eras witnessed a return to saintly localism. During the invasions of the ninth and tenth centuries the inhabitants of besieged towns resorted to the protection of saints' relics just as they had during the first wave of barbarian incursions. In 885 the relics of Saint Geneviève and Saint Germanus saved the inhabitants of Paris, and in 903 those of Saint Martin saved Tours.[48]

A tenth-century marginal note in a liturgical manuscript from Saint-Martin provides the bare facts concerning the Viking attack on Tours in June 903: under their leaders Heric and Baret the Vikings burned the basilica of Saint-Martin, along with twenty-eight other churches and the faubourg. The note makes no mention, however, of the crucial role Martin's relics played in saving the walled cathedral town from destruction.[49]

It was a bishop—Radbod of Utrecht—who, in a sermon intended to comfort his congregation in the midst of the chaos of their time, set down the narrative describing Martin's divine intervention. Radbod, who had studied at Saint-Martin in Tours and whose episcopal town looked to Martin as a special patron, provides a poignant example of the persisting relationship between Martin's cult and the themes of

47. *Brevis historia Sancti Juliani Turonensis*, 226; Mabille, *Pancarte noire de Saint-Martin*, no. 143, p. 187; Oury, "Reconstruction monastique dans l'Ouest," 75–77. On the elevation of Tours to an archbishopric and the burial of archbishops, see Crozet, "Recherches sur la cathédrale et les évêques de Tours," 193–95.

48. Herrmann-Mascard, *Reliques des saints*, 217–18; Abbo, "De bello Parisiaco," 84–87; Gasnault, "Tombeau de Saint Martin," 62.

49. Gasnault, "Tombeau de Saint Martin," 62. The text of the marginal note (from Tours, Bibliothèque Municipale, MS. 106) is reproduced in *Catalogue général des manuscrits des bibliothèques publiques de France*, 37:2:68–69. Pierre Gasnault points out that Radbod's own dating of the event was basically consistent with that of the marginal note from Tours: "'Narratio in reversione beati Martini a Burgundia,'" 162–63.

civic unity, localism, and royal patronage.[50] His sermon also merits
close attention because it inspired some of the legitimizing stories that
would be invented in the twelfth century.

The circumstances of the siege of 903 encouraged an external form
of civic unity: the canons of Saint-Martin sought refuge for themselves and their saint inside the walls of the cathedral town, and they
deposited Martin's relics in a church they possessed inside the city
walls.[51] In his account of the siege, Radbod depicted this unity in
idealized terms. Like Gregory and Paulinus of Perigord, he blurred
distinctions within the community of Tours, and especially within its
ecclesiastical community. His narrative created the impression that the
entire city worked together and that Martin belonged to everyone in
Tours: while the armed men of the city fought as best they could,
women, children, and old men joined the clerics in praying for divine
assistance. Radbod provided no details. The clergy were not of any
particular house, and the appeal for assistance—"Martin, saint of
God, why do you sleep so soundly?"—took place at an unspecified
church that housed Martin's relics.[52]

Radbod did, however, distinguish the clergy from the laity. The
clergy as a unit took control of the relics, carrying them to the ramparts. And when the relics arrived, the armed townsmen as a unit
regained "both their bodily strength and their audacity of spirit."[53]
Like Paulinus of Perigord's account of the annual pilgrimage to Marmoutier, Radbod's sermon made no mention of the bishop or of
hierarchical arrangements. Nevertheless, he described a drama that
took place within the ramparts of the cathedral town. For this reason
his vague language concerning the church where the events took
place, and his assumption that the clergy acted as a single unit, suggested that the cathedral and its clerics, if not the bishop himself, were
involved in the drama.

In Radbod's sermon, the Carolingian rulers played no role as protectors of Tours; Martin, the local patron saint, took their place.
Radbod further underscored the resort to localism in his depiction of
the appeal to Martin. The people of Tours almost chastised their
saint, reminding him that he had worked miracles for foreigners but
now, in their hour of peril, he seemed to have forgotten the men and
women of his own town: "Behold, we are to be handed over to pagans

50. Radbod of Utrecht, *Libellus de miraculo S. Martini*, 1243; *Vita Radbodi*, 569–71;
Ewig, "Culte de Saint Martin à l'époque franque," 16.

51. Gasnault, "Tombeau de Saint Martin," 63–64.

52. "Sancte Dei Martine, quare tam graviter obdormisti?" (Radbod, *Libellus*, 1243).

53. "Simul et corporis vires et animi audaciam resumpserunt" (Radbod, *Libellus*, 1243).

and led away as captives . . . and you feign not to know these things. Have pity . . . you who once displayed so many signs for foreigners, do at least the same for your own, and free us."[54] The people then turned from admonishments to passive threats, warning that if Martin did not help them they would perish, "and your city will be reduced to solitude."[55] Without inhabitants, Tours would be an empty shell; no one would glorify Martin's tomb, and his relics might even be lost. The underlying assumption was that the relationship between the saint and his town was reciprocal: just as the town depended on the protection of the saint, the glory of the saint ultimately depended on the well-being of the city and its inhabitants.

Through the mouths of the people of Tours, Radbod depicted the resurgence of urban localism, but he did not himself forget the broader political unit of the Carolingian rulers. As bishop of Utrecht, Radbod did not view Martin's relationship to Tours in quite the same way Perpetuus and Gregory had. Although he asserted that the inhabitants of Tours were indeed fortunate in possessing Martin's relics, "that most precious gem," he maintained as well that the brightness of that gem irradiated the whole world.[56] As a former resident of the court of Charles the Bald, Radbod emphasized that Martin's relationship to the royal family strengthened the rulers themselves rather than binding them in obligation to the city of Tours.[57] In his concern for the welfare of the ruling dynasty, Radbod employed some of the imagery that had been developed at the court of Charlemagne. But there was one crucial difference: for Charlemagne's circle Christianity was a source of power and confidence; for Radbod it was a pious refuge and a consolation.

The writings of Charlemagne's court had stressed that the Franks were the new Israelites, God's chosen people, and that Charlemagne was a new King David. Divine favor implied worldly success: as the laudes regiae proclaimed, "Christ conquers, Christ reigns, Christ rules."[58] Radbod made a weak attempt to emulate these themes. He declared that Christianity had now conquered the whole world, including those who once seemed to have superior power, and that the

---

54. "En tradendi sumus paganis, en captivi abducendi. . . . Et tu haec omnia te nosse dissimulas. Ostende . . . pietatem . . . qui multa quondam pro alienis signa fecisti, saltem unum fac modo pro tuis, ut liberes nos" (Radbod, *Libellus*, 1243).

55. "Alioquin et nos peribimus, et civitas tua redigetur in solitudinem" (Radbod, *Libellus*, 1243).

56. "Gemma illa pretiosissima" (Radbod, *Libellus*, 1241).

57. On Radbod's relationship with Charles the Bald, see *Vita Radbodi*, 569.

58. "Christus vincit, Christus regnat, Christus imperat" (Kantorowicz, *Laudes Regiae*, 21 ff., 56–57).

religion thus deserved to be called *imperatrix* and *domina*. His story of God's action through Saint Martin implied that though the barbarian invaders sometimes appeared to have the upper hand, God continued to support the Christian Franks. Radbod went so far in his imperial imagery as to compare the miraculous deliverance of Tours to the divine assistance that had supported the military successes of the Christian Roman emperors Constantine and Theodosius.[59] But Radbod's sermon failed to evoke real confidence. He portrayed Christians and their rulers as passive victims. Saint Martin—the "unconquered warrior, most powerful fighter, divine contender"—was his only hero.[60]

Radbod transformed the earlier assertion that the Frankish kings were the leaders of God's chosen conquering people into a desperate plea that through Martin's intercession "the line of Charlemagne" would "never eclipse" and the kingdom of the Franks would be always "feared, loved, venerated, and strengthened."[61] According to Radbod, God had sent the invaders to punish the Franks for their sins. It was suffering and punishment, not success, that now indicated to Radbod and his contemporaries that God had a special relationship with the Franks.[62] Although he maintained his loyalty to the Carolingian order, Radbod apparently had limited faith in its effectiveness.

Radbod's account of the Viking attack on Tours was the swan song of early medieval representations of the relationship between the cult of Saint Martin and the royal and civic orders. During the ninth and tenth centuries the Carolingian political and ecclesiastical order crumbled: while the Robertian/Capetian dynasty competed with and then replaced the Carolingian dynasty, effective royal power almost disappeared from many parts of France, public power fused with private domain, ecclesiastical property and institutions fell into the hand of powerful secular families, and the hierarchical ordering of the diocese broke down.

In Tours in the late tenth and eleventh centuries, the Capetian king

59. Radbod, *Libellus,* 1240, 1242.
60. "Bellator invictissime, athleta fortissime, agonista divine" (Radbod, *Libellus,* 1244).
61. "Esto igitur ubi es et semper intercede pro nobis, statumque regni Francorum, prole Magni quondam Karoli nunquam deficiente, tuis intercessionibus erige, quo in hac vita nec visibilis nec invisibilis hostis sibi addicat nec expugnare praevaleat, sed te patrocinante timeatur et ametur, veneretur et firmetur" (Radbod, *Libellus,* 1244).
62. Radbod, *Libellus,* 1242; Radbod, *Carmina,* 164; Haenens, *Invasions normandes: Une catastrophe?* 72–77.

was often limited to simply aligning himself with either the count of Blois or the count of Anjou.[63] This position of relative weakness affected the king's relationship with religious institutions. Hugh Capet inherited from his Robertian ancestors the position of lay abbot of Saint-Martin, a position the Capetian kings never relinquished. Throughout most of the eleventh century and even the early years of the twelfth, however, the men who held the positions of dean and treasurer of Saint-Martin (the two most important offices there) were usually *fideles* of the counts of Blois or of the counts of Anjou.[64]

At Marmoutier the situation was somewhat different: in 985, apparently with the consent of Hugh Capet, who had been lay abbot of both Saint-Martin and Marmoutier, Marmoutier was placed under the authority of the count of Blois, who called on monks from Cluny to reform it. When Count Geoffrey Martel of Anjou extended his power over Touraine in 1044, the counts of Blois retained their relationship with Marmoutier. In effect, however, the new political situation placed Marmoutier in a position of relative independence. And because Marmoutier gained a widespread reputation in the eleventh century as a model of reformed monasticism, the counts of Anjou, the dukes of Normandy, and the Capetian kings, as well as the counts of Blois, called upon it to reform other religious houses.[65]

The ascendency of powerful princely families, such as those of Blois and Anjou, represents one aspect of the breakdown of the Carolingian order. Another aspect was the monastic reform movement, which successfully challenged the hierarchical ordering of the diocese. As I recount in the next chapter, in the late tenth century the canons of Saint-Martin began a new era of resistance to the jurisdictional rights of their archbishop, and they were joined in the early eleventh century by the monks of Marmoutier. Both houses were ultimately successful in their efforts, largely because they aligned

---

63. Halphen, *Comté d'Anjou*, 30–33, 45 ff. On Capetian alliances with Angevin and Blésois counts, see Bachrach, "Angevin Strategy of Castle Building in the Reign of Fulk Nerra," 540; Bachrach, "Geoffrey Greymantle, Count of the Angevins," 28–29.

64. Boussard, "Trésorier de Saint-Martin de Tours"; Griffiths, "Capetian Kings and St. Martin of Tours." I am grateful to Professor Griffiths for sending me his article before it appeared in print. Olivier Guillot does not agree with Boussard's analysis of the fact that the treasurers of Saint-Martin were *fideles* of Anjou and Blois. Boussard, he suggests, went too far in assuming the king's loss of control over the house (*Comte d'Anjou*, 1:114 n. 506).

65. On the reform of Marmoutier, see introduction to part 2, and chapter 6. On Angevin, Capetian, and Blésois relations with Marmoutier, see Guillot, *Comte d'Anjou*, 1:173–93. On Marmoutier and Duke William of Normandy, see Martène, *Histoire de l'abbaye de Marmoutier*, 1:392, 439.

themselves, in the second half of the eleventh century, with the emerging papal monarchy.[66]

By the middle of the eleventh century, when the pattern of post-Carolingian fragmentation began to yield to a reemergence of more centralized secular and ecclesiastical governments, the stage had been set in Tours for the story I tell in the following chapters. Tours was a meeting ground for Angevin, Capetian, and to a lesser extent Blésois influence. Châteauneuf and Saint-Martin were under the jurisdiction of the Capetian kings, who nevertheless continued to favor Angevin allies for offices there, at least until the early years of the twelfth century.[67] After 1068 the Capetian kings were able to assert their influence over archiepiscopal elections in Tours, but the cathedral town itself, as well as the entire region, was under Angevin control.[68] The counts of Blois, in the meantime, shifted their primary political attention to the regions of Chartres and Champagne, but they retained their role as patrons and protectors of Marmoutier.[69] In the ecclesiastical sphere, by 1050 the monastic exemption movement had already begun to upset the traditional ecclesiastical hierarchy of Tours. By the end of the century the archbishop's right to control, or even to visit, the basilica of Saint-Martin and the abbey of Marmoutier had been severely limited.

The canons of Saint-Martin, the monks of Marmoutier, the counts of Blois and Anjou, and the archbishops of Tours all played important roles in the development of Martin's cult between the mid-eleventh century and the mid-thirteenth century. But the story included one other important group as well: the burghers of Châteauneuf. The rise of trade and commerce in the post-Viking era, the location of Tours on the Loire, and the popularity of Martin's tomb all contributed to the growth in Châteauneuf of a population of prosperous burghers, whose wealth was unmatched by that of the inhabitants of other parts of Tours. Throughout the twelfth and thirteenth centuries these burghers, whose prosperity depended on Saint Martin, demonstrated

66. See chapter 2. For a summary of the various arguments concerning the relationship between monastic exemption and feudal decentralization, see Rosenwein, *Rhinoceros Bound: Cluny in the Tenth Century*, 2.

67. Griffiths, "Capetian Kings and St. Martin of Tours," 115, 119 n. 10.

68. On the archbishops, see Bienvenu, "Réforme grégorienne dans l'archidiocèse de Tours," 79. On the Angevin victory of 1044 that led to the count's control of Touraine, see especially Boussard, "Eviction des tenants de Thibaut de Blois par Geoffrey Martel," 141–49; on the count's residence in the cathedral town, see Galinié, "Résidence des comtes d'Anjou à Tours."

69. On relations between the counts of Blois and Anjou and Marmoutier see introduction to part 2, and chapters 3 and 4 below. On the counts of Blois in general, see Bur, *Formation du comté de Champagne*.

their self-confidence by resisting the seigneurial authority of the canons of Saint-Martin.

When the monks of Marmoutier and the canons of Saint-Martin directed their attention, between 1050 and 1250, to the cult of their common patron saint, they portrayed Martin's relationship to the community in ways that were fundamentally different from those of Perpetuus, Gregory of Tours, and Radbod of Utrecht. As I argue in the next chapter, neither the monks nor the canons represented Saint Martin as the patron of a single community united under the archbishop. Their legends and rituals represented Tours as a fragmented community. Nor, as I show in chapters 3 and 4, did the monks agree with the canons that Martin and his town had a special relationship with the Capetian kings. Finally, as parts 2 and 3 suggest, the monks and canons drew on Martin's prestige to enhance the local collective interests not of the town as a whole, but of their particular religious institutions.

That the cult of Saint Martin reflected a conflict-ridden community in the eleventh, twelfth, and thirteenth centuries does not mean there was more actual violence and rivalry in that period than there had been in the early Middle Ages. Rather, more people had access in the later period to the written medium and recognized its power; cultural expressions were thus more open to contestation. No single group could retain a monopoly on the cult of the saints as bishops had done in the Merovingian period.

2

Excluding the Center:
Monastic Exemption and Liturgical
Realignment in Tours

Beginning in the late tenth century and continuing throughout the eleventh, the canons of Saint-Martin and the monks of Marmoutier struggled to gain exemption from the hierarchical authority of their archbishop. They achieved their goals by the second decade of the twelfth century, and as a result the cultic unity of the city, which had survived at least in part from the fifth century through the early tenth, was definitively dismantled. The archbishop lost his position at the liturgical hub of Tours: he was no longer free to make ceremonial visitations to Saint-Martin and Marmoutier and to preside over services at those two houses. Marmoutier and Saint-Martin, by contrast, established a network of lateral alliances, which they underscored with elaborations in the cult of Saint Martin. A new legend and a new liturgical celebration, both commemorating the role Martin's relics had played during the Viking invasions, simultaneously emphasized the bond between the two religious houses and deemphasized, or indirectly denigrated, the authority of the archbishop. In symbolic terms, Tours became two communities. On the one hand there was the archbishop's town, now excluded from Martin's patronage and cult. And on the other hand there was Martin's community, which consisted of Marmoutier, Saint-Martin, and Châteauneuf.

The Demise of Episcopal Dominance

The tenth- and eleventh-century monastic exemption movement emerged in the 990s when the monks of west Francia, and most especially Abbot Abbo of Fleury, began to chafe under the temporal and disciplinary interference of lay and ecclesiastical lords. These were the early years of the Capetian dynasty, when Carolingian order was breaking down. Monasteries were vulnerable to the depredations of local magnates, including bishops, who were attempting to increase their temporal and banal powers. In an effort to seek protection from those depredations, monks like Abbo turned to the papacy.[1]

In 991 Abbo became engaged in the deliberations at the Council of Saint-Basle in Verzy concerning a bishop who had been accused of treason against King Hugh Capet. Abbo argued that it was not appropriate for the council of Frankish bishops to judge the case, which should be referred to Rome instead. His support of papal prerogatives was perhaps partially a matter of self-interest. Fleury possessed papal privileges that the archbishop of Orléans would have liked to ignore, and he would have felt more at liberty to do so once papal prerogatives fell into doubt.[2]

It was, in fact, the archbishop of Orléans—Arnulf—who took the leading role at Saint-Basle in defending the prerogatives of the Frankish council. After the council, relations between Abbo and his archbishop continued to sour, and Abbo soon resolved to step up his efforts to gain exemption for his abbey from episcopal interference. He spent the years between 991 and 997 gathering several collections of texts—based largely on letters of Gregory the Great—to provide general support for his position on monastic rights. Abbo needed to base his case on the statements of illustrious "fathers," because the bishops of Gaul were arguing that the statements of a current pope had no validity if they overturned the positions of earlier, more illustrious popes. But Abbo also needed to support general theory with specific evidence concerning his own abbey, and to this end he, or someone close to him, forged a papal privilege for Fleury sometime before 997.[3]

In 997 Abbo succeeded in obtaining from Pope Gregory V a grant of exemption for Fleury. Henceforth all archbishops, bishops, and clerics were forbidden to visit Fleury, to make ordinations there, or to celebrate mass there without the consent of the abbot. Bishops were to have no authority over monks they ordained, and abbots who were accused of crimes were to be judged by provincial councils or, if they wished, by the pope himself. Fleury thus became, in the words of Jean-François Lemarignier, "a quasi-independent islet in the heart of the diocese of Orléans."[4]

1. Lemarignier, "Political and Monastic Structures in France"; Lemarignier, "Exemption monastique," 301 ff.; Head, *Hagiography and the Cult of the Saints,* chap. 6.

2. Lemarignier, "Exemption monastique," 303; Mostert, *Political Theology of Abbo of Fleury,* 46–47; Head, *Hagiography and the Cult of the Saints,* chap. 6.

3. Lemarignier, "Exemption monastique," 303–11; Head, *Hagiography and the Cult of the Saints,* chap. 6; Mostert, *Political Theology of Abbo of Fleury,* 48–76.

4. Lemarignier, "Exemption monastique," 311.

Even before Abbo attained his abbey's exemption in 997, the canons of Saint-Martin in Tours made their own attempt to resist episcopal authority: they refused the blessing of their archbishop, Archambald (980–1005).[5] Archambald reported the incident to Archbishop Gerbert of Reims, who informed the canons that they should either reconcile themselves with their archbishop or come to the Council of Chelles to explain themselves.[6] The canons of Saint-Martin, whose treasurer, Herveus, had studied with Abbo, turned to that abbot for support. Abbo offered the canons general statements concerning monastic privileges—based again on letters of Gregory the Great—but he also assumed that Saint-Martin's claim rested on an established local precedent. It was not until a much later date, in the 1080s or 1090s, that the canons of Saint-Martin produced forgeries establishing such a precedent. Only then were their claims to exemption finally recognized.[7]

A bishop's authority to bless and ordain the clerics and monks in his diocese was a fundamental aspect of his spiritual authority, and indeed nothing in the 997 privilege for Fleury called this episcopal right into question. Nevertheless, in 998 or 999 the monks of Cluny received a privilege of exemption that did just that: not only were bishops forbidden to visit Cluny unless invited, but the monks were granted the right to ask *any* bishop, from whatever diocese, to bless new abbots. Cluny thus became totally independent of its diocesan bishop. Such a privilege was unknown in Tours until the end of the eleventh century, when Urban II granted it to the monks of Marmoutier.[8]

Our first hint of Marmoutier's possible involvement in the exemption movement comes from a decree issued by Archbishop Arnulf of Tours (1023–52) deploring a violent incident that broke out during Arnulf's annual Easter visitation to Marmoutier. Although Arnulf did not explain what provoked the incident, it is reasonable to assume that the issue of exemption loomed in the back of people's minds during and after the event.

In his decree, Arnulf stated that some of the laymen and clerics

5. Gerbert, Letter 209, *PL* 139:262–63; Lemarignier, "Exemption monastique," 314–15.

6. Gerbert, Letter 211, *PL* 139:263.

7. Abbo, Letter 5, *PL* 139:423–24; Lemarignier, "Exemption monastique," 314; Gasnault, "Etude sur les chartes de Saint-Martin," 39. Cousin, *Abbon de Fleury,* 160–61. Cousin mistakenly accepted as authentic a forged papal privilege from Gregory V to Saint-Martin (see Gasnault on its forged nature). On Saint-Martin's privilege from Urban II, see below. On the relationship between Abbo and Herveus of Saint-Martin, see Oury, "Idéal monastique dans la vie canoniale: Le bienheureux Hervé de Tours," 4–8.

8. Lemarignier, "Exemption monastique," 314–15. On Marmoutier, see below.

(probably canons of the cathedral) who participated in his Easter visitation "left the mass, violently broke into the cloister of the monastery, and violated the solitude of the monks without any reverence for God. Moreover, they demanded . . . food for themselves in places ordained for the divine cult."[9]

Despite his silence concerning the motivations for this act of aggression, Arnulf's language pointed to the issue of monastic exemption. He emphasized that his annual visitation on the fourth day after Easter was a long-standing tradition, but he was not referring to the tradition of pious veneration that Paulinus of Perigord had described in the fifth century. Rather, Arnulf invoked the universal right and responsibility of bishops to visit the monasteries within their jurisdictions and to provide pastoral care in those places by preaching and imposing discipline.[10] The archbishop was asserting an episcopal prerogative to intervene in the internal governance of monasteries, and it was precisely this prerogative that monks throughout west Francia were resisting.

In Tours, Arnulf's prelacy was marked by at least two insults to his episcopal honor. First, the monks of the abbey of Saint-Julian resisted Arnulf's appointment of his own father as their abbot. And second, the monks of Marmoutier asked him to give up his right to episcopal exactions at a parish church they had built. The request by the monks of Marmoutier was not necessarily a challenge to episcopal authority—other bishops were granting monasteries temporal rights over parishes. Nevertheless, Arnulf responded to this request with anger.[11]

The context of a general movement for monastic exemption, cou-

9. "Plerique enim eorum, qui mecum tanquam sanctae celebritatis gratia se venire simulabant tam ex laico, quam etiam ex clericali ordine adeo totius honestatis obliti erant, ut contemptis, quae Dei sunt, Missarumque celebrationibus relictis, claustra ipsius Coenobij violenter irrumperent, secretumque Monachorum absque Dei reverentia violarent, epulasque sibi in locis divino cultui ordinatis exhiberi consueta redhibitione fronte pudoris nescia exigerent" (Arnulphus, "Decretum," 249). The decree is undated, but Arnulf was archbishop from 1023 to 1052: *Gallia Christiana,* 14:58–61; Mas-Latrie, *Trésor de chronologie,* 1502.

10. "Sancta, et satis religiosa Presulum consuetudo tam in Rom. quam etiam in ceteris per orbem terrarum diffusis Ecclesiis hactenus fuisse cognoscitur, ut in precipuis solemnitatibus Monasteria, que in Civitatibus, et in Suburbiis earum sita erant circuirent missasque publicas in eis agerent, ut scilicet populis ad ea conuenientibus, opportunius verbum praedicationis seminarent, et si quid in locis eisdem reprehensionis vidissent, pia admonitione corrigerent" (Arnulphus, "Decretum," 248–49).

11. *Brevis historia Sancti Juliani Turonensis,* 230; *Chronicon rhythmicum Sancti Juliani Turonensis,* 250–51; Boussard, "Evêques en Neustrie avant la réforme grégorienne," 176; *Gallia Christiana,* 14:56, 59; *Marmoutier, Cartulaire Blésois,* 35, (notice, dated 1060), p. 45. On the franchise of monastic parishes, see Lemarignier, *Etude sur les privilèges d'exemption,* 107–10 and passim.

pled with Arnulf's perception that he had problems in his own diocese, may have provided the provocation for the Easter incident at Marmoutier. It is quite likely that the perpetrators were allies of Arnulf and canons of the cathedral and that they wished to convey a message to the monks of the diocese that power and dominion still resided in the cathedral.

Archbishop Arnulf condemned the insult to Marmoutier, but he acknowledged no causal connection between the transgressions of individuals and the practice of episcopal visitation that enabled them to take action. Indeed, given the goals of the exemption movement, Arnulf's stress on the "charitable" and "paternal" nature of episcopal visitation is significant. By emphasizing the inherent value of visitation, Arnulf conveyed the message that the aggressive incident was merely an isolated case rather than a symptom of structural problems: "Desiring to put an end to these miseries, I establish that no one is to contrive in any way to demand or carry out the things that we have described, but as the apostle says, let all things be done with charity since our coming to holy places should be able to be called a paternal visitation rather than a tyrannical depredation or a hostile incursion."[12]

Arnulf's relations with the monks in his diocese were not always peaceful, but he was archbishop at a time when the ultimate outcome of the exemption movement was not clear and when the balance of power between bishops and monasteries was still relatively equal. In Tours this balance was disrupted by the growth of papal government, which began with the reform councils of Leo IX about 1049. Through their disciplinary actions against simony and their intervention in episcopal elections, the popes and their legates imposed their will on bishops, thereby subordinating local ecclesiastical power to that of the Holy See.[13] Moreover, some reforming popes, such as Urban II (1088–99), tended to favor monastic exemption, both because they held the morality of the episcopacy in low esteem and because they aimed to strengthen their own position by placing monasteries directly under the authority of Rome.[14] The popes were not

12. "Ego finem his miserijs imponere cupiens, statuo ut haec quae prediximus a nullo penitus ulterius expetantur, vel perpetrentur, sed omnia, ut ait Apostolus, ex charitate fiant, quatenus adventus noster ad sancta loca potius dici possit paterna visitatio, quam tyrannica depredatio, vel hostilis incursio" (Arnulphus, "Decretum," 249).

13. Imbart de la Tour, *Elections épiscopales,* 378–91, 476–512; Benson, *Bishop-Elect.*

14. Lemarignier, "Exemption monastique," 289. Lemarignier, *Etude sur les privilèges d'exemption,* 179–81; Fliche, *Règne de Philippe Ier,* 451, 459–60; Cheney, *Episcopal Visitations of Monasteries,* 17–53.

entirely free to dissolve traditional relationships between bishops and religious houses, however. For this reason, it appears, the monks of Marmoutier and the canons of Saint-Martin invented precedents for their claims to exemption and exaggerated the transgressions of their archbishops. Toward the end of the eleventh century both houses attained bulls of exemption from Pope Urban II, but Marmoutier did not finally resolve its struggle for exemption for another twenty years.

It was during the primacies of Archbishop Ralph of Langeais (1073–ca. 1093) and Archbishop Ralph of Orléans (ca. 1093–1118) that the papal reformers assumed a central role in the struggle for ecclesiastical exemption at Tours.[15] These two archbishops also faced a conflict of interest between their traditional loyalty to the king of France and the reformers' attempts, which accelerated in 1074, to extract the church from the king's control.[16] The position each bishop took in the conflict between church and state may have affected the papal party's decisions concerning monastic exemption. The first Ralph tended to favor the papal reformers rather than the king, and in turn the reformers tended to back him rather than Saint-Martin and Marmoutier. The second Ralph, by contrast, remained a close ally of King Philip I, whose divorce and remarriage placed both king and archbishop in disfavor with the papal reformers. Ralph II's alliance with the king may have contributed to Urban II's persistent support of Marmoutier and Saint-Martin. Urban, however, was inclined to favor monastic exemption anyway.[17]

The beginning of Ralph I's archiepiscopal career did not mark him as a likely ally of papal reform: he gained his archbishopric through an indirect form of simony. And soon after he assumed office he associated with Count Fulk Rechin of Anjou, who was under a sentence of excommunication at the time. Pope Gregory VII admonished Ralph for associating with Fulk and commanded him to come to Rome in November 1074. The visit apparently sealed a working relationship between Ralph and Gregory, who in 1078 overturned the

15. For the dates of the two archbishops, see *Gallia Christiana,* 14:63–76. On Gregory VII as the turning point for papal activity in France, see Fliche, *Règne de Philippe Ier,* 387–423. On the local evidence, see the discussion that follows.

16. Fliche, *Règne de Philippe Ier,* 390; citing Gregory VII's letter of 1074 to the French bishops, *Bibliotheca rerum Germanicarum,* 2:113–17.

17. On Philip's divorce and remarriage, see Fliche, *Règne de Philippe Ier,* 40–77. Archbishop Ralph II crowned Philip in 1098, against the orders of a papal legate: see Ivo of Chartres, Letters 66, 67, *PL* 162–83, 87; Fliche, *Règne,* 94. Urban II made it clear at the Council of Clermont in 1095 that he favored monastic exemption: see Lemarignier, *Etude sur les privilèges d'exemption,* 190; on his support for Cluny, see Fliche, *Règne,* 459–60.

decision of his legate, Hugh of Die, that Ralph should be deposed for his act of simony.[18]

By 1082 Archbishop Ralph I had apparently become, in the eyes of King Philip I, too sympathetic to the program of papal reform, which was undermining Philip's control of bishoprics in his realm. Philip convinced Count Fulk of Anjou to expel Ralph from his bishopric, and as a consequence Fulk was excommunicated, as were the canons of Saint-Martin. For reasons the documents do not explain, the canons were implicated in the count's actions. Gregory VII wrote to the excommunicated canons urging them to restore the archbishop's property, to obey the papal legates, and to avoid associating with Fulk of Anjou.[19] By 1083 Ralph was back in Tours.[20]

In a propagandistic account of their struggle with the archbishop, which they probably wrote for Urban II about 1096, the canons of Saint-Martin claimed that the traditional liberty of Saint-Martin (a royal house) had been a central issue in Fulk's ousting the archbishop. Fulk had expelled the archbishop, they claimed, "because of the injuries that Ralph, the enemy of God, perpetrated against the king, and especially against the canons of Saint-Martin."[21] The canons also

18. On the call to Rome in 1074 and the relationship that followed, see "Analekten zur Geschichte des Reformpapsttums," 37–42. On Fulk's excommunication (1067–94), see Guillot, *Comte d'Anjou,* 1:110, 116. On Ralph's deposition by Hugh and reinstatement by Gregory, see Letter of Hugh of Die (January 1078) and Gregory VII (March 9, 1078—Jaffé 3805), in *Recueil des historiens des Gaules,* 14:615, 618; Guillot, *Comte d'Anjou* 1:253 n. 236.

19. Halphen, *Comté d'Anjou,* 185–86, 199–201; Gregory VII, Letter to Archbishop Ralph, "Trois lettres de Grégoire VII," 559; Gregory VII, Letter to Tourangeaux and Angevins, Letter to canons of Saint-Martin (December 4, 1082—Jaffé, 3944–45, J.-L. 5231–32), in *Recueil des historiens des Gaules,* 14:654–55. These last two letters were described by Leo Santifaller, but he did not reedit them: see *Quellen und Forschungen zum Urkunden- und Kanzleiwesen Papst Gregors VII,* 1:242, no. 204. On the king's annoyance with Ralph's attitude toward papal legates, see *Narratio controversiae inter capitulum S. Martini Turonensis et Radulphum,* 459; however, this is a biased and slightly later account (see note 21 below).

20. Halphen, *Comté d'Anjou,* 201, 314.

21. "Propter injurias quas Regi, maxime autem Ecclesiae Canonicisque S. Martini, Radulfus Dei inimicus intulerat" (*Narratio controversiae,* 459). I suggest the date of 1096 because the document misrepresents Gregory VII's stance toward the canons, so it was probably written after Gregory's death in 1085, and because it established false precedents concerning rights to refuse papal legates, which were finally granted by Urban II in 1096: see "Bulla pro canonicis S. Martini Turonensis," in *Recueil des historiens des Gaules,* 14:719–20, and *PL* 151:449–50. To support the false precedents, the canons produced forged papal privileges from Adrian I and Gregory V: see Gasnault, "Etude sur les chartes de Saint-Martin," 39. The canons would have needed to invent a case for their rights to refuse legates only before Urban actually granted them that right. Louis Halphen argued (*Comté d'Anjou,* 198 n. 3, 313) that this inaccurate work may not have been written until the mid-twelfth century. Although he was right about the propagandistic distortions, he exaggerated the factual errors, especially those concerning the identity and kinship of Geoffrey and Ralph of Langeais: see Guillot, *Comte d'Anjou,* 1:252 n. 232, 253–54, 2:222.

claimed that Gregory VII had upheld their right not to provide a solemn reception for the papal legate Amatus, and they attributed a speech to Gregory in which he recognized the basilica's long-standing liberties: "Many of my predecessors—Gregory, Sergius, Stephen, Adeodatus, Leo—. . . established Saint-Martin free and undisturbed from all custom and subjection, and they confirmed these things so that the church would never be placed under the domination of any pontiff, because of the dignity of [Saint Martin] the worthy confessor."[22]

The canons went on, in this work of propaganda, to describe the rupture in relations between the cathedral and the basilica. Public rituals, which symbolized both the rift between the cathedral and the basilica and the autonomy of the canons, played a central role in their narrative. During the height of the tensions, the canons claimed, an exchange of excommunications replaced processional exchanges that had once expressed the concord between the cathedral and the basilica. When the archbishop and papal legate excommunicated the canons, the canons flaunted their defiance, excommunicating the archbishop in turn and continuing with their customary round of ceremonial visitations to churches other than the cathedral:

> At that time, by the advice of the sons of priests who were canons at the church of Saint-Maurice [the cathedral], all concord between the bishop of the city and the clergy of Saint-Martin was destroyed. . . . But this discord arose out of the jealousy of their city, so that they did not make processions to us, nor we to them, as was established by ancient custom. That same year Archbishop Ralph and the legate Amatus excommunicated the Tourangeaux and the people of Anjou from all Christian office. And we, the canons of Saint-Martin, celebrated the mass at Saint-Julian on the first day of rogations, against their will, and on the second day at Saint-Mary of Beaumont, and we made all the stations, just as the ancient custom prescribes. Moreover, William Bassus, the chaplain of Saint-Martin, excommunicated Ralph, the enemy of God.[23]

22. "Multi . . . praedecessores mei, Gregorius, Sergius, Stephanus, Adeodatus, Leo . . . ab omni consuetudine et ab omni subjectione liberam et quietam fecerunt; et ut in perpetuum nullius dominationi Pontificis subdita foret Ecclesia sanxerunt, propter dignitatem tanti Confessoris" (*Narratio controversiae,* 459); and on Gregory's respect for the refusal to receive legates and other visitors, 459–60.
23. "Hoc tempore, consilio filiorum Sacerdotum qui erant Canonici in Ecclesia S. Mauritii, dissipata est et destructa concordia omnis inter Episcopum civitatis et Clerum S. Martini, et ut omnia simul concludam, inter nobiles ipsas duas Ecclesias. Haec autem discordia orta est ex invidia ipsorum civitatis, ita ut neque illi ad nos in processionem veniant, neque nos ad illos, sicut antiqua consuetudo statuerat. Ipso anno excommunicavit Radulphus Archiepiscopus et Amatus Legatus populum Turonorum et Andegavorum ab

In their account of the events, the canons of Saint-Martin misrepresented the stance of Gregory VII, who had actually supported Archbishop Ralph. Yet there is no reason to doubt their depiction of their persistent desire to gain institutional autonomy (from the archbishop and papal legates, if not from the king) and to circumscribe the rituals that would have symbolized their own hierarchical subordination. They ultimately won that autonomy in 1096, when Urban II issued a bull recognizing their right not to offer solemn receptions to anyone except the king, the pope, and—once during each prelacy—the archbishop of Tours. That each archbishop could make only one ceremonial visit to Saint-Martin was an indication of the pontiff's loss of dominance. This exclusion of the archbishop from the liturgical life of Saint-Martin was still in effect in the first third of the thirteenth century.[24]

After his reinstatement in 1083, Archbishop Ralph I became preoccupied with Marmoutier's struggle for exemption, which, like that of Saint-Martin, tended to focus on rituals—both the archbishop's ceremonial visitations to the abbey and the ceremony of blessing a new abbot, when the archbishop was accustomed to demand an oath of obedience from the abbot. The hostilities between the archbishop and Marmoutier apparently first emerged in conjunction with Ralph's reinstatement as archbishop. Like the canons of Saint-Martin, the monks of Marmoutier were, for unexplained reasons, implicated in Fulk of Anjou's aggression against the archbishop: the bishops of the province of Lyons included the monks in their excommunication of the count in 1082.[25]

Even though they were implicated in Fulk of Anjou's action, the monks of Marmoutier probably had an agenda independent of those of both Fulk and King Philip. Sometime after the Council of Clermont in 1095, the monks wrote a retrospective and biased account of their struggles with the archbishop. According to that account, the archbishop's Easter visitation (which had first become a problem under Archbishop Arnulf) resurfaced as a source of tension during the

omni officio Christianorum. Et nos canonici S. Martini celebravimus Missam, primo die Rogationis ad S. Julianum, contra voluntatem ejus; et altero die ad S. Mariam de Bellomonte, et omnes stationes, sicut lex antiqua praeceperat. Willelmus etiam Bassus Capellanus S. Martini excommunicavit Radulfum Dei inimicum" (*Narratio controversiae*, 461).

24. "Bulla pro canonicis S. Martini Turonensis," in *Recueil des historiens des Gaules*, 14:719–20, and *PL* 151:449. Evidence for the early thirteenth century comes from *Consuetudines ecclesiae beati Martini*, 148–49. According to this customal the archbishop made a procession to Saint-Martin on the day of his consecration, but otherwise "archiepiscopus Turonensis non debet ibi cantare vel praedicare vel aliud pontificis officium exercere." On the date of the customal (after 1226) see Source Appendix, II-B.

25. "Episcoporum Lugdunensis provinciae ad Episcopos et Clerum provinciae Turonensis," in *Recueil des historiens des Gaules*, 14:673–74.

prelacy of Archbishop Ralph I. Tensions over this visitation gave rise, the monks claimed, to their subsequent problems with both Ralph I and Ralph II. The monks claimed that the annual visitation had developed as an expression of pious veneration and that recent abuses of it made a mockery of such piety. They made no reference to Arnulf's position, that the Easter visitation was a manifestation of the pontiff's right to exercise pastoral care and discipline over monks in his diocese:

> It had grown up, we do not know when or for what reason—except perhaps out of love and veneration for the ancient place—that the archbishop would solemnly celebrate a paschal station in our monastery. And though many evil things had occurred, even to the point of homicide [a reference to the language in Arnulf's decree], neither our fathers nor we ourselves had ever resisted this visitation until, under the license of the things that had been conceded, they began to demand illicit things, and what ancient religion had preserved for the sake of devotion their modern abuse subverted to derision and buffoonery.[26]

The monks claimed that the resulting quarrel over this visitation led to their excommunication. They were probably referring to the excommunication of 1082.

In 1084 there arose a second issue, which became a source of persistent dispute between the archbishop and the monastery, involving the consecration of Marmoutier's abbot. At the time of his consecration in 1084 Abbot Bernard promised his subjection to the archbishop. This promise apparently angered some of the monks, who attempted to unseat Bernard, calling his legitimacy into question because, they claimed, he had been consecrated while the archbishop was under a ban of excommunication.[27] Nevertheless, Bernard remained in office until his death in 1100.[28]

26. "Illud tamen quod ex qua nescimus consuetudine vel ex quo tempore inoleverit, nisi forsitan pro antiqua loci veneratione et dilectione, ut in monasterio nostro paschalem archiepiscopus solemniter celebret stationem, nec patres nostri nec nos eis hactenus negavimus, cum exinde multa mala, etiam usque ad homicidia, evenisse doleremus: donec sub concessa licentia exigere coeperunt illicita; et quod ad devotionem antiqua consueverat religio, in derisionem et scurrilitatem moderna eorum subvertit abusio" (*Notitia seu libellus de tribulationibus . . . Majori-monasterio injuste illatis,* 93–94). The text mentions Urban's investigation of the monks' claims at the Council of Clermont (November 1095) but not the defense of the monks' case, which he made in March 1096 at the time of the dedication of the abbey's new church (see below, note 30).

27. "Relatum enim est mihi quosdam e fratribus adversus fraternitatem vestram insurrexisse, qui dicerent curam vobis commissam non legitimum habuisse principium, his de causis, quod ab eo qui dicebatur excommunicatus esse, benedictionem acceperitis, et subjectionem debitam metropolitanae sedi ante benedictionem promiseritis" (Ivo of Chartres, Letter 73 [to Bernard, abbot of Marmoutier], *PL* 162:92).

28. Martène, *Histoire de l'abbaye de Marmoutier,* 1:471–537.

Even during the sixteen years of Bernard's tenure, however, tensions persisted between the cathedral and the monastery. In 1089 Urban II granted Marmoutier a bull of exemption, specifying that bishops could neither make visitations to Marmoutier nor perform public masses there. He stated in addition that only the pope could excommunicate the abbey or its monks, and newly elected abbots were not required to make a profession of "subjection" (*professio*) to the consecrating archbishop. If the archbishop was obstinant, he continued, the abbot could receive his consecration from some other bishop.[29] Urban thus granted Marmoutier privileges resembling those granted to Cluny at the end of the tenth century.

Despite this papal exemption, however, the archbishop of Tours continued to vex Marmoutier, and he was excommunicated for this reason in 1094. In November 1095 Urban heard both sides of the case at the Council of Clermont and again ruled in Marmoutier's favor. Three months later, when he dedicated Marmoutier's new church, Urban felt compelled to reprimand the canons of the cathedral, who he maintained had tyrannized the monks for a decade.[30]

When Abbot Bernard died in 1100, the monks of Marmoutier avoided a confrontation over the oath of subjection by electing a former bishop to their abbacy. Since he had already been consecrated, the new abbot did not need to receive the archbishop's blessing. But when that abbot died only four years later, the conflict exploded anew. Anticipating trouble from the canons of the cathedral, the monks arranged for the archbishop to bless the new abbot on relatively neutral territory, at the monastery of Saint-Julian. In the middle of the ceremony, however, the monks realized that the archbishop intended to demand the abbot's oath of subjection. They interrupted

29. "Missas sane publicas per archiepiscopum aut episcopum quemlibet in prefato monasterio celebrari aut stacionem fieri omnimodo prohibemus, ne in servorum Dei recessibus popularibus occasio prebeatur ulla conuentibus. Adicientes etiam et precipientes, ne quisquam ulterius archiepiscopus aut episcopus beati Martini monasterium aut ipsius monasterii monachos excommunicare presumat, sed omnis eorum causa grauior ex apostolice sedis iudicio pendeat . . . Electus [the abbot] a Turonensi archiepiscopo consecrationem accipiat, si gratiam et communionem apostolice sedis habuerit et si eam gratis et sine prauitate exhibere uoluerit professionis exactione seposita; si quod autem horum obstiterit, abbas aut ad Romanum pontificem consecrandus accedat aut a quocumque uoluerit catholico episcopo consecratur" (Urban II, Bull of December 19, 1089, in *Papsturkunden in Frankreich*, n.s. 5, no. 21, p. 84).

30. Lemarignier, *Etude sur les privilèges d'exemption*, 189; *Notitia . . . de tribulationibus*, 97–98. The monks of Marmoutier wrote an account of Urban's speech at the dedication of 1096: "Atque adversariorum nostrorum canonicorum non minus exsecrans conversationem, ac praecipue ipsorum detestans in nos actam decennio tyrannidem" (*Textus de dedicatione ecclesiae Majoris monasterii*, 339).

the service and eventually took their abbot to Rome, where he was consecrated by Pascal II.[31]

Sometime after 1118, when Gislebert succeeded Ralph II as archbishop, and before 1124, Marmoutier and the cathedral reached a compromise on the abbot's oath. According to their agreement, the archbishop was to bless the abbot "without a written or oral profession of subjection." Still, the abbot was to "promise as much obedience to the archbishop and his church as to a mother, save for the obedience and authority of the Roman see." The working distinction seems to have been between an oath demanded by the archbishop and an oral promise freely offered by the abbot.[32]

The agreement between Archbishop Gislebert and the monks of Marmoutier also stipulated that the pontiff could not make visitations to Marmoutier.[33] The abbey, like the basilica of Saint-Martin, had finally achieved recognition of its goals of exemption, and in so doing it succeeded in circumscribing not only the power but also the ritual behavior of the archbishop.

The Rhetorical Exclusion of the Archbishop

In the course of their struggles with the archbishop of Tours, the monks of Marmoutier and the canons of Saint-Martin not only removed the archbishop from the center of their city's liturgical life, they also created a rhetorical universe that disassociated him from the Christian community and from the cult of Saint Martin. Whereas Martin became the special patron of Marmoutier and of Saint-Martin, rather than of Tours as a whole, the archbishop became the enemy of God and of God's people.

In the retrospective works of propaganda presented to Urban II, the canons of Saint-Martin implied that any threat to their liberty represented an insult to the "dignity" of Saint Martin. Similarly, the monks of Marmoutier associated their right of exemption with the "summit of the ancient dignity" of the "place always loved by the

31. The events of 1100 and 1104 are narrated in "De professionibus abbatum," 188; Ivo of Chartres, Letters 108, 234–35, *PL* 162:126–27, 236–38; Martène, *Histoire de l'abbaye de Marmoutier*, 1:551–60, 2:3–4.
32. "Electum nostrum [abbot] benedicendum coram archiepiscopo offeremus, quem ipse sincere benedicet absque scrutinio, absque scripto, absque professione; antequam vero fiat benedictio illa, vel postquam facta fuerit, tantum promittet abbas obedientiam ei et ecclesie sue sicut matri, salva ex integro obedientia et auctoritate Romane sedis" (*Cartulaire de l'archevêché de Tours*, 1:94, no. 43 [1118–24]).
33. *Cartulaire de l'archevêché*, 1:94, no. 43.

Blessed Archbishop Martin."[34] These claims had an ironic twist, since the archbishop whose authority the monks and canons were undermining was himself an heir to Martin's dignity. Nevertheless, the arguments seem to have influenced Urban II, who maintained that he supported Marmoutier's exempt status "both out of devotion and reverence for the Blessed Confessor Martin and because of the prerogative of your religious life."[35]

Although the monks and canons appropriated Martin's dignity for themselves alone, they represented the archbishop as an evil opponent of both Martin and God. According to the canons, Archbishop Ralph I was the "enemy of God."[36] According to the monks he was Amalek, the enemy of Israel, and Saint Martin, in the role of Moses, helped defeat him: "Unless God had looked upon us and aided us, perhaps [Ralph and the canons of the cathedral] would have swallowed us alive; and unless our Moses, that is the Blessed Martin, had stood in the breach for us in his sight [Ps. 105:25], perhaps they would have dispersed us among peoples; and unless, with our provoking, our own mother of God had extended her hands, perhaps Amalek would have extinguished the people of God [Ex. 17:12]."[37] The monks also evoked parallels between the archbishop and the Viking invaders—the pagan enemies of Christian Europe. Like the Vikings, the archbishop and his allies were sent by God to punish his people,

34. "Et ut in perpetuum nullius dominationi Pontificis subdita foret Ecclesia illa sanxerunt, propter dignitatem tanti Confessoris" (Narratio controversiae, 459 [Saint-Martin]). In an invented account of Maiolus of Cluny's recognition of Marmoutier's rights of exemption, written at Marmoutier probably sometime before 1095, Maiolus declared, "Non me tanti estimo, nec ratio suffragatur, ut meae parvitatis temeritas domini papae statutis obviare audeat, et locus beato archipraesuli Martino semper dilectus dignitatis antiquae per me culmen amittat" (Narratio de commendatione Turonicae provinciae, ed. Salmon, 314, with corrections from Charleville, MS. 117, fol. 106v). On the dates of this text, see Source Appendix, I-B. This passage resembled a false charter written at the end of the tenth century, which had served in Marmoutier's attempt to extract itself from Cluny's domination: "Habemus namque non minima imperatorum et regum praecepta necnon et apostolicorum perplurima privilegia quibus hic noster locus, pro veneratione pii patris nostri domni Martini qui eum fundavit, specialem obtinet dignitatem et gloriam et nunquam ab aliquo regum nisi aut regi aut proprio abbati Sancti Martini subjectus fuit" (Lévêque, "Trois actes faux ou interpolés . . . en faveur de l'abbaye de Marmoutier," 300). For discussion of this document, see chapter 6 at notes 3 ff.

35. "Cum pro beati confessoris Martini deuocione et reuerencia tum pro uestre religionis prerogatiua" (Urban II, Bull of 1089, in Papsturkunden in Frankreich, n.s. 5, no. 21, p. 83).

36. "Dei inimicus" (Narratio controversiae, 459, 461).

37. "Nisi enim Dominus respexissit et adjuvisset nos, forsitan vivos absorbuissent nos; et nisi noster Moyses, B. videlicet Martinus, stetisset in confractione pro nobis in conspectu ejus, forsitan disperdissent nos in nationibus; et nisi Dei genitrix et nostra nobis lacessentibus manus suas extendisset, forsitan populum Domini Amalec extinxisset" (Notitia . . . de tribulationibus, 93).

and they reduced cultivated land to desolate wilderness.[38] Moreover, the monks claimed, in the midst of their peril Jesus "slept," and they had to "awaken" him. In 903 it was Martin who had slept while the inhabitants of Tours clamored to awaken him.[39]

The rhetoric of the monks and canons represents a serious departure from the representation of civic unity and episcopal authority that had originated with Perpetuus and Gregory and survived through the time of Radbod, whose description of the Viking attack of 903 was still read aloud at Saint-Martin during one, or possibly two, of Martin's feasts.[40] At a time when the archbishop was losing his right to visit Saint-Martin and Marmoutier and to perpetuate the traditional Easter procession to Marmoutier, the monks and canons rhetorically banished him from the community and exiled him as an enemy of God, of Israel, and of Christian Europe.

Martin's New Community: The Feast of May 12

In 1115, three years before Marmoutier finally came to terms with the archbishop of Tours, Marmoutier and Saint-Martin established liturgical arrangements that reinforced the archbishop's exclusion from Martin's cult and from the center of the city's liturgical order. The arrangement between the monks and canons also emphasized that the two houses were associated in a lateral bond of fraternity, which contrasted significantly with the vertical ties the archbishop wished to preserve. In a charter claiming to renew their alleged "ancient association" (a reference, in all likelihood, to the institutional ties between Marmoutier and Saint-Martin before Marmoutier's tenth-century reform), the monks and canons agreed to participate in

38. *Notitia . . . de tribulationibus,* 93–94. For examples of the perception that the Vikings were instruments of God's judgment, see chapter 1 at note 62. On the theme of reducing cultivated land to wilderness, see *Narratio de commendatione,* 306 ("Atque subversis habitationibus regionum olim florentissimarum, partem, per loca immensa innumeraque, quam plurimam inanis desertam vastitatis solitudinemque redegit horrendam"). See chapter 6 for further discussion of this text.

39. "Interea tumescentibus undis et super capita nostra exsurgentibus, Jesus dormiebat . . . sed exclamavimus et excitavimus eum" (*Notitia . . . de tribulationibus,* 94). "Sic conclamabant, 'Sancte Dei Martine, quare tam graviter obdormisti?'" (Radbod, *Libellus de miraculo S. Martini,* 1243).

40. Tours, Bibliothèque Municipale, MS. 1018 (eleventh-century) fols. 208–17v. The text is divided into nine lessons. A thirteenth-century lectionary (Tours, Bibliothèque Municipale, MS. 1021, fols. 111v, 155v) indicates that Radbod's sermon was read on Martin's feasts of December 13 and May 12—both of which were linked to the Viking invasions. It is not clear, however, that the link between the invasions and the May feast had been established in the late eleventh century; see discussion below.

each other's funerals and to commemorate each other's dead. In addition, they established that thirty of Marmoutier's monks would participate in rogation processions at Saint-Martin.[41]

Even more important were the new arrangements for one of Saint Martin's feasts, that of May 12. On that day the monks of Marmoutier were to make a procession to the basilica, where their abbot would celebrate mass.[42] This arrangement apparently served to upgrade the importance of the May feast, which probably originated in 919 when the archbishop of Tours translated Martin's relics from the cathedral town to the newly rebuilt basilica. By the middle of the twelfth century, however, a new explanation for that feast had emerged. According to a legend written between about 1137 and 1156—*Saint Martin's Return from Burgundy*—the feast celebrated the events of 903, when Martin's relics delivered Tours from the Vikings.[43] It is quite plausible that this new interpretation of the feast resulted from, or helped prompt, the agreement of 1115.

As far as I know, the charter of 1115 marks the first time (at least since the reform of Marmoutier) the monks of that abbey came to be included in the observance of Martin's cult at the basilica.[44] At a time when tensions between Marmoutier and the archbishop had not yet been resolved, the two most defiant houses in his diocese made a lateral agreement to celebrate together a feast of the city's patron saint. According to that agreement, the abbot of Marmoutier had the annual right to celebrate mass at Saint-Martin, something the archbishop could no longer do.

41. "Antiqua . . . societas," original parchment, Bibliothèque Nationale MS. lat. 12875, fol. 607; copied by Housseau, Bibliothèque Nationale, Collection Housseau, MS. 4, no. 1356, fol. 159. On Marmoutier's status in the ninth and tenth centuries, see Lévêque, "Trois actes faux ou interpolés . . . en faveur de l'abbaye de Marmoutier," 62, 64–66, 294–97, and Lévêque, "Histoire de l'abbaye de Marmoutier," 95–99.

42. "Ordinatum est atque statutum ut in illa Beati Martini festivitate quae est IIII idus maii faciant monachi annis singulis processionem unam cum Abbate et conventu suo ad ipsam Beati Martini et eorum ecclesiam, in qua nimirum missam abbas ipse celebrabit" (Bibliothèque Nationale, MS. lat. 12875, fol. 607; Bibliothèque Nationale, Collection Housseau, MS. 4, no. 1356, fol. 159).

43. The 903 event actually took place in June: see chapter 1 at note 49. Two thirteenth-century sources, the *Chronicon Turonense auctore anonymo canonico* (col. 982) and the *Chronicon Turonense abbreviatum* (p. 184), cited May 13, 919 (possibly the date of dedication, one day after the translation), as the date of Martin's translation from the cathedral town to the new basilica. Mabille (*Invasions normandes dans la Loire*, 41 n. 2) cited two contemporary charters that placed this translation between June 918 and March 920. The earliest known source associating May 12 with the siege of 903 was the *Return from Burgundy* (*De reversione beati Martini*), written between about 1137 and 1156. See Source Appendix, I-A.

44. See Vaucelle, *Collégiale de Saint-Martin*, 363–64, on the earlier involvement of the canons and monks of Saint-Pierre, Saint-Venant, and Saint-Julian in the celebration of Martin's feasts at the basilica.

During the siege of 903, Martin's relics were deposited in a church inside the cathedral town, and from there the saint was carried to the ramparts of the episcopal city, where he won the day by striking fear into the hearts of the Vikings. The celebration of the May 12 feast, however, circumvented the cathedral town. The juxtaposition of the commemorative ritual, which excluded the cathedral town, with the memory of the actual event, which had taken place there, thus highlighted the archbishop's exclusion.

We do not know how the monks of Marmoutier made their procession to Martin's basilica on May 12 in 1116 (the year after they formed the new liturgical agreement with Saint-Martin). By 1180–81, however, when the dean and treasurer of Saint-Martin wrote a letter describing their observance of all four of Martin's feasts, the monks were making their procession to the basilica by boat.[45] The boats may have served as a physical reminder of the Viking raiders, or they might have been intended as an inverted revival of the pious Easter visitation to Marmoutier that Paulinus of Perigord described in the fifth century. Both Paulinus's Easter procession and the May 12 procession took place in the spring, both involved a boat trip, and both honored Saint Martin. But Paulinus's procession was probably orchestrated by Bishop Perpetuus; the May 12 procession excluded the archbishop. Besides, the use of boats enabled the monks to avoid the bridge across the Loire that would have directed their procession route through the cathedral town. The path of their procession defined a new version of "Martin's town," which included Marmoutier, Saint-Martin, and Châteauneuf but excluded the cathedral town (see map 4).[46]

The letter of 1180–81 suggests that the May feast defined yet another version of Martin's town. The feast functioned as an urban patronal feast, thereby placing Martin and the basilica at the hub of the symbolic order of Châteauneuf. The rituals for the feast helped define Châteauneuf as a distinct town with its own identity and jurisdiction, beyond the reach of the archbishop and the cathedral town.[47]

The association of the May feast with the events of 903 and the public enactment on that day of a lateral tie between the monks of Marmoutier and the canons of Saint-Martin served to highlight the

45. "De cultu Sancti Martini apud Turonenses extremo saeculo XII," 236.

46. On Paulinus of Perigord, see chapter 1 at note 26. By the thirteenth century an Easter procession to Marmoutier had been revived, but there is no necessary reason to believe it involved the archbishop: see Péan Gatineau, *Vie monseignor Saint Martin de Tors,* lines 68–71, p. 4. On the dates of this text, see Source Appendix, II-C.

47. See chapter 9 at notes 68 ff.

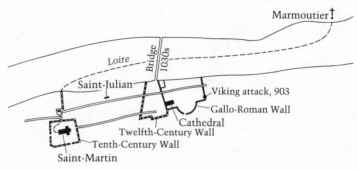

Loire

Bridge

1030s

Marmoutier †

Saint-Julian

Viking attack, 903

Gallo-Roman Wall

Cathedral

Twelfth-Century Wall

Tenth-Century Wall

Saint-Martin

— — — Monks' procession route on May 12

MAP 4. Procession route on May 12. Adapted from Vivier and Millet, *Pour comprendre et visiter Tours,* 10.

fact that the archbishop of Tours was no longer at the hub of the liturgical life in his town and that his access to Martin's cult was now severely limited. That this Martinian feast coincided with the commemoration of two other saints, Maiolus and Maurice, further underscored the theme of monastic liberty and the secondary position of the cathedral in Martin's town.

On May 12 the monks of Marmoutier devoted a number of readings to Saint Maiolus of Cluny, whose feast was on May 11. According to a legend written at Marmoutier, probably just before 1095, Maiolus had played an important historical role in recognizing Marmoutier's liberty. Originally, the legend claimed, the abbot of Cluny had attempted to assert Cluny's dominance over Marmoutier, but he then bowed to the monks' claims that Martin's abbey had always been independent.[48] By honoring Maiolus on May 12, the monks of Marmoutier thus made an indirect reference to an important (albeit legendary) moment when the continuous tradition of the abbey's freedom had been successfully defended and preserved.

Martin's feast also coincided with a local feast honoring Saint Maurice. Indeed, as a result of the agreement of 1115, Martin's May

48. On Maiolus's feast day see Hourlier and Celleti, "Maiolo," 566. On the readings at Marmoutier on May 12, see thirteenth-century breviary from Marmoutier: Tours, Bibliothèque Municipale, MS. 153, fol. 72v. On Maiolus and Marmoutier's liberty, see chapter 6 at note 21.

feast began to overshadow that of Maurice, at least at Marmoutier and Saint-Martin. Moreover, when the dean and treasurer of Saint-Martin wrote their letter in 1180–81, they recounted a legend about Maurice's feast that enhanced the symbolic subordination of Maurice and the cathedral to Martin and the basilica. They claimed that Saint Maurice and his Theban legion (Roman soldiers who were martyred for their beliefs) were commemorated at Tours on May 12 because it was on that day that their relics were translated to Tours from Agaune (now in Switzerland). It was Saint Martin who translated the relics, after he discovered them in a miraculous way. When he returned to Tours, Martin deposited only a portion of the martyrs' relics in the cathedral, retaining another portion for himself. In recent days, the dean and treasurer continued, the canons had discovered Martin's portion of the relics in the basilica. The new legend thus attributed the origin of Maurice's feast to Saint Martin and indicated that Martin's basilica was at least equal to the cathedral in possessing the relics of the cathedral's patron saint.[49]

It is frequently difficult to trace the history of liturgical practices, and for this reason the charter of 1115, the legend of *Saint Martin's Return from Burgundy,* and the letter of 1180–81 represent, despite their many silences, particularly rich sources for the development of Martin's feast of May 12. Although it is not possible to determine precisely when the feast of May 12 became associated with the Viking events or at what point the May procession began to take place on boats, the sources show that on many levels the ritual practices and legendary interpretations of the May feast underscored the message that the archbishop was now excluded from the rituals of Châteauneuf and Marmoutier and thus was no longer at the center of the ritual life of Tours as a whole. *Saint Martin's Return from Burgundy* and the letter of 1180–81 indicate that this message persisted as an underlying theme even after the conflict over monastic exemption had subsided.

49. The evidence of liturgical manuscripts indicates that through the end of the twelfth century Maurice's feast of May 12 was observed primarily at Tours; see Leroquais, *Sacramentaires et les missels manuscrits,* 1:148, 218, 243, 289, 315. It first appears in liturgical manuscripts from the eleventh century: see Rouen, Bibliothèque Municipale, MS. 243; Bibliothèque Nationale, MS. lat. 9434 (the notation for May 12 is in a later hand) and Tours, Missel from the Petit Seminaire (see, on this last manuscript, Bosseboeuf, "Missel de Marmoutier"). For the twelfth-century legend about Martin's translation of Maurice's relics, see *Traditio Turonensium de sanguine sanctorum Thebaeorum,*" with additions in "De cultu Sancti Martini," 223–24; now reedited in *Guiberti Gemblacensis epistolae,* 73–75. In the fourteenth century Saint Gatien, the first bishop of Tours, became the patron saint of the cathedral: see Leclercq, "Tours," 2632.

Legendary Realignment: *Saint Martin's Return from Burgundy*

In addition to reiterating the story of the delivery of Tours in 903, *Saint Martin's Return from Burgundy* recounted a second story concerning the role Martin's relics played during the Viking invasions, and like the first, this one underscored the message that Martin's cult stood in opposition to the power of bishops. The second story described the destruction of Marmoutier by the Vikings and the translation of Martin's relics to Burgundy, where his guardians hoped to find a safe refuge for the saint and his reliquary. While in Burgundy the monks of Marmoutier and the canons of Saint-Martin encountered their worst enemy not in pagan Vikings, but in a selfish bishop. The unfriendly hierarchical relations the bishop attempted to impose on the monks and canons of Tours contrasted sharply with the fraternal love and compassion the monks and the canons gave to each other.

According to the legend, the Vikings returned to Touraine fifteen years after Martin's relics saved Tours. This time the flooded waters of the Loire prevented the invaders from approaching the city itself, so they turned their attention to Marmoutier, destroying it and massacring 116 of its monks. Only Abbot Herbern, along with twenty-four monks who had hidden in Marmoutier's caves, managed to survive. The canons of Saint-Martin gave shelter to these survivors, who remained at the basilica for six months, until rumors of another incursion compelled the canons to entrust the relics of their patron saint to Abbot Herbern, the twenty-four monks, and twelve of their own canons. Accompanied by twelve burghers from Tours, these monks and canons carried Martin's relics to the city of Auxerre in Burgundy, where they remained for thirty-one years.[50]

Although real recollections from the period of the invasions stood behind this new legend, it included a number of fabrications and distortions as well. The Vikings had indeed devastated Marmoutier, but no contemporary accounts report that they massacred its inhabitants. And Martin's relics were indeed translated from Tours to safer locations, including Burgundy, but there is no evidence that they were ever taken to Auxerre.[51]

50. *De reversione beati Martini,* 21–25, 34.

51. Emile Mabille pointed to contemporary chronicle evidence for the destruction of Marmoutier as well as Saint-Martin of Tours in 853: see *Invasions normandes dans la Loire,* 17–26; Lévêque, "Histoire de l'abbaye de Marmoutier," also argued for a destruction in 903 and possibly one in 868. Like other monastic sources, especially those written over a century later, the *Return from Burgundy* probably exaggerated the extent of murder and torture by the Vikings, who were essentially interested in obtaining treasure: see Haenens, *Invasions normandes: Une catastrophe?* 29–36; Haenens, *Invasions normandes en Belgique,* 80–92.

More important than the legend's inaccuracies and exaggerations were its projections of twelfth-century concerns onto the earlier period. In its description of the assistance the canons extended to the surviving monks of Marmoutier, the legend reinforced the idea that the two houses were joined in a fraternal bond. Indeed, its language added a dimension of compassion and empathy to the theme: "Wrapped in the mantle of sadness and mourning . . . as is the custom with those who suffer empathically," the canons of Saint-Martin went to Marmoutier, sought out its survivors, and brought them back to their own church.[52]

The claim that the canons of Saint-Martin and the monks of Marmoutier cooperated in translating Martin's relics to Burgundy further reinforced the theme of the fraternal bond. This aspect of the story served as a reminder that the bond between the two houses rested on a common relationship with their patron saint. Nevertheless, the account is more representative of Marmoutier's interests than of the basilica's, and it is thus reasonable to assume that it was a monk of Marmoutier who wrote the legend. The highly improbable assertion that Abbot Herbern headed the party of Martin's guardians established a precedent that might have undermined the canons' exclusive rights to the possession of those relics.[53]

In its account of the thirty-one years that Martin, the canons, and the monks spent in Burgundy, *Saint Martin's Return from Burgundy* emphasized not a fraternal bond but an oppositional relationship between the religious community of Tours and that of Auxerre. The clerics of Auxerre greeted their guests from Tours with jealousy and selfishness rather than compassion and empathy. Saint Martin's miracles attracted numerous pilgrims to Auxerre, and the churchmen of

---

For a critique, see Wallace-Hadrill, "Vikings in Francia"; but see also Frank, "Viking Atrocity and Skaldic Verse." On the actual translations of Martin's relics, see Gasnault, "Tombeau de Saint Martin et les invasions normandes," 55–59.

A martyrology from Marmoutier, copied by Housseau in the eighteenth century (Bibliothèque Nationale, Collection Housseau, MS. 20, fols. 50–61v), has a commemoration on November 8 for 126 monks of the abbey who were killed by the Vikings. Mabille (*Invasions normandes dans la Loire*, 25–26) thought this corroborated the *Return from Burgundy* (*De reversione beati Martini*), even though the numbers were slightly different (126 rather than 116). This was, however, a late martyrology, with entries for fifteenth-century saints. The most plausible explanation for the commemoration of monks killed by the Vikings is that it was based on the *Return from Burgundy*.

52. "Moestitiae igitur et moeroris pallio amicti . . . sicut moris est compatientium" (*De reversione beati Martini*, 22).

53. The assertion that the author of the *Return from Burgundy* was a monk of Marmoutier is my own, based not only on the author's ascribing a central role in the guardianship of Martin's relics to the monks, but also on his close attention to the destruction of Marmoutier (see below, chapter 6 at notes 49 ff., and Source Appendix, I-A).

PLATE 2. The contest in Auxerre. According to the twelfth-century legend *The Return from Burgundy,* the clerics of Tours and Auxerre attempted to establish which of their patron saints was curing pilgrims in Auxerre by having a leper lie for one night between the relics of Saint Martin and Saint Germanus. In the morning the leper had been cured only on the side closer to Saint Martin, thus proving that Martin was performing the other miracles as well. The story was repeated in several late medieval texts, including this early printed book, *Vie et les miracles de Monseigneur Saint Martin,* lviii. Photograph courtesy Bibliothèque Nationale.

that city wanted a share in the pilgrims' alms. They claimed, there-fore, that their own saint, Germanus, was performing half of the miracles. Knowing this was not true, Martin's guardians devised a contest to prove that Martin alone was responsible for the miracles: a leper was to lie for one night between the relics of Saint Martin and Saint Germanus. If he was cured on only one side, the saint on that side was to receive credit for all the miracles. When the clerics of the two cities put their patrons to the test, Martin alone provided the cure. The dispute was thus resolved in favor of Martin's guardians (see plate 2).[54]

But a second dispute arose when the monks and canons finally decided to return to Tours. This time their opponent was the bishop

54. *De reversione beati Martini,* 23–25.

of Auxerre, who declared that since his church had already been "adorned" with Martin's relics when he became bishop, he did not want it "to be defrauded of such a great treasure."[55] The bishop's intransigence forced the monks and canons to seek armed assistance from Count Ingelger of Anjou, who succeeded in convincing the bishop to relinquish the relics. In mid-December the party returned to Tours, where Martin's reentry was marked by a miraculous display of blooming trees, ringing bells, and self-igniting candles. Already in the eleventh century, December 13 was known, in Tours, as the feast of Saint Martin's return from Burgundy.[56]

This depiction of the events in Burgundy conformed in many ways to a genre of monastic legends that proliferated in the eleventh and twelfth centuries. Those legends drew on the historical fact that a number of religious communities had translated their saints' relics to protect them from the invaders of the ninth and tenth centuries. It is significant, however, that eleventh- and twelfth-century authors took such great interest in the earlier events, even to the point of inventing translations and disputes that never took place.[57]

Like the *Return from Burgundy*, a number of these legends described disputes that arose over the rights to relics.[58] The original inspiration for this agonistic theme may have been Gregory of Tours's account of the fight in Candes over Saint Martin's body.[59] Whereas Gregory described a struggle between the inhabitants of two cities, however, the eleventh- and twelfth-century legends tended to depict struggles between particular religious communities. These legends suggest that ecclesiastical strife and the narrowing of representations of religious community were widespread in the eleventh and twelfth centuries.

Although the *Return from Burgundy* resembled other translation legends in its portrayal of disputes between religious communities, I have found no other translation legend that focuses on a struggle

55. "Nolo ecclesiam meam tanto thesauro defraudari, quam, episcopus factus, eo vestitam inveni" (*De reversione beati Martini*, 26).

56. *De reversione beati Martini*, 27–34. On the December 13 feast, see below, chapter 9 at notes 83 ff.

57. On invented legends about the Viking invasions, see Haenens, *Invasions normandes en Belgique*, 164–68.

58. For instance, *Gesta episcoporum Cameracensis* (eleventh century), bk. 1, chap. 76, p. 429; *Historia Sancti Florenti Salmurensis* (thirteenth century), 223 ff.; Theodoric of Amorbach, *Illatio Sancti Benedicti* (early eleventh century). This incomplete edition must be supplemented with passages from Bibliothèque Nationale, MS. lat. 17641, which are printed in *Catalogus codicum . . . Parisiensi*, 3:422–23, and Vidier, *Historiographie à St.-Benôit-sur-Loire*, 178. On the broader genre of monastic translation legends, see Heinzelmann, *Translationsberichte*.

59. See chapter 1 at notes 36 ff.

between a religious community (or in this case two religious communities, Saint-Martin and Marmoutier) and an archbishop or bishop. Here, it seems, the author found his inspiration not in the topoi of his genre but in the historical experiences of his own abbey. Although the opponent in the *Return from Burgundy* was the bishop of Auxerre rather than the archbishop of Tours, he represented the kind of episcopal oppression and opposition that the monks of Marmoutier and the canons of Saint-Martin met during their struggles for exemption. Indeed, the legend actually endowed the bishop of Auxerre with characteristics that had already been attributed to Archbishops Ralph I and Ralph II.

Like Marmoutier's and Saint-Martin's retrospective accounts of their actual struggles, the *Return from Burgundy* portrayed the oppressing bishop as an enemy of God's chosen people. In their complaint to Ingelger of Anjou, the guardians of the relics compared the bishop of Auxerre to Pharaoh: "Because the heart of this obstinate priest is hardened and he is made like another Pharaoh, he does not want to send away the man of God except to an armed band."[60]

The image of Pharaoh, like that of Amalek, placed the bishop outside the Christian community. Indeed, it placed him outside God's realm altogether, since Pharaoh frequently represented the devil in discussions of baptism and the monastic vocation. Like Pharaoh in Egypt, the devil lorded it over the worldly realm; but just as Pharaoh could not pursue the chosen people when they crossed the Red Sea, the devil was unable to maintain his hold on those who crossed the threshold of baptism or who joined the monastic life.[61]

According to the author from Marmoutier, Pharaoh represented both a threat to an entire community and a threat to individual believers. For Martin's guardians—the monks, canons, and burghers of Tours—he was an external oppressor of the community as a whole. For the Christians of Auxerre, however, he was a subversive influence

60. "Quoniam igitur obstinati illius antistitis cor induratum est et quasi alter Pharao factus non vult dimittere virum Dei nisi in manu forti" (*De reversione beati Martini*, 28).

61. On baptism, see Danielou, *From Shadows to Reality: Studies in the Biblical Typology of the Fathers*, 175–201. On monastic typologies, see Penco, "Tema dell'Esodo nella spiritualità monastica," 340. Examples by a monk from Marmoutier and a former monk from Marmoutier are Sermon for Saint Benedict's Day (twelfth century), Bibliothèque Nationale, MS. lat. 12412, fol. 111; Adam of Perseigne, Letter 5, PL 211:596. See also an earlier example from the monastery of Charroux cited by Landes, "Dynamics of Heresy and Reform in Limoges," 468.

On the Moses/Egypt imagery in the ceremony of making a catechumen (taken from two manuscripts from Tours), see *De antiquis ecclesiae ritibus*, bk. 1, chap. 1, art. 7, ordo 4, reprint ed., 1:44. On the identity of Martène's manuscripts (Bibliothèque Nationale, MS. lat. 9434; Tours, Bibliothèque Municipale, MS. 184), see Martimort, *Documentation liturgique de Dom Edmond Martène*, 253.

who threatened to undermine the faith of every believer. Thus Count Ingelger of Anjou told him he was not worthy of the title pontiff: "Since the name of pontiff [*pontificis*] and its honor delight you, why, having lost its etymology, do you subvert rather than make [*facis*] a bridge [*pontem*] of virtues? Why, having become a model of deception and trickery for your flock, do you hurl the one clinging to your footsteps from the way of sublime truth and compel him to go to the precipice of perdition?"[62]

As an external oppressor who refused to recognize the rights of Martin's guardians, the bishop of Auxerre represented the kind of opposition that Saint-Martin and Marmoutier had met in the archbishop of Tours. In creating this image of the bishop, the author of the *Return from Burgundy* reiterated views that had arisen both at Marmoutier and at Saint-Martin during their struggles for exemption. The discussion of the bishop's corrosive influence on individuals, however, is more representative of the monks' perspective.

The monks of Marmoutier were concerned with the spiritual welfare of individuals, and they wished to convey the impression that the cloister provided the most propitious environment for preserving and nurturing that welfare. To do so, they maintained, the cloister had to remain intact, its walls impermeable. Episcopal visitations undermined the isolation of the monastery and disrupted the "monastic peace."[63] When the members of Archbishop Arnulf's party "violated the solitude of monks," they did not merely infringe upon the material liberties of Marmoutier as an institution; they demonstrated as well that undesired contact with the secular world inevitably exposed the monks and their way of life to pollution, which infected people like a disease.[64]

The evil bishop of Auxerre symbolized the dangers of such contact. He harbored a disease that the monks claimed they could avoid, and he was able to infect individual members of the lay community because that community had no effective system of quarantine. Proponents of Marmoutier's monastic way of life stressed that as long as the abbey remained free and independent its cloister could offer pro-

---

62. "Pontificis nomen cum te et honor delectet cur, hujus praenominis etymologia perdita, virtutum pontem non facis sed subvertis; et gregi tuo factus forma deceptionis et doli, vestigiis tuis inhaerentem a sublimi veritatis via dejicis et in perditionis praecipitium ire compellis?" (*De reversione beati Martini*, 28–29).

63. "Quietem monasticam" (*Notitia . . . de tribulationibus*, 93).

64. In their defense of monastic liberty the monks of Marmoutier stated, "God . . . commanded that his sabbaths should be kept, and that they should not be polluted in any way by servile work—that is, by a secular way of life"; "Dominus . . . praecipiat ut sabbata ejus custodiantur, nec servili opere, hoc est saeculari conversatione, ullatenus polluantur" (*Notitia . . . de tribulationibus*, 93).

tection against pollution. In 1182, for instance, Guibert, a monk from the abbey of Gembloux in the Low Countries, claimed that abbatial elections at Marmoutier were uncorrupted because no outside power—secular or ecclesiastical—intervened, and thus no one who had been "defiled with the leprosy of the simoniacal heresy" was ever "violently forced" upon the monks. Marmoutier's cloister was, in the image the monks projected, a haven from the diseases of worldliness and corruption.[65] The chapter of secular canons of Saint-Martin did not offer such protection. Its members were in constant contact with the city around them.

The *Return from Burgundy* gave legendary expression to the changes in the liturgical boundaries and alliances of Tours that had resulted from the movement for monastic exemption. It portrayed a bishop as an oppressor who stood in opposition to the Christian community and the cult of Saint Martin, and it depicted a fraternal bond between Saint-Martin and Marmoutier. Its representation of Martin's guardians—twenty-four monks, twelve canons, twelve burghers—pointed to the three parts of Martin's new community: Marmoutier, Saint-Martin, and Châteauneuf.

Although these themes were of interest to both Marmoutier and Saint-Martin, the author of the legend was a monk of Marmoutier, and his interests did not revolve exclusively around the problem of exemption, which had already been resolved. In the character of Count Ingelger, the author both glorified the ancestry of his abbey's patrons and presented a role model for those patrons. In his discussion of the monks who survived Marmoutier's destruction, he strengthened a sense of Marmoutier's historical continuity, which was fundamental to its identity as a community. Finally, in the discussion of the bishop of Auxerre, he gave implicit expression to an underlying conviction that spiritual well-being was incompatible with exposure to the secular world. The legend points, therefore, to some of the themes of part 2 of this book: Marmoutier's relations with noble patrons, its identity as a community, and its nurturing of the spiritual lives of individuals.

---

65. "Nullus enim umquam abbas ibi violentur intruditur, nullus lepra haereseos symoniacae respersus assumitur: quia nemo ab aliqua, vel saeculari, vel ecclesiastica potestate, quae per pecuniam corrumpi possit, aliquando statuitur, sed libera et irreprehensibili electione, qui ordinandus est promovetur" (Guibert, Abbot of Gembloux, "Epistola ad Philippum, archiepiscopum Coloniensem," 608–9). On Guibert's life and chronology, see Delehaye, "Guibert, Abbé de Florennes et de Gembloux." For a general discussion of the frequent metaphorical association of heresy with leprosy and promiscuousness, see Moore, *Formation of a Persecuting Society*, 62–63.

PART 2

Marmoutier

Introduction

Marmoutier and Saint-Martin shared a common goal in the late eleventh and twelfth centuries—gaining exemption from the control of the archbishop of Tours. Because their interests in the realm of ecclesiastical politics were similar, they worked together to undermine the traditional image of Tours as a single community united under its patron saint and its bishop. In the realm of secular politics, however, the two houses had different agendas: whereas the canons of Saint-Martin retained an intimate tie with the Capetian kings of France, Marmoutier developed close patronage relations with the principal rivals of the Capetians—the comital lines of Blois and Anjou. Between the late eleventh century and the early thirteenth the monks even represented the Blésois and Angevin lines—rather than the kings of Francia—as the principal lay patrons and beneficiaries of Martin's cult. One of those legends explicitly indicated that because the king of Francia failed to exercise his responsibilities toward Martin's cult, the count of Anjou stepped in to take his place.

The monks of Marmoutier differed from the canons of Saint-Martin not only in their political alliances, but also in their spiritual goals and in the nature of their common life. And again, in the years between the late eleventh century and the early thirteenth, they described their spiritual goals and communal concerns in legends and historical works about Saint Martin and his cult.

The twelfth century was an age of great spiritual and intellectual fervor, and it saw an efflorescence of monastic historical writings as well.[1] On one level, then, it is not surprising to discover that Marmoutier's monks energetically wrote new legends about their secular and saintly patrons and about the nature of their religious community. It is important to note, however, that this was also an age of

---

1. On monastic historical writing, see chapter 6.

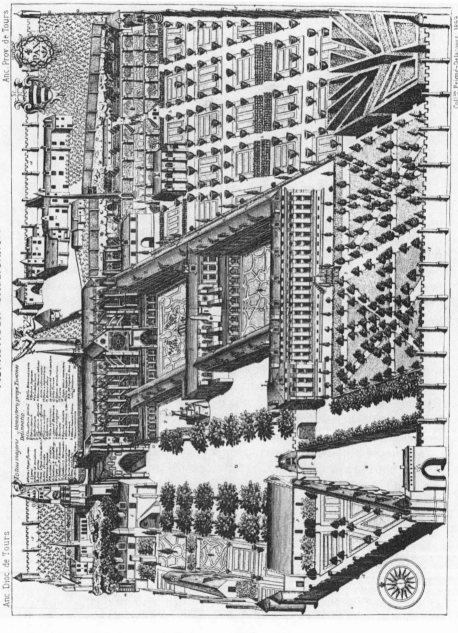

Anc. Prov. de Tours

Anc. Dioc. de Tours

Totius majoris — Monasterii prope Turonas
Delineatio

ABBAYE DE MARMOUTIERS

Coll⁹ Peigné-Delacourt 1869

economic, social, and political change and that those changes gave rise to new forms of spiritual and intellectual endeavor. By the mid-thirteenth century most Benedictine monasteries—including Marmoutier—suffered a decline, and the roots of that decline were already present in the twelfth century.[2]

Marmoutier's legendary and historical writings demonstrate that its monks made their own contribution to the cultural flowering of the twelfth century. But those writings also demonstrate that the monks were conscious of—and attempting to address—the social and cultural changes that threatened to render obsolete their spirituality and their way of life and to undermine the bonds of their religious community. To understand their legends about the Angevin and Blésois counts (the subject of chaps. 3 and 4), it is necessary first to discuss the origins of the abbey's patronage relations in the late tenth and early eleventh centuries and the transformations those relations underwent in the twelfth century. I will give a fuller explanation of the monks' spiritual and communal concerns at the beginning of chapter 5.

Marmoutier and Its Patrons

In 985 secular jurisdiction over Marmoutier passed from Hugh Capet—the patriarch of the Capetian royal line—to Count Odo I of Blois. Within a year, Odo ousted the secular canons who had resided

---

2. For a general discussion of Benedictine decline, see Southern, *Western Society and the Church*, 230–40. Despite his position that the Benedictines did not decline in the twelfth century, John Van Engen acknowledges that the new orders emphasized a more inward and personal piety, which eventually came to predominate, and that by the end of the twelfth century the older Benedictines were no longer at the center of Western spiritual life: see "'Crisis of Cenobitism' Reconsidered," esp. 303–4. On Marmoutier's decline in the thirteenth century, see Martène, *Histoire de l'abbaye de Marmoutier*, 2:209–38, and Robinet, "Conflit entre pouvoir civil et pouvoir ecclésiastique." The struggle Robinet recounts certainly marked the end of an era: the count of Blois (who was related to the twelfth-century counts through the female line) actually imprisoned Marmoutier's abbot for a number of years. Eventually, the monks of Marmoutier paid 3,500 livres so that King Louis IX would place the abbey under direct royal protection (see my Conclusion).

PLATE 3. (opposite) Marmoutier in the seventeenth century. This engraving from the *Monasticon Gallicanum* depicts Marmoutier's Gothic church, which was begun about 1218 and completed in the mid-fourteenth century. To the right of the cloister (which is in the immediate foreground of the abbatial church) is the Romanesque chapel of Saint Benedict (marked with the letter I). The monks were brought to this chapel when they were dying. On the dates of the Gothic church, see Lelong, "Observations et hypothèses sur l'église abbatiale." See plate 4 for further discussion of the chapel of Saint Benedict, which was dedicated in 1162. Photograph courtesy State University of New York, Binghamton.

at Marmoutier since the ninth century and replaced them with monks from Cluny.[3] Odo also endowed the abbey with a sizable gift from his family property, thus providing the material means for the abbey's future independence and prosperity. Like other monasteries, Marmoutier had declined both materially and spiritually during the chaotic ninth and tenth centuries, and it needed this gift, as well as subsequent ones from Odo, his descendants, and other noble benefactors (for an outline of Blésois gifts to Marmoutier, see table 1).[4]

Tenth- and eleventh-century monastic reform curtailed direct lay interference in the internal governance of monasteries. In 909 Cluny's founder, Duke William of Aquitaine, granted Cluny immunity from outside taxation and control. He also stipulated that the monks were to live according to the Benedictine *Rule* and to elect their own abbot as they pleased, without the intrusion of any outside power. These ideas about monastic liberty were not original, but the Cluniacs and their supporters pursued them with particular vigor.[5] In 985 or 986 the Cluniac monks who came to Marmoutier introduced the idea of monastic liberty to Marmoutier. Thus, sometime between 985 and 987 Odo I of Blois ceased to call himself the "rector" of Marmoutier (the term for lay abbots) and began to call himself its "instructor" and "defender" instead.[6]

Although reformed monasticism entailed a degree of internal independence from lay intervention, the lives of monks and their patrons remained intimately intertwined. Thus we find that in 998, when the monks of Marmoutier (or perhaps the young Count Odo II or his stepfather, King Robert the Pious) ousted the Cluniac monks from their house, it was a member of the Blésois family, Gauzbert, who became its new abbot. And it appears that Abbot Albert of Marmoutier, who was elected sometime between 1028 and 1037, was probably the Blésois count's favored candidate.[7] In the 1020s and

3. On Marmoutier's transformation into a house of canons in the ninth century, see Semmler, "Benedictus II," 15 n. 28; Lévêque, "Histoire de l'abbaye de Marmoutier," 96. On the refoundation, see Guillot, *Comte d'Anjou*, 1:173–74; Lévêque, "Trois actes faux ou interpolés . . . en faveur de l'abbaye de Marmoutier," 76–77.

4. On the general pattern of tenth- and eleventh-century monastic foundations and refoundations, which were sponsored more often by nobles than by the king, see Lot, *Etudes sur le règne de Hugues Capet*, 229–30.

5. Rosenwein, *Rhinoceros Bound: Cluny in the Tenth Century*, xvii, 43; Cowdrey, *Cluniacs and the Gregorian Reform*, 3–15; "Charter of the Abbey of Cluny," ed. Henderson, in *Select Historical Documents*, 329–32.

6. Guillot, *Comte d'Anjou*, 1:174.

7. On Gauzbert's family background and his introduction as abbot of Marmoutier, see Oury, "Reconstruction monastique dans l'Ouest," 72–77, 90–95. Oury does not take into account that Odo I, the reformer of Marmoutier, had died in 996, his widow had married Robert the Pious, and Thibaud, the young count, was the protégé of the king: see Dun-

TABLE 1   Blésois relations with Marmoutier

ODO I (d. 996)
Gift: Part of hamlet of Chamars (later a priory; *CD*, 4)
Restores to Marmoutier: Villa of Coutures (originally given in ninth century; *CB*, 1, 4)
Gift by his widow, Bertha: Exemption from river toll at Blois (*CB*, 5)
Burial at Marmoutier (along with mother and brother; *CD*, 92)

ODO II (d. 1037)
Personal: Gauzbert, abbot of Marmoutier in 998, is from the Blésois family (see text at note 7)
Personal: Albert, elected abbot of Marmoutier between 1028 and 1037, is closely tied to Odo (Guillot, 1:175 no. 190)
Gift: Part of forest of Blémars (later priory of Mesland; *CB*, 6, 35)
Gift: Church of Saint-Medard (later a priory; *CV*, 13)
Gift: Land at Mercuriole (Martène, 1:279)
Gift (at urging of his wife, Ermengard): Rights to wood at forest of Chaumont (on the Loire, near Mesland) and fishing rights at Fontcher (*CB*, 55)
Restores to Marmoutier: Church of Chouzy (later a priory; *CB*, 7)
Spreads Marmoutier's influence: At his command, election of the abbot of Saint-Florent of Saumur follows the discipline of Marmoutier (Guillot, 1:176)
Spreads Marmoutier's influence: On his deathbed, gives Marmoutier the right to watch over the abbatial election at Montier-la-Celle (Guillot, 1:184)
Burial at Marmoutier (*CD*, 92)

THIBAUD III (d. 1089)
Retains rights over Marmoutier after 1044, when he loses Touraine (*CD*, 92)
Gift (after 1044): More land in forest of Blémars (later priories of Mesland and Orchaise; *CB*, 20, 32, 36)

STEPHEN (d. 1102)
Gift (at request of his wife, Adele): Priory of Fréteval (*CD*, 92)
Gift: Priory of Francheville-Morée (widow, Adele, later gives more wooded land there and writes to ask her son Thibaud to defend the monks' right to a tithe there; *CD*, 77, *CB*, 146)
Gift by widow, Adele: Forest near Maroles (*CB*, 111)

THIBAUD IV (d. 1152)
Spreads Marmoutier's influence: At urging of his mother, Adele, asks Marmoutier to reform College of St.-Martin-au-Val (Martène, 2:68–69, BN MS. lat. 12879, fol. 74)

THIBAUD V (d. 1191)
Modest gift: Rent of £10 on fulling mills of Blois, to found perpetual anniversary (*CB*, 179)

LOUIS (d. 1205)
Modest gift: Founds chapel of Pontigou in the forest of Blémars and endows it with £20 rent to support two monk-priests who will perform divine services there; later adds £20 to endow daily masses for himself, his father, and his children (*CB*, 189, 203)

CB	= *Marmoutier, Cartulaire Blésois*
CD	= *Cartulaire de Marmoutier pour le Dunois*
CV	= *Cartulaire de Marmoutier pour le Vendômois*
Guillot	= Guillot, *Comte d'Anjou et son entourage*
Martène	= Martène, *Histoire de l'abbaye de Marmoutier*
BN	= Bibliothèque Nationale

1030s Odo II of Blois encouraged the spread of Marmoutier's reformed influence to other abbeys. In 1037, however, just after Odo's
death, this favoritism produced results that Odo himself might not
have liked: Abbot Albert introduced to the abbey of Montier-la-Celle
the idea that laymen (and women) could invest new abbots only with
the symbols of temporal, not spiritual, power.[8]

Even though Marmoutier was now engaged in a reform program
that had the potential to undermine the political power of noble princes, the Blésois counts continued to favor the abbey. When Geoffrey
Martel of Anjou defeated Thibaud of Blois in 1044, thereby extending
his power over Touraine, Thibaud "valued [Marmoutier] so much"
that he kept it in his "proprium dominium" rather than relinquishing
it to Geoffrey along with the rest of Touraine.[9] Thibaud, his son
Stephen, and his daughter-in-law Adele continued to shower gifts on
Marmoutier into the early years of the twelfth century. Their descendants maintained the tradition, though on a more modest scale, until
the early years of the thirteenth century (see table 1).

Like other powerful princes in the eleventh century, the counts of
Blois had a vested interest in maintaining close contact with and some
degree of influence over the monasteries they patronized. After all,
they were turning these establishments into wealthy and powerful
landed institutions, and they did not wish to see the monks' wealth
and power slip away from them. But the nobles were also dependent
on the monks for spiritual assistance, and for this reason many of
them, including the counts of Blois, encouraged monastic reform.

These laymen sought the spiritual assistance of monks because they
were anxious about their own actions in the political and social
realms. During the tenth and early eleventh centuries, territorial
lords, such as the counts of Blois, were usurping royal powers that the
king was too weak to exercise. Although they necessarily filled a
political void, these nobles could not act with complete confidence,
since they lacked the legitimacy that belonged to the king by virtue of
his royal blood and sacred anointing. Moreover, the violence that
nobles exercised among themselves was, as the church began to emphasize in Odo I's generation, inherently sinful. According to the
theology of the time, violent nobles needed to appease God by doing
penance for the sins they committed as a consequence of filling and

---

babin, *France in the Making*, 191–92. I am grateful to Bernard S. Bachrach for alerting me to
the political situation in 998. On Abbot Albert, see Guillot, *Comte d'Anjou*, 1:175 n. 190.

   8. Guillot, *Comte d'Anjou*, 1:176, 183.

   9. "In tantum caram habuit" (*Cartulaire de Marmoutier pour le Dunois*, 92, p. 80);
Guillot, *Comte d'Anjou*, 1:175.

maintaining their positions in society. But they had no time to perform the requisite acts themselves, so they gave large tracts of lands to
monasteries, whose inhabitants were to spend their time corporately
performing vicarious penances and intercessory prayers. As two of
Marmoutier's benefactors stated, they desired the monks' prayers "so
that when the day of death comes to us, the pestiferous enemy will
not rejoice in our souls."[10]

The tenth- and eleventh-century patrons of Marmoutier expected
not only the intercessions of the abbey's monks, but also the assistance of its patron saint, Martin. Thus, like his mother, his brother,
and eventually his son, Odo I of Blois hoped that burial at Marmoutier would assure Martin's help in attaining a desirable after life:
"Remembering the enormity of my evil deeds and becoming very
afraid of the Day of Judgment . . . and especially because I desire,
when I pay my debt to death, to rest at Marmoutier so that [Martin],
the confessor, will snatch my soul from the infernal flames . . . I,
Count Odo, restore and return in perpetuity to all my faithful monks
serving God at Marmoutier the manse of Couture, which belongs to
their abbey but has long been separated from it."[11]

Like the counts of Blois, the Angevin counts often enjoyed a symbi-
otic relationship with Marmoutier (see table 2). Even before Geoffrey
Martel gained control over Touraine in 1044, he and his father Fulk
Nerra—who established his dynasty's power by acquiring new territory, building fortified castles, and allying himself with the church—
nurtured a positive relationship with Marmoutier. In 989 Fulk Nerra
granted Marmoutier some fishing rights, and in 1020 he invited monks
from Marmoutier to inhabit the abbey of Saint-Nicholas of Angers,
which he had just founded. About 1040, Geoffrey Martel and his wife

---

10. "Tradimus supradicto loco beatissimi Martini, et monachis ibi degentibus . . . ut
semper memoriam nostri in suis orationibus habeant, et pro nobis peccatoribus Dei clementiam exorent, ut cum nobis dies mortis aduenerit, non gaudeat de animabus nostris pestifer
inimicus" (Charter of Salomon of Lavardin and Adele, his wife [1032–47], in *Marmoutier,
Cartulaire Blésois,* 14). Although the pious expressions in charters were somewhat for-
mulaic, they represented genuine concerns. For a general discussion of monastic foundations and the anxieties of nobles, see Southern, *Western Society and the Church,* 223–28;
Duby, "Laity and the Peace of God," in Duby, *Chivalrous Society,* 122–33; Rosenwein,
Rhinoceros Bound, 30–56, 101–12.
11. "Ego . . . Odo comes . . . quandam villam, quae Culturas dicitur, et ad abbatiam
sancti Martini majoris monasterii pertinet, sed longe retroactis temporibus separata est,
meorum enormitatem reminiscens scelerum, et districti examinis diem pertimescens . . . et
praecipue quia debitum mortis exsolvens, ibi requiescere cupio, ut jam dictus confessor
animam meam ab infernalibus eripiat flammis . . . cunctis meis fidelibus monachis inibi
Deo famulantibus restituo et in perpetuum reddo" (Charter of Odo I of Blois [ca. 986], in
Marmoutier, Cartulaire Blésois, 8). On Blésois burials at Marmoutier, see *Cartulaire de Marmoutier pour le Dunois,* 92, p. 80.

TABLE 2   Angevin relations with Marmoutier

FULK NERRA (d. 1040)
Gift: Fishing rights at Bocé (Marchegay, 60, Guillot II:C8)
Spreads Marmoutier's influence: Invites Marmoutier's monks to inhabit Saint-Nicholas
  of Angers, which he founded, but later expels them (Guillot, 1:177–78)

GEOFFREY MARTEL (d. 1060)
Gift: Domain of Carbay (later a priory; Guillot, 2:C209)
Gift: Exemption from land tolls and tolls on the Loire (Marchegay, 50–52)
Spreads Marmoutier's influence: Asks Marmoutier's monks to inhabit Trinity of
  Vendôme (Johnson, 37–38)
Possible hostile relations: Marmoutier introduces reform of abbatial elections and of lay
  investiture to Saint-Florent of Saumur (which passed from Blésois to Angevin
  patronage in 1044; Guillot, 1:181–83)

GEOFFREY THE BEARDED (deposed 1067–68)
Hostile relations: Attempts to impose lay investiture on Marmoutier, lays waste its
  property (see text at note 14)

FULK RECHIN (d. 1109)
Gift: Forest of Canevosa (desired burial at Marmoutier when he made the gift; Guillot,
  2:C347; Martène, 1:482–83)
Special status: Urban II places Marmoutier under Fulk's protection (see text at note 20)

FULK V OF JERUSALEM (d. 1142)
Gift: Priory of Trôo (Martène, 2:49)

Guillot   = Guillot, *Comte d'Anjou et son entourage*
Johnson   = Johnson, *Prayer, Patronage and Power*
Marchegay = "Prieurés de Marmoutier en Anjou," ed. P. Marchegay
Martène   = Martène, *Histoire de l'abbaye de Marmoutier*

Agnes invited monks from Marmoutier to help establish a new abbey,
Trinity of Vendôme; in 1050 he gave a landed gift to Marmoutier. The
night before he died in 1060, Geoffrey, like other nobles of his time,
decided to join a monastery *ad succurrendum.* He entered the abbey of
Saint-Nicholas of Angers, but it was a monk from Marmoutier who
gave him medical care during his final hours there. In gratitude,
Geoffrey granted Marmoutier an exemption from paying tolls on the
Loire river.[12]

  In the eleventh century, the counts of Blois and Anjou alleviated
their spiritual anxieties and bolstered their secular power by establishing relationships with the monks of Marmoutier. The Angevins,

---

  12. Halphen, *Comté d'Anjou,* 86–87, 127 n. 2; Guillot, *Comte d'Anjou,* 1:177–81,
2:C209; Johnson, *Prayer, Patronage and Power: The Abbey of La Trinité, Vendôme,* 37; Fulk
Rechin, *Fragmentum historiae Andegavensis,* 236–37; *Chronica de gestis consulum Andegavorum*
(additions by John of Marmoutier), 150–51; "Prieurés de Marmoutier en Anjou," 51–52,
60.

however, like the archbishops of Tours, found that the monastic and Gregorian reforms interfered with their political interests. About 1032, when Baudry, the first abbot of Saint-Nicholas of Angers, retired, another monk from Marmoutier replaced him, but the newly chosen abbot fled the abbey before his benediction. Apparently the abbot could not accept the conditions that the Angevin count was imposing on Saint-Nicholas. Neither would the count tolerate Marmoutier's conditions: after the new abbot fled Saint-Nicholas, Fulk Nerra expelled Marmoutier's monks from the abbey and introduced a monk from Saint-Aubin as the new abbot.[13]

Two decades later, in 1055, Marmoutier introduced to the Angevin abbey of Saint-Florent of Saumur the reforming idea that a layman could not invest an abbot with the symbols of spiritual authority. After this date Geoffrey Martel ceased to found new monasteries. And in 1064 Geoffrey Martel's successor, Geoffrey the Bearded—whose own power had diminished in the face of the duke of Normandy, the king of France, and the reforming papacy—attempted to claim the right to invest Marmoutier's abbot with the pastoral staff, the symbol of the abbot's spiritual authority. When the monks of Marmoutier resisted Geoffrey's attempt, the count retaliated by attacking and laying waste Marmoutier's possessions.[14]

The monks of Marmoutier responded to Geoffrey the Bearded's aggressions with the kinds of cultic responses they employed during their struggles with the archbishops of Tours. First they made a procession to the tomb of Saint Martin. Accompanied by lepers and other feeble people—"whose prayers they believed prevailed above many before God"—the monks proceeded in bare feet to the "body of their patron Saint Martin," where they implored God to temper the count's behavior before he could destroy the abbey and thus earn his own damnation.[15] This procession did not produce immediate

13. Guillot, *Comte d'Anjou,* 1:177–78, 2:C36, C77; charter recounting the events of 1020 to ca. 1036 at Saint-Nicholas, *PL* 155:481. There are some dating problems with the charter, but it is basically correct (see Guillot, 2:C77).

14. Halphen, *Comté d'Anjou,* 139–40; Guillot, *Comte d'Anjou,* 1:106, 173–93; *Chronica de gestis consulum* (additions of MS. B), 152–55.

15. "Monachi autem, cum hec diu cum patientia tolerassent nec jam possent pericula imminentia sustinere, orationes quas pro suis persecutoribus juxta evangelii effundebant preceptum, statuerunt devotius ampliare nudatisque pedibus ad corpus patroni sui beati Martini processerunt, assumptis secum debilibus et leprosis quos de victu vel vestitu monasterii sustinebant et quorum preces apud Deum valere quamplurimum confidebant. Ubi unanimiter in orationibus persistentes, implorabant Domini et sancti merita ut pestem illam tam sevissimam sua misericordia temperaret, ne locum illorum persequutor ille destrueret, unde ipse postmodum in infernum penas luiturus descenderet" (*Chronica de gestis consulum* [additions of MS. B], 153–54).

results. In 1067, however, Geoffrey the Bearded was imprisoned by his brother, Fulk Rechin, and deposed by the pope, who was probably reacting at least in part to Geoffrey's aggression against Marmoutier.[16] In their retrospective account of these events the monks of Marmoutier interpreted Geoffrey's fall from power as a sign that God had come to their assistance. As in their struggles with the archbishop of Tours, the monks represented their opponent—Geoffrey—as the devil's agent and the enemy of the people of God.[17]

Although the monastic and papal reform movements threatened the counts of Anjou and the archbishops of Tours in similar ways, the Angevins healed their rift with Marmoutier much more quickly than did the archbishops. Indeed, in his own relationship with Marmoutier, Count Fulk Rechin benefited from the continuing struggle between the abbey and the archbishop. Fulk became indirectly entangled in the exemption struggle at Tours when he forced Archbishop Ralph to leave his see in 1082.[18] The count was excommunicated for this action, and it was not until fourteen years later that he became reconciled with the reform papacy. In the meantime, however, Fulk fell ill and made a generous gift to Marmoutier. Apparently fearing he was going to die, the count called Saint Martin his "patron" and "defender" and indicated that he wanted to be buried at Marmoutier.[19]

16. Halphen, *Comté d'Anjou*, 139–40, 143–51; Guillot, *Comte d'Anjou*, 1:107–11, 193.

17. "Diabolus, cujus cibus et delectatio est a mundi principio sancta depravare, pacifica perturbare, bonis operibus obviare, electionem Bartholomei abbatis Majoris monasterii atque benedictionem sincerissime factam molitus est modis quibus potuit infestare. Instigavit igitur comitem Andegavensium, nomine Gaufredum, cognomento Barbatum, ut locum Majoris Monasterii suo dominatui subjugaret et abbatem loci cogeret ut de manu illius baculum pastoralem reciperet. . . . Porro Deus, qui *erigit elisos* et *sperantes in se non deserit*, non dormitabat, custodiens Israel spiritualem, et afflictioni servorum suorum, qui, ut scriptum est, jam duplicia pro peccatis suis receperant, misereri ultra non distulit" (*Chronica de gestis consulum* [additions of MS. B], 152, 154).

Halphen and Poupardin acknowledged that this addition in Breton of Amboise's redaction of the *Deeds of the Counts of Anjou* had to have come from Marmoutier: see *Chroniques des comtes d'Anjou*, xxxvii–xxxviii. The best evidence that this was from a Marmoutier source is that Breton's addition included a passage borrowed from an interpolated charter from Marmoutier: see Lévêque, "Trois actes faux ou interpolés . . . en faveur de l'abbaye de Marmoutier," 54–82, 209–305; esp. 300. Hildebert of Lavardin also gave an account of Marmoutier's struggle with Geoffrey the Bearded, but only the Marmoutier text associated Geoffrey with the devil and his imprisonment with God's just retribution on behalf of the people of God: see Hildebert of Lavardin, *Vita S. Hugonis Abbatis Cluniacensis*, 5:33, pp. 70–71.

For a useful discussion of the differences between the problems that Geoffrey the Bearded and Fulk Rechin had with papal reform and the positive relationship that Thibaud of Blois was able to forge with the reformers, see Dunbabin, *France in the Making*, 189, 193–94.

18. See chapter 2 at note 19.

19. Guillot, *Comte d'Anjou*, 2:C347; Martène, *Histoire de l'abbaye de Marmoutier*, 1:482–83.

Fulk recovered from this illness, and in 1096, when Urban II dedicated Marmoutier's new church, the pope made peace with the count. Urban chastised the canons of the cathedral of Tours for tyrannizing the monks of the abbey, proclaimed the monks' innocence "to the ears of Fulk, the distinguished count of Anjou," and placed Marmoutier under the protection of Fulk, along with several other lay leaders.[20] To Urban, Fulk Rechin was an ally of Marmoutier in its struggle with the archbishop and the cathedral.

By the end of the eleventh century, then, the monastic and papal reforms had effectively limited the direct control that local lords could exercise over monasteries like Marmoutier. No outside magnate—lay or ecclesiastical—could impose an abbot on Marmoutier, and no layperson could invest new abbots with the symbols of spiritual authority. Marmoutier was more independent than it had ever been. Indeed, with over one hundred priories in northern and western France and several in England as well, it was at the height of its prosperity, prestige, and influence.

Well into the twelfth century, and even into the thirteenth, Marmoutier maintained its stellar reputation as a model Benedictine abbey, whose prayers for the dead were especially efficacious.[21] Like other traditional Benedictine houses, however, it began to face a number of difficult challenges. First, new monastic orders—such as Cîteaux, Prémontré, Fontevrault, and Grandmont—began to offer spiritual alternatives to the older, more ritualized spirituality of the black Benedictines. Individuals seeking a more rigorous form of religious "poverty" or a more introspective and personal spirituality might join one of these orders, or they might found their own hermitages. Laypeople who were impressed by the poverty, simplicity,

20. "Adversariorum nostrorum canonicorum non minus execrans conversationem, ac praecipue ipsorum detestans in nos actam decennio tyrannidem, innocentiam nostram in auribus tam egregii Andegavorum comitis Fulconis Junioris et procerum ejus, qui sermoni ipsi intererant, quam omnium qui illuc undecumque confluxerant, ipse papa exposuerat et assignaverat. . . . et, ad ultimum, coenobio nostro et nobis praefato comiti ac proceribus ejus, caeteroque populo commendatis benedixerat, ex praefatorum privilegiorum tenore, et absolverat omnes qui nos et universa nostra custodirent fideliter et tuerentur, atque honorarent" (*Textus de dedicatione ecclesiae Majoris monasterii*, 339–40).
For a general discussion of Urban II's reconciliation with Fulk Rechin, see Guillot, *Comte d'Anjou*, 1:116–17. It was during this trip that Urban gave Fulk the Golden Rose, a token of special favor: see Fulk Rechin, *Fragmentum historiae*, 238.
21. Guibert of Gembloux, a Benedictine from the Low Countries, had the highest praise for Marmoutier in the 1180s: see chapter 6, especially at note 74. An early thirteenth-century Cistercian work included a story illustrating Marmoutier's continuing reputation as a center for efficacious prayers for the dead: see *Exordium magnum ordinis Cisterciensis*, 6:5, PL 185:2:1188–90.

or rigor of the new houses and orders began to patronize them—either instead of or along with the older Benedictines. And in all their benefactions, laypeople became more circumscribed. By the second half of the twelfth century the age of large landed gifts had drawn to a close, and religious institutions had to adapt to (and learn to administer) modest sources of income—such as tithes, oblations from parish churches, and rents from small properties.[22] As I show in chapter 4, the transition to modest gifts was closely tied to a new theology that placed responsibility on the individual. An interior sense of remorse, theologians now maintained, was all that was necessary to save a sinner from eternal damnation. But if that was so, what role was there for monastic suffrages for the dead? One of the aims of Marmoutier's twelfth- and thirteenth-century legends was to answer this question.

Marmoutier's monks encountered the new religious institutions of the late eleventh and twelfth centuries in a number of arenas. The forests of the diocese of Tours became dotted with new hermitages—Fontaines-les-Blanches, Aiguevive, Gastine, Baugerais, Turpenay, Bois-Aubry. Fontevrault, moreover, was just west of the diocese of Tours and had two priories within the diocese.[23] By the second half of the twelfth century Marmoutier's most influential patrons—the Angevin and Blésois counts—were favoring the new orders. Fulk V of Anjou was a major benefactor of Fontevrault, his daughter became its second abbess, and his grandson, King Henry II of England, was buried there, as were Henry's wife and son. Similarly, Thibaud IV of Blois became an intimate associate of Bernard of Clairvaux.[24] The Blésois counts continued to give gifts to Marmoutier until the end of the twelfth century, but their donations became more modest; the Angevins apparently ceased to bestow gifts on Marmoutier after 1124 (see tables 1 and 2). By the second half of the twelfth century, however, Marmoutier's monks were learning that the patronage of powerful secular rulers was not limited to landed gifts. Representatives of Marmoutier now spent a great deal of time in secular and episcopal courts defending their abbey's claims to property, sometimes against the newer religious orders. Powerful lords, including the Angevin kings and the Blésois counts, could show goodwill toward Mar-

22. Southern, *Western Society and the Church*, 232–33, 240–71.
23. Oury, "Erémitisme dans l'ancien diocèse de Tours"; Devailly, "Expansion et diversité du monachisme du XIᵉ au XIIᵉ siècle," 66–72.
24. Dunbabin, *France in the Making*, 314–15, 339–40; Bezzola, *Origines et la formation de la littérature courtoise*, 2:2:289, 291, 292 n. 1.

moutier by reaching judicial decisions that favored the abbey.[25] It paid
to have friends in high places, and Marmoutier's monks attracted and
reciprocated the favors of powerful men not only by praying for their
souls, but also by writing flattering historical works. As the discussion in chapter 3 suggests, John of Marmoutier's role as a prominent
historian and biographer in the court of King Henry II was potentially
beneficial for his monastery.

There is no evidence that Marmoutier suffered a major decline
during the twelfth century—indeed, it probably remained the most
impressive religious house in Touraine. And the visitation records of
Bishop Odo of Rouen reveal that even in the thirteenth century Marmoutier's priories maintained a higher standard of the monastic life
than did many other monastic institutions.[26] Nevertheless, the
monks had to adapt to changing patterns of generosity, to new spiritual concerns, and to evolving cultural tastes. They needed to convince both themselves and their potential patrons that they still had
something to offer society. They made a strong case for themselves in
their writings about the Angevin and Blésois counts.

25. On Marmoutier's monks in judicial courts, see White, *Custom, Kinship, and Gifts,*
83, 264 n. 208. Cases decided by Henry II of England and Thibaud V of Blois include
Marmoutier, Cartulaire Blésois, 187, p. 173, and Martène, *Histoire de l'abbaye de Marmoutier,*
2:118. Cases involving new religious orders include *Cartulaire de Marmoutier pour le Perche,*
67, pp. 84–85 (settlement between priory of Bellême and Cistercian house of La Trappe);
Marmoutier, Cartulaire Blésois, 167, p. 157, 243, p. 222 (settlements between Marmoutier and
Premonstratensian house of Stella); 257, p. 234 (settlement between Marmoutier and Pig-
nardière, a priory of Fontevrault).

26. Odo Rigaldus, *Register of Eudes of Rouen,* 96, 102, 524.

3

History, Legitimacy, and Motivation in Marmoutier's Literature for the Angevins

Between about 1137 and 1175 Marmoutier's monks wrote three works that served in part to enhance the status and legitimacy of the counts of Anjou. The first of those works glorified Ingelger, the legendary tenth-century patriarch of the Angevin line; the second, a history of the counts of Anjou, gave a series of brief biographies beginning with Count Ingelger and continuing through Count Geoffrey the Fair (d. 1151); and the third provided a laudatory biography of Geoffrey the Fair.

These three works reflect a growing interest, in the eleventh and twelfth centuries, in noble ancestry. Medieval people tended to believe that charged moments in the past—especially origin points, the times when patriarchs lived—provided blueprints and exemplary models for the present. But by the twelfth century they had also become convinced that tangible links should join the past with the present and that individuals derived their status and personality from their bloodlines. As the discussion in chapter 6 shows, this aristocratic concern with genealogy and linear continuity spilled over into monastic histories as well.

Legitimizing stories about the ancestors of a count or king not only could enhance that man's reputation but could also mold him, telling him who he was and how he should behave. Over the course of the twelfth century, Marmoutier's writings about the Angevins showed an increasing concern with molding behavior and affecting the conscience of the individual. This interweaving of an interest in collective reputation with an interest in interior motivation points to the close linking in this period of group consciousness and notions of the self, the one enhancing the other. Indeed, both the concern with group legitimacy and the awareness of individual responsibility were related, at least in part, to the mounting complexity of society.

Because they served persuasive purposes, Marmoutier's legends about the Angevins had the potential of meeting not only the Angevins' needs, but also those of the monks. Through their legends the monks offered moral advice, and they informed the counts of Anjou and the first Angevin king of England how to maintain reciprocal relations with the abbey. The monks portrayed these ideal relations at a time when the Angevins were turning to the newer religious orders for spiritual solace. It is possible that the monks saw in these texts (and especially in the *Return from Burgundy*) a way to draw the Angevins' attention back to Marmoutier and Martin's cult. Even if the monks failed in the end to outshine the newer religious orders in the Angevins' eyes, they could still benefit from the favor of their rulers in courts of law. By presenting the Angevins with the "gift" of flattering histories, the monks may have hoped to merit the reciprocal gift of favorable legal decisions if ever the need arose.

Dynastic Legitimacy: *Saint Martin's Return from Burgundy*

Marmoutier's first work concerning the counts of Anjou, the *Return from Burgundy*, was written by an anonymous monk between about 1137 and 1156.[1] This legend enhanced the reputation of the counts of Anjou in three ways: it simultaneously associated their patriarch with the cult of Saint Martin and disassociated the Capetian king from that cult; it contrasted the heroism of Count Ingelger of Anjou with the ineffectual behavior of the king of Francia; and it made a substantial contribution to the Angevins' genealogical literature.

The criticism of an earlier king of France in the *Return from Burgundy* reflected the political stance of the Angevins in the years after 1128. Before 1128 the Angevins had frequently changed sides in the political struggles of the times, sometimes allying with the Capetian kings and sometimes lining up against them. In 1128, however, a new phase of Angevin history began. Fulk Junior's son Geoffrey the Fair became engaged to Mathilda, the daughter of Henry I of England, and the Angevins turned their attentions to England.[2] When Henry II, the son of Geoffrey and Mathilda, assumed the English throne in 1154, Touraine became part of the Angevin empire, and it did not fall under the French king's domain until 1204.

In its focus on the prestige of the Angevins and its implicit crit-

1. On the date of the *Return from Burgundy* (*De reversione beati Martini*), see Source Appendix, I-A.
2. Guillot, *Comte d'Anjou*, 1:56–101; Chartrou, *Anjou de 1109 à 1151*, 1–25.

icism of the French throne, the *Return from Burgundy* differed from the work that had inspired it—Radbod of Utrecht's sermon describing the siege of Tours in 903. Whereas Radbod's sermon had assumed that the community of Christian Franks was united and that it directed its hostility toward external enemies, the *Return from Burgundy* emphasized hostilities among Christians, thereby highlighting the twelfth-century author's perception that both the church and Christian society in general were divided into competing communities or groups.

According to the legend, the special relationship between the Angevins and the cult of Saint Martin originated when Ingelger, allegedly the first count of Anjou, stepped in to fill a void left by the king, who through his inactivity implicitly forfeited his association with Martin. Abbot Herbern and the other men who had carried Martin's relics to Auxerre sought the assistance of the king, the legend claimed, when they learned that the bishop of Auxerre would not allow them to carry the relics back to Tours. The king, however, was reduced to inaction by his desire to avoid prejudicing one part of his kingdom in favor of another. He told the saint's custodians that both Tours and Auxerre were in his realm and that the evidence of possession seemed to favor Auxerre's claims: "Since both cities are under royal authority and in both we serve that authority indifferently, we consider it unworthy that with the violence of prejudice we should despoil Auxerre, which possessed the treasure, and that we should give it to Tours, which up until now has relinquished its possession."[3] In the face of such unjust equanimity, the *Return from Burgundy* implied, it was better to turn to local patrons. Indeed, when the Tourangeaux turned to Count Ingelger for assistance, he immediately responded to their dilemma. Backed by the armed might of six thousand men and horses and assisted by several bishops, the count convinced the bishop of Auxerre to relinquish Martin's relics. He then accompanied Martin's party in its glorious procession back to Tours.[4]

Earlier facts and traditions concerning the Angevin line had already established a special relationship between the Angevin line and Saint Martin's cult and basilica. Fulk the Red (+940) had probably been the treasurer of the chapter of Saint-Martin (although this seems to have been forgotten by the twelfth century); Fulk the Good (+960) had, so

3. "Cum utraque civitas regii sit juris, et ab utraque nobis indifferenter serviatur, indignum ducimus ut Autissiodorum, quae de thesauri hujus possessione saisita est, praejudicii violentia spoliemus, et Turonum vestram, quae huc usque illius investituram amisit, investiamus" (*De reversione beati Martini*, 26).

4. *De reversione beati Martini*, 28–34.

the twelfth-century *Deeds of the Counts of Anjou* claimed, such special devotion for the church of Saint-Martin that he was made an honorary canon there and frequently sang in the choir; Geoffrey Greymantle was buried at Saint-Martin; and Geoffrey Martel (as well as his descendants) carried the saint's banner into battle.[5] Nevertheless, legendary historiography now established that Ingelger was the patriarch of the Angevin line. Thus, because the prevailing historical consciousness of the period assumed that points of origin provided blueprints for subsequent time, Ingelger's relationship with Martin's cult was normative in a way that those of Fulk the Good, Geoffrey Greymantle, and Geoffrey Martel were not.[6]

Furthermore, unlike the remembered devotion of Fulk the Good, the burial of Geoffrey Greymantle, and the use of Saint Martin's banner by Geoffrey Martel (who fought as an ally of the Capetian king the first time he carried Martin's banner, in 1044), the *Return from Burgundy* indicated that the formation of the relationship between the Angevins and Saint Martin's cult was linked to the king's failure to live up to his responsibilities toward the saint.[7] Indeed, it appears that the author of the *Return from Burgundy*, mindful of his patron's com-

5. On Fulk the Red as treasurer of Saint-Martin, see John of Salerno, "Vita Sancti Odonis," 1:11, 1:21, *PL* 133:48, 52. John does not state outright that Fulk was the treasurer, but the actions he describes (Fulk gave Odo a cell at Saint-Martin and a canonry, and he took two gold vessels from the treasury) lend themselves to that conclusion. I am grateful to Barbara H. Rosenwein and Bernard S. Bachrach for alerting me to these passages. On Fulk the Good's honorary canonry, see *Chronica de gestis consulum Andegavorum*, 36. This twelfth-century passage, perhaps an invention, may have been based on the fact that Guy, the brother of Fulk the Good, was indeed a canon at Saint-Martin: see Guillot, *Comte d'Anjou*, 141 n. 49; *Chroniques des comtes d'Anjou*, 33 n. 2. On Geoffrey Greymantle's burial, see Fulk Rechin, *Fragmentum historiae Andegavensis*, 233. On Geoffrey Martel and his descendants carrying the banner of Saint-Martin, see Ralph Glaber, *Historiarum libri quinque*, 5:2, pp. 129–30; Vaucelle, *Collégiale de Saint-Martin*, 170; Du Cange, *Glossarium*, S.V. "Vexillum S. Martini," 6:796.

6. On the identification of Ingelger as the Angevin patriarch, see text below at note 20 ff. On historical consciousness and the importance of blueprints from the past, see Duby, "French Genealogical Literature: The Eleventh and Twelfth Centuries," in Duby, *Chivalrous Society*, 134–57, esp. 156; Spiegel, *Chronicle Tradition of Saint Denis*, 40, 44–45; Chenu, "Monks, Canons and Laymen in Search of the Apostolic Life," in Chenu, *Nature, Man and Society in the Twelfth Century*, 202–38; Benson, "Political *Renovatio*: Two Models from Roman Antiquity"; Constable, "Renewal and Reform in the Religious Life"; Southern, "Aspects of the European Tradition of Historical Writing: 4. The Sense of the Past." Brian Stock associates both the preoccupation with anterior models or precedents and the efflorescence of genealogical literature with the growing importance and predominance of literacy: see "Medieval Literacy, Linguistic Theory, and Social Organization," 19, 25–26. But already in the early eleventh century there had been a concern with presenting the distant past as a blueprint for the present. See Landes, "Dynamics of Heresy and Reform in Limoges," 480.

7. On Geoffrey Martel's relations with King Henry I of France in 1044, see Guillot, *Comte d'Anjou*, 1:57–58.

petitive stance toward the Capetian kings, was trying to promote a relationship between Saint Martin and the counts of Anjou that both rivaled the one between the Capetian king and Saint Denis and appropriated for the house of Anjou a saint who had traditionally been associated with the kings of Francia.

To a certain extent the Capetian kings themselves had already begun to abandon Martin's cult as they grew closer to the cult of Saint Denis. About a generation before the *Return from Burgundy* was written, during the reign of Louis VI, the link between the Capetian kings and Saint Denis began to receive greater attention than before. In 1124, under the threat of attack by the emperor Henry V, Louis visited the abbey of Saint-Denis, just outside Paris. There he declared that Denis was the special patron and protector of the realm and took up the saint's banner, which he intended to carry into battle. By the end of the twelfth century this banner was identified with the oriflamme, which Charlemagne had carried in the *Song of Roland,* and it remained a central royal symbol until the end of the Middle Ages.[8]

But Louis might have chosen another saint. His predecessor Philip I, for instance, had favored Saint Remi's relationship with the crown and had chosen to be buried at Fleury, near Saint Benedict, who was also a long-standing favorite of the Frankish rulers.[9] It is significant, however, that Louis VI, with the encouragement of Abbot Suger and other monks of Saint-Denis, chose a saint who resided within the immediate royal domain. Even though the events of 1124 gave rise to an unusual amount of unity between the king and his vassals, Louis VI's most direct sphere of activity remained his private domain—land in the region immediately around Paris.[10] Such was the state of the feudal monarchy in the late eleventh and early twelfth centuries. By the time the king finally extended his unrivaled power over Touraine in 1204, Saint Denis had gained an unquestionable position as the royal patron.

Changes in the manuscripts of the liturgical acclamations of the king, the laudes regiae, may well reflect the twelfth-century rise of Saint Denis's royal status vis-à-vis that of Saint Martin. Eighth-

---

8. Spiegel, *Chronicle Tradition of Saint Denis,* 30; Spiegel, "Cult of St. Denis and Capetian Kingship," 58–59. Erdmann (*Origins of the Idea of Crusade,* 273–74) also maintained that the turning point in Denis's relationship with the king came in the eleventh and twelfth centuries, especially with the new role of Denis's banner.

9. Spiegel, *Chronicle Tradition of Saint Denis,* 28.

10. Hallam, *Capetian France,* 114–19. On the role Suger and the monks of Saint-Denis played in promoting Denis's cult, see Bournazel, "Suger and the Capetians." See also Spiegel, "Cult of St. Denis and Capetian Kingship," 58–59.

century Carolingian laudes had equated the two saints, associating them, as well as Saints Hilary and Maurice, with the Frankish army. In these manuscripts, and in one from the eleventh century as well, the king was associated with Saints Mary, Michael, Gabriel, Raphael, John, and Stephen. But in a twelfth-century manuscript the king was associated with Denis alone.[11] Although the basilica of Saint-Martin of Tours remained a royal abbey and twelfth-century chansons de geste, such as the *Couronnement de Louis,* perpetuated the idea of the king's relationship with Martin, before the middle of the twelfth century Saint Denis attained a privileged position as the preeminent royal patron saint.[12]

The monks of Marmoutier thus promoted an association between Saint Martin and the Angevins one generation after Louis VI and the monks of Saint-Denis began to stress with new fervor the relationship between Denis and the Capetian line. The efforts of both the monks of Marmoutier and those of Saint-Denis reflect a general intensification in the use of legitimizing legends and rituals. These resulted at least in part from the competitive relationship between princely magnates and the Capetian kings, whose power—from the time of Louis VI on—was growing at the expense of those magnates. In Tours, in the period when the *Return from Burgundy* was written, the Angevins were feeling the direct effects of the expansion of Capetian power. Between 1044, when Geoffrey Martel gained control over Touraine, and the early part of the twelfth century, the men who were appointed deans and treasurers of the chapter of Saint-Martin tended to be close allies of the Angevins. The treasurer who assumed office about 1139, however, and possibly the dean who assumed office about 1154, were sons of King Louis VI. And all their successors, at least until the end of the thirteenth century, were close allies of the Capetian kings.[13]

In addition to associating the count of Anjou with Saint Martin's cult, the *Return from Burgundy* contributed to the status and prestige of the Angevins by portraying the founder of the line as a hero of the Viking era and by contrasting his heroism with the king's ineffectual behavior. The legend described Ingelger as an "energetic count" (*comes impiger*) and juxtaposed the count's energy with the "slothfulness"

11. Kantorowicz, *Laudes Regiae,* 15 (citing Bibliothèque Nationale, MS. lat. 13159, eighth century), 46 n. 118 (citing Rouen, Bibliothèque Municipale, MS. 537, twelfth century), 116 n. 16 (citing Bibliothèque Nationale, MS. lat. 9949, eleventh century).

12. For Martin's relationship with the king in the chansons de geste, see *Couronnemente de Louis,* line 1467, p. 68; Frappier, *Chansons de geste du cycle de Guillaume d'Orange,* 2:149.

13. Griffiths, "Capetian Kings and St. Martin of Tours," 115–17, 126–27.

(*pigra segnities*) that prevented the king from protecting the interests of the Tourangeaux.[14]

In focusing on a hero of the era of Viking and Saracen invaders, as well as in contrasting a vigorous count with a passive sovereign, the *Return from Burgundy* resembled a number of chansons de geste, also written in the first half of the twelfth century. The *Couronnement de Louis,* for example, portrayed the emperor Louis the Pious as a thoroughly incompetent ruler whose realm was held together and protected by Count William of Orange, who fought the Saracen invaders and defended both the Christian faith and the principle of justice.[15]

Some critics have argued that the portrayal of a weak king in many of the chansons de geste represented the perspective of powerful territorial lords who either threatened or were threatened by the increasing effectiveness of the French kings. Twelfth-century vernacular literature promoted the interests of these rivals to the Capetians by reducing the sovereign to a weak figurehead or portraying him as an unjust antagonist.[16] The *Return from Burgundy* can also be understood in this way. It was written at the same time as these chansons de geste, it glorified a comital family that was in direct competition with the Capetians, and it juxtaposed an energetic count, who performed his heroic deeds during the mythical age of Viking and Saracen invaders, with an ineffective and slothful king.

But Ingelger's heroism represents more fundamental intellectual shifts as well. Unlike Radbod's tenth-century sermon, in which the Franks were passive victims and only God and his saints played active roles, the *Return from Burgundy* portrayed men as actors. Ingelger proved his faith with acts of prowess and bravery. In Radbod's account, the appearance of Martin's relics had caused a "vehement stupor" to strike the Danes; in the *Return from Burgundy,* by contrast, it was at the appearance of Ingelger's armed band that "the city of Auxerre was stupefied."[17] This emphasis on men as causal agents

14. *De reversione beati Martini,* 27–28. For a similar eleventh-century portrayal of the lazy king, see the *Annales de Vendôme,* cited by Dunbabin, *France in the Making,* 133.

15. *Couronnement de Louis;* Frappier, *Chansons de geste du cycle de Guillaume d'Orange,* 2:51.

16. Calin, *Old French Epic of Revolt,* 131; Bezzola argues that the noble criticism was not that the king had too much power, but that he could not maintain control: see "De Roland à Raoul de Cambrai." R. Howard Bloch sees in all the epics more a criticism of war as a means of solving problems in the post-feudal age than a criticism of monarchy (*Medieval French Literature and Law,* 100–103).

17. "Danis e contrario stupor vehemens incussus est" (Radbod, *Libellus de miraculo S. Martini,* 1243); "Stupet Autissiodorum civitas armato milite ex insperato se repleri" (*De reversione beati Martini,* 28).

points to one of the salient characteristics of spiritual and secular writings from the period that began about 1000—optimism.[18]

Insofar as it reflected the competition between the French king and the princely magnates of his realm, the *Return from Burgundy* resembled not only certain themes in the chansons de geste but also new historical writings.[19] Such writings, which emanated from both royal and noble circles, also served legitimizing purposes. The most important innovation within this genre entailed the emergence of noble genealogies and genealogical histories, to which the *Return from Burgundy* contributed.

Between the seventh century and the eleventh century the only genealogies recorded in continental Europe were produced for royal dynasties. At the end of the eleventh century, however, a few powerful noble families—those of the counts of Anjou and Flanders and that of the duke of Normandy—began to record or commission their own genealogies. In these works the powerful magnates claimed (whether or not it was true) that their lineages had originated in Carolingian times and that they thereby owed their power and office not to the Capetian king but to their own connections with the Carolingians, which had been preserved through the unbroken links of their continuous family lines.

The initial function of the new genealogies was to illustrate the continuity of a patrimony, passed on through a single bloodline. In the twelfth century, however, the circle around the Angevins, like those around other powerful nobles, became interested in recording the deeds of ancestors who had bequeathed to them an inheritance of valor as well as a patrimony. Indeed, the accounts of these deeds suggested that it was by virtue of their heroic accomplishments in the mythical age of Carolingian rulers and pagan invaders that legendary ancestors had obtained their patrimonies. Twelfth-century family histories like those concerning the Angevins both borrowed from and provided material for the chansons de geste.

The gradual elaboration of the historical accounts concerning In-

18. This new confidence in man as actor is implicit in several discussions of the twelfth-century renaissance and twelfth-century spirituality. See, for example, Southern, *Making of the Middle Ages*, 219–57; Chenu, "Nature and Man," in Chenu, *Nature, Man, and Society in the Twelfth Century*, 1–48.

19. For the following discussion, see Duby, "Structure of Kinship and Nobility" and "French Genealogical Literature," in Duby, *Chivalrous Society*, 134–57; Spiegel, "Genealogy: Form and Function," 45–53; Spiegel, *Chronicle Tradition of Saint Denis*, 40, 44–45; Lewis, *Royal Succession in Capetian France*, 119–20. On the development of patrilineal consciousness in twelfth-century Germany, see Freed, *Counts of Falkenstein*.

gelger illustrates the stages of development of these family histories. Ingelger's historical existence is affirmed by a ninth-century charter in which he is identified as the father of Fulk the Red, the first historical count of Anjou.[20] More than a century after Ingelger's death, the Angevins began to take an interest in recording the history of their line. Not surprisingly, however, their memory of the family patriarch was weak. To be sure, they still knew who Ingelger was: his name appeared on one of the earliest Angevin genealogies, written at the abbey of Saint-Aubin of Angers toward the end of the eleventh century.[21] Even so, Fulk Rechin, who wrote a short history of his family in 1096, said he could record the "virtues and deeds" neither of Ingelger nor of Ingelger's two successors, Fulk the Red and Fulk the Good, "because they lived so long ago that we do not even know where they are buried."[22] Nevertheless, Fulk Rechin contributed to, and perhaps initiated, the family mythology concerning Ingelger, claiming that it was a descendant of Charlemagne, rather than an ancestor of the Capetians, who had bestowed the position of count on Ingelger. Fulk Rechin also claimed that Ingelger, as well as his earliest descendants, had liberated Anjou from pagans: "These four counts [Ingelger, Fulk the Red, Fulk the Good, and Geoffrey Greymantle] held the honor of Anjou, having seized it from the hands of pagans. . . . And Ingelger, the first count, held that honor from the king of France—not from the race of the impious Philip [who had recently won over and married Fulk's wife] but from the stock of Charles the Bald, who was the son of Louis, the son of Charlemagne."[23]

During the first half of the twelfth century, historians of the Angevin line elaborated the legends concerning Ingelger. According to

20. Halphen, *Comté d'Anjou*, 3; *Cartulaire de l'abbaye de St. Aubin d'Angers*, 177; Werner, "Untersuchungen zur Frühzeit des französischen Fürstentums," 266–79. For a recent assessment of Werner, with some discussion of Ingelger and Fulk the Red, see Bouchard, "Origins of the French Nobility," 514–16.

21. *Genealogiae comitum Andegavensium*, 247.

22. "Quorum quatuor consulum [Ingelger, Fulk the Red, Fulk the Good and Geoffrey Greymantle] virtutes et acta, quia nobis in tantum de longinquo sunt ut etiam loca ubi corpora eorum iacent nobis incognita sint, digne memorare non possumus" (Fulk Rechin, *Fragmentum historiae*, 233). Although Fulk included Geoffrey Greymantle in this statement, he went on to explain that Geoffrey was an exception because he was the most recent of the four, and indeed, Fulk knew where Geoffrey was buried.

23. "Isti autem quatuor consules tenuerunt honorem Andegavinum et eripuerunt eum de manibus paganorum et a christianis consulibus defenderunt. Et ille primus Ingelgerius habuit illum honorem a rege Francie, non a genere impii Philippi sed a prole Caroli Calvi, qui fuit filius Hludovici filii Caroli Magni" (Fulk Rechin, *Fragmentum historiae*, 232–33). On the earlier evidence concerning the first Angevin counts and the Capetians, see Bouchard, "Origins of the French Nobility," 515.

the first redaction of the *Deeds of the Counts of Anjou,* written before 1115 and rewritten after 1151, Ingelger defeated the Vikings in battle, thereby earning himself a noble wife, additions to his patrimony, and the position of count. Concerning Ingelger's chivalric behavior, this work noted that while he was still a youth, Ingelger successfully defended in one-on-one combat his godmother, who had been falsely accused of adultery.[24]

The *Return from Burgundy* augmented the Angevins' corpus of genealogical literature and elaborated the themes that had been important to Fulk Rechin and the first author(s) of the *Deeds of the Counts of Anjou.* Like the earlier histories, it rooted the family memory in the age of Carolingians and Vikings and portrayed the patriarch of the line as a chivalric hero. It enhanced those themes by demonstrating that the association between the Angevins and the cult of Saint Martin began with Ingelger.

But unlike Fulk Rechin's fragment and the first version of the *Deeds of the Counts of Anjou,* the *Return from Burgundy* was written from a decidedly monastic perspective. As I argued in chapter 2, the legend helped support the interests of Marmoutier and Saint-Martin in their struggles with the archbishop of Tours. Even while glorifying Marmoutier's Angevin patrons, moreover, the legend attempted to mold those patrons by instructing them that they should protect the monks and canons who guarded Saint Martin's cult. The message applied to both Marmoutier and Saint-Martin. By emphasizing that the party in Auxerre was headed by Abbot Herbern of Marmoutier, however, the author highlighted the relationship between Marmoutier and the counts.

The monastic perspective of the *Return from Burgundy* is perhaps best illustrated by the fact that the monks themselves (along with their companions from Saint-Martin) were the principal beneficiaries of the deeds and miracles in the story. This had not been so in earlier stories about the Angevins' relations with the cult of Saint Martin or in the earlier histories of the Angevins. In an eleventh-century account of Geoffrey Martel's victory in 1044 over the count of Blois, the miracles of Saint Martin benefited the count: in 1044 when Geoffrey first carried Martin's banner into battle, he won the battle without

---

24. *Chronica de gestis consulum,* 29–31. On the dates of the first redaction (which was written by Thomas of Loches, chaplain for the Angevin count, and then rewritten by a certain Robin), see *Chroniques des comtes d'Anjou,* xviii–xxxix, and Martin, "Autour de Thomas Pacitius, prieur de la collégiale de Loches." Martin argues that Thomas must have written before 1115 because he would have softened his harsh portrayal of Bertrade—who left Fulk Rechin to marry King Philip—once she became a prioress at Fontevrault in 1115.

shedding any blood because Thibaud of Blois's men were frightened by Geoffrey's army, which looked completely white.[25] Similarly, in Fulk Rechin's historical fragment and in the first version of the *Deeds of the Counts of Anjou*, Ingelger's actions were beneficial to himself, bringing him wealth, property, and the position of count. In the *Return from Burgundy*, Ingelger's action served the monks, the canons of Saint-Martin, and the saint himself. And the miracles in that legend reinforced the idea that Ingelger's service and the consequent return of the saint's relics to Tours were pleasing to God and to Martin. When the saint reentered his parish, bells rang, candles ignited, and trees turned green in mid-December.[26]

In its representation of the heroic patriarch Ingelger, the *Return from Burgundy* emphasized the layperson's responsibility to protect the interests of religious institutions. Nevertheless, like the more secular works about heroic ancestors, the legend concentrated on external behavior and external signs of status. Like an epic hero, Ingelger established his reputation through actions: we know nothing about his motivations or sentiments.[27] Ingelger's external accomplishments devolved, as an almost physical inheritance, upon the Angevin counts who succeeded him. But the legend about Ingelger was also an exemplary and exhortatory tale establishing a set of expectations for those who inherited the patriarch's position. Thus the author of the *Return from Burgundy* implied that a good count did not simply inherit his status; rather, he chose to conform to the model of his ancestors. John of Marmoutier would go much further in this exhortatory and motivational direction.

Group Legitimacy and Individual Motivation: The Writings of John of Marmoutier

In his writings about the Angevin line John of Marmoutier, like the author of the *Return from Burgundy*, legitimized his secular patrons while at the same time adding a monastic perspective. Also like the earlier author, John strengthened the links between his Angevin patrons and the cult of Saint Martin. Unlike the earlier author, however, John shifted his preoccupations away from heroic behavior, and his desire to mold the individual character of his patron, King Henry II of

25. Ralph Glaber, *Historiarum libri quinque* 5:2, pp. 129–30.
26. *De reversione beati Martini*, 32.
27. For a general discussion of epic heros and external concerns, see Southern, *Making of the Middle Ages*, 241–46.

England, was more explicit. John consciously employed the art of persuasion to incite Henry to be a good man. Although John's discussions of motivation and persuasion did not bear directly on the cult of Saint Martin, his interest in these themes merits our attention, since parallel discussions recurred in texts from Marmoutier that did involve Martin's cult.

Both of John's works—his revised and expanded version of the *Deeds of the Counts of Anjou,* which he wrote between 1164 and 1173, and his biography of Geoffrey the Fair, written after 1173—contributed to the corpus of Angevin genealogical literature.[28] Furthermore, John gave the Angevins' relationship to Martin's cult a central place in the family's genealogical memory by incorporating the *Return from Burgundy* into his redeaction of the *Deeds of the Counts of Anjou.*[29]

John's inclusion of the earlier legend in the family's continuous linear history strengthened the implication that because the family patriarch was linked to Saint Martin's cult, so were all his descendants. And John reinforced this message of continuity by making a new claim that not only Ingelger, but also his first two descendants—the three ancestors whose bodies had been lost to Fulk Rechin seventy-five years earlier— were buried at Saint-Martin.[30]

John also asserted, as the *Return from Burgundy* did not, that the relationship between Ingelger and Martin's cult was reciprocal: he claimed that after Ingelger accompanied Martin's relics to Tours he was given a prebend at the basilica of Saint-Martin and designated its defender, tutor, and treasurer. Fulk the Red, the actual patriarch of the Angevin line, probably was the treasurer of Saint-Martin. But he apparently used the position on occasion to plunder the chapter's resources rather than to serve the house. Thus John's example differed from the historical precedent (which he may not have known anyway), in that he portrayed Ingelger as the defender of Saint-Martin.[31]

Not only in his narrative about Ingelger but also in his biography of Geoffrey the Fair, John was able to demonstrate that both the count and the religious houses of Marmoutier and Saint-Martin benefited

---

28. On the dates of John's works, see *Chroniques des comtes d'Anjou,* xxvi, xl, lxxxiv.

29. *Chronica de gestis consulum,* 30 n. d.

30. *Chronica de gestis consulum,* 31 n. a; 34 n. a; 37 n. a; and introduction, *Chroniques des comtes d'Anjou,* xi, xlvi.

31. Herbernus, Archbishop of Tours (attributed), *Miracula beati Martini, PL* 129:1035. This passage was either written by John of Marmoutier and borrowed by the author of the collection of miracles or vice versa. On the Herbernus collection, see Van der Straeten, "Recueil de miracles de S. Martin attribué à Herberne." John put this passage at the end of the passages that he borrowed from the *Return from Burgundy:* see *Chronica de gestis consulum,* 30, n. d. On Fulk the Red, see above at note 5.

from their association. According to John, the archbishop of Tours threatened to excommunicate Geoffrey during one of their frequent altercations. But Geoffrey remained unruffled, reminding the archbishop that he was (honorarily, at least) both a canon of Saint-Martin and a monk of Marmoutier. "And thus," since both houses were now exempt from the archbishop's power to excommunicate, "the wise man both evaded the unjust sentence of the pontiff and proved how highly the pontiff should hold the privileges of churches."[32]

Although John directed much of his discussion to inner motivation, he continued to praise the exterior and manly virtues of the Angevins in terms reminiscent of the *Return from Burgundy*. In his life of Geoffrey the Fair, for example, he portrayed Geoffrey as a valorous count—like Ingelger, a "comes impiger." And like the author of the *Return from Burgundy*, John contrasted the count's vigor with the weakness of a king. This time, however, the weak king was not the king of France but Stephen, the "false king" of England, who in his struggle to retain the throne "waned" each day, while his rival Geoffrey grew "more robust."[33]

John described Geoffrey as a leader who met the traditional criteria of manly virtues. Nevertheless, he stressed that Geoffrey's most important traits were wisdom, mercy, and justice. In his prologue to Geoffrey's *Life,* John wrote that because Geoffrey manifested these traits, he proved himself an ideal ruler, even though he was not actually a king: "For who did not know either his clemency toward those who had been overthrown, or his mercy toward the wretched, his justice toward rebels, his strength in fighting enemies, his skill in managing things?"[34]

In emphasizing Geoffrey's intellectual and moral virtues, John built on earlier twelfth-century versions of the Angevin family history. Even in the *Return from Burgundy*, Ingelger employed a certain rhetorical skill when he pointed out to the bishop that he was not living up to the etymology of his title, *pontifex*. Moreover, the first redaction of the

32. "Sic vir sapiens et injustam pontificis evasit sententiam et quanti haberet ecclesiarum privilegia comprobavit" (John of Marmoutier, *Historia Gaufredi ducis Normannorum et comitis Andegavorum,* 192–93).

33. "Facta est longa concertatio inter Stephanum pseudoregem et Gaufredum Andegavorum consulem: Gaufredus proficiens et semper in seipso robustior, Stephanus decrescens quotidie" (John of Marmoutier, *Historia Gaufredi,* 226, 230–31).

34. "Quis enim non noverit vel clementiam predicti viri in prostratos vel in miseros misericordiam vel justitiam in rebelles vel in hostes fortitudinem vel in rebus gerendis astutiam?" (John of Marmoutier, *Historia Gaufredi,* 173). C. Stephen Jaeger has cited John's descriptions of Geoffrey as "clemens" and "mitis" as a sign that the laity was adopting the courtly manners of the clerics in their midst (*Origins of Courtliness,* 150).

Deeds of the Counts of Anjou portrayed Fulk the Good as "peacemaking, tranquil and mild" and noted that Geoffrey the Fair was "admirable in his uprightness, notable in his justice, devoted to military deeds, extremely literate, the most eloquent among both lay and clerical persons, and generally endowed with all good morals."[35]

This interest in the moral, intellectual, and—as C. Stephen Jaeger has argued—courtly virtues of the Angevins seems to have grown in increments during the twelfth century.[36] John of Marmoutier, however, was the first historian of the Angevin line who explicitly attributed these traits to Ingelger. John made it clear that Ingelger was a wise and literate ruler, and in so doing he wedded an interest in rational and interior traits of rulership with an interest in mythological points of origin: "This Ingelger [was] most profound in counsel, catholic in faith, exceedingly learned in letters, strenuous in arms and great in counsel and strength."[37] Because Ingelger, the only patriarch of the family, was both learned and wise, the entire Angevin line was by implication blessed with these traits.

John of Marmoutier's interest in the moral and intellectual virtues of the former counts of Anjou was linked to his rhetorical interest in affecting the interior motivations of his contemporary audience. He wrote not simply to enhance the reputation of the Angevin line, but to instruct and move his audience as well. Indeed, in his *Life of Geoffrey the Fair* he presented Geoffrey as an exemplar upon whom Henry II could model his own behavior.

The earlier authors who wrote about the counts of Anjou showed some interest in moral persuasion, but their primary intention was to enhance the reputation of the Angevins—to convince an outside au-

---

35. "Iste fuit pacifici et tranquilli et mitis ingenii," "probitate admirabilis, justitie insignis, militie actibus deditus, optime litteratus, inter clericos et laicos facundissimus, fere omnibus bonis moribus repletus" (*Chronica de gestis consulum*, 34, 71). See Jaeger's insightful discussion, which anticipated much of what I have to say here (*Origins of Courtliness*, 203–6). Jaeger, however, attributed this passage to Breton of Amboise (who wrote between 1155 and 1173) rather than to Robin, who continued the first redaction of the chronicle. I am following Halphen and Poupardin in attributing the passage to Robin.

36. *Chronica de gestis consulum*, 35–36; additions of MS. B (redaction of Breton of Amboise, who wrote between 1155 and 1173), p. 140. This latter is the passage in which Fulk the Good sends the famous note to the king, "Rex illiteratus est asinus coronatus." On the use of this proverb in the twelfth century (by William of Malmesbury and John of Salisbury and then by Breton), see Galbraith, "Literacy of the Medieval English Kings," 212–13. Georges Duby sees in Breton's passage an elaboration of the secularization of princely values and the appropriation of kingly virtues by the Angevins (*Three Orders*, 289–90).

37. "Hic itaque Ingelgerius, consilio profundissimus, fide catholicus, litteris apprime eruditus, armis strenuus, magno consilio et fortitudine" (*Chronica de gestis consulum*, additions of MS. C, p. 30 n. d).

dience of the glory and legitimacy of the dynasty. Fulk Rechin declared in his prefatory remarks, which seem to reveal a desire to justify his somewhat irregular succession, that he wanted to describe how he and his ancestors came to possess and retain their position.[38] And the introduction to the first redaction of the *Deeds of the Counts of Anjou* emphasized unambiguous praise: it opened with a quotation from Sallust about the need to preserve the memory of those whose "virtue is considered glorious and eternal."[39] The author of the *Return from Burgundy* made no clear statement of his intentions, but the legend emphasized heroic and legitimizing deeds more than motivation and moral concerns.

Despite their preoccupation with reputation, however, the first authors of the *Deeds of the Counts of Anjou* helped pave the way for John's interest in instruction and motivation. At several points in their work they acknowledged that the dynasty's history was not one of continuous glory, that stories from the past could help mold the character of individuals in the present, and that family characteristics did not absolutely determine one's destiny. For example, in the last sentence of his version of the *Deeds of the Counts of Anjou* (which ended with Fulk Rechin, who died in 1109), the first author of the first redaction explained that he had collected the record of the counts' deeds not only to glorify the Angevins but also to edify them and provide models for their imitation: "While I found these things written in hidden volumes, I could not bear to bury them with fruitless silence. Therefore I composed their deeds just as I perceived them for the honor of our lords the counts of Anjou, and I entrusted the established deeds for the edification of successors, imploring that our labor would be able to find fruit in the imitation of the best of our predecessors by our contemporaries."[40]

John of Marmoutier built on these precedents, but he went much

---

38. "Volui commendare litteris quomodo antecessores mei honorem suum adquisierant et tenuerant usque ad meum tempus et deinde de me ipso quomodo eumdem honorem tenueram adjuvante divina misericordia" (Fulk Rechin, *Fragmentum historiae*, 232). Fulk's succession was irregular: he became count after he imprisoned his brother, Count Geoffrey the Bearded, who was subsequently deposed by the pope. Moreover, his brother had succeeded their uncle, Geoffrey Martel, so his succession did not follow the regular father-son pattern either: see Halphen, *Comté d'Anjou*, 133–34, 143–51.

39. "Cum *vita* nostra *brevis sit, memoriam* eorum *quam maxime longam efficere* debemus quorum *virtus clara et eterna habetur*" (*Chronica de gestis consulum*, 25). Italicized words were borrowed from Sallust, *Catilina*, 4:3.

40. "Hec ego dum in voluminibus abditis invenissem scripta, non sum perpessus infructuoso silentio tegi. Ad honorem igitur dominorum nostrorum Andegavorum consulum sicut gesta eorum agnovi conscripsi et ad edificationem successorum credidi destinanda, obsecrans ut labor noster in optimorum antecessorum imitatione a modernis valeat fructum invenire" (*Chronica de gestis consulum*, 67).

further. By placing his discussion of edification and imitation in the preface rather than in a concluding sentence, he framed his entire work in a motivational way. In that preface John directly addressed the man—King Henry II of England—whose behavior he wanted to influence, suggesting that the king would find in the Angevins' family history not a continuous succession of virtuous men and glorious deeds, but a set of bad men, whose behavior he should avoid, and good men, whom he could choose to imitate. The authors of the first redaction of the *Deeds of the Counts of Anjou* had made a similar point, but only when they needed to justify their reasons for discussing the less exemplary members of the line, Geoffrey the Bearded and Fulk Rechin.[41]

John also moved beyond the earlier authors in his explicit assertion that although his history provided models for imitation and examples for edification, those models could take effect only if they penetrated the surface of behavior, affecting the king's interior motivations. John wanted to *instigate* imitation and *kindle* caution. His use of these words, which appear in other works by his contemporaries at Marmoutier as well, placed new emphasis on the inner self and the role persuasion could play in moving that inner self:

> When good history refers to good things, the solicitous listener should be instigated to imitate the good or, recollecting the bad deeds of the depraved, the religious and pious listener or reader will be kindled, nonetheless, to avoid what is noxious or perverse, to execute more clearly those things that are good and that he knows to be worthy to God.
>
> These things, my lord king, I . . . wrote down for the honor of the counts of Anjou, our lords, and for the utility of those who hear them and for the instruction of your character, so that you will assume a good example and a better end from the good ones, and from the bad ones you will be made aware of a bad entrance or path lest you come to the same bad end.[42]

41. *Chronica de gestis consulum*, 62–63. Along similar lines, Guibert of Nogent indicated that he wrote his *Memoirs* to edify others by providing bad and good examples: *De vita sua*, 129–30.

42. "Sive enim historia de bonis bona referat, ad imitandum bonum auditor sollicitus instigatur, seu mala commemorans de pravis, nichilominus religiosus ac pius auditor sive lector de vitando quod noxium est ac perversum, ipse solertius ad exequenda ea que bona sunt ac Deo digna esse cognoverit accenditur," "Hec ego . . . ad honorem Andegavorum consulum, dominorum nostrorum, et ad utilitatem audientium et instructionem morum tuorum, domine mi rex, conscripsi, scilicet ut ex bonis bonum sumas exemplum et meliorem exitum et ex malis malum caveas introitum sive incessum, ne incidas in eorum pessimum finem vel exitum" (*Chronica de gestis consulum* [additions, preface of John of Marmoutier], 163, 164).

John of Marmoutier was not the only author in Henry II's circle who took an interest in internal motivation. Indeed, it is not surprising that people in the king's entourage addressed this issue. Henry and his associates helped lead the way in the twelfth-century revival and expansion of legalistic and bureaucratized forms of government.[43] Bureaucratic governments have their advantages, but they also have their costs: government officials, as John of Marmoutier was well aware, may not always behave in ways that serve the interests of their ruler and of the people.[44] Such men exercised many of their official functions in the absence of the ruler himself; their loyalties to him were more impersonal and attenuated than were those of feudal vassals. Because sophisticated forms of political organization rely on impersonal ties, a desirable goal for twelfth-century rulers and intellectuals was to mold people—potential bureaucrats, ordinary subjects—who would behave in accordance with principles of law and justice even when the eye of the ruler was not watching and when the policing arm of the government was not striking. Internal motivation, rather than mere external restraint, was a desirable form of inhibition for the society that was taking shape in the mid-twelfth century.

The differences between John's preoccupations and those of earlier authors who wrote about the counts of Anjou point to a mounting interest in interior concerns. Note, however, that Henry II's court was not the only context for John of Marmoutier's ideas. As I show in chapters 4 and 5, Marmoutier's twelfth-century literature abounded with discussions of internal motivation.

This growing interest in internal motivation did not supplant or stand in opposition to the interest in group legitimacy. Rather, Marmoutier's monks explored the two themes simultaneously. The multiplicity of competing groups in twelfth-century society meant that one's place in the world and one's code of behavior were not necessarily predetermined. The individual was left with choices: whether to become a black Benedictine or a Cistercian, whether to side with the cathedral of Tours or the abbey of Marmoutier, whether to ally with the Angevin count or the French king. Some of the vernacular epics of the period successfully portrayed these multiple perspectives, giving equal weight, for example, to the demands of feudal ties and of family.

43. On the growth of government in the twelfth century, see Warren, *Governance of Norman and Angevin England,* and Dunbabin, *France in the Making,* 277–86.

44. John of Marmoutier, *Historia Gaufredi,* 185–91: Geoffrey demonstrates his liberality by giving ear to a poor man, who tells him that his agents are mistreating and cheating his subjects. For discussions of this well-known passage, see Dunbabin, *France in the Making,* 285–86, and Duby, *Three Orders,* 280–82.

These works suggested that conflicting loyalties—to overlord and family, to church and king—forced the individual to recognize that the world did not provide a perfect system of order. Men and women had to find that order within themselves.[45]

John of Marmoutier's writings do not represent a break with earlier notions of group legitimacy or with aristocratic notions that blood helped shape who one was. Aristocratic ideas about blood and class were intensifying at the end of the twelfth century, and John's writings were thoroughly consistent with these developments.[46] Nevertheless, John portrayed his royal patron in active dialogue with his heritage and group identity. Henry II had the advantage of inheriting the blood of the illustrious Angevin counts, but he also had the responsibility of shaping his own career and character within the limits defined by his dynasty's history. The king was privileged to be the descendant of special men of a special dynasty, but he was also responsible for his own choice to live up to the potential his heritage provided and to follow the examples of the good men who had preceded him.

45. See discussion of epics of revolt in Bezzola, "De Roland à Raoul de Cambrai," 191–213; Calin, *Old French Epic of Revolt*, esp. 116, 140 ff. For similar discussion of alienation in twelfth-century romance literature, in which the individual had to resolve conflicting codes of behavior, see Morris, *Discovery of the Individual*, 133–38

46. Duby, *Three Orders*, 271–92.

4

Marmoutier and the Salvation of the Counts of Blois

Between the end of the eleventh century and the early part of the thirteenth, anonymous monks from Marmoutier wrote three versions of a legend concerning the refoundation of Marmoutier by Odo I of Blois in the late tenth century. Unlike its writings about the counts of Anjou, Marmoutier's legends about Count Odo stressed the salvation of the individual over the collective legitimacy of a dynasty. Nevertheless, these stories developed along lines that paralleled the Angevin writings: they moved from an emphasis on external deeds to an emphasis on internal character and motivation, and they exhibited increasing interest in persuasion.

Like the writings about the Angevins, the legends about Odo of Blois helped explain how monks and their patrons could and should sustain mutually beneficial relations in a changing society. The twelfth-century stories about the Angevins portrayed a lateral and mutually beneficial exchange of noble protection for monastic legitimization. This relationship replaced the one of domination that eleventh-century nobles frequently tried to impose on monastic institutions. The stories about Odo of Blois encouraged and explained the benefits of modest gifts to monasteries. Such gifts began to predominate after the first quarter of the twelfth century as nobles grew more conservative in their generosity toward monasteries.[1] The later stories about Odo suggested, moreover, that despite a new theology of salvation, which

1. See White, *Custom, Kinship, and Gifts*, 22–23 and table 3-1, which shows a sharp decline in gifts to monasteries after 1125. Table 3-1B (p. 214) gives statistics for Marmoutier (based on five of its cartularies): 2 gifts between 1000 and 1024, 37 gifts between 1025 and 1049, 143 between 1050 and 1074, 101 between 1075 and 1099, 52 between 1100 and 1124, 14 between 1125 and 1149, 8 between 1150 and 1174, and 23 between 1175 and 1199.

Marmoutier had at least 151 priories in the early thirteenth century. Of those, 4 were founded at the end of the tenth century, 110 in the eleventh, and 37 in the twelfth: see Gantier, "Recherches sur les possessions et les prieurés de l'abbaye de Marmoutier," 55(1965): 71–79.

put greater stress on the intention of the individual, lay patrons could continue to benefit from monastic prayers for the dead.

In two of the three Blésois legends, the count's wife, Ermengard, played a central role. Archival records concerning this remarkable woman—actually the wife of Odo II rather than Odo I—provided some of the inspiration for including her in the legend. But the monks were also attempting to explain and promote new roles that women could assume in a changing society. Developments in the economy of benefactions and a new interest in the social benefits of persuasion were opening up new possibilities for women's influence and action.

The First Legend: Odo and Ermengard as Archetypal Benefactors

The first legend about Odo I and Ermengard was included in a brief history of Marmoutier that the monks apparently presented to the council of Clermont in 1095 (see Source Appendix, I-B). According to the legend, the reform and refoundation of Marmoutier began when Ermengard, a "venerable matron," encountered in the church at Marmoutier the concubine and child of its sacristan. The concubine told Ermengard that she had assumed the responsibility of bellringer for the church because there was no one else to do it.[2] Deeply grieved that "the *opus Dei* was negligently performed by shameless servants," Ermengard rode to her husband's court, where she threw herself at his feet. After gaining the support of the knights and common people who were present at the count's court, she compelled her husband to promise he would reform the abbey.[3] Odo fulfilled his promise by convincing the king to give him jurisdiction over Marmoutier then expelling the canons who occupied the abbey. "With God making the

2. "Cumque introisset ecclesiam, adolescentula quaedam . . . filio . . . posito, signum pulsabat. Reverenda vero matrona sacristidem inconsuetam videns sancto pudore suffusa est. Dissimulato que dolore, quaerit ab ea diligenter quaenam esset, quisve pueri pater existeret. Cui mulier ait: capicerii hujus ecclesiae concubina ego sum, et utriusque nostrum parvulus iste filius est. Propter absentiam vero famulorum id officii mihi usurpavi, et ex necessitate, neglegentiae reatum exclusi" (*Narratio de commendatione Turonicae provinciae*, 310, with corrections from Charleville, Bibliothèque Municipale, MS. 117, fol. 103v).

3. "Ingemiscens itaque comitissa opus Dei ab impudicis servitoribus negligenter agi" (*Narratio de commendatione*, 310, with corrections from Charleville 117, fol. 103v). The printed version of the story uses Ermengard's name here and in the passage quoted below. The manuscript mentions her name only once, just before the passage quoted above.

suggestion through his amiable wife, Ermengard," he established thirteen monks from Cluny in their place.[4]

Although this first legend about Odo did not directly mention the cult of Saint Martin, it resembled the *Return from Burgundy* in that it associated a distant ancestor of a comital dynasty with Marmoutier while it disassociated the French king from the monastery. Unlike the *Return from Burgundy*, however, the legend about Odo was not directly critical of the king. It simply reiterated the circumstances of Marmoutier's reform, which took place only after secular jurisdiction over the abbey had passed from the king to the count.

Although it did not portray the count as a chivalric hero, this legend did emphasize that he carried out a commendable deed. Indeed, like Ingelger in the *Return from Burgundy*, Odo became a role model for other nobles, who could learn from his example how they should behave toward monastic institutions. Unlike Ingelger, Odo I was not the actual patriarch of his dynasty. Nevertheless, he was involved in Marmoutier's refoundation—its second point of origin— and for this reason his generosity toward the abbey provided a normative blueprint for subsequent relations between the Blésois line and Marmoutier.[5]

In developing his portrait of Odo, the author of the legend simply reiterated the known historical record. In developing Ermengard's role, however, he manipulated the record. The surviving documents concerning Ermengard provided more exemplary material than did the documents concerning Bertha, the real wife of Odo I.[6] But Bertha had lived at a more normative, archetypal time. By pushing the real Ermengard back to the time of Marmoutier's refoundation, the author of the legend transformed her into a role model for other women who married into the Blésois dynasty as well as for noble women in general.

Our sources for the actual Ermengard, who flourished in the 1030s, come from Marmoutier's charters—records that the monks kept when nobles bestowed property on them. These charters indi-

---

4. "Suggerente Deo amabili uxore sua" (*Narratio de commendatione,* 310–12, with corrections from Charleville 117, fol. 105).

5. On the theme of the abbey's second foundation, see chapter 6. The patriarch of the Blésois line was Thibaud the Trickster, Odo I's father: see Mas-Latrie, *Trésor de chronologie,* 1562.

6. About 986 Bertha cosigned one of Odo's gifts to Marmoutier. After 995 she acted as his widow, along with her young sons. For the sake of their souls and that of Count Odo I, they exempted Marmoutier from the toll at the port of Blois: see *Marmoutier, Cartulaire Blésois,* 4, 5, pp. 9, 10. Bertha, who was the daughter of the king of Burgundy, married King Robert the Pious after Odo's death: see Dunbabin, *France in the Making,* 191.

cate that Ermengard was one of the rare women (and my examination of the abbey's charters has revealed only one other, Countess Adele of Blois) whose ability to influence their husbands' decisions actually impressed the monks. Unlike other charters, in which women usually appear as co-donors, or simply assenting to the gifts of their husbands, fathers, or brothers, the charters involving Ermengard—as well as Adele—report that while the husband officially disposed of the property, the wife provided the initial impetus toward generosity.[7]

Ermengard exercised this rare influence at a critical time, when the consolidation of noble property under the control of tightly constructed male lineages resulted in the decline of women's power within the noble family. Daughters were losing their shares in patrimonial inheritances, and wives, as the charters of Marmoutier make clear, were losing control over conjugal properties, including their own dowries.[8] Ermengard apparently impressed the monks of her own time, as well as those of a later generation, because she managed so well within the new system. Again and again she exhibited her favor toward religious institutions and causes by acting *through* her husband: at her "entreaty" Odo gave a gift to Marmoutier; with her "insistence and labor" he built a bridge at Tours, to put a stop to the frequent drownings there; and with her "incitement" and "the inspiration of God" he decided not to charge a toll for the use of the bridge.[9]

Ermengard represented to the monks of Marmoutier a way noble women could continue to exercise influence, despite their loss of official power within the noble family. In their charters the monks of

7. This assertion is based on an examination of *Marmoutier, Cartulaire Blésois; Cartulaire de Marmoutier pour le Dunois; Cartulaire de Marmoutier pour le Perche;* and *Cartulaire de Marmoutier pour le Vendômois.*

8. In a number of Marmoutier's charters husbands alienated or attempted to repossess their wives' dowries, and in the settlements the husbands were sometimes paid more for the dowries than were the wives: see *Cartulaire . . . Dunois*, 34, p. 32 (1064–73); 38, pp. 35–36 (1084–1100); 55, p. 50 (1084–1100); 83, pp. 74–75 (1108); 105, pp. 97–98 (ca. 1042); 129, pp. 119–20 (ca. 1064, 1080); 160, pp. 149–50 (1100–1104); *Cartulaire . . . Perche*, 10, p. 21 (ca. 1067); *Cartulaire . . . Vendômois*, 10, pp. 15–16 (1032–64); 11, pp. 16–19 (1072); 44, pp. 71–72 (eleventh century); 73, pp. 115–17 (1064–77); 120, pp. 200–203 (eleventh century); 121, pp. 203–6 (before 1062); *Marmoutier, Cartulaire Blésois*, 122, pp. 120–21 (1106). On the general pattern of women's loss of property rights or of men's greater control in the eleventh and twelfth centuries, see White, *Custom, Kinship and Gifts*, 119, 121, 245 n. 53; Duby, *Medieval Marriage;* Duby, *Knight, the Lady and the Priest*, 99–106, 235; Duby, *Chivalrous Society*, 72; Hughes, "From Brideprice to Dowry in Mediterranean Europe," 276 ff.

9. "Deprecatione" (*Marmoutier, Cartulaire Blésois*, 55 [charter dated 1083, but with internal evidence pointing to 1032–37], p. 65); "instantia ac labore," "Dei instinctu . . . uxorisque meae hortatu" (Charter of Count Odo II [1033], printed in Rabory, *Histoire de Marmoutier*, 522).

Marmoutier drew special attention to Ermengard's remarkable abilities. And in their legends, beginning with this one from the end of the eleventh century, they presented her as a normative role model.

It appears that the author of this legend wrote about Ermengard because he wanted to encourage another influential countess of Blois: Adele, daughter of William the Conqueror and wife of Count Stephen (1089–1102).[10] Adele gained a reputation as a pious, independent benefactress of Marmoutier after 1096, when Stephen departed for the Holy Land. Indeed, she became more than a mere benefactress. She presided in the seigneurial court of Blois, and through her decisions there she emerged as a major protectress of Marmoutier. For this reason the monks addressed her as "our most sweet lady," "the most fervent lover of Marmoutier," and—in an expression of admiration for her ability to exercise manly power and independence—"virago."[11]

But even before Stephen's departure in 1096, Adele disclosed her favorable disposition toward Marmoutier by exercising influence over her husband. Stephen began to consider making a gift to Marmoutier when his father died, six years before the beginning of the First Crusade. He consulted Adele as well as other members of his family and household, and he listened to the frequent exhortations of two monks from Marmoutier, whom he called his "familiars." Finally, just before he left for the Holy Land, Stephen bestowed his gift, acting "not only with [Adele's] assent and admonition, but also at her request."[12] During a six-year period, then, the two monks from Marmoutier had come to know, and perhaps to encourage, a second influential countess of Blois. It was during this period, moreover, that one of the abbey's monks composed the first legend about Odo and Ermengard, and it is therefore probable that the author had Adele in mind when he chose to write about her influential predecessor.

But the author of this legend may have had a more general female audience in mind as well, one that included the wives of all potential noble patrons. This was the period when both noble and urban women were beginning to demonstrate a remarkable enthusiasm for re-

---

10. Mas-Latrie, *Trésor de chronologie*, 1563.

11. "Dulcissimae dominae nostrae," "Majoris monasterii amatrix ferventissima" (*Cartulaire . . . Dunois*, 161 [1104], p. 150; 67 [1101], p. 60; similarly, 76 [1104], p. 67; 68 [1101], p. 62). The theme that women were "manlike" was not unusual in the twelfth century: William of Malmesbury also referred to Adele as a "virago" (*De gestis regum Anglorum*, 3:276, ed. Stubbs, 2:333); and Hildebert of Lavardin said of a virtuous countess, possibly Adele, that she had "nothing in her of feminine inconstancy": "In se femineae nil levitatis habens" (Hildebert of Lavardin, *Carmina miscellanea*, 34, PL 171:1394).

12. "Familiares," "non solum assensu ejus et ammonitione, sed etiam prece" (*Cartulaire . . . Dunois*, 92 [1096], 80–81).

ligious life and practice. Just west of Tours, for example, Robert of
Arbrissel began his itinerant preaching career in 1095, attracting a
large following of converts of both sexes. To accommodate this following he founded, in 1100 or 1101, the double monastery of Fontevrault on the border of Touraine. The abbey, which was ruled by an
abbess of noble background and became a favorite of the prominent
noblewomen of the region, also provided accommodations for former prostitutes. Largely because it met women's growing spiritual
needs, it was extremely successful. By the middle of the twelfth
century it had close to forty priories.[13]

Throughout the twelfth century, women continued to seek outlets
for their religious enthusiasm. We find nuns on the institutional
fringes of the new male religious orders of Cîteaux and Prémontré
and individual recluses in monasteries and towns.[14] At Marmoutier,
sometime around 1130, the monks made an effort to meet women's
religious needs by converting the abbey's eremitical retreat on the
island of Saint-Nicholas into an informal religious house for
noblewomen.[15]

Noblewomen of the late eleventh and twelfth centuries demonstrated their religious sentiments not only by renouncing family life,
but also by exercising religious and moral influence within the family.
Churchmen who frequented the courts of prominent nobles and
kings began to acknowledge and encourage this female role in the
civilizing process. The monastic chronicler Orderic Vitalis associated
"sweet speech" or eloquence with pious wives, saintly monks, and
effective preachers. Other clerical authors praised Adele of Blois for
her erudition and proclaimed that she exceeded her father and brothers in her appreciation of poetry and of manners.[16]

13. Gold, *Lady and the Virgin*, 93–115; Little, *Religious Poverty and the Profit Economy*, 79.
On the general pattern of women's growing religious enthusiasm, see Bynum, "Religious
Women in the Later Middle Ages"; Bolton, "Mulieres Sanctae," 77–85.

14. Bolton, "Mulieres Sanctae"; Gold, *Lady and the Virgin*, 76–93; Leclercq, "Solitude
and Solidarity: Medieval Women Recluses"; and Rosof, "Anchoress in the Twelfth and
Thirteenth Centuries." In 1213, four women from Tours, two of them nuns from the abbey
of Beaumont, began living an eremitical life under the Cistercian rule. Three years later
they and sixteen others moved into a stone structure built for them by a burgher named
Péan Hermenardus, who later founded the local Franciscan house: see *Chronicon Turonense
auctore anonymo*, col. 1048–49, 1065.

15. Oury, "Erémitisme à Marmoutier aux XIᵉ et XIIᵉ siècles," 322–25; "Prieurés de
Marmoutier en Anjou," 47–49.

16. Orderic Vitalis, *Historia ecclesiastica*, 4, 6:8, 6:9, 8:7, ed. Chibnall, 2:294; 3:256, 272;
4:166; Baudry of Bourgueil, *Oeuvres poetiques*, poem 196, lines 31–38, p. 198; Hugh of
Fleury, *Historia ecclesiastica*, 349, 353. For a general discussion of these positive views of
noble women, see Farmer, "Persuasive Voices: Clerical Images of Medieval Wives," 538–
43. See also, on relations between clerics and queens in this period, Huneycutt, "Medieval
Queenship," 16–22; Huneycutt, "Idea of the Perfect Princess: The Life of St. Margaret."

Churchmen recognized that the women of Adele of Blois's generation wielded cultural and moral influence in aristocratic courts, but
they were also aware that women seldom had the power to alienate
noble property on their own. It was thus in the interest of the monks
of Marmoutier to encourage whatever means of control women could
continue to exercise over the disposal of family properties.[17] The
legendary description of Ermengard of Blois, who compelled her
husband to reform Marmoutier by falling at his feet and refusing to
rise until her petition had been granted, both mirrored actual gender
interactions in Adele's generation and provided encouragement for
even bolder behavior by pious wives.[18]

The Second Legend: The Judgment of Odo

The first version of the legend about Odo and Ermengard, which
presented the count and his wife as exemplary role models, had the
potential of enhancing the status of the Blésois counts, just as the
writings about the counts of Anjou enhanced the status of the Angevins. The second legend shared none of these legitimizing characteristics. Rather than lauding Odo of Blois as a chivalric hero or an
ideal ruler, the second legend portrayed him as a depraved sinner who
abused his position of power. It associated the count of Blois with
Marmoutier and the cult of Saint Martin, but unlike the *Return from
Burgundy* it did not imply that the association glorified the comital
line. Like the writings of John of Marmoutier, this legend offered
moralistic advice for secular lords and showed some interest in internal motivation. But unlike John, who portrayed Geoffrey the Fair as
an ideal ruler, the author of this legend offered only a negative image
of Odo of Blois.

According to this anonymous author, who wrote sometime in the
twelfth century, Count Odo I was a sinful man, "totally given over to
the world" and "carried away" with the desire to expand his earthly
glory and possessions.[19] This portrait of Odo's sinful character drew

17. For further elaboration of this argument, see Farmer, "Persuasive Voices."
18. "Non surgam ait donec petitionis meae pandam secretum, sed tam diu provolvar in
pulvere, usque dum erigar exhilarata exauditione" (*Narratio de commendatione*, 310, with
corrections from Charleville 117, fol. 104).
19. "Laetorum prosperitate abutens successuum, ad dilatandos laudis et gloriae secularis
titulos, et ampliandos possessionum terminos, multiplex animo ferebatur. . . . Totus mundo deditus" (*Liber de restructione Majoris monasterii*, 355, with corrections from Charleville
117, fol. 124v–125). On the dates of this redaction and the longer one, see Source Appendix, I-C.

upon original charters in which Odo I asserted, for example, that "the enormity" of his "evil deeds" made him fear the Day of Judgment; for that reason the count sought the aid of Saint Martin, who might succeed at "snatch[ing]" the count's soul "from the infernal flames."[20] While drawing on these concepts, the author of this legend also manipulated the historical record, basing his narrative on the fact that Odo II, not Odo I, had earned an unsavory reputation as a result of his breach with King Robert the Pious and his untimely death at the battle of Bar-le-Duc, where he had attempted to gain control of the Burgundian kingdom.[21] Like the first legend about Odo I, which associated Odo I with Ermengard, the wife of Odo II, this legend conflated the lives of the two men, and the confusion, whether conscious or accidental, suited the author's purposes.

The author of this legend lent dramatic tension to his narrative by implying that Odo's chances for salvation were precarious even though he felt last-minute remorse. Just before he "exhaled the final breath of life," Odo felt repentance for his sins and privately confessed them to the "eternal priest." But this was not a manifest confession given to a priest, and so the devil, "whom the light of truth never illuminates," claimed Odo's soul for himself and his demons.[22]

Nevertheless God, whose "mercy for those who fear Him lasts forever," was mindful of the good deeds Odo had performed during his life, especially his refounding of Marmoutier.[23] Therefore he sent Saint Martin to assist the count. Martin challenged the demons, claiming they could not take possession of the count's soul because he had not yet been fairly judged. The demons then proposed that Odo's fate be determined by weighing his virtues against his vices. In the ensuing contest, it seemed at first that the demons would prevail: even though they included the refounding of Marmoutier, Odo's virtuous deeds only just managed to equal the weight of his enormous heap of sins. Saint Martin, however, successfully averted the demons' victory by adding to the weight of the count's good deeds the vicarious assistance the monks of Marmoutier were offering for him: "[The

20. See Introduction to part 2 at note 11.

21. *Liber de restructione Majoris monasterii*, 360; Dunbabin, *France in the Making*, 191–92; Arbois de Jubainville, *Histoire des ducs et des comtes de Champagne*, 1:316–44; Ralph Glaber, *Historiarum libri quinque*, 3:37–38, pp. 85–87. Some of Glaber's language seems to have inspired the author from Marmoutier: according to Glaber, Odo II was "rerum ditissimus, licet fide pauper."

22. "Ante ultimum vitae exhalat spiritum," "aeterno sacerdoti," "quem lux veritatis nunquam irradiat" (*Liber de restructione Majoris monasterii*, 360).

23. "Cujus misericordia . . . ab aeterno usque in aeternum super timentes eum" (*Liber de restructione Majoris monasterii*, 363).

two sides] are almost even, but lest . . . the occasion for treachery be offered to the adversaries, Martin [and his assistants] add both his own prayers, vigils, fasts, acts of charity, and other aids of penitence as well as the supplemental sacrifice of prayers for him, which the brothers of the abbey did not cease busily to procure for his seizing; as well as the daily celebration of the divine mystery. . . And with that done the left dish of the scales, outweighed by the right, springs up as if it is empty."[24] The presumptuous demons were thus routed, and having saved the count from eternal damnation, Martin arranged for his "soul to be transferred to the purgatorial college" where he could be "fully purged."[25]

Certain aspects of this story—the description of Odo's final moment of contrition and private confession, the reference of God's mercy, and the assertion that after Odo was saved from hell he underwent purgation—reflect spiritual changes and theological developments that transformed the relations between monks and their lay patrons in the twelfth century.

Two of the most salient features of twelfth-century spirituality were its optimism and its emphasis on internal and personal experience. Late tenth- and eleventh-century sources—including the actual charters of Odo I—stressed God's judgment and the impending threat of eternal punishment for those who had not done penance for their sins. Twelfth-century sources, by contrast, increasingly emphasized God's mercy and the promise that even sinners could attain eternal salvation. In the eleventh century the corporate and external actions of monks provided vicarious intercession for sinful laypeople. In the twelfth century theologians became convinced that individual sinners earned God's forgiveness by feeling sincere sorrow—inner contrition—for their misdeeds.[26]

The growing emphasis on God's mercy and on the personal and

24. "Fit pene aequalitas, sed ne . . . causa calumniae praeberetur adversariis, Martinus et sui orationes et vigilias, jejunia et eleemosynas et caeteras auxiliatrices poenitentiae que illius suppletivas precum hostias, quas supradicti fratres coenobii pro ipsius ereptione sedulo procurare non cessabant, apponunt, quotidianam quoque divini celebrationem mysterii. . . . Quo facto patera sinistrae partis trutinae, ac si vacua esset dextera praeponderante in sublime resilit" (*Liber de restructione Majoris monasterii,* 368–69, with corrections from Charleville 117, fol. 127–27v).

25. "Martinus ereptam Odonis animam in loco ei competenti ubi plenius purgaretur, et deinceps ad purgatorum transferretur collegium disponit" (*Liber de restructione Majoris monasterii,* 369, with corrections from Charleville 117, fol. 128).

26. On the general shifts and the optimism, see Southern, *Making of the Middle Ages,* 219–58. On the earlier emphasis on vicarious prayer, see Southern, *Western Society and the Church in the Middle Ages,* 225–28. On intention in ethics, see Anciaux, *Théologie du sacrement de pénitence au XIIe siècle;* Teetaert, *Confession aux laïques dans l'église latine,* 99–100; Tentler, *Sin and Confession on the Eve of the Reformation,* 3–27.

internal nature of spiritual experience contributed to the rising importance of the doctrine of purgatory, which reached its fullest articula-
tion in the twelfth century. According to the new theology of penance, sinners were absolved of their guilt as soon as they felt contrite,
but they were still obliged to confess their sins and make satisfaction—pay off the debt—for them. Contrition alone now earned the
promise of salvation, yet contrite sinners who died before completing
their satisfaction could expect to spend time in purgatory until the
debt was paid off. Formerly the somber threat of eternal damnation
loomed darkly on the horizon for sinners who failed to complete the
penitential works that compensated for their sins. Now, though external works of penance were still obligatory, the message was optimistic, and it was an internal emotion—genuine sorrow for one's
sins—that earned salvation for the individual.[27]

The doctrine of purgatory, as Jacques Le Goff has argued, represents an affirmation of life and a growing sense that men and women
had control over their own destinies and even over the destinies of the
dead. Like the *Return from Burgundy*, this theological development
points to the characteristic twelfth-century stress on men and women
as actors.[28] Like the writings of John of Marmoutier, moreover, it
shows a shift in emphasis from deeds to motivations, from external to
internal concerns.

The story about the weighing of Odo's virtues and vices shows
signs of the new theology of salvation: Odo feels contrition; God is
merciful, but Odo must still undergo purgation after he has been
saved from hell. Nevertheless this legend is only partially imbued
with the new theology and its implications. Like the tenth-century
charters of Odo I, it still notes that the external deed of founding
Marmoutier, coupled with the intervention of Martin and the
vicarious assistance of the monks, saves Odo from hell. Odo's contrition, in this legend, has no real effect. And despite the reference to
God's mercy, the legend dwells on the less optimistic idea that Odo's
chances for salvation are precarious. The threat of the demons and the
dramatic contest, in which Odo's virtues almost fail to outweigh his
vices, dominate the emotional landscape of this tale.

The predominant message of this legend, definitively monastic in

27. Le Goff (*Birth of Purgatory*) has argued that we should not read the fully articulated
doctrine of purgatory back into patristic and early medieval sources. Scholars have generally
agreed with Le Goff's overall thesis, though a number have argued convincingly that Le
Goff pinpoints the change about a century later than it actually occurred; and they have
pointed to different reasons for the change as well: see Southern, "Between Heaven and
Hell," 652; Bernstein, review of Le Goff.

28. Le Goff, *Birth of Purgatory*, 230–34.

its perspective, was that secular lords needed monasteries even more than monasteries needed secular lords. Like the tenth-century charters from Marmoutier, it suggested that sinful nobles—and who among them could claim he was less sinful that Odo?—should anticipate God's imminent judgment with a sense of terror.[29] This pessimistic message was tempered by references to God's mercy, to contrition, and to purgatorial punishments. Yet the legend did not complete the task of transforming the traditional monastic message for the laity in light of the new theology of salvation.

The Third Legend: Odo's Purgatory, Ermengard's Persuasion, and Social-Economic Change

Toward the end of the twelfth century or sometime in the thirteenth, the author of a third legend about Odo of Blois accommodated the new theology more thoroughly. By adding interpolated passages to the second legend, he transformed the earlier redaction in two ways.[30] First he softened the theological edges, emphasizing that God's mercy was available to all contrite sinners and distinguishing purgatorial and eternal punishments. In this way the author clarified the new theology of salvation. At the same time, however, he emphasized that monastic suffrages for the dead could continue to assist lay patrons: although it was the personal contrition of sinners that now saved them from damnation, the vicarious assistance of monks was still of use, especially in easing the burden of purgatorial punishment.

The second change in the story entailed the integration of Marmoutier's first legend about Odo—the story about Ermengard and the refounding of Marmoutier—into the story about Odo's virtues and vices. Ermengard, in this third legend, played a more developed role than in the first: she became even more pious, persuasive, and economically influential. Cultural, economic, and theological developments contributed to these new representations of a pious wife.

The author of the interpolated legend showed much more clearly than the author of the second that God exercised not only judgment but also mercy. This aspect of God's nature, the author made clear,

29. The author opens with a description of his epoch, "in which we all dissolve like wax in sin," and in which it is virtually impossible to find someone who has not been puffed up by the "eminence of nobility" and "the affluence of riches": "Si quis hominum his praesertim inveniatur temporibus, quibus omnes ut cerei in vitia solvimur, quem non et nobilitatis eminentia et divitiarum affluentia extollat" (*Liber de restructione Majoris monasterii*, 355).

30. The later interpolation of the *Liber de restructione Majoris monasterii* is the text edited by Salmon: see Source Appendix, I-C.

was a mystery to the demons, who understood only judgment. Because they had not "penetrated the abyss of God's compassion," the demons mistakenly thought they had jurisdiction over Odo's soul.[31] Odo, however, was eligible for God's compassion, which is available to anyone who puts hope in it: those with "changed hearts" experience mercy, which "will enfold the one who hopes in the Lord."[32] Odo's moment of true contrition ensured his ultimate salvation because it qualified him for God's mercy and for the benefits of Christ's death on the cross.

Because contrition plays such an important part in this legend, the drama of Odo's trial becomes almost redundant, and the threat of the demons diminishes. During the interlude before Martin actually arrives to assist Odo's soul, the narrator of the story asks God what has happened to his promise to save repentant sinners. But even as he poses the question, the narrator implies that God will indeed keep his promise: "Where [God] is that faithful promise, in which you say, 'Whenever the sinner sighs he will be saved?' O most pious Lord, be mindful of this healthful word of yours, in which you gave hope to the penitent."[33]

God's judgment is still in effect in this legend, but it functions as a prelude to mercy, purifying souls and thereby qualifying them for deliverance: "His judgment leads them through fire and water, his mercy leads them into the cooling. His judgment melts and purifies them, cleaning them out and purging them like gold and silver. It cooks out all dross of their sins. His mercy restores them as before, leading them back to the lost fellowship of the citizens of the heavens."[34] It is, in fact, for purgatorial purposes that God first allows

31. Martin says to the demons, "An abyssum miserationum Dei penetrastis? . . . Vos exclusi a luce veritatis extrinsecus" (*Liber de restructione Majoris monasterii*, 365). The later interpolation (which is four times the length of the earlier redaction) includes twenty-seven instances of words referring to mercy—*misericordia, misereri, miserator, misericors, miseratio;* the earlier version includes only two instances.

32. "Homines vero receptibiles qui . . . mutato corde convertuntur ad Deum, . . . misericordia coronantur," "sperantem in Domino misericordia circumdabit" (*Liber de restructione Majoris monasterii*, 366, 362).

33. "Ubi promissio tua fidelis illa qua dicis, cum ingemuerit peccator salvus erit? O Domine piissime, memor esto hujus salutaris verbi tui in quo poenitentibus spem dedisti" (*Liber de restructione Majoris monasterii,* 363). Again, on p. 366 the author employs another form of the expression, which was a favorite among twelfth-century theologians: "Quacumque hora peccator ingemuerit salvus erit." On the uses of this phrase in the twelfth century, see Anciaux, *Théologie du sacrement de pénitence,* 52, nn. 2, 3.

34. "Per judicium traducit eos per ignem, et aquam; per misericordiam educit in refrigerium. Per judicium conflans et colans eos emundat et purgat ut auram et argentum, et excoquit omnem scoriam peccatorum eorum, per misericordiam restituens illos, sicut antiquitus, ad amissam supernorum civium societatem reducit" (*Liber de restructione Majoris monasterii,* 366).

Odo to be frightened by the devil and his demons.[35] We no longer have the impression, as we did in reading the earlier version, that Odo's contest is real, that he may not attain salvation.

The emphasis on contrition and mercy in this interpolated legend renders problematic the rationale for weighing Odo's virtues and vices. Indeed, when Martin assents to the contest he already knows that Odo will be saved not by the weight of his own good deeds, but by Christ's death on the cross. The redemptive power of Christ, which is available to the contrite, is now much more important than good works. We no longer have the sense that sinners have to pay back the price—or counter the weight—of bad works to attain salvation:

> Martin, according to Isaiah, not uncertain that "he would scorn the scornful" [Prov. 3:34] and that [the demons] depend upon an ineffective explanation, confidently assents [to the weighing of Odo's virtues and vices], secure in the incomparable weight of that unique price that will not be wanting on his side. Which weight, poised in the balance of the cross and outweighing the sins not only of one man but even of the whole world, redeems the general captivity of the human race and restores it to the inheritance of paradise, which was taken away by judgment.[36]

Only the demons mistakenly believe that Odo's virtues and vices really count for something. They do not realize that Christ's death on the cross outweighs the sins of humanity.

Nevertheless, Odo is not a passive participant in the drama of his own salvation. As soon as he sighs the sigh of true contrition—as soon as his heart changes its inclinations—he makes himself eligible for the benefits of Christ's death and for the boundless depths of God's mercy. Odo attains salvation not by performing good deeds but by feeling contrition. The author develops this new theme by building around the earlier text: without eliminating the passages in which the monks' vicarious assistance plays an important role in

---

35. The author addresses Odo just after he dies: "[Deus] abscondit quidem ad modicum faciem suam a te, et sine adjutorio nudum et exspoliatum inter hostes deseruit, ut territus purgeris, et purgatus aliquem obtineas locum inter eos quorum remissae sunt iniquitates" (*Liber de restructione Majoris monasterii*, 362).

36. "Martinus, secundum Isaiam, non incertus quod illusores ipse deluderet et inefficaci niti eos diffinitione, praesumptione assentitur facillime de illius singularis pretii in parte sua non defuturi incomparabili securus pondere, quod in statera crucis libratum, non solum unius hominis, sed et totius mundi peccatis praeponderando, generalem humani generis captivitatem redemit, et abjudicatam illi paradisi haereditatem restituit" (*Liber de restructione Majoris monasterii*, 367–68).

counterbalancing the weight of Odo's sins, he encompasses the earlier message within a new one.

But though the new theology of salvation, contrition, and the redemptive power of the cross now overshadows the monks' vicarious assistance and the deed of refounding Marmoutier, good deeds and prayers for the dead still have their place. They now help to ease the burden of purgatorial punishments. Relatives of the dead can turn to monks, asking them to offer assistance for those in purgatory.

The author of this legend expounds the theme of vicarious assistance for those in purgatory in his discussion of Ermengard, who now plays a much more instrumental role than in the first legend. She wields economic influence not only by working *through* her husband, but also by spending money and bestowing property independently. Through her independent actions, Ermengard is able to assist Odo in purgatory. Moreover, her persuasive powers now influence not only Odo's *act* of refounding Marmoutier, but also his internal moral conscience, and she is thus implicitly connected to the turn of conscience by which Odo saves himself from damnation.

In contrast to the first legend about Odo and Ermengard, this last legend portrays the personalities of the foundress and her husband in completely polarized terms. Odo, on the one hand—until his final moment of remorse—is a hopeless sinner. Indeed, the author even equates Odo with an unbeliever, "for even if he did not wander away from the Christian profession with words, he did with deeds," and he belonged with those "who confess to know God, but who nevertheless deny God with their actions."[37] Once again Ermengard convinces her husband to reform Marmoutier, but the author emphasizes that Odo's action is "kindled by his wife's unwearied diligence more than by his own intention or ardor" and that he never deserts his love for the secular realm, the realm of "Egypt."[38] Odo's sins include, just as they did in the shorter version of the story, vainglory and desire for fame. But the author now stresses Odo's desire for wealth and mentions "how difficult it is for a rich man to be saved."[39]

37. "Infidelis enim et hic erat qui et si non verbis, operibus tamen a professione christiana aberrabat, necdum a numero illorum exceptus qui confitentur se nosse Deum, factis autem negant" (*Liber de restructione Majoris monasterii*, 356).
38. "Ille indefessa conjugis assiduitate magis quam propria intentione vel alacritate successus," "mente semper ad Aegyptia . . . intenderet" (*Liber de restructione Majoris monasterii*, 358, 359).
39. "Quam difficile salvari divitem" (*Liber de restructione Majoris monasterii*, 359). The emphasis on avarice recurs in the author's address to Odo's soul after he has died: "Quare non audisti: nolite sperare in iniquitate, et rapinas nolite concupiscere, divitiae si affluant nolite cor apponere? Quare non audisti quod de divite scriptum est: aeger dives habet nummos, se non habet ipsum; et item: *Dives obit, sua pompa perit, quam flamma cremabit.* Vel certe illud psalmistae: cum interierit non sumet omnia, neque descendet cum eo gloria ejus.

Opposite the unbelieving, sinful Odo, the author of this legend places Ermengard—a saintly evangelizer. In passages that reveal a growing interest in the spiritual capacity of laypeople, the legend portrays Ermengard as leading a virtually monastic life: she is chaste, she fasts frequently, and she engages in continuous prayers. In her relations with her husband she plays the role of Saint Cecilia, an early Christian woman who converted her pagan husband to Christianity: Ermengard constantly attempts to change her husband, and through her persuasive efforts she fulfills Saint Paul's precept that "an unbelieving man will be saved [*salvabitur*] by a believing wife" (1 Cor. 7:14). "Powerful in her manner of speaking and in works," Ermengard "soften[s]" (*mitigabat*) her husband's "ferocity."[40]

In this legend Ermengard's persuasive powers affect much more than her husband's economic behavior. Her spiritual influence—her ability to "soften" and "kindle" her husband—saturates his conscience, though it does not finally turn around until his moment of death. Like John of Marmoutier, the author of this legend was interested in internal motivation, and for that reason he encouraged and explored the rhetorical efforts by which one individual could "kindle" the conscience of another.

Parallels between the later Ermengard legend and Scholastic discussions of persuasion within marriage suggest that the anonymous author from Marmoutier was aware of Parisian theological discussions and that he himself was responding to the social and economic changes that influenced the Parisians. Like the Scholastic theologians, who discussed preaching wives and the moral sway that wives of usurers could exercise over their husbands, the author from Marmoutier emphasized spiritual influence within marriage, the wife's words, and her softening effect. Like Thomas of Chobham and other Scholastic theologians, Marmoutier's author juxtaposed the moral persuasion of a wife with the sinfulness of her husband and equated that sinfulness with unbelief. Like Thomas of Chobham he even rephrased 1 Cor. 7:14, indicating that a husband "was saved" by his persuasive wife rather than that he "was consecrated." Finally, like the Scholastics, he highlighted the sin of greed, although he did not exclusively equate Odo's sinfulness with greed for wealth.[41]

Quare Odo, confisus es in virtute tua, et in multitudine divitiarum tuarum?" (*Liber de restructione Majoris monasterii,* 361).

40. "Salvabitur vir infidelis per mulierem fidelem," "potens sermone et opere . . . a saevitia mitigabat" (*Liber de restructione Majoris monasterii,* 355–56).

41. For further discussion of the Scholastic interest in marital persuasion, see Farmer, "Persuasive Voices," and Farmer, "Softening the Hearts of Men: Women, Embodiment, and Persuasion in the Thirteenth Century."

This new interest in interior conscience and persuasion was related in part to the greater role individuals were able to play, in a more complex society, in determining their life circumstances. Growing towns and thriving urban schools drew their numbers from the countryside; new crafts, professions, and burgeoning bureaucracies provided new options for the uprooted and the ambitious.[42]

Marmoutier's monastic empire both benefited from and helped stimulate the changing economic and organizational structures that gave rise to the twelfth-century interest in choice, internal motivation, and persuasion. In the countryside the monks helped to expand the interior frontiers of western Francia, establishing the priories of Fréteval, Orchaise, Fontaine-Mesland and Saint-Laurent-en-Gâtines in forests that had formerly been uncleared. Marmoutier's monks founded rural settlements and markets, stimulating rural commerce and providing new and better opportunities for the peasantry.[43] In addition, they engaged in long-distance trade, moving their boats up and down the Loire from Nantes to Blois.[44] Because they needed to manage their vast empire, in the second half of the eleventh century and the early years of the twelfth the monks of Marmoutier had to develop increasingly sophisticated forms of administration.[45] Through John of Marmoutier and others like him, they had firsthand knowledge of the growth of bureaucratic government. Indeed, by the mid-twelfth century more and more of their property disputes were being resolved by formal legal procedure in episcopal and comital courts.[46]

Marmoutier's monks also had direct ties to the growth of towns. In Tours the prosperity of the monastery helped stimulate the commercial growth of the suburb of Saint-Symphorian. The monks, moreover, owned residential and commercial property in Châteauneuf, and they had intimate relations with some of the prominent mer-

42. For some discussion of the effects of the shift to urban life, see Little, *Religious Poverty and the Profit Economy*, 19–29. On the new social mobility, see Murray, *Reason and Society in the Middle Ages*, 81–109. On more extensive and bureaucratized government, see Strayer, *On the Medieval Origins of the Modern State;* Dunbabin, *France in the Making*, 277–86; Warren, *Governance of Norman and Angevin England*.

43. Gantier, "Recherches sur les possessions et les prieurés de l'abbaye de Marmoutier," 53(1963): 105; 55(1965): 39–44.

44. *Marmoutier, Cartulaire Blésois*, 5, p. 10 (exemption from toll at the port of Blois, granted after 995); "Prieurés de Marmoutier en Anjou," 51, 58 (in 1060 Count Geoffrey Martel of Anjou remits to Marmoutier all levies on their boats on the Loire, from Nantes to Tours; in 1090 Daniel of the Palace gives up his customs on Marmoutier's boats at Nantes).

45. Gantier, "Recherches sur les possessions et les prieurés de l'abbaye de Marmoutier," 53(1963): 98–99; 54(1964): 56–64. See also chapter 5 below.

46. White, *Custom, Kinship, and Gifts*, 83.

chants there.[47] They even promised on at least one occasion to provide daily board for a man who thought he might pursue his studies in Tours, apparently at the cathedral school.[48] Marmoutier's urban connections, moreover, were not limited to Tours. The monks had priories in York (England), Amiens, Reims, Nantes, and Paris.[49] Affinities between the language of the third Odo legend and some of the writings of Thomas of Chobham suggest that the monks also had intellectual ties with the Parisian Scholastics.[50]

Economic and governmental growth provided men and women with more opportunities and choices than they would have known in the early Middle Ages, and the burden of those choices frequently weighed heavily on their consciences. Awareness that individuals could choose their destinies helped foster an interest in moral persuasion. The experience and perception that people had options and that they could change carried over into the moral sphere, where preachers and teachers became increasingly interested in persuading laypeople to follow the precepts of the church or to convert—to make a conscious change—to a life of repentance. A number of Marmoutier's own monks joined the abbey's ranks because they experienced this kind of conversion.[51]

The greater complexity of urban life and of more extensive and centralized forms of government also fostered an interest in internal motivation by putting a premium on self-discipline. Unlike their

47. Chevalier, "Cité de Tours et Châteauneuf," 239–40 (Saint-Symphorian); 242 (sometime around 1090 a merchant named David, who had held from Marmoutier a large residence with a workshop in Châteauneuf, died. The abbot of Marmoutier called David his "friend" and "familiar" and thanked him for everything he had done for him and the monastery); Martène, *Histoire de l'abbaye de Marmoutier*, 1:239 (in the early eleventh century King Robert the Pious gave Marmoutier some land in the faubourg of Châteauneuf).

48. *Cartulaire . . . Vendômois*, 28, pp. 44–45 (ca. 1066).

49. Martène, *Histoire de l'abbaye de Marmoutier*, 1:394, 475; Gantier, "Recherches sur les possessions et les prieurés de l'abbaye de Marmoutier," 55(1965): 71–74 and map.

50. Thomas of Chobham, the latter Ermengard legend, and two early thirteenth-century Cistercians—Caesarius of Heisterbach and the author of the *Exordium magnum ordinis Cisterciensis*—all used the verb *salvare* rather than the usual *sanctificare* when citing 1 Cor. 7:14 ("an unbelieving man will *be saved* by a believing wife"): Thomas of Chobham, *Summa confessorum*, 4:2:7:6, p. 150; *Liber de restructione Majoris monasterii*, 356; Caesarius of Heisterbach, *Dialogus miraculorum*, 12:24, ed. Strange, 2:335–36; *Exordium magnum ordinis Cisterciensis*, 5:12, PL 185: 2:1147–49. See Farmer, "Persuasive Voices," at nn. 35, 50, 51 for further discussion.

51. For a review of the literature on twelfth-century interest in interior motivation, see Bynum, "Did the Twelfth Century Discover the Individual?" in Bynum, *Jesus as Mother*, 82–109. On clerical persuasion, see Little, *Religious Poverty and the Profit Economy*, 146–219, and Baldwin, *Masters, Princes and Merchants*, 1:161–309. The most noteworthy story of a dramatic conversion leading an individual to join Marmoutier is that of Evrard of Breteuil, the viscount of Chartres, who became a charcoal maker and then took the monastic habit at Marmoutier: see Guibert of Nogent, *De vita sua*, 1:9, pp. 54–57.

predecessors in the tenth and early eleventh centuries, people who lived in the twelfth and thirteenth centuries were much less likely to remain in face-to-face communities where the mere possibility of being observed and recognized served as a deterrent against violating collective norms. Larger towns and more extensive and depersonalized forms of government lent greater anonymity to the individual's day-to-day activities, and the smooth functioning of society now depended on an internalization of the community's norms.[52] The church's interest in internal motivations and its fostering of popular exhortatory preaching, which appealed to those motivations, indicates not only that it wanted to inculcate the laity with its values, but also that it was attempting to address the problems of larger and more depersonalized urban and political communities.[53]

Persuasion also became a concern in the twelfth and thirteenth centuries because the greater complexity of society had both increased the importance of communication and rendered it more difficult. People's experiences were more diverse than in small, face-to-face communities, and they were more aware that attempts to communicate had to begin with the perception of diversity and with the willingness and ability to bridge the gulf between one's own experiences and those of others. Scholastic argumentation, which was built around the attempt to reconcile apparently contradictory texts, represents one effort to deal with diversity and establish common grounds for understanding. The new interest in the art and methods of persuasion represents another such effort.[54]

Interiority and persuasion, then, were integrally related to the growing complexity of twelfth- and thirteenth-century society. They reflected and helped shape a world in which individuals who were free to make choices had to cooperate, negotiate, and live together peacefully.

In its emphasis on internal contrition and persuasion and its asso-

---

52. I am drawing here, in part, on Ruth Benedict's distinction between shame cultures (which "rely on external sanctions for good behavior") and guilt cultures (which rely on an internalized sense of guilt): see *Chrysanthemum and the Sword*, 222–27. For one discussion of the demise of face-to-face groups in this period, see Brown, "Society and the Supernatural: A Medieval Change"; but see also the important response of Bartlett, *Trial by Fire and Water: The Medieval Judicial Ordeal*. Charles M. Radding has also suggested that the growing importance of intention was linked to the growing complexity of society ("Evolution of Medieval Mentalities," 591).

53. On practical moral theology and popular preaching, see Little, *Religious Poverty and the Profit Economy*, 146–219; Baldwin, *Masters, Princes and Merchants*, 1:161–309.

54. On Scholastic methods, see Southern, *Making of the Middle Ages*, 203 ff. On developments in rhetorical theory, see Murphy, *Rhetoric in the Middle Ages*, 301 ff. See also Constable, "Papal, Imperial and Monastic Propaganda."

ciation of Ermengard's persuasion with Odo's avarice, the third legend about Odo and Ermengard reflects social and economic changes of the twelfth and thirteenth centuries. This is true as well of the legend's treatment of Ermengard's financial independence. Ermengard not only works through her husband, as she did in the first legend, convincing him to found Marmoutier, she also works independently: she gives alms in Odo's behalf while he lives, and after he dies she gives some landed estates to Marmoutier so that the monks will perform masses to help deliver Odo from the punishments of purgatory.[55]

This portrayal of Ermengard's independent economic behavior, like the portrayal of her moral persuasion and her husband's avarice, was not unique. Other clerical authors from the late twelfth and early thirteenth centuries wrote stories that demonstrated the spiritual efficaciousness of women's alms and the role their pious observances and modest benefactions could play in spiritually assisting the dead and the living.[56] The actual economic choices available to the women in these stories did not mark a striking departure from the eleventh and early twelfth centuries. Noble wives frequently managed the household finances. Theoretically, then, they had always had the opportunity to give alms. And throughout the eleventh and twelfth centuries widows—like Ermengard in this last legend—exercised more freedom in disposing of noble property than did married women.[57] What was most significant in these stories was the assertion that the independent economic actions available to women—even while their husbands were alive—could render spiritual benefits. The wealth that married women, and even widows, could control independent of their husbands and relatives was limited. But the church was now more interested in limited assets, including those of women.

The author from Marmoutier, like several of his contemporaries, wanted to perpetuate the message that modest feminine alms were spiritually beneficial. This message reflects the changes monasteries had undergone since the tenth and eleventh centuries, when nobles like Odo I, Odo II, and even Stephen of Blois founded monasteries and monastic priories, often because they wanted to avoid the eternal punishments of hell. Necessarily, these monastic endowments and

---

55. *Liber de restructione Majoris monasterii,* 356, 370.

56. Thomas of Chobham, *Summa confessorum,* 7:2:15, p. 375; Caesarius of Heisterbach, *Dialogus miraculorum,* 12:5, 7, 24, ed. Strange, 2:318–23, 335–36.

57. Herlihy, "Land, Family and Women in Continental Europe," 24, 31–34; Huyghebaert, "Femmes laïques dans la vie religieuse des XIᵉ et XIIᵉ siècles dans la province ecclésiastique de Reims," 374–75, 375 n. 134.

priories drew on major portions of patrimonial properties—the cost of avoiding hell was high in the tenth and eleventh centuries. By the second half of the twelfth century, however, noble families had become more protective of their patrimonies, and the money economy enabled religious institutions to draw on new sources of income in the form of tithes, modest rents, and fees collected for providing pastoral care. Modest gifts became increasingly important, and noble benefactors—including Marmoutier's Blésois patrons—began to endow anniversary masses and perpetual chantries rather than priories. They paid for these masses and chapels with modest estates and rents (see table 1).[58]

Along with the new doctrine of contrition, the church's growing interest in smaller sources of income may have contributed to the crystallizing of the doctrine of purgatory. The cleansing fires of purgatory, more circumscribed than the eternal punishments of hell, fit the new, more modest religious-economic system: it was far less costly to help a soul out of purgatory than to prevent its damnation.[59]

Stories concerning the efficacious actions of independent wives suggest that monks either perceived or wanted to create a link between small, feminine gifts and purgatory: Ermengard endowed masses to deliver Odo from purgatorial punishments; a usurer's wife, according to Caesarius of Heisterbach, fasted, performed vigils, said prayers, and gave alms to deliver her husband.[60] Significantly, the author of this final legend about Odo and Ermengard maintained a distinction between the spiritual effects of Odo's economic behavior—the traditional act of founding a monastery—and the spiritual

58. On the transition from avoiding hell to avoiding purgatory, see Southern, "Between Heaven and Hell," 652. On tithes, see Constable, *Monastic Tithes.* On monks and pastoral care, see Berlière, "Exercice du ministère paroissial par les moines." On the transition from large gifts to modest gifts, see Southern, *Western Society and the Church,* 245–50; Bouchard, *Sword, Miter, and Cloister,* 131–208. On the growing importance of endowed masses and anniversaries, see Marot and Lemaître, *Répertoire des documents nécrologiques français,* 19 ff., and McLaughlin, "Consorting with Saints: Prayer for the Dead in Early Medieval French Society," chap. 7.

Developments at Marmoutier after the middle of the twelfth century included growing numbers of endowed anniversary masses and chapels, more charters defining the abbey's rights to oblations in parish churches, and a new concern with convincing noble patrons to relinquish their rights of procuration at Marmoutier's priories: see *Cartulaire . . . Perche,* 33, pp. 49–50 (parish oblations, 1185–90); 35, pp. 51–52 (parish oblations, 1203); *Marmoutier, Cartulaire Blésois,* 168, pp. 157–58 (parish oblations, 1160); 170, pp. 159–60 (parish oblations, 1163); 179, p. 166 (anniversary, 1182); 189, p. 175 (chapel, 1194); 191–92, pp. 177–78 (procuration, twelfth century); 194, pp. 178–79 (procuration, twelfth century); 202, pp. 188–89 (procuration, 1202); 203, p. 189 (chapel, same as 189); 215, p. 198 (procuration, 1218); 232, pp. 209–10 (anniversary, 1233).

59. Southern, "Between Heaven and Hell," 652.

60. Caesarius of Heisterbach, *Dialogus miraculorum,* 12:24, ed. Strange, 2:336.

effects of Ermengard's new independent efforts. According to this interpolated legend, Odo's restoration of Marmoutier (the material from the earlier redaction) was now relatively superfluous, since his own contrition and Christ's death on the cross were what truly mattered in saving the count from hell. By contrast, the countess's benefactions to the abbey were essential. Ermengard learned from a visionary hermit that Odo had been saved from damnation but was still undergoing purgatorial punishments, and it was with the specific intention of delivering her husband that she endowed some masses at Marmoutier.[61]

In their legends about Odo and Ermengard of Blois, the monks of Marmoutier channeled their concerns and anxieties about the social and cultural consequences of an increasingly complex society. More important, they attempted to demonstrate how, in this new society, monks and laypeople could maintain mutually beneficial relations. There was an optimistic emphasis, in the final legend about Odo and Ermengard, on the moral and spiritual capacities of laypeople and on their relative autonomy. Odo's own act of contrition, rather than the assistance of the monks of Marmoutier, saved him from damnation. Similarly, Ermengard's independent economic actions and her pious persuasion brought about spiritually efficacious results. Yet the story stressed that men and women still needed to recognize their interdependence: Ermengard's moral example and persuasive role bound her to her husband on levels that transcended the lineage concerns of the noble family; the actions of Ermengard and the monks of Marmoutier assisted the count in paying off his purgatorial punishments.

With stories about spiritual interdependence the monks of Marmoutier suggested that laypeople still needed monastic intercession. But the monks' preoccupation with interdependence involved much more than their need to attract lay benefactors. The complexity of society had rendered older notions and experiences of community problematic, and the monks—as I argue in the next chapter—were searching for new ways to feel connected to one another.

61. *Liber de restructione Majoris monasterii*, 363–70.

5

Individual Motivation, Collective Responsibility: Reinforcing Bonds of Community

In their literature about the counts of Anjou and Blois the monks of Marmoutier exhibited a growing interest in treating the group or community in tandem with the individual and in complementing discussions of exterior reputation with discussions of the inner person and his or her motivation. These wedded themes of community and self recur as well in Marmoutier's twelfth-century literature for and about the monks and their community.

Personal motivation and fraternal connection were important themes in the intellectual awakening of the twelfth century, and they were central to the spirituality of the newer religious orders. But in assessing the literature from Marmoutier we should not assume that the black monks merely responded to ideas and concerns that originated elsewhere. A rhetorical concern with the internal experiences of the individual may have been introduced to the Benedictines from outside their own order. Nevertheless, like other people in the twelfth century, they perceived that their community was becoming increasingly complex. Their appeals to internal experience represent their own attempts to meet the challenges of a society that created new kinds of social experience and threatened to undermine the traditional bonds of the Benedictine community. To understand the problem as the monks of Marmoutier perceived it in the twelfth century, we must first examine the traditional Benedictine ideals of community; then we must look at the monastic function of intercessory prayer and its impact on Benedictine ideals and realities.

Thoughts and Deeds

Although the founder of Benedictine monasticism, Benedict of Nursia (ca. 480 to ca. 550), directed his attention to the inner faith of the individual monk, the primary focus of his *Rule* was the relationship between the individual and his community. The central themes of the *Rule* were humility and obedience—on the one hand, a personal attitude of both body and heart, and on the other hand, a relationship to authority. Within the monastery, as Benedict portrayed it, the watchful eyes of the abbot and the community—the "workshop of virtue"—gently yet sternly compensated for the human frailty of the individual monk, providing him with external sources of conscience, will, and judgment.[1] Physical presence, external observability, and the way the monks moved together through a daily and yearly cycle of prayers and activities were essential to Benedict's communal system, and indeed these seem at times to overshadow his attention to the inner self. A monk's attitude might remain hidden, but his posture and actions could serve as indications of whether he was attempting to attain sufficient humility. By molding the external behavior of a monk, the community and its abbot might leave an imprint on his conscience. Because actions reflected attitudes, even physical accidents—such as breaking a dish while washing it or stumbling over a word while praying—were punishable errors. Punishment usually involved a public ritual by which the offender was brought before the community's gaze and its collective judgment. Even an excommunicated monk, who had been excluded from the oratory and the common table, could not escape this collective gaze. "Visibly present in his absence," the excluded monk still lived within the abbey's walls and daily called attention to his shameful status by prostrating himself before the other monks as they left the oratory.[2]

Tenth-century sources suggest that in the early stages of Cluniac reform the black monks continued to adhere to Benedict's depiction of the relations between individual and community, thoughts and deeds. John of Salerno's *Life* of Abbot Odo of Cluny (927–42) provides ample evidence for an emphasis on deeds, for literal adherence to various external actions prescribed by the *Rule*, and for the central role the abbot played in the spiritual development of individual monks. Similarly, in a sermon for the feast of Saint Martin, Odo himself (who had been a canon at Saint-Martin of Tours) articulated his version of a Benedictine emphasis on external deeds: "Therefore while we have the time let us do good works and let us not add sin to

---

1. *RB 1980: The Rule of Saint Benedict*. On humility of body and heart, 7:62, pp. 48–49; on purity of heart, 20:3, pp. 64–65; on obedience, exterior source of judgment and will, chap. 5, pp. 34–37.
2. *RB 1980*, chaps. 44–46, pp. 92–95. The quotation is from Fulton, "Liminal Status of the Excommunicated Monk."

sin. . . . For if perverse thoughts depart from God, how much more do perverse deeds depart from him? If on the Day of Judgment we are going to give an account for our idle words, what will it be for perverse works?"[3] In addition to stressing the importance of correct action, Odo of Cluny, like Benedict before him, was mindful of the internal experience of the monk. He hoped his own spiritual writings could move other monks to be vigilant—"lest we harden our hearts"—and to reflect upon the fate of their own souls.[4]

Despite the similarities between Odo of Cluny's monastic ideals and those of the Benedictine *Rule*, however, monastic life and practice in the tenth century differed in at least one fundamental way from what had been described in the *Rule*: the daily life of monks had come to focus on providing vicarious intercessions for the souls of the dead. While knights fought and peasants labored in the fields, Benedictine monks prayed for the souls of benefactors, of kin, and most especially, for the souls of their fellow monks—not only those of their own abbey, but also those of abbeys to which their houses were joined in confraternity.[5]

This intercessory function, which first became important in the

3. "Ergo dum tempus habemus operemur bonum, nec adjiciamus peccatum super peccatum. . . . Perversae namque cogitationes separant a Deo, quanto magis perversa opera? Si de verbis otiosis redituri sumus rationem in die judicii, quid erit de perversis operibus?" (Odo of Cluny, "Sermo in festo Sancti Martini," *PL* 133:750); John of Salerno, "Vita Sancti Odonis," *PL* 133:43–86, trans. Sitwell, 1–88; Rosenwein, *Rhinoceros Bound: Cluny in the Tenth Century,* 84–100.

4. "Charissimi Patres et fratres; in quantum justi, Patres, in quantum peccatores, socii et fratres, admonendo et obsecrando dico, ne obduremus corda nostra" (Odo of Cluny, "Sermo in festo Sancti Martini," *PL* 133:750).

5. Monks in western Europe began offering intercessory prayers even before the time of the Carolingians. Nevertheless, Benedict of Aniane was a central figure in passing that function on to ninth- and tenth-century monasticism. See, on Benedict of Aniane, Semmler and Bacht, "Benedikt von Aniane," and Semmler, "Benedictus II." Drawing on Semmler's work, Barbara Rosenwein has depicted a fundamental distinction between the monastic ideals of the Carolingian Benedict of Aniane and the ideals of the tenth-century Cluniacs. Benedict of Aniane included liturgical offices that were not in the Benedictine rule, but his central goal was to *pare down* the liturgical practices of the monasteries of his day. By contrast, the spirit of Cluny in the tenth century was one of eclecticism and liturgical expansion. Benedict of Aniane had cut the number of psalms recited each day to under 75; the Cluniacs in the tenth century expanded the number to at least 138: see Rosenwein, "Rules and the 'Rule' at Tenth-Century Cluny"; Rosenwein, *Rhinoceros Bound,* 84–100. Other discussions of the Carolingian roots of Cluniac liturgy include Bishop, *Liturgica Historica,* 214–21; Schmitz, "Liturgie de Cluny"; Schmitz, "Influence de Saint Benôit d'Aniane"; Molinier, *Obituaires français au Moyen Age,* 21 ff.; Bredero, "Cluny et le monachisme carolingien."

For a discussion of the distinctively central role that intercession for the dead played at Cluny, see Le Goff, *Birth of Purgatory,* 124–27, and Neiske, "Vision und Totengedenken," 164–79, 184; Heath, *Crux Imperatorum Philosophia: Imperial Horizons of the Cluniac Confraternitas;* Wollasch, "Überlieferung cluniacensischen Totengedächtnisses"; Huyghebaert, *Documents nécrologiques.*

seventh and eighth centuries, was largely responsible, in the tenth and eleventh, for the enormous success of the black monks. Laypeople seeking relief for their sins showered abbeys like Marmoutier with landed gifts, and as a result the monastic liturgy expanded to the point that it virtually filled the entire day. At Cluny, during the abbacy of Saint Hugh (1049–1109), the monks prayed each year for ten thousand individually remembered souls, and at all such abbeys the prayers escalated to the point that the monks' life became an almost constant round of ritualized liturgical offices.[6]

The enormous growth of the liturgy of the black monks, and of the landed gifts that nobles bestowed upon them so they would pray for their souls, began to peak in the second half of the eleventh century.[7] About the same time, certain religious reformers represented as a problem the institutional expansion of the black monks, including the intercessory function that stood behind it. Ritualized deeds, they maintained, threatened to overwhelm the inner life of monks. Saint Anselm observed of Cluny that monks there were so busy performing the liturgy that they had no time to study; Peter Damian noted that they had barely a half-hour to themselves each day.[8] Along similar lines, the Carthusians, whose order had its beginnings in 1084, and the Cistercians, whose order arose in 1098, proclaimed their return to the original purity of the Benedictine *Rule*, with its much more restricted horarium; their detachment from entanglements with the secular realm, including incomes associated with intercessory prayer; and their devotion to apostolic poverty, which meant—in intentional contradistinction to the "poverty" of the black monks—simplicity in architecture, in clothing, and in liturgical decoration. Although the Cistercians did not directly attack the black monks' intercessory function or totally eliminate offices for the dead, many of their criticisms of liturgical extravagance and worldly

6. In the mid-tenth century the monks at Cluny chanted 124 psalms each day. By the second half of the eleventh century they were reciting 250 each day: see Peter the Venerable, *Statuta*, p. 66 n, citing Schmitz, "Liturgie de Cluny," 89, and John of Salerno, "Vita Sancti Odonis," 1, *PL* 133:43–86, trans. Sitwell, p. 33 and n. 1). See also Hunt, *Cluny under Saint Hugh*, 99–123, and McLaughlin, "Consorting with Saints." On the remembrance of ten thousand souls at Cluny, see Heath, *Crux Imperatorum*, 80; Wollasch, "Cluniacensisches Totenbuch aus der Zeit Abt Hugos von Cluny." For further discussion of Cluniac liturgy and remembrance, see Hallinger, *Gorze-Kluny*, 1:26 ff.; Bishop, *Liturgica Historica*, 228–29.

7. Noreen Hunt treats Abbot Hugh's tenure (1049–1109) as a major turning point in the abbey's size and empire and sees Hugh himself as the last of the abbots to retain an earlier spirit of simplicity: see *Cluny under Saint Hugh*. Marmoutier's turning point in terms of the number of priories and possessions came under Abbot Albert (1032–64): see Gantier, "Recherches sur les possessions et les prieurés de l'abbaye de Marmoutier," 53(1963): 100.

8. Eadmer, *Life of Saint Anselm*, p. 9; Peter Damian, *Epistolae*, 6:5, *PL* 144:380.

entanglements arose because they envisioned the monastic life more as a quest for personal salvation than as one of corporate intercession.[9] They even curtailed the burden of intercessory responsibilities by avoiding the practice of individual remembrances. The Carthusians went still further in their disengagement. They recorded the names of no donors in their martyrologies, performed no anniversary masses, and did not encourage visitors.[10] In conjunction with their avoidance of liturgical accretions and obligations toward the outside world, the new orders placed considerable importance on the individual reflection and personal devotion of each monk. Cistercians especially produced numerous lyrical and insightful accounts of interior spiritual experiences and mystical devotion.

Despite the criticisms of zealous reformers and the personal conversions of individual monks such as Adam of Perseigne, who left Marmoutier sometime after 1180 to become a Cistercian, black monks continued to provide a vital service in the twelfth century, and they were hardly prepared, nor would they have found it possible, to unburden themselves of their lands, their architectural monuments, and their intercessory obligations.[11] Still, there were in their midst voices of reform and renewal: Peter the Venerable, abbot of Cluny

9. John Van Engen makes the point about the Cistercian emphasis on personal salvation rather than liturgical intervention: see "'Crisis of Cenobitism' Reconsidered," 296–97, and his *Rupert of Deutz*, 314–22. Bernard of Clairvaux and Hugh of Pontigny criticized Marmoutier's proprietorship of parish churches: see Bernard of Clairvaux, Letter 397, *PL* 182:606–9.

10. On Cistercian prayers for the dead, see Laurent, "Prière pour les défunts et les obituaires dans l'ordre de Cîteaux." On the Cistercian reform, see Lackner, *Eleventh-Century Background of Cîteaux*, 217–73; Bishop, *Liturgica Historica*, 228–29. On Cistercians and Carthusians, see Little, *Religious Poverty and the Profit Economy*, 84–87, 90–96. On the Carthusians, see anonymous monk of La Grande-Chartreuse, "Doctrine monastique des coutumes de Guigues." For contemporary observations and criticisms (implicit and explicit) of the shortened Cistercian liturgy, see Peter Abelard, *Epistolae*, 10 (to Bernard of Clairvaux), *PL* 178:339; Wilmart, "Riposte de l'ancien monachisme au manifeste de Saint Bernard," 334–35; Talbot, "Date and Author of the Riposte," 72–80; Van Engen, *Rupert of Deutz*, 300–306; Hunt, *Cluny under Saint Hugh*, 48; Folz, "Pierre le Vénérable et la liturgie," 152. On the liturgies of the Carthusians and Cistercians, see King, *Liturgies of the Religious Orders*, 1–157.

11. Jean Bouvet, who edited Adam of Perseigne's letters, was not absolutely certain that Adam resided at Marmoutier, but he was unaware of Guibert of Gembloux's statement that a defense of the epithet "par apostolis," which was applied to Saint Martin, had been written "ab armario Majoris Monasterii, domno Adam." It was Adam (later of Perseigne) who provided that discussion in his letter 10. Bouvet was also misled by his assumption that Guibert did not visit Marmoutier until 1194, when Adam was already abbot of Perseigne. Guibert's visit, however, took place in 1180–81: see "De cultu Sancti Martini apud Turonenses extremo saeculo XII," 244; Adam of Perseigne, *Lettres*, ed. Bouvet, 7–29, 163 n. 1, 164–79; Delehaye, "Guibert, Abbé de Florennes et de Gembloux." Gerald of Alne, another Cistercian abbot, may also have begun his monastic career at Marmoutier: see Martène, *Histoire de l'abbaye de Marmoutier*, 2:87.

between 1122 and 1156, and Rupert, abbot of Deutz between 1120 and 1129, advocated a renewed fervor and commitment in fulfilling the task of monastic prayer and intercession. Black monks graciously welcomed those who aspired to the more personal and ascetic accomplishments of the eremitical life: Abbot Hugh of Cluny encouraged the hermit Anastasius to come to Cluny so he would serve as an example to its monks; and Peter the Venerable created a space within the monastery, forbidden to all outsiders, where the monks could "assiduously burn in God's presence with the holy and secret perfume of prayers . . . as if they were in the desert."[12]

Peter the Venerable also felt compelled to cope with the length of the liturgical offices at Cluny by cutting out pauses between psalms. Like his predecessor Abbot Hugh, he set aside special days for the commemoration of the dead, possibly, as Noreen Hunt suggested, in an attempt to ameliorate the burden of individual remembrances by consolidating them on special days.[13] Peter's attempts to reform the liturgy at Cluny may have been motivated in part by his desire to respond to the criticisms of the new religious orders and by his perception that the monks at Cluny should be allowed the opportunity to develop a more inward, meditative religious life.[14] But Peter's statutes also indicate that the length of the liturgy at Cluny was a real problem. Most of the monks' commemorative and intercessory responsibilities were performed on behalf of fellow monks of the abbey.[15] Thus that Cluny had grown from one-hundred monks in the mid-eleventh century to four-hundred in Peter's day suggests that liturgical burdens increased about fourfold.[16] Peter the Venerable noted that the material aspects of commemoration—distribution of food to the poor on behalf of monks who had recently died—could impoverish the abbey, and he claimed, when he cut out the pauses between psalms,

12. "Ubi sancta et secreta orationum aromata deo assidue accenderent . . . velut in heremo" (Peter the Venerable, *Statuta,* 53, p. 83); Constable, "Monastic Policy of Peter the Venerable," 126–38; Van Engen, *Rupert of Deutz,* 300–306; Hunt, *Cluny under Saint Hugh,* 48; Folz, "Pierre le Vénérable et la liturgie," 150–61.

13. Hugh set aside January 31 for the commemoration of dead monks and the Monday after Trinity Sunday for those buried in the cemetery. Peter the Venerable added the vigil of Saint Michael's Day for the commemoration of Cluny's monks and the vigil of the Conversion of Saint Paul for the commemoration of the parents of monks: see Hunt, *Cluny under Saint Hugh,* 104; Ulrich of Cluny, *Antiquiores consuetudines,* 1:26, *PL* 149:673; Peter the Venerable, *Statuta,* 8, pp. 47–48.

14. Orderic Vitalis accused Peter of "rivaling the Cistercians and other seekers after novelties" (*Historia ecclesiastica,* 13:13, ed. Chibnall, 6:426–27).

15. This is evident in Cluniac necrologies, which listed many more names of monks than of *familiares:* see Wollasch, *Synopse der cluniacensischen Necrologien,* vol. 2.

16. On the size of Cluny, see Hunt, *Cluny under Saint Hugh,* 82–89.

that "neither the hours of the day nor those of the night would be able to suffice" if the monks were to allow time for the desired pauses.[17]

Although statistics are not available for the number of monks at Marmoutier, we know that its success paralleled that of Cluny and that the mother house must have been large in the twelfth century, since it provided the personnel for the abbey's extensive priories and deaneries, which numbered (on the Continent alone) 114 by 1100 and 151 by the early thirteenth century.[18] Liturgical adjustments also suggest that Marmoutier, like Cluny, was feeling the pressure of internal growth. The author of Marmoutier's customal, writing sometime after 1124, stated that it had once been the custom at his abbey to recite Psalms 5 and 14 for each dead brother for a total of thirty days, "but because of the great multitude of the dead, for whom it was most difficult to observe a trental, it was decided that these psalms would be said at all times and at all hours without intermission." The psalms were now recited every day, not for specific dead brothers, but for whomever had recently died.[19]

17. "Quia ad istud nec diurnae horae, nec nocturnae, visae sunt posse sufficere" (Peter the Venerable, *Statuta*, 1, pp. 41–42). On distributions of food, see statute 32, pp. 66–67, and Peter's "Dispositio rei familiaris Cluniacensis," cited by Constable in the note to that statute. For general discussion of Peter's reforming decrees, see Knowles, "Reforming Decrees of Peter the Venerable"; Constable, "Monastic Policy of Peter the Venerable," 129–30; Folz, "Pierre le Vénérable et la liturgie," 149–50; Van Dijk, "Historical Liturgy and Liturgical Studies," 174–77.

Already about 1083, Ulrich of Cluny observed that there was virtually never a time when the monks of Cluny did not have to perform commemorative offices for those who had recently died: see Ulrich of Cluny, *Antiquiores consuetudines*, 1:3, 7, PL 149:647, 652 (on Ulrich's date, see Hunt, *Cluny under Saint Hugh*, 12).

18. There are no sources for the size of Marmoutier, but the assertion by the author of the *Return from Burgundy* that Marmoutier had 140 monks plus one abbot at the time of the Viking invasions could well have been a projection into the past of his own experience at the abbey. Since most abbeys were growing in the first half of the twelfth century and monks were aware of this, the author may have projected into the past a number that was somewhat smaller than the size of the abbey at the time he wrote: see *De reversione beati Martini,* 21. It was Ursmer Berlière who surmised that the number of monks at Marmoutier must have been quite large in the twelfth century to provide the personnel for the priories and deaneries ("Nombre des moines dans les anciens monastères," 246–47). On the number of Marmoutier's priories, see Gantier, "Recherches sur les possessions et les prieurés," 55(1965):71–79.

19. "Consuetudinis enim erat antiquitas ut haec duo, idest *Verba mea* minus, et psalmus *Voce mea* pro unoquoque fratre nostro triginta diebus dicebantur, sed pro nimia multitudine morientium, quorum trigenaria observare difficillimum erat, difinitum est ut omni tempore per omnes horas absque intermissione dicantur" (*Antiquae consuetudines Majoris monasterii,* chap. 48, fol. 111). The *Verba mea* was said every day after matins, the *Voce mea* during the familiar psalms. According to this customal (which was written after 1124), sometime after 1104 a vespers for the dead was set aside on the feast of the Purification of the Virgin, on behalf of the parents of all the monks. The passage concerning the vespers for parents of monks mentions the parents of Abbot William, who became abbot in 1104 (ibid., chap. 45, fols. 108v–109).

There were tensions, then, between the black monks' desire to partake of the new, more meditative spirituality and their continued liturgical obligations. Nevertheless, like the members of the newer orders, the black monks began to express themselves with the language of inner experience. The spiritual readings and devotional writings of the older Benedictines began to assimilate and resemble those of the Cistercians. Twelfth-century libraries of older Benedictine houses, including Marmoutier, possessed copies of Cistercian sermons.[20] Peter the Venerable's collection of miracle stories—the *De miraculis*—anticipated those of Cistercians such as Caesarius of Heisterbach. Both Peter and Caesarius recounted ghost stories, propagandized the Christian sacraments, and attempted to communicate the needs and implications of an inner spirituality that emphasized sincere contrition and the fate of souls that had been saved but still needed to be purged of their sins.[21]

At Marmoutier, too, the monks attempted to open up new spaces for interior fervor and personal expression. Toward the beginning of the twelfth century, several monks of Marmoutier retired to the nearby island of Saint-Nicholas (on the Loire), where they apparently built a wooden chapel and began to live an eremitical life. In 1123 they gained permission to build a stone hermitage, which continued to provide a place of meditation for Marmoutier's monks until about 1130, when the site became a religious refuge for women.[22] Several of Marmoutier's monks retired to the abbey's priories to live ere-

20. Chibnall, *World of Orderic Vitalis,* 91–92; Tours, Bibliothèque Municipale, MS. 344. This manuscript, which includes sermons of Bernard of Clairvaux, has the following note at fol. 193v: "Liber iste est Sancti Martyni Majoris monasterii . . . factus est tempore Guillelmi, armarii, anno octavo Hervei abbatis [1187]" (*Catalogue général des . . . bibliothèques publiques de France,* 37:1:265–66). Other twelfth-century manuscripts that were in Marmoutier's library in the eighteenth century contain works by Isaac of Stella, Bernard, and other Cistercians, but I have no direct evidence that these manuscripts were at Marmoutier in the twelfth century: see Tours, Bibliothèque Municipale, MSS. 137, 246; *Catalogue général,* 37:1:87–90, 175–77.

21. Peter the Venerable, *De miraculis;* Caesarius of Heisterbach, *Dialogus miraculorum;* Schmitt, "Revenants dans la société féodale"; Le Goff, *Birth of Purgatory,* 177–81, 300–310; Ward, *Miracles and the Medieval Mind,* 192–200; Patin and Le Goff, "A propos de la typologie des miracles dans le *Liber de miraculis* de Pierre le Vénérable," 181–89; Constable, *Cluniac Studies,* introduction, iii–iv. The ghost stories of Peter the Venerable and Caesarius drew on a long tradition stretching back to the early Christian period, which had been considerably expanded in the eighth and ninth centuries. Earlier Cluniac ghost stories had also focused on the special relationship between the returning souls of the dead and their requests for spiritual assistance: see Neiske, "Vision und Totengedenken," 137–85. In their collections of miracles and ghost stories, however, Peter the Venerable and Caesarius of Heisterbach emphasized contrition and confession in ways that the earlier works had not.

22. Oury, "Erémitisme à Marmoutier," 322–24.

mitical—or simply quieter—lives.[23] In 1187 Abbot Hervé of Ville-preux retired to the grotto of the seven sleepers, a cave above the abbey's main church, where he continued to lead an eremitical life for another sixteen years.[24] Finally, a work titled *Deeds of the Abbey of Marmoutier in the Eleventh Century* presented the monks with examples of those who, while remaining among the other brothers, quietly exceeded the devotional requirements of the abbey's customs. John, who was ten years old, never laughed as children do, and he outdid the other boys in the abbey by rising for vigils even though the younger members of the abbey were allowed to sleep at that hour; a sacristan secretly served the others at night, drawing water and filling the lavatories; a monk wore out his knees with genuflections during his frequent private devotions.[25]

In the language of their sermons the monks of Marmoutier paid close attention to the issues of intention and sincerity. An anonymous author of a collection of sermons from the second half of the twelfth century emphasized, in a way that Sulpicius Severus had not, Saint Martin's role as a preacher. "With words, examples, and miracles," the saint "provoked and converted thousands of men"; his teaching "illuminated" unbelievers "with the light of truth."[26] Some of the language in these passages was inspired by Carolingian spiritual writings, yet it is significant that the twelfth-century monk chose to portray his patron saint as a master of speech at a time when rhetoric,

23. Abbot Baudry of Saint-Nicholas returned to his mother house of Marmoutier before 1033, then went on to the priory of Tavant to lead an eremitical life: see Charter of Fulk of Anjou, *PL* 155:482; Guillot, *Comte d'Anjou*, 2:C77. Odo Rigaldus's episcopal visitations to some of Marmoutier's priories in the thirteenth century suggest that they still provided a place of quiet retirement for sick and elderly monks: see Odo Rigaldus, *Register of Eudes of Rouen*, 96.

24. *Chronicon abbatum Majoris monasterii*, 324; Oury, "Erémitisme à Marmoutier," 321–22. Hervé may have written a collection of sermons (Bibliothèque Nationale, MS. lat. 3823): see Leclercq, "Recherches sur d'anciens sermons monastiques," 8–10. Arnold of Bonneval, friend and biographer of Bernard of Clairvaux, and indeed one of the great spiritual thinkers of his age, began his monastic career at Marmoutier. On the one hand, this suggests that Marmoutier may have provided him (and possibly Adam of Perseigne as well) with a relatively good education. On the other hand, Arnold's career suggests there was probably more room for inner development at a Benedictine house of smaller proportions than Marmoutier: see Canivez, "Arnaud de Bonneval"; Prévost, "Arnaud, Arnold, et Ernaud de Bonneval."

25. *De rebus gestis in Majori monasterio*, 398, 402–3, 404–5. On the dates and manuscripts of this work, see Source Appendix, I-D.

26. "Verbis pariter exemplis atque miraculis multa hominum milia provocavit atque convertit," "Homines autem luce veritatis . . . illuminabat" ("In translatione beati Martini, sermo secundus," Bibliothèque Nationale, MS. lat. 12412, fol. 105v, col. 1; ibid., "Sermo primus," fol. 105, col. 1).

popular preaching, and the possibility of changing the hearts of men and women were becoming major concerns in Scholastic circles.[27]

The author of Marmoutier's sermons stressed Saint Martin's preaching, but he also recognized, as had ancient and early Christian theorists of rhetoric, the difficulty of bringing about a motivational change with words alone.[28] Thus he attributed the success of Martin's preaching not only to his words but also to his example and miracles, which reinforced the sincerity and truth of his spoken message.[29] This author understood that while words can convey the content of deep spiritual truths, they can also serve as masks, disguising the real self. Receptivity to the Christian message cannot be demonstrated with words alone, since it frequently occurs, as the Lord himself declared, that "the people honor me with their lips but their heart is far from me [Is. 29:13, Matt. 15:8, Mk. 7:6]."[30] A confession of faith, the author of the sermons insisted, must be accompanied by deeds, which are signs of an inner piety, one which arises from the "root of faith" or "from the heart."[31]

Even works, which are more trustworthy than words alone in serving as outward signs of sincerity, are not infallible signifiers of the inner self, and they do not suffice for a true piety. In the end, the author of these sermons suggested—and here we encounter the chasm separating his own spirituality from that of Odo of Cluny—only God can perform the final test of sincerity, because a piety of deeds must always be accompanied by the proper attitude. The monks of Marmoutier can imitate the virtue of their patron Saint Martin, but they must couple an imitation of his voluntary poverty with faith—the confidence that they are saved by God's grace. They must strive to ensure that their meekness, a visible mien they assume in their relations with other men, is accompanied by true humility, which is visible only to God.[32] On one level the author of these sermons was consistent with the dual themes—interior and exterior—of the *Rule* of Saint Benedict. But

27. Alcuin, "De vita S. Martini" and "Sermo de transitu S. Martini," *PL* 101:657–64. For further discussion of the background to this theme, see my dissertation, "Societal Change and Religious Expression: Saint Martin's Cult at Tours," 278 ff.

28. Romilly, *Magic and Rhetoric in Ancient Greece;* Murphy, *Rhetoric in the Middle Ages,* 286–94; Farmer, "Softening the Hearts of Men: Women, Embodiment, and Persuasion in the Thirteenth Century."

29. "In translatione beati Martini, Sermo secundus," Bibliothèque Nationale, MS. lat. 12412, fol. 105v, col. 1.

30. Ibid. fol. 105, col. 2. The second legend about Count Odo and Countess Ermengard described Odo in a similar manner: see above, chapter 4.

31. "Corde," "ex fidei radice" (ibid., fol. 105, col. 2).

32. "De transitu beati Martini, Sermo quartus," ibid., fol. 156, col. 2; "De transitu beati Martini, Sermo quintus," ibid., fol. 107v. col. 1.

whereas Benedict had emphasized that monks must answer outwardly
to their abbot and community, this author emphasized instead that each
must answer to God, who alone knows the true inner self.

Individual and Community

In the Benedictine *Rule* and the writings by and about Odo of
Cluny, the idea that outward deeds reflected the true inner character
of the monk was closely related to the ideal that the community could
serve as the outward conscience of the individual. Abbots were to
keep careful watch over their charges, measuring inward spiritual
progress by observing outward bearing. The difference between the
earlier writings and the later ones from Marmoutier thus points not
only to a new emphasis on inner spiritual experience, but also to a
perception that relationships between persons in positions of authority and those who answered to them, or indeed between the individual
and the community, were problematic. No monk or abbot, the author of Marmoutier's sermons implied, can truly know the soul of his
neighbor.

This new assessment of the problem of knowing the heart of another is representative of changed perceptions that resulted at least in
part from the language of interiority that the Cistercians and others
like them were promulgating. More important, however, this new
attention to the possibility of a disjunction between deeds and character reflects the fact that the monastic community of the twelfth
century was a different physical and psychological entity than the one
Benedict and Odo of Cluny had envisioned and experienced. It could
no longer be assumed that the members of a monastic community
would share the same physical space, the same rhythm of liturgical
activities.

It was the escalating growth of these monastic houses, especially
the more successful ones such as Cluny and Marmoutier, that transformed the nature of the community. As their liturgical and administrative responsibilities expanded, the monks needed to distribute
their human resources across large distances and to divide up their
liturgical and organizational labor. Members of the mother house
could be sent out to distant priories or deaneries, and they might not
see their brothers for months or years. Even those who remained at
home were expected to fulfill some of their collective responsibilities
in places or at times when no one else was around. The watchful gaze
of the community became less and less evident in the daily lives of the
monks.

We might expect that the intensification and expansion of the monks' liturgical obligations would have enhanced the effectiveness of the authority that both the community and the abbot were supposed to hold over the wills of the monks. The monitoring of every action of the individual was, after all, an inherent aspect of collective liturgical activity, and participation in an elaborate ritual life served to merge the identity of the individual with that of the community as a whole. But the actual results of liturgical expansion were quite different. Since the eighth century, monasteries had been fulfilling their intercessory functions not only by expanding the conventual liturgy but also by encouraging, or requiring, monks who were priests to perform private, intercessory masses. The proliferation of side altars in monastic churches (we know of at least three in Marmoutier's Romanesque church, but there were certainly more) and the increase in the number of monks who were priests indicates that within monasteries private masses were steadily gaining importance from the eighth century on. By the tenth century about 55 percent of monks were priests. By the time of Peter the Venerable, the percentage at Cluny must have been much higher, since he complained that at times the celebration of private masses threatened to reduce attendance at the abbey's conventual offices to one-quarter of the abbey's monks.[33] Statistics are not available for the number of priest-monks at Marmoutier, but the author of the Deeds of the Abbey of Marmoutier proclaimed that the "numerous priests" of the abbey offered the mass continuously from "dawn until the dinner hour."[34]

Private masses represent, at least on one level, a division of labor in the liturgical sphere. At Cluny, whenever a monk died, six of the

33. Peter the Venerable, Statuta, 6, pp. 46–47; see also statute 72 on p. 102; Hunt, Cluny under Saint Hugh, 108–9; Folz, "Pierre le Vénérable et la liturgie," 156–57. On the percentage of monks who were priests in the earlier period, and on the role that private masses played in monasteries, see Vogel, "Vie quotidienne du moine en Occident à l'époque de la floraison des messes privées." On side altars, see Conant, Benedictine Contributions to Church Architecture, 20–21. We know very little about the plan of the Romanesque church of Marmoutier that was dedicated in 1096 and probably completed after that date. Between 1218 and about 1350 a Gothic structure was built over the Romanesque one, which was eventually demolished. In 1818–19 the Gothic structure was demolished: see Lelong, "Recherches sur l'abbatiale de Marmoutier à l'époque romane," and his "Observations et hypothèses sur l'église abbatiale gothique de Marmoutier." Although the physical evidence is lacking, the written sources show that at least three eleventh-century abbots of Marmoutier were buried next to different side altars: see Chronicon abbatum Majoris monasterii, 318–19.

34. "Mos erat ipsius cenobii ut a prima aurora usque in horam prandii propter sacerdotum copiam continua missarum celebratio protraheretur" (De rebus gestis in Majori monasterio, with corrections from Charleville 117, which are printed in Van der Straeten, "Recueil de miracles de S. Martin dans le manuscrit 117 de Charleville," 90).

abbey's priests were to take turns performing masses until the dead monk had received the thirty masses that were owed to him. At Marmoutier all priests were obliged to perform private masses for a deceased monk until his body was buried; after the burial, priest-monks chose to perform private masses for the dead monk in order to pay off personal obligations.[35]

Even as private masses gained importance, the conventual hora-rium continued to grow, and as it did, further division of labor became necessary. More and more monks were granted exemptions from participating in the common liturgy. These included not only priests who performed private masses (although Peter the Venerable attempted to draw them back to the common liturgy by insisting that they could not perform private masses during the conventual mass), but also monks who were responsible for the smooth functioning of the abbey—cooks, refectorians, even scribes working on important manuscripts.[36]

Another change that led to the transformation of the religious community was the monks' residing, sometimes alone and often in groups of less than six, away from their abbeys in the granges and smaller priories that served as administrative and spiritual centers on parcels of dispersed landed property. Marmoutier's numerous prio-ries were situated all over western and northern France and even in England (see map 5). This system of priories and granges had already begun to take shape at Marmoutier and Cluny in the tenth century, but it did not lead to an administrative restructuring until the middle of the eleventh century.[37] In the twelfth century, when the number

35. According to Ulrich, all the priests sang mass on the day a brother was buried, but after the burial six priests shared the remaining responsibilities: see Ulrich of Cluny, *Anti-quiores consuetudines*, 3:29, PL 149:775. The parallel distinction at Marmoutier was that before the burial all priests performed private masses "pro gratia" rather than "pro debito" (presumably this second expression meant "for personal debts"). After a monk had been buried, whoever said masses for the dead monk paid off such personal debts: "Quamdiu corpus super terram fuerit, omnes sacerdotes missas privatas pro eo singulariter debant cantare. Nulla tamen illarum missarum pro debito repulsabitur, sed pro gratia. Tumulato autem corpore, quisquis pro eo cantaverit a debito solvi incipiet" (*Antiquae consuetudines Majoris monasterii*, fol. 110v).

36. Hunt, *Cluny under Saint Hugh*, 108–9; *Antiquae consuetudines Majoris monasterii*, fol. 116 (scribes exempt from certain liturgical offices). See also Leclercq, *Aux sources de la spiritualité occidentale*, 114–20.

37. On Marmoutier's priories, see Gantier, "Recherches sur les possessions et les pri-eurés de l'abbaye de Marmoutier." Gantier observed that the prioral organization did not emerge until the second quarter of the eleventh century and that the word for "prior" did not appear in the charters before about 1075. On the priories in England, see Martène, *Histoire de l'abbaye de Marmoutier*, 1:393.

Hunt (*Cluny under Saint Hugh*, 55–56) argued that deans were a new development in the mid-eleventh century and that the major concern in the customals of that time was to

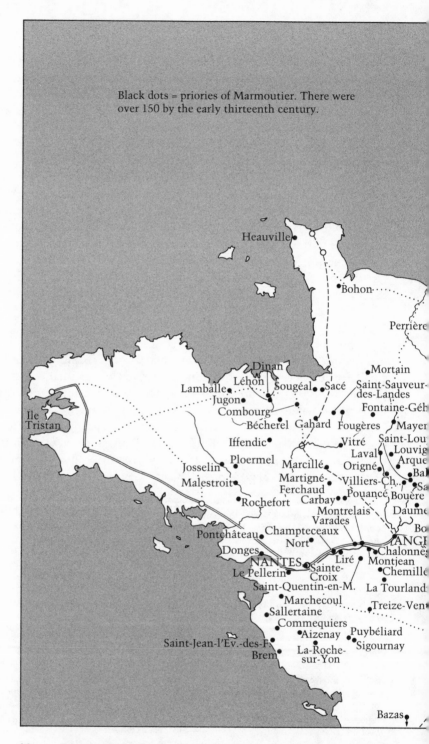

Black dots = priories of Marmoutier. There were over 150 by the early thirteenth century.

Heauville

Bohon

Perrière

Dinan
Mortain
Léhon
Lamballe   Sougéal   Sacé   Saint-Sauveur-
Jugon   des-Landes
Combourg   Fontaine-Géh
Ile   Bécherel Gahard   Fougères   Mayer
Tristan   Iffendic   Vitré   Saint-Lou
                                 Laval   Louvig
             Ploermel   Origné   Arque
Josselin   Marcillé   Ba
Malestroit   Martigné- Villiers-Ch...   Sa
             Ferchaud   Pouancé Bouère
             Rochefort Carbay   Daume
                        Montrelais   Bo
                        Varades
             Champteceaux   ANGI
Pontchâteau Nort   Chalonne
Donges,   Liré Montjean
             NANTES   Chemillé
Le Pellerin Sainte-   La Tourland
Saint-Quentin-en-M. Croix
             Marchecoul   Treize-Ven
Sallertaine
Commequiers
             Aizenay   Puybéliard
Saint-Jean-l'Ev.-des-F   Sigournay
Brem   La-Roche-
            sur-Yon

Bazas

MAP 5. Priories of Marmoutier about 1200. Adapted from Gantier, "Recherches sur les . . . prieurés."

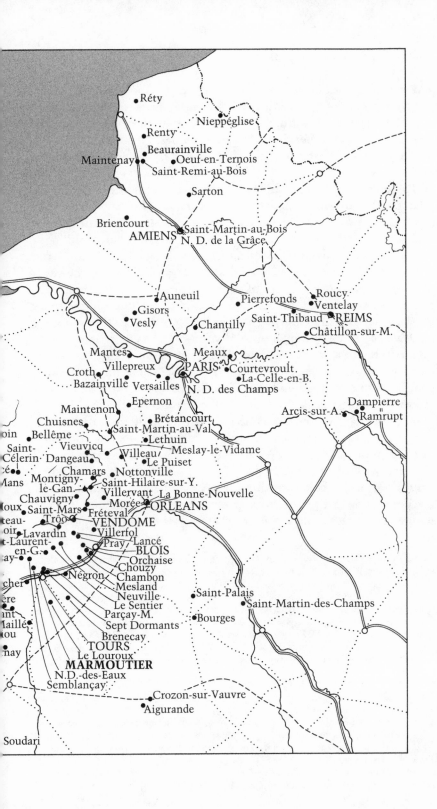

Réty
Nieppéglise
Renty
Beaurainville
Maintenay
Oeuf-en-Ternois
Saint-Remi-au-Bois
Sarton
Briencourt
Saint-Martin-au-Bois
AMIENS
N. D. de la Grâce
Auneuil
Roucy
Pierrefonds
Ventelay
Gisors
Saint-Thibaud
REIMS
Vesly
Chantilly
Châtillon-sur-M.
Mantes
Meaux
Villepreux
PARIS
Courtevroult.
Croth
Bazainville
Versailles
La-Celle-en-B.
N. D. des Champs
Epernon
Dampierre
Maintenon
Arcis-sur-A.
Ramrupt
Chuisnes
Brétancourt
oin
Bellême
Saint-Martin-au-Val
Saint-
Vieuvicq
Lethuin
Célerin
Dangeau
Villeau
Meslay-le-Vidame
cé
Le Puiset
Mans
Chamars
Nottonville
Montigny-
le-Gan
Saint-Hilaire-sur-Y.
Chauvigny
Villervant
La Bonne-Nouvelle
oux
Saint-Mars
Morée
ORLEANS
eau-
Fréteval
oir
Trôo
VENDOME
Lavardin
Villerfol
t-Laurent-
Lancé
en-G.
Pray
ay-
BLOIS
Orchaise
cher
Chouzy
Négron
Chambon
ère
Mesland
nt
Neuville
Saint-Palais
aillé
Le Sentier
Saint-Martin-des-Champs
ou
Parçay-M.
Bourges
nay
Sept Dormants
Brenecay
TOURS
Le Louroux
MARMOUTIER
N.D.-des-Eaux
Semblançay
Crozon-sur-Vauvre
Aigurande
Soudari

and size of donations declined, administrative responsibilities probably continued to grow. Endowed anniversary masses, which became
especially popular toward the end of the twelfth century, required
new kinds of record keeping. Dispersed modest gifts complicated the
problems of administration, and they frequently needed defending in
court.[38]

There was a significant difference of scale between the "empires" of
Cluny and Marmoutier in the tenth century and those of the twelfth.
The monks of the later period were confronted with a much more
extensive problem of holding the system together and instilling a
sense of community in those monks who resided at the outlying
posts, often far from the mother house. It was difficult for the community to serve as a "school of virtue," a source of judgment, will,
and conscience for the monks who were scattered about in the tinier
of Marmoutier's and Cluny's enclaves. The pious Abbot Baudry may
have wished to pursue an eremitical vocation when he retired, sometime before 1033, to Marmoutier's priory at Tavant, but the twelfth-
century author of the *Deeds of the Abbey of Marmoutier* was more
concerned that men would behave like Ulrich, the irresponsible steward of the same priory.[39] Similarly, the statutes for the priories and
granges of Marmoutier, which may have been written in the twelfth
century, indicate that Marmoutier's leaders were anxious to ensure
that the priors and monks of the subject houses and granges would
continue to fulfill their liturgical duties and that they would retain
their distance—in behavior, dress, and eating habits—from the secular countryside that seemed to encroach upon them. The author of the
statutes encouraged the monks in the priories to avoid being alone,

---

regulate this unusual situation for monks—to ensure that monastic discipline would be
maintained as fully as possible. Jacques Dubois concurred that the remarkable expansion of
dispersed centers of administration (deaneries and priories) took place in the eleventh and
twelfth centuries, but he also reported that Cluny had thirty-two deaneries at the end of the
tenth century ("Vie des moines dans les prieurés du Moyen Age"). For a good discussion of
the bureaucratization of a monastery, which resulted from the growth in the number of
priories, see Johnson, *Prayer, Patronage and Power: The Abbey of la Trinité, Vendôme*, 52 ff. She
wrote that at La Trinité the number of monks holding office rose from 29 percent in the
eleventh century to 61 percent in the twelfth and that the reason for this increase was the
proliferation of priories.

38. McLaughlin, "Consorting with Saints," chap. 7; Marot and Lemaître, *Répertoire des
documents nécrologiques français*, 1:19–21; Constable, *Monastic Tithes*, 144 (on Marmoutier
defending its tithes in courts); White, *Custom, Kinship, and Gifts*, 83 (on Marmoutier's
monks spending time in court); Southern, *Western Society and the Church*, 232–36.

39. Charter of Fulk of Anjou, PL 155:482 (see Guillot, *Comte d'Anjou*, 2:C36, C77, on
the date and authenticity of this charter); *De rebus gestis in Majori monasterio*, 400. During the
abbacy of Barthelemy of Marmoutier (1063–84) there were eighteen monks at Tavant: see
Martène, *Histoire de l'abbaye de Marmoutier*, 1:429, and Bibliothèque Nationale, MS. lat.
12878, fol. 299 (copy from Marmoutier's Touraine cartulary).

because they could provoke each other "by word and example" to keep regular observances, and their company could thus provide an important antidote to the temptations of secular life.[40] Saint Benedict was apparently correct in assuming that human flesh is weak and that individuals are more likely to adhere to an ascetic way of life when they have someone nearby—not just the Divine Father—to whom they must answer for their behavior.

Just as the distance separating monks from each other expanded, so did the distance between the abbot and his charges. At home in the mother house, the abbots of Benedictine monasteries the size of Marmoutier and Cluny were consumed with administrative duties. It is thus unlikely that they continued to live up to the image of the discerning shepherd that the Benedictine *Rule* had portrayed and Odo of Cluny had attempted to emulate. Benedict's abbot was a wise teacher, a stern taskmaster, and a tender father who responded appropriately to the variety of temperaments among his monks, assisting each to achieve the level of personal piety he was capable of while at the same time providing him with an external source of conscience and authority.[41] How, though, could the abbot of a prestigious and prosperous twelfth-century house, such as Marmoutier or Cluny, carry out such intimate scrutiny and judgment? He had hundreds of monks under his immediate care and many more to account for in the deaneries and dependent priories. To keep tabs on the priories, Abbot Albert (1037–64) established a yearly chapter general of the priors of Marmoutier's dependent houses and cells (and in doing so, he anticipated the abbot of Cluny by at least sixty-eight years). But despite the annual meetings, Marmoutier's abbots needed to make frequent visits to the priories.[42]

Guests, too, intruded upon Benedictine houses, making demands

40. "Immo cum sociis sint frequenter, et vos provocent ad regulares observantias pro modulo suo, verbo pariter et exemplo, servantes cum eis honestatem et communem vitam in victu et vestitu" ("Statuts des prieurés de Marmoutier," p. 11, chap. 12, with emendations from Tours, Bibliothèque Municipale, MS. 94, fol. 39v; see also pp. 7, 8, 10). For my argument that the Tours manuscript of the statutes may represent a version from the twelfth century, see Source Appendix, I-G. In three of his statutes Peter the Venerable attempted to deal with the abuses and potential abuses in the priories. His primary strategy was to attempt to ensure that in as many cases as possible individual priories would have at least twelve monks: see Peter the Venerable, *Statuta*, 41, 42, 46, pp. 75, 78.

One example of how the countryside infringed on Marmoutier's priories is the way benefactors frequently reserved rights of procuration at the priories and employed them as virtual hunting lodges: see Gantier, "Recherches sur les possessions et les prieurés de l'abbaye de Marmoutier," 54(1964): 17, 134–35.

41. *RB 1980*, chaps. 2, 5, pp. 18–27, 34–37.

42. *Chronicon abbatum Majoris monasterii*, 318; Martène, *Histoire de l'abbaye de Marmoutier*, 1:348; Gantier, "Recherches sur les possessions et les prieurés," 54(1964): 64; Hunt, *Cluny under Saint Hugh*, 174; Johnson, *Prayer, Patronage and Power*, 51.

on their abbots' time. The Benedictine *Rule* had indicated that abbots were supposed to eat with their guests separately from the other monks, but in an apparent effort to prevent the abbot's loss of contact with his flock both Marmoutier and Cluny decided that he should always eat in the main refectory with the other monks.[43] By breaking with one specific command of the *Rule* these abbeys were attempting to salvage its essence, which rested so firmly on the bond between abbot and community. Their efforts, however, point to the strains of success. Because of their stellar reputations, both Marmoutier and Cluny had a steady stream of important ecclesiastical and secular visitors, among them popes and kings. Their abbots may have continued to eat with the monks, but they could not ignore the presence of such eminent visitors. In the course of the twelfth century, moreover, the abbots of Marmoutier and Cluny built separate sleeping quarters for themselves and showed an ever-growing propensity for ceremonialism and display. As a result, the gap between them and their monks widened.[44]

Finally, because abbeys like Marmoutier and Cluny had international reputations, their abbots played key roles in ecclesiastical and political affairs, which pulled them away from their internal responsibilities. Similarly, because the affairs of a monastery were now tied to larger ecclesiastical politics, its abbot had to spend time in Rome and at church councils defending his house and its rights. Marmoutier's own struggle for exemption, for instance, compelled various abbots to make trips to Rome and to church councils.[45]

The *Deeds of the Abbey of Marmoutier*, written between 1137 and the

43. Hunt, *Cluny under Saint Hugh*, 49–50; Peter the Venerable, *Letters of Peter the Venerable*, 28, vol. 1, p. 74; Guibert, Abbot of Gembloux, "Epistola," 609. See also Peter the Venerable, *Statuta*, 23, p. 60, for evidence of frequent visitors at Cluny.

44. Abbot Hugh of Cluny slept in the common dormitory, but a separate abbot's house was built in the twelfth century. Hugh maintained simplicity, but later abbots cultivated display. At Marmoutier, Abbot Robert of Blois (1165–76) built a separate chapel and sleeping quarters for the abbot, and the burial of Abbot Hugh of Rochecorbon (1210–27) was carried out "more solemnly" than that of any previous abbot: see Hunt, *Cluny under Saint Hugh*, 49 ff.; *Chronicon abbatum Majoris monasterii*, 321, 326. Penelope Johnson also traces an evolution at La Trinité of Vendôme during the eleventh and twelfth centuries from the image of the abbot as father to that of the abbot as lord (*Prayer, Patronage and Power*, 50–51).

45. Hunt, *Cluny under Saint Hugh*, 52. Marmoutier's abbots attended the following church councils: Clermont in 1095, Poitiers in 1105, Loudun in 1109, Reims in 1130, and Tours in 1162. Moreover, in 1196 Abbot Geoffrey was one of the major guarantors in the peace settlement between Richard the Lion-Hearted and Philip Augustus: see Martène, *Histoire de l'abbaye de Marmoutier*, 1:521, 2:10, 15, 79, 125, 174; Charter of Alexander III of 1162, in *Papsturkunden in Frankreich*, n.s. 5, no. 117, pp. 206–9. In 1184 Abbot Herveus of Marmoutier was delegated by the pope to adjudicate in the dispute between the canons of Saint-Martin and the burghers of Châteauneuf: see chapter 9 at note 8.

end of the twelfth century, shows that at least one monk from that abbey attempted to address the attenuation of fraternal bonds that resulted from the growth of Marmoutier's empire and the division of labor within its walls. Like the collection of sermons, the *Deeds of the Abbey of Marmoutier* suggests that the abbey's monks were attuned to the new inward piety of the twelfth century. But this text also represents an attempt to create an adhesive that would bind together the dispersed community, whose existence could no longer rest on coincidence of time, place, and collective activity. That adhesive was the internal motivation of every monk.

In many ways the *Deeds of the Abbey of Marmoutier* closely resembles Peter the Venerable's *De miraculis,* and in both collections we can detect a preoccupation with contrition, purgatory, and the fate of the individual soul.[46] But whereas Peter the Venerable's stories served a variety of rhetorical purposes for a variety of audiences—nobles who might contemplate seizing monastic property, heretics, monks of Cluny—the author of Marmoutier directed his message almost exclusively to his fellow monks there. And whereas Peter the Venerable wanted to demonstrate the efficacy of the sacraments in general, the author of Marmoutier focused, in his prologue and in ten of his fifteen stories, on monastic assistance for the dead and dying.[47] For Marmoutier's author, assistance to the dead and dying was at the heart of his abbey's spirituality and was central to its sense of community as well.

In its focus on the salvation of the soul and its message that Marmoutier and its patron saint could expedite that salvation, the *Deeds of the Abbey of Marmoutier* was a traditional text. Since the tenth century the monks of both Marmoutier and Cluny had attempted to turn the minds of men and women to the fate of their souls and to convince them that favorable relationships with the monks and their saint would provide the best assurance for a comfortable afterlife. Like earlier works from Cluny, the *Deeds of the Abbey of Marmoutier* depicted the visitations of dead men who wanted, and indeed received, vicarious assistance from the monks of those two houses.[48]

In the earlier works, however, the horror of the Day of Judgment

46. *De rebus gestis in Majori monasterio;* Peter the Venerable, *De miraculis, PL* 189:851–954.

47. *De rebus gestis in Majori monasterio,* paragraphs 1–6, 8–11, 16, pp. 395–401, 404. The printed edition has sixteen stories (paragraphs 2–17), but paragraph 15 is not in the twelfth-century manuscript, Charleville 117, so I have not included it in the total.

48. For examples from Marmoutier in the tenth century, see introduction to part 2 at notes 10 and 11. On Cluny, see above at note 5 and Heath, *Crux Imperatorum Philosophia,* 98 ff. On ghost stories from Cluny, see Neiske, "Vision und Totengedenken," 164 ff.

loomed much larger than it did in the twelfth century. There is no discussion at all, in the *Deeds of the Abbey of Marmoutier,* of the possibility of damnation. Purgation, in this world or in the next, is the only punishment at issue. Demons are so powerless, or perhaps we should say men are so powerful, that a mere declaration by a dying monk that he places his faith in the cross can cause the devil and his entourage to "vanish like smoke."[49] Even Saint Martin's power recedes as the personal faith of the individual becomes more efficacious. In their tenth-century charters the monks of Marmoutier had described the passive hope that its benefactors could place in Saint Martin, who had the ability to "snatch" their souls "from the infernal flames."[50] Martin, in tenth-century depictions, was a symbol of charity and mercy. Nevertheless, the word "mercy" attained much more prominence in twelfth-century writings, where it was directly associated with the individual believer's decisive acts of faith and contrition. Hence, though Martin remained, in the *Deeds of the Abbey of Marmoutier,* a symbol of God's mercy and a special tutor and assistant of Marmoutier's monks, the believing monk himself (like Count Odo, in the third legend about him) now effected his own soul's salvation. This new focus on the will—not only of the individual who sought salvation but also of the community of other individuals who assisted him—set the *Deeds of the Abbey of Marmoutier* apart from tenth- and early eleventh-century monastic literature.

In its opening frame the *Deeds of the Abbey of Marmoutier* briefly addresses Marmoutier's reputation, which rests on the abbey's efficacy in assisting the souls of sinners who are "not yet worthy to possess the joys of the heavenly kingdom."[51] That reputation places Marmoutier on a par with other great monasteries of the age. Indeed, in an effort to enhance Marmoutier's comparative status, the author opens his own collection of stories with two he has borrowed from other authors: from Guibert's *Life of Pope Leo IX,* an anecdote about a

49. *De rebus gestis in Majori monasterio,* 6, p. 397.
50. See introduction to part 2 at note 11. See also Odo of Cluny, "Sermo de combustione basilicae beati Martini," *PL* 133:748; "Hymnus de Sancti Martini archiepiscopi," *PL* 133:515; "Hymnus in Honorem S. Martini," *PL* 133:516. In these works Odo developed the idea that Martin's cape (which he originally shared with a poor man in an act of charity) could clothe his devotees on the Day of Judgment, providing them with "a garment of justice" so that their "shamefulness" would not "be revealed before the highest judge." For the evidence that the "Sermo de combustione" was written by Odo, see Source Appendix, II-A.
51. "Animas caelestis regni gaudia nondum meritas possidere" (*De rebus gestis in Majori monasterio,* in Charleville 117, fol. 108). The phrase is in a passage borrowed from Guibert, *Vita Leonis IX papae,* in *Acta sanctorum,* April, 2:662.

troop of ghosts who made a penitential pilgrimage from Marmoutier to the abbey of Farfa, near Rome; and from Ralph Glaber, a story about an African anchorite who declared to a traveler from Marseilles that one abbey in the entire Roman world exceeded all the others in liberating souls: "For the frequent offering of the vivifying sacrifice thrives so greatly there that hardly a day goes by in which such commerce does not snatch souls from the power of the evil demons." Ralph had written these words about Cluny; the author of Marmoutier found it convenient to apply them instead to his own abbey.[52]

In his commentary on these two stories, the author linked Marmoutier's efficacy to one of its traditional sources of legitimacy—the patronage of Saint Martin, who "by means of the merits of his humility" was able to obtain absolution for sinners who turned to the abbey of Marmoutier for assistance. But the author also gave credit to the "zeal" of the brothers, who performed private masses almost continuously.[53] Thus the abbey's external reputation depended in part on the will of each monk to maintain it.

Having dealt briefly with Marmoutier's intercessory service for the world at large, the author turned to the subject of most of his stories—the monks' task of assisting each other in their quest for a peaceful hereafter. The author's underlying message was that the monks actualized their community by fulfilling, through vicarious acts of penance, the biblical injunction to "bear one another's burdens" (Gal. 6:2). They could fulfill this command only if each of them was endowed with sufficient motivation and compassion. Deeds alone were not enough—they needed to be grounded in the proper attitude.

52. "Tanta enim viget in eo vivifici sacrificii frequens immolatio ut nulla pene dies pertranseat in qua non de potestate malignorum demonum tale commercium animas eripiat" (*De rebus gestis in Majori monasterio,* in Charleville 117, fol. 107, and Bibliothèque Nationale, MS. lat. 13899); Ralph Glaber, *Historiarum libri quinque,* 5:1, p. 125. Even in one of the manuscripts of Glaber's *History* someone scratched out the word for Cluny and replaced it with "Majoris monasterii": see Ralph Glaber, *Historiarum libri,* p. 125, note, citing Bibliothèque Nationale, MS. lat. 6190. On Guibert's *Life* of Leo IX see the preceding note.

53. "Quidni enim illic votorum obtineatur effectus, ubi patrocinatur prepotens et sublimis ille sacerdos Martinus, qui humillimi magistri Iesu Christi humilis et constans imitator, maxime humilitatis meritis . . . inibi fideliter oratum venientibus obtinere potest a peccatis absolutionem? Nec incongrue etiam revelante Deo predictus heremita de studio et efficacia fratrum eiusdem monasterii circa cultum et frequentationem sacramentorum, que supra retulimus, vel vidit vel effudit . . . mos erat ipsius cenobii ut a prima aurora usque in horam prandii propter sacerdotum copiam continua missarum celebratio protraheretur" (*De rebus gestis in Majori monasterio,* p. 395, with corrections from Charleville 117, which are printed in Van der Straeten, "Recueil de miracles de S. Martin dans le manuscrit 117 de Charleville," 90).

According to the author, the monks who resided at Marmoutier in the eleventh century had possessed this attitude, and his own contemporaries at the abbey would do well to imitate their "wondrous ardor of love":

> Neither do we think that we should leave out the praiseworthy and imitable custom they observed on behalf of their dead brothers. Whenever one of them had recently died, his confessor was questioned in public regarding the penance imposed on him. And when it was heard, you would have seen the burden of the dead brother eagerly taken up with wondrous compassion by the brothers. This one seized for himself [the recitation of] psalms, this one masses, another fasts, and another disciplining with whips. Truly with a wondrous ardor of love that apostolic saying was fulfilled, "bear one another's burdens and thus you will fulfill the law of Christ." And when the dead brother had been exonerated from the imposed satisfaction he passed on, as we believe, to the place of rest and the convent procured more abundant grace.[54]

The author of the *Deeds of the Abbey of Marmoutier* reinforced his message concerning internal motivation and spiritual interdependence with stories about miraculous visions in which the monks maintained intimate contact with those in the hereafter: with Saint Martin, the personal protector of contrite monks and the corporate patron of the abbey as a whole; with angels, who came to carry away the souls of dying monks; and with dead monks who were undergoing purgatorial punishment for their sins.[55]

The efficacy of the vicarious spiritual assistance that the monks provided depended on the faith and sincerity of the one receiving it. Each had to recognize for himself the mercy of God, and each had to feel truly sorrowful for his sins. These attitudes were requisites for salvation. Indeed, as the story about a monk who disavowed the religious life at Marmoutier makes clear, they were the only requisites, even for the most depraved of sinners.

54. "Unde nec laudabilem et imitandam eorum circa fratres defunctos antiquitus observatam consuetudinem pretereundam censemus. Cum enim aliquis fratrum nuper obisset, confessor eius in communi super indicta ei penitentia inquirebatur. Qua audita, mira compassione videres certatim a fratribus defuncti fratris onus suscipi: hic psalmos, ille missas, alius ieiunia aliusque disciplinas verberum sibi rapiebat. Implebatur profecto miro caritatis ardore apostolicum illud: 'Alter alterius onera portate, et sic adimplebitis legem Christi'" (*De rebus gestis in Majori monasterio,* no. 1, p. 395, following variations in Charleville 117, which are printed in Van der Straeten, "Recueil de miracles . . . de Charleville," 90).

55. On the genre of monastic ghost stories, see Le Goff, *Birth of Purgatory,* 177–81, 300–310; Schmitt, "Revenants dans la société féodale"; and Neiske, "Vision und Totengedenken."

The former monk, who served as a secular priest after he left Marmoutier, had become well "versed" in the ways of the world.[56] He accumulated much wealth, and he lived with a concubine who bore him several children. His soul might have been lost, except that God's kindness "wondrously . . . and mercifully" awoke him from his stupor.[57] The concubine and children died, the renegade monk fell ill, and at last, "with great contrition of the heart" he "returned to himself."[58] Thinking at first that it was too late to make amends, the sinner cried abundant tears, but then he gained confidence, exclaiming to himself, "I believe and I have faith that He who mercifully supported the thief who confessed to him on the cross will not reject me, who am also truly penitent."[59] He then called the monks of Marmoutier to his side, asked to be flogged with whips as an appropriate form of satisfaction for his sins, and requested that they dress him, for a second time, in the monastic habit.

After these things had been done according to his wishes, the sick man had a vision in which the devil proclaimed to Saint Martin and Saint Benedict that they had unjustly accepted into their midst a man whose "tears of only one hour" followed upon a long life of sin.[60] But Martin replied with the favorite phrase of twelfth-century theologians that "in whatever hour the sinner sighs, all his iniquities will be handed over to oblivion."[61] The saint then absolved the man, exhorting him to sin no more. He told him that he would recover from his illness and return to Marmoutier, where he should carry out whatever discipline of satisfaction his master should impose on him, because his death was not far off. The sinner did as he was told, and though he saw the devil once again, lurking near his deathbed, he died with a joyful face, confidently proclaiming, "I have protectors against you—Martin, the Miracle Worker [*signipotens*], and Father Bene-

56. "Mundana non mediocriter callebat prudentia" (*De rebus gestis in Majori monasterio*, no. 11, p. 400).

57. "Cum benignitas divina mirabiliter eum simul et misericorditer visitavit" (*De rebus gestis in Majori monasterio*, no. 11, p. 400, with corrections from Charleville 117, fols. 117–117v).

58. "Tunc demum in se reversus . . . cum magna cordis contritione excogitare cepit" (*De rebus gestis in Majori monasterio*, no. 11, p. 400, with corrections from Charleville 117, fol. 117v).

59. "Credo enim et confido, qui et latronem in cruce se confitentem misericorditer suscepit, me quoque veraciter poenitentiam non abjiciet" (*De rebus gestis in Majori monasterio*, no. 11, p. 401, with corrections from Charleville 117, fol. 117v).

60. "Unius horae lacrymas" (*De rebus gestis in Majori monasterio*, no. 11, p. 401).

61. "In quacumque hora peccator ingemuerit, omnes iniquitates ejus oblivioni tradentur" (*De rebus gestis in Majori monasterio*, no. 11, p. 401, with corrections from Charleville 117, fol. 118v).

dict. . . . 'I do not fear what man will do to me' [Heb. 13:16]."[62]

In a number of ways this story resembles the third legend about Count Odo of Blois. Both stories distinguish the worldly reputation and outer appearance of these sinners from their sinful state: Odo was one of those insincere believers "who confess to know God, but who nevertheless deny God with their actions"; the renegade monk "carried himself guiltily before God . . . but honestly before men."[63] Both stories portray a fight between Saint Martin and the devil over the soul of the sinner, and both refer to the doctrine of true inner contrition by citing the twelfth-century phrase about the efficacy of the sinner's sigh.[64] In both stories the emphasis is on God's mercy and Martin, the patron of Marmoutier, serves as its agent. Finally, both stories indicate that though contrition qualifies one for God's mercy and removes the threat of damnation, the sinner is still required to make amends, either by undergoing the discipline of satisfaction in this life or by suffering purgatorial punishment in the next.

Despite the similarities between the two stories, however, one salient aspect of the anecdote about the renegade monk distinguishes it from the legend about Count Odo and highlights the central characteristics of the *Deeds of the Abbey of Marmoutier:* Odo's legend dealt with spiritual interdependence among laypeople as well as between laypeople and monks; the story about the renegade monk, by contrast, like another seven of the fifteen stories in the same collection, dealt exclusively with interdependence among monks.[65] The central message of the *Deeds of the Abbey of Marmoutier* was that Marmoutier could provide—as long as the monks continued to will it—a desirable and safe environment for the dying and the dead. Those in the secular realm could best reap the benefits of the abbey by undergoing conversion and joining its ranks. Even a last-minute conversion was better than none. Indeed, the story about the renegade monk was not the only one concerning the custom of joining the abbey *ad succurren-*

62. "Protectores habeo contra te. Adest Martinus signipotens, adest et pater Benedictus, non timeo quid faciat mihi homo" (*De rebus gestis in Majori monasterio,* no. 11, p. 401). The epithet "signipotens" was apparently applied exclusively to Saint Martin: see Du Cange, *Glossarium,* 7:483.

63. "Confitentur se nosse Deum, factis autem negant" (*Liber de restructione Majoris monasterii,* 356); "etsi coram Deo culpabiliter . . . coram hominibus tamen honeste se agebat" (*De rebus gestis in Majori monasterio,* no. 11, p. 400, with corrections from Charleville 117, fol. 117). Like the author of the anonymous sermons from Marmoutier, the author of the *De rebus* emphasized that only God can know the true inner man: see above at notes 35–37.

64. See chapter 4 at note 33.

65. *De rebus gestis in Majori monasterio,* nos. 2–5, 9, 10, 16, pp. 395–97, 399–400, 404. Only the prologue and no. 12 mention spiritual relations with outsiders.

dum in order to die as a monk. The author also described a layman and two other priests who donned the religious habit as their final hour approached.[66] Within the haven of the abbey, the author indicated, "Father" Benedict and Martin—the abbey's "guardian" and "provider"—offered special protection.[67] Clothed in Marmoutier's habit, flagrant sinners could make appropriate satisfaction for their sins, and as the ghost of a dead monk made clear, it was better to make such satisfaction on this side of the grave than on the next, since even the greatest mortal punishment would seem light compared with the purgatorial fires.[68] Finally, and most important of all, Marmoutier's monks provided each other with assurance, vicarious strength, and spiritual assistance during illnesses, at the moment of death, and as long as help was still needed after death. The man who joined the abbey ad succurrendum gained spiritual power by dying in that holy place, surrounded by the other monks (see plate 4). At the critical moment when the soul left the body, the prayers of the other monks would "confirm" the strength of the convert's own faith and even chase away demons. And after the convert's death his brothers would do for him what they would do for any member of the abbey—they would complete whatever satisfaction he still owed for his sins.[69]

The purpose of the *Deeds of the Abbey of Marmoutier* was to arouse a sense of obligation in the monks, so that they would continue to provide this assistance to the dead and dying. The author told ghost stories to heighten the monks' awareness of their interdependence, and he appealed to the emotions to strengthen the complex network of relationships that constituted the community. He attested, moreover, that the bonds of community did not end at death's door.

The first emotion the author appealed to was fear—fear that those who did not live up to their responsibility to others would know not

66. *De rebus gestis in Majori monasterio,* nos. 5, 6, 8, pp. 396–99.

67. "Pater," "tutor," "provisor" (*De rebus gestis in Majori monasterio,* nos. 10 and 6, pp. 401 and 397). Despite the emphasis on Martin's role in delivering and guarding God's mercy, the author of the *De rebus* gives him epithets that underscore his power and formal role ("signipotens," "tutor") rather than the name father, which is applied to him in the anonymous sermons (see below, chap. 6 at notes 45 ff.). One possible explanation for this attention to Martin's power is that the *De rebus* was a work of propaganda meant to kindle the zeal of the monks, and an emphasis on Martin's fatherhood would have enhanced the monks' confidence rather than admonishing them to do better. Also, even when he is delivering mercy Martin must protect his tutees from the devil, and his power is thus required.

68. *De rebus gestis in Majori monasterio,* no. 8, p. 399.

69. "Quantum prosit fides propria, probat aliena" (*De rebus gestis in Majori monasterio,* no. 3, p. 396, with corrections from Charleville 117, fol. 109v).

PLATE 4. Floor of the chapel of Saint Benedict. The decorated floor of Marmoutier's infirmary chapel (dedicated in 1162 and destroyed in 1699; see Lelong, "Etudes sur l'abbaye de Marmoutier," 290, 301) gave visual expression to assistance for the dead and dying, which held a central place in the spirituality of Marmoutier. The life-sized image of a dying monk was flanked by one monk making a gesture of mourning and a second praying for him. In accordance with Saint Martin's assertion that "it is not decent for a Christian to die in any way except lying on ashes" (Sulpicius Severus, *Epistolae*, 3:14), monks were apparently placed on this image, which had been covered with ashes from Ash Wednesday. The inscription read (here I follow Dom Martène's notes [*Histoire*, 2:124] rather than the slightly different inscription depicted by Housseau): "Cum dabor exire de mundo, jussus obire, Hic peto finire, precor hinc mihi detur abire" ("When, bidden to die, I am given to exit from this world, I desire to meet my end here, I pray that I may be able to leave from here").

The style of the floor was Gothic, perhaps of the thirteenth century. On the custom of dying on ashes, see Gougaud, *Anciennes coutumes claustrales*, 81. I thank Walter Caen of Yale University for this advice concerning the date of the floor. Bibliothèque Nationale, Collection Housseau, MS. 5, fol. 139. Photograph courtesy Bibliothèque Nationale.

only God's mercy but also his judgment. That judgment would be meted out to individuals, not—as in many tenth- and early eleventh-century monastic stories—to the community as a whole.[70] All the monks owed service to each other and to the dead, but each was responsible, as an individual, for bearing his share of the burden. And the dead themselves could demand and administer punishment for those who had been judged irresponsible in meeting their collective responsibilities.[71]

Two ghosts who visited Abbot Bartholomew (1063–84), for example, sent a warning to those monks who were not "zealous enough for their dead brothers," that each of them owed a debt to the dead, which he had to pay off while he was alive. If any of them failed to do so, the suffrages performed for him after his death would benefit not him, but the dead to whom he was still indebted.[72] Each monk ran a personal risk of incurring punishment, each accumulated or paid off his own debt to the dead. And each had to consider the possibility that punishment would come not from a distant God, but from a brother who had eaten in the same refectory, slept in the same dormitory, prayed in the same oratory. Indeed, it is significant that the ghosts in the *Deeds of the Abbey of Marmoutier* tended to visit brothers who knew them and to come alone or in pairs rather than in large groups.[73]

Ulrich, the monk who served as the steward of Tavant, encountered two such brothers. Apparently Ulrich had yielded to the temptations of a life of relative independence while he was living at the priory of Tavant. He thought no one would know, so he cheated his dead brothers of Marmoutier of some of the income that had been designated for the benefit of their souls. Ulrich's living brothers were

70. For an example of collective punishment, see Odo of Cluny, "Sermo de combustione," *PL* 133:729–49.
71. There were some precedents in ninth- and tenth-century ghost stories for the theme of the punishment of those who neglected to live up to their obligations to the dead: see Neiske, "Vision und Totengedenken," 153, 161. I am not aware, however, of any works that focused exclusively on relationships among monks of the same abbey or that showed the same concern for a sense of monastic community.
72. "Qui defunctis dum vivit quod debet non exsolvit, quod ei defuncto ab aliis exsolvetur, non in eius, sed defunctorum proficiet utilitatem" (*De rebus gestis in Majori monasterio*, no. 2, p. 395, with corrections from Charleville 117, fol. 109v).
73. *De rebus gestis in Majori monasterio:* in nos. 2, 4, 9, and 10 one or two dead monks visit an individual monk in some kind of intimate setting; in no. 8 a secular priest who had become a monk at Marmoutier before he died visited the priest who had succeeded him at his post, again in an intimate setting. In all these cases except no. 10, the author makes it clear that the living men recognized the dead men, and in no. 10 recognition seems implicit to the story. In nos. 11 and 17 Saint Martin is accompanied by "a troop" of monks, but in these stories the theme is not the encounter between the living and the dead but Martin's and the saints' assistance or glorious presence.

not aware of what he was doing, but his dead brothers knew, and they demanded their just deserts:

> And therefore it happened that two brothers who had been freed from the body appeared to him in a dream and rebuked him with very harsh words for this injury to the dead. But he was hardened and considered what he had seen as nothing, as if it were a dream. Appearing to him once more, they announced that punishment for his contempt was imminent. Nonetheless, he remained uncorrected. Having returned a third time, they gave him so many floggings that he remained in bed for half a year tortured by the most severe pains. In time he recuperated, but just barely, and he was never able to recover his original vigor.[74]

Lest the other monks of Marmoutier should miss the point of Ulrich's story, the author went on to address them directly: "From this you should infer, reader, what those defrauding their obligations [*debita*] to the dead can expect in the future punishment, if someone who had not yet departed from the temporal life deserved to be flogged in this way."[75]

The ghostly visitations to Bartholomew and Ulrich served to elicit the monks' sense of obligation to all their brothers. This obligation was more intimate than that owed to outsiders, but perhaps, in an age when Marmoutier and its empire had become so large, it was not intimate enough. In other stories the author appealed to more personal relationships, suggesting that each monk was at the center of his own community, which grew out of his special ties with other individuals. Those ties could be familial, affective, or contractual.

One dead monk appeared to his confessor seeking reassurance that his confession had been effective and that he was indeed freed from the penalty for his sins. The confessor responded that he himself would answer for the dead man on the Day of Judgment, and at that

74. "Contigit igitur ut ei dormienti duo fratres a corpore soluti per somnium apparerent, et pro hac defunctorum iniuria durissimis eum verbis increparent. Induratus ille quasi somnium nichili pendit quod viderat. Cui denuo apparentes illi pro contemptu vindictam sibi imminere denuntiant. At ille nichilominus incorrectus permansit. Tercio reversi tantis eum verberibus affecerunt ut per annum dimidium lectulo decubans gravissimis doloribus torqueretur. Vix tandem convaluit, quamvis pristinam corporis alacritatem nullatenus recuperare potuerit" (*De rebus gestis in Majori monasterio*, no. 10, p. 400, with corrections from Charleville 117, fols. 116v–117). For similar stories about ghostly punishments, see William of Malmesbury, *De gestis regum Anglorum*, 3:293, ed. Stubbs, 2:345–46, and Othloh of Saint Emmerman, "Liber visionum," chap. 16, PL 146:371–72.

75. "Hinc conice lector quid in futuro vindicte mortuorum debita defraudantibus immineat si sic flagellari meruit qui nondum temporali decessarat vita" (*De rebus gestis in Majori monasterio*, p. 400, with corrections from Charleville 117, fol. 117).

point demons who had been demanding the dead monk's punishment disappeared.[76] The ghost of a usurious priest who had joined Marmoutier ad succurrendum appeared to complain that a mendacious business associate was prolonging his purgatorial punishment. That man, who had borrowed money from the dead usurer, had promised that within a year of the latter's death he would donate to Marmoutier the full amount of the loan. The year came and went, but the promise—sealed with the kiss of peace on a repentant sinner's deathbed— had not been kept.[77] Finally, in a third story, a monk who had been sent to England (apparently to one of Marmoutier's priories there) by Marmoutier's abbot appeared on the day of his death to his brother by birth, also a monk at Marmoutier, asking that "with the intuition of brotherly love" he announce the death to the other monks and request that they perform the office of the dead.[78]

In this final story the living monk was stirred by the request of his dead brother, but he hesitated to announce the death, assuming that no one would believe his vision and that the monks in England would eventually send the proper written announcement. Still, the author suggested, God worked to reinforce the proper bureaucratic process.[79] Miraculously, a messenger arrived from England with the written announcement of the death, and the monks all assumed that it was the anniversary of the monk's death. At that point the brother informed the others of the miracle that had just occurred, convincing them that this was the very day of his brother's death.

These stories about broken promises and anxious requests that obligations be met despite the obstacles of time and distance point to the incremental changes that had been transforming the monastic community since the middle of the eleventh century. Like the secular world around it, Marmoutier had changed from an intimate community or set of communities into a complex society, held together not by concrete ties of kinship and dependence, not by exchanges of service, not by physical proximity of time and space, but by abstract concepts, bureaucratic organization, written documents, promises,

---

76. *De rebus gestis in Majori monasterio*, no. 4, p. 396.

77. *De rebus gestis in Majori monasterio*, no. 8, pp. 398–99.

78. "Germanae dilectionis intuitu" (*De rebus gestis in Majori monasterio*, no. 9, pp. 399–400).

79. "Dissimulabat tamen adhuc, reputans quod si vere obisset, fratres cum quibus moratus fuerat eius obitum nuntiare eis non different. Estimabat enim non facile sibi credi potuisse maxime a viris qui somniorum imaginationibus non satis movebant" (*De rebus gestis in Majori monasterio*, Charleville 117, fol. 116). The printed edition (9, p. 400) says the dead monk's brother did make the announcement, but the officers of the abbey replied: "Non est . . . consuetudinis nostrae, ut alicui debitum exsolvamus nisi breve allatum fuerit."

contracts, and money.[80] A monk continued to belong to Marmoutier not because he lived within its walls and physically engaged with the other monks in its tangible round of prayers and meals, but because his name, inscribed on a piece of parchment in England, could be carried over land and sea to the mother house, which would then fulfill its obligations to his departed soul. A piece of property, such as that at Tavant, belonged to Marmoutier even though the abbot could not physically survey it regularly. Rather, the written record of its administration and the income from its crops could be transported across a considerable distance to the mother house. Money and writing stretch out our relations; they connect us to those who are far afield and make possible bonds and contacts between individuals who are not present to one another and may never meet.[81] Indeed, it is significant that one of the most salient features of the twelfth-century spiritual revival, the cult of monastic friendship, was characterized by written vows of "intimate" association and commitment and that such vows could be made by men who never met face to face.[82]

Money and written records are the prerequisites for bureaucratic organization and abstract community. But in a world in which they

80. For a similar discussion of the rise of abstract relations in this period, see Marvin Becker, *Medieval Italy*. On the increased role of written records, see Clanchy, *From Memory to Written Record,* and Stock, *Implications of Literacy,* 3–10.

81. The role of money and written records in holding together a monastic empire was already evident when Ulrich wrote his custumal of Cluny about 1083. Although a simple transport of agricultural produce tied the closest priories and deaneries to the mother house, those that were too far away sent money: "His . . . villis quae tam longe sunt positae ut nec vinum nec annona . . . possit ad nos pervenire, ibidem venditur, et pretium camerario defertur" (Ulrich of Cluny, *Antiquiores consuetudines,* 3:11, PL 149:751. A charter from Marmoutier's priory of Laval (ca. 120 km from Marmoutier) says that Marmoutier's priories also sent money to the mother house: see Gantier, "Recherches sur les possessions et prieurés de l'abbaye de Marmoutier," 55(1965): 68.

Written records, *Breves,* that were sent around to the mother house and the priories and deaneries to announce the death of a brother provided the mechanism that held the monastic system together spiritually: see Ulrich of Cluny, *Antiquiores consuetudines,* 3:30–33, PL 149:775–77; *Antiquae consuetudines Majoris monasterii,* fol. 109v; Marot and Lemaître, *Répertoire des documents nécrologiques,* 1:20. On the transformation of Cluny into a money economy in the generation after Ulrich, see Duby, "Budget de l'abbaye de Cluny entre 1080 et 1155." See also, on the effects of writing (the loss of the association of words with actuality and presence), Ong, *Presence of the Word.*

I do not mean to suggest that writing and money had not existed and been used in the earlier period; indeed, written documents—*libri memoriales*—made possible the numerous bonds that bound Carolingian and Cluniac monasteries to the laity through the obligation of intercessory prayers for the dead. I am suggesting, instead, that as administrative and bureaucratic organization became more sophisticated, written documentation and liquid wealth were used more and became more necessary functionally, not only for the monastery's external relations, but also for its internal life.

82. Morris, *Discovery of the Individual;* McGuire, *Friendship and Community: The Monastic Experience.*

were becoming increasingly necessary, it was often difficult to have faith that promises would be kept, obligations honored. The author of the *Deeds of the Abbey of Marmoutier* apparently sensed this problem of faith and was perplexed by it as well. He suggested that the newer forms of association could be reinforced by older, more concrete, ties such as those of kinship. His description of the appeal to the "brotherly" love between two monks who were also related by blood calls to mind that many new forms of business association—partnerships, companies, banks—were built upon ties of kinship.[83] In a brave new world of long-distance trade, risk, and abstract association, these older, more organic relations might reinforce abstract ties, thereby ensuring that promises would be kept. In the same story about the blood brothers, however, the monastic author also offered some reassurance that the abbey's bureaucratic system would work. The appearance of the divine messenger, who bore the necessary written document, suggested that though Marmoutier's monks might end up dying in England they could be confident that they still belonged to Marmoutier and that God himself was working to hold this detached community together.

The story about the two brothers appealed to and attempted to strengthen a sense of faith—faith that somehow this system, however abstract, however extended, was going to work. In other stories, though, the author's rhetorical aim was not to incite faith but to inculcate guilt, to mold the monks into the kinds of individuals who would themselves uphold this system because they were trustworthy.

Trustworthiness was a central problem in this new world of detached relationships. Why should a man join Marmoutier ad succurrendum, thus entrusting both his property and his soul to the monks, and why should a creditor lend out money if, in this world of greater independence, debtors could escape without making their payments? If abstract relationships were to take hold and flourish, men and women in both the secular and the monastic worlds needed the proper conscience, the sense that even when no one was present the eye of justice and the will of an associate would still prevail.[84] Belief in purgatory and stories about returning ghosts could help create a sense that sanctions were at work to enforce this new system of rela-

---

83. Lopez, *Commercial Revolution of the Middle Ages*, 74–75; Herlihy, *Medieval Households*, 89 ff.

84. The closest parallel to my discussion here is that of R. Howard Bloch, who argues that in the twelfth century interiority served the purposes of the centralizing monarchy, which needed to create self-governing individuals (*Medieval French Literature and Law*, 223–48). Becker sees an association between interiority and commercial culture, but he does not explain it (*Medieval Italy*, passim).

tionships. Those beliefs and stories conveyed the message that partnerships, debts, and promises would be carried over and upheld beyond the threshold of death. The bonds of community, affection, and
association between the living and the dead helped strengthen and
reinforce the bonds of community, affection, and association among
the living.

The ghost stories from Marmoutier indicate that its monks were
interested both in inner motivation and in emotional bonds. It would
be misleading, however, to assume that these concerns simply paralleled the spirituality of the new religious orders. Marmoutier's monks
were searching for, or attempting to mold, more self-conscious individuals, but they were still much more deeply entrenched in feudal
society and in the ritual life of the older Benedictines than were the
new monks.

Even the language of the ghost stories is more literal and concrete
than the lyricism of, say, Cistercian mystical writing. Like the authors
of epics, the author of Marmoutier's ghost stories employed few
metaphors or figures of speech.[85] His stories could move the monks
emotionally, but their persuasive force lay in their concrete realism,
not in the emotional or poetic power of their language. A graphic
description of the changes in a monk's appearance, for example, communicated the intensity of his struggle with invisible demons: "His
eyes swelled with bloody veins and offered, as they twisted around, a
horrible appearance. His distorted mouth vomited forth foam colored
with blood, while his limbs enjoyed no rest."[86] Passages like this
certainly evoke emotional response, but they retain a simplicity and
directness in their depiction of inner experience. The author alludes to
subjective experience only through external signs. Bitter tears and
sighs signify sincere contrition, weeping signifies despair, shaking
signifies fear.[87] This is the kind of language that came to predominate
in the exempla—edifying tales that communicated the church's moral
lessons to the laity.[88] Such language remained much closer to the
logic and psychology of oral culture than did the metaphorical language of the Cistercians and of romance literature.

85. Bloch, *Etymologies and Genealogies*, 101, 116.
86. "Oculi venis intumescunt sanguineis, et versati terribilem praebent intuitum. Os
distortum in partes spumas sanguine infectas evomit, cum membra quidem reliqua nulla
quiete fruantur" (*De rebus gestis in Majori monasterio*, no. 5, p. 397, with corrections from
Charleville 117, fol. 111v).
87. *De rebus gestis in Majori monasterio*, nos. 8, 11, pp. 398–99, 401.
88. On the genre and its realism, see Brémond, Schmitt, and Le Goff, "*Exemplum*,"
esp. 79–80.

In its approach to emotional bonds, as in its language, the *Deeds of the Abbey of Marmoutier,* like other literature from Marmoutier, differed from that of the newer religious orders. Like the members of the new orders, the monks of Marmoutier were interested in a spirituality that emphasized the "wondrous ardor of love." In their actual discussions of relationships, however, the monks of Marmoutier did not go beyond the insights of the earlier monastic tradition of friendship; they did not, like the Cistercian Aelred of Rievaulx, distinguish the special relationships among intimate friends from generalized Christian charity.[89]

Nevertheless there were important similarities, both in content and in intent, between the treatment of relationships in Marmoutier's ghost stories and the one we find in the twelfth-century cult of friendship. In both cases we can detect attempts to reinforce the new community with personal bonds. Marmoutier's author, however, probably focused more narrowly on the community of Marmoutier and its empire than did many of the others. Aelred of Rievaulx's literature on friendship tended to address the monks in his own abbey, but Cistercians as well as others could take vows of friendship—which entailed obligations of prayer—with men they had never seen. The intimacy of daily contact was not present in these cases, but the intimacy of mutual intellectual and spiritual concerns, which could be shared through letters, took its place.[90] Unlike the author of the *Deeds of the Abbey of Marmoutier,* the most self-conscious men of the day explored a form of intimacy that took place on an intellectualized, nonsensory level. Indeed, it appears that in many cases they embraced and extolled the emotional possibilities of detached communities that were bound together by written documents. The primary concern of the author from Marmoutier, by contrast, was to ameliorate some of the problems the more abstract social bonds created. Marmoutier's author shared with the others, however, the sense that the monastic role of "bearing one another's burdens" was now a personal responsibility that each monk assumed for those with whom he as an individual had special ties and obligations. Peter Damian even wrote a ghost story that resembles those of Marmoutier, except that it was about two monks who were joined by a pact of friendship. That pact was so effective that when the more irreproachable of the two friends died he had to undergo punishment for the sins of the other.[91]

89. McGuire, *Friendship and Community;* Fiske, *Friends and Friendship in the Monastic Tradition.*
90. Morris, *Discovery of the Individual;* Southern, *Saint Anselm and His Biographer,* 72–76.
91. Peter Damian, *Epistolae,* 8:20, PL 144:403–4.

Still very much embedded in the old world, the ghost stories of Marmoutier point to the new, and they suggest just how profoundly the older life and traditions of the countryside, the nobility, and the Benedictines could be transformed by the logic and psychology of long-distance relationships and bureaucratic organization. By the twelfth century Marmoutier was far from being a local institution with purely local ties. Itself an empire, its well-being was tied in part to its relations with two other empires—Angevin and papal. Though a landed institution, it was nevertheless an active force in the new money economy, and the management of both its properties and its intercessory function required a sophisticated organization and division of labor. Its circle of associations was greatly extended, and its contacts, even those within the monastic community, were often rendered impersonal. In this kind of world, with these kinds of activities and relationships, not only urban dwellers, not only bankers and Scholastics, but also black monks were searching for new ways to affect individual behavior and to bind people together. The monks of Marmoutier saw one avenue of approach in the appeal to the conscience, motivation, and emotions of the individual. As part 3 of this book demonstrates, however, the appeal to the individual's conscience was not the only way of dealing with the problems of complex social organization and order.

Before we turn, in that section, to a discussion of the canons of Saint-Martin, we must look at another problem the monks of Marmoutier faced in the twelfth century—the problem of preserving their past. In an age of rapid change, the abbey's links to the time of Saint Martin seemed increasingly tenuous. Nevertheless, their collective identity rested upon their inheritance from that remote past.

6

Preservation through Time:
Historical Consciousness at Marmoutier

As chapter 3 showed, the monks of Marmoutier were active participants in a widespread twelfth-century endeavor: the reconstruction and invention of the past. This was an age when "blueprints" from the past served as justifications for new claims in the present and when a consciousness of noble lineage stimulated the construction of linear histories. Like their noble patrons, the monks of Marmoutier thought of themselves as a kind of family, with origins in a remote and glorious past, and they were interested in enhancing their status and reputation in the present. Thus it is not surprising to learn that they invented legitimizing histories not only for their lay patrons but also for themselves, and that they conceptualized their collective history in ways that resembled noble family histories.

In their efforts to promote their monastery and its interests the monks of Marmoutier claimed that the abbey's status and privileges had been established at the time of its founding by Saint Martin. Nevertheless, in the twelfth century their heightened historical consciousness brought the monks face to face with the disturbing knowledge that the links between their own time and the archetypal age of the founder were tenuous. The exaggerated memory of the Viking destruction of Marmoutier and the belief that after the destruction secular canons had come to replace the monks of the abbey suggested that there was no continuity in Marmoutier's history—that whatever tradition Saint Martin established in the fourth century had not necessarily survived into the late eleventh and twelfth centuries. This problem of discontinuity was exacerbated because the monks of Marmoutier did not possess Martins' relics. They could not point to his physical presence—a tangible remnant from the past—as evidence that their institutional tradition had survived the calamities of the intervening centuries.

These problems contributed to a sense of historical distance at

Marmoutier and stimulated an interest in constructing bridges that could span the temporal chasm separating the past from the present. It was not enough to know—or presume to know—what the golden age of Saint Martin had been like. The monks of Marmoutier wanted to prove to themselves and to others that the qualities of Martin's golden age had somehow been preserved through time. To do this, they developed four metaphors for historical continuity—the linear metaphors of spiritual and biological genealogy and the cyclical metaphors of typological repetition and seasonal renewal.[1] The monks elaborated these ideas incrementally, in four historical works produced between the late eleventh century and the early thirteenth. Their interest in a "golden age," as well as the ideas of spiritual continuity and typological repetition, had precedents in early medieval texts. Their more organic and natural ideas of biological genealogy and seasonal renewal, however, point to preoccupations and modes of thought that gained prominence in the twelfth century.

A number of historians have argued that the twelfth-century interest in the two organic metaphors resulted from a new consciousness of secular time, historical distance, and natural causation. Although this was indeed the case, the early medieval notions of typological repetition in history and of spiritual continuity through time provided some precedents for these perceptions. More important, though twelfth-century thinkers certainly became increasingly conscious of historical development, significant features distinguished their conceptions of history from our own. Monks especially—and they were the most prolific recorders of history at that time—were conservative in their attitudes toward time.[2] They emphasized *preservation* rather than change, and this conservative stance points both to their identification with an aristocratic outlook and to their monastic ideal of separation from the "secular" realm, the realm dominated by change.

An interpolated document from the end of the tenth century provides a useful starting point for examining historical writing at Marmoutier. At that time Marmoutier's inhabitants already looked to the age of Saint Martin as a golden age, and they indicated that they had successfully preserved certain aspects of that age. The tenth-century

1. It might seem that linear and cyclical conceptions of history are in conflict. As Edward Said has suggested ("On Repetition"), however, genealogical histories, while apparently linear, have an internal theme of the cyclical repetition of generations.

2. Leclercq, *Love of Learning and the Desire for God*, 190; Guenée, *Histoire et culture historique dans l'Occident médiéval*, 46–55; Southern, "Aspects of the European Tradition of Historical Writing: 4. The Sense of the Past."

document was based on an original notice from the year 912 concerning a request that Herbern, archbishop of Tours, made to Robert, count of Paris, Touraine, and Anjou (who was also the son of Robert the Strong, the lay abbot of Saint-Martin and Marmoutier and grandfather of the first Capetian king, Hugh Capet). Archbishop Herbern wanted to compensate for his losses during the Viking incursion of 903 by taking over the possessions of Marmoutier. According to the original notice, Count Robert considered granting this request, but in the end he changed his mind.[3]

The later interpolator enhanced the material from the original document with his own additions, in which the canons of Marmoutier defended the autonomy of their institution by claiming to possess papal and royal privileges that exempted Marmoutier from the jurisdiction of anyone except the king and the abbot of Saint-Martin. This stipulation—that only the king or the abbot of Saint-Martin could hold jurisdiction over Marmoutier—was an inaccurate representation of Marmoutier's actual institutional status in the ninth and tenth centuries. The author's interest in making this claim suggests that he was probably a canon who had resided at Marmoutier before 985–87 but who was writing sometime after that date. That is to say, he created his interpolated document after Odo of Blois became the proprietor of Marmoutier and introduced Cluniac monks to the abbey. The claims in the document apparently served the interests of Marmoutier's original canons, who wished to evade Odo's reforms by suggesting that Hugh Capet did not have the right to relinquish his jurisdiction over Marmoutier to Odo or to anyone else. After he became king in 987 Hugh was both king and abbot of Saint-Martin—thus, according to the interpolated charter, only he could hold jurisdiction over Marmoutier.[4]

It is difficult to imagine any other point in Marmoutier's history when this interpolated document could have been written. A number of anachronisms make it clear that the interpolator was not actually writing in 912, the date of the original notice.[5] Moreover, before Hugh Capet gave the abbey to Odo of Blois there was no need to

3. Lévêque, "Trois actes faux ou interpolés . . . en faveur de l'abbaye de Marmoutier," 55, 64, 299–300.

4. Although Marmoutier and Saint-Martin sometimes shared the same abbot in the ninth and tenth centuries, no royal or papal documents made this a requirement. Lévêque, "Trois actes faux," 64–66, 66 nn. 2, 3, 75–88, 289–305; Voigt, *Karolingische Klosterpolitik*, 97; Oury, "Reconstruction monastique dans l'Ouest," 90 n. 99. On the date of Marmoutier's reform, see the introduction to part 2.

5. The most blatant anachronism is the interpolator's assumption that the Viking incursion of 903 immediately preceded the archbishop's attempt in 912 to appropriate the abbey's possessions: Lévêque, "Trois actes faux," 64, 299–300.

claim that jurisdiction over Marmoutier belonged exclusively to the king and the abbot of Saint-Martin (and indeed it was not the case). After the abbey's reform successfully took root, the monks of Marmoutier consistently avoided lay interference in their internal governance, and thus they would have rankled at the idea that the lay abbot of Saint-Martin had jurisdiction over them. It is not clear, however, how long after 985–87 the kind of resistance represented in this charter—that of canons who wanted to return to Capetian jurisdiction—continued. In 998 the monks of Marmoutier rebelled against their Cluniac abbot, and they may have looked to the Capetian king for help, since he was the protector of Thibaud of Blois at the time. Nevertheless, Marmoutier remained a reformed abbey, and the ousting of the Cluniac abbot tied it even more closely to the comital family of Blois.[6]

The author of this document based his claims for Marmoutier's status on invented historical precedent and on the abbey's relationship with Saint Martin. Earlier emperors, kings, and popes, he claimed, had protected Marmoutier from every jurisdiction except those of the king and the abbot of Saint-Martin, and they did so out of respect for Martin:

> Stunned and confused by [Archbishop Herbern's plans to appropriate Marmoutier's lands] the flock of that monastery began to ponder and to ask how it could be possible that in modern times the regal power—so great and so long lasting—and the always special glory of lord Martin . . . could be subdued to the dominion of anyone except the king, as had always been the case, or of its own abbot. . . . "We have [the canons argued] significant commands of emperors and kings, as well as several apostolic privileges by which our place—out of veneration for our pious Father Lord Martin, who founded it—possesses special dignity and glory; and it was never subjected to any ruler except the king or its own abbot, the abbot of Saint-Martin, just as it was removed from the dominion of every bishop, except as is necessary for the ordaining of canons.[7]

6. See the introduction to part 2.

7. "Grex ejusdem monasterii stupefactus ac mente confusus ex tam inaudita hactenus ratione cogitare cepit ac dicere quomodo fieri posset ut tanta et tam longa regalis potestas et specialis semper domni Martini gloria . . . modernis temporibus alicujus dominio nisi regio, sicut semper, aut abbati proprio subderetur. . . . habemus namque non minima imperatorum et regum praecepta necnon et apostolicorum perplurima privilegia quibus hic noster locus, pro veneratione pii patris nostri domni Martini qui eum fundavit, specialem obtinet dignitatem et gloriam et numquam ab aliquo regum nisi aut regi aut proprio abbati Sancti Martini subjectus fuit, qualiter etiam ab omni praesulum est dominio nisi in quantum in ordinandis canonicis necessitas cogit ecclesiae sequestratus, cum quibus ne id fiat satis defendere possumus" (Lévêque, "Trois actes faux," 300).

In his account of Count Robert's response to these arguments, the late tenth-century author reiterated the idea that Marmoutier's status and glory were rooted in the status and glory of Saint Martin. Robert, he claimed, honored the abbey's privileges, "lest the honor and glory of such a father, which always grows in heaven and has, until now, always been kept inviolably by so many kings, fathers, and princes, should seem to diminish in some way on earth."[8]

According to these passages, Martin's saintly status flowed into the abbey; and so, conversely, did the abbey's status flow back into the saint. Any insult to the abbey was an insult to Martin's dignity. But Martin was more than a source of status for the abbey; he was also a historical actor who drafted the blueprint for Marmoutier's institutional inviolability by appointing "its own abbot, by the name of Walbert."[9] This is the earliest reference we have to Walbert, and the author's attention to—or invention of—this detail suggests that he considered it very important. Indeed, the author even asserted that Walbert's burial place, a tangible remnant from the past, was still known at Marmoutier.[10] Walbert's story demonstrated that even while Martin was bishop of Tours, Marmoutier possessed its own abbot. Thus, because it had always been the case, the abbey should remain outside "the dominion of every bishop except as is necessary for the ordaining of canons." Had Martin simultaneously presided as bishop of Tours and abbot of Marmoutier, he would have provided a legitimizing precedent for later prelates (such as Archbishop Herbern, in 912) who wished to claim dominion over the abbey; and if archbishops could extend their tendrils over Marmoutier, so could the abbot of Cluny and the count of Blois. The best way to protect Marmoutier's autonomy, this author assumed, was to demonstrate that Martin himself established its autonomy by giving it an abbot.

Like later historians at Marmoutier, this author projected into the golden age of Saint Martin rights that he desired for Marmoutier in the present. Unlike the later authors, however, he did not perceive— or at least he did not wish to represent—differences between Marmoutier as it existed in Martin's time and Marmoutier as it existed in his own time. A vague sense of identity and continuity joined the two ages. Marmoutier's privileged status was established "from the begin-

---

8. "Ne honor et gloria tanti patris quae semper crescit in celis, aliquatenus minorari videretur in terris, a tantis hactenus semper inviolabiliter conservata regibus, patribus atque principibus" (Lévêque, "Trois actes faux," 301).

9. "Martini . . . qui dum adviveret proprium ibi abbatem esse constituit, nomine Walbertum" (Lévêque, "Trois actes faux," 300).

10. "Qui nunc ibidem humatus quiescit" (Lévêque, "Trois actes faux," 300, 65 n. 1).

ning" and had remained so "ever since."[11] This author acknowledged no significant differences between Walbert, the original abbot, and Count Robert, the lay abbot in 912; no significant differences between the monks who first inhabited Marmoutier and the canons who occupied the abbey in the tenth century. And he avoided mentioning that Marmoutier and Saint-Martin could not have shared a single abbot in the time of Saint Martin, since the basilica was not built until after the saint died.

Historical distance was not an issue for this author, because he did not want to acknowledge change and decline. The idea of "reform" (which he was resisting) implies a recovery of, or return to, pristine beginnings—but as far as this author was concerned, nothing had been lost, hence nothing needed to be regained. Even the Viking invasions did not represent a break in the abbey's history: the canons who occupied the abbey in 903 simply took refuge behind the walls of Tours; and though an undesirable change would have occurred had the archbishop succeeded in subordinating the abbey to his power, that change was successfully avoided.

What this author proposed—what the resistant canons at Marmoutier apparently desired—was the preservation of the status quo as it existed at Marmoutier before 985. His strategy for achieving that end was to represent the abbey as an unchanging institution whose status had always remained exactly as Saint Martin had established it at some vague point in the past. Distance and separation from Marmoutier's point of origin would become issues, he implied, only if Count Odo of Blois and the monks from Cluny were to succeed in taking over the abbey and reforming it.

Of course Odo and the Cluniacs did reform Marmoutier, and the success of their reform helps explain some of the differences in perspective between the monks who resided at Marmoutier from the late eleventh century to the early thirteenth and the author of the tenth-century document. Unlike the earlier author, the monks of the later period looked favorably upon Marmoutier's tenth-century reform, and since they recognized that a reform had taken place, they had to acknowledge that some kind of decline preceded it. They could not ignore, therefore, the gulf that separated them from Saint Martin's age.

The monks attempted to deal with this gulf in two ways: they

---

11. "Ex priscis et ex suis etiam ipsis temporibus . . . hucusque" (Lévêque, "Trois actes faux," 300).

employed the theme of cyclical repetition to leap across it, and they created a sense of linear continuity to narrow it. In turn, their linear accounts contributed to an even greater sense of distance: the vague and compressed continuity of Marmoutier's past—the "from the beginning" and "ever since"—stretched out into a linear duration, a series that in its most fully articulated stage rendered the distance in time between Martin and themselves almost measurable.

The first of the later works about Marmoutier's past was a rudimentary history of the abbey, apparently written after the monks became entrenched in their struggle for exemption from the spiritual domination of the archbishop of Tours but before the Council of Clermont resolved the issue in the abbey's favor in 1095 (see Source Appendix, I-B). This was the work that included the first version of the story about Odo of Blois and Ermengard. The internal evidence in the history suggests that its author wanted to convince Pope Urban II or one of his legates that Marmoutier's foundation in the fourth century, and its refoundation at the end of the tenth, provided blueprints for its independent status vis-à-vis the archbishop.[12]

Like the tenth-century interpolator, the eleventh-century author supported his abbey's autonomy. The earlier author, however, took a defensive position in an attempt to block the innovations introduced by Cluny and Odo of Blois. The later author, by contrast, took the offensive: his claim that Marmoutier was exempt from the traditional jurisdictional powers of the archbishop was—whether conscious or not—an innovation. The monks at Marmoutier were inventing new rights for their abbey, but they portrayed them as traditional rights.

Not only in his claim to be preserving Marmoutier's autonomy, but also in some of his strategies, the eleventh-century author resembled the tenth-century interpolator. Both authors elaborated the known record concerning Marmoutier's original foundation; both described a recent attempt to infringe on the abbey's autonomy; and both reported that the recent attempt had ended when the aggressor was compelled to recognize Marmoutier's rights and the dignity it derived from Saint Martin.

The eleventh-century historian elaborated the record of Marmoutier's golden age by adding a prehistory to the abbey's founda-

---

12. *Narratio de commendatione Turonicae provinciae,* 302–3, 305–6, 309–14. Salmon's published edition is of a later, interpolated text. The earlier one is to be found in a twelfth-century manuscript: Charleville, Bibliothèque Municipale, MS. 117. For further discussion, and for my argument that the text in Charleville 117 dates from about 1095, see Source Appendix, I-B.

tion, which pushed its roots back from the time of Martin, who was the third bishop of Tours, to that of Gatien, its first bishop:

> Therefore we faithfully hold from ancient authors, and find in histories, that Gatien, who was the first bishop of Tours, sent by Cornelius, the twenty-second bishop of the Roman see, preached to the innumerable multitudes of all of Tours, converting them to the faith of Christ. And at that time some of these, fleeing the company of the faithless, lest their lives should be tainted by profane rites, hastened to this place, which was so secluded and remote that they desired no better solitude, and there most of them remained, carving out caves for themselves with their own hands. And when a convent of Christians had grown up there, they built a church for themselves . . . at which they all assembled at the hour of prayer . . . returning afterward to their caves, where they occupied themselves with sacred readings and divine meditations. And they are known to have held such a custom until the coming of blessed Martin.[13]

Despite the claims in this passage, it was probably Saint Martin who introduced monasticism to Gaul, and it was certainly he who founded Marmoutier.[14] Indeed, even this author did not wish to deny Martin's key position in the history of Marmoutier: Martin remained for him, as for all subsequent authors at Marmoutier, the real founder and patriarch of the abbey.

Nevertheless, the story about Gatien's followers served a useful purpose: it indicated that Marmoutier was virtually as old as the cathedral. Eleventh- and twelfth-century bishops often argued that younger institutions (such as monasteries) derived their existence from older institutions (cathedrals) and that the younger institutions participated in the apostolic tradition only through the older ones.[15]

---

13. "Itaque ab antiquis fideliter tenemus et in historiis invenimus quod a tempore beati Gatiani [Charleville 117 has Gratiani] qui primus Turonorum pontifex missus a beato Cornelio vicesimo secundo Romanae sedis antistite totius Turoniae multitudines innumeras praedicando ad fidem Christi convertit, extunc plurimi fugientes consortia perfidorum, ne vitam suam profanis eorum ritibus macularent, ad locum hunc properabant, eo quod tam secretus esset et remotus ut meliorem non desiderarent solitudinem, in quo plurimi propriis manibus cavantes sibi receptacula congrua morabantur. Cum autem conventus christianorum illic excrevisset, construxerunt sibi ecclesiam . . . ad quam omnes conveniebant ad horam orationis. . . . Postea revertentes ad suam quisque cavernulam, sacris lectionibus et meditationibus divinis occupantur, et usque ad adventum beati Martini hujusmodi consuetudinem tenuisse noscuntur" (*Narratio de commendatione,* 303, with corrections from Charleville 117, fol. 102v–103).

14. On Martin and Gallic monasticism, see chapter 1 at note 6.

15. See, for example, Lemarignier, *Etude sur les privilèges d'exemption,* 196–200, on the struggle between the archbishop of Rouen and the abbey of Fécamp, and Fécamp's literary attempts to establish the abbey's greater antiquity. In a similar ninth-century case the

By employing such arguments, bishops claimed jurisdiction over monasteries in their dioceses. The intention of Marmoutier's author, therefore, was to suggest that Marmoutier was virtually as old as the cathedral and that its link to the apostles did not depend upon the cathedral of Tours.

By itself, however, the claim that Bishop Gatien's followers founded Marmoutier was not enough to establish Marmoutier's independence, since it still implied that the abbey derived its foundation from the cathedral. But the author managed to undermine the claim that the cathedral provided Marmoutier with its crucial link to the apostles. He made it clear that though the cathedral's connection to the apostles extended through twenty-two bishops of Rome, Marmoutier had direct apostolic connections because Saints Peter and Paul, and even the Virgin, had spiritually visited Saint Martin in his cell at the abbey.[16] He also suggested that, unlike the cathedral, Marmoutier preserved the tradition of Bishop Gatien continuously until the time of Saint Martin. Gregory of Tours had noted that a thirty-seven-year gap separated the see of Gatien from that of Litorius, the second bishop of Tours; but according to this author Gatien's followers, who became hermit-monks at Marmoutier, inhabited the site of the abbey without a break until the time of Saint Martin.[17] Thus in the diocese of Tours it was Marmoutier, rather than the cathedral, that had the most direct and continuous links with the apostles.

Although the Gatien story was important for strategic reasons, it was Martin who gave Marmoutier its identity and prestige. Thus, in his account of Marmoutier's tenth-century reform, the author stated that the refounders carefully preserved the inheritance of freedom that had been given to the abbey by Saint Martin. Avoiding any reference to the period between 985–87 and 998, when Marmoutier was actually under the domination of Cluny, this author claimed instead that the thirteen Cluniac monks who refounded the abbey in 985–87 immediately attained papal and royal privileges of exemption and compelled Abbot Maiolus of Cluny to recognize those privileges when he tried, but failed, to extend Cluny's domination over Marmoutier. The privileges the monks attained forbade "that the church of Marmoutier be subjected to anyone or to any person—archbishop,

---

invented evidence from the past supported the argument that the abbey of Saint-Calais should be subordinated to the bishop of Le Mans: see Sot, *Gesta episcoporum, gesta abbatum*, 50.

16. *Narratio de commendatione*, 303.

17. Gregory of Tours, *Historia francorum*, 10:31, pp. 526 ff.; *Narratio de commendatione*, 303.

bishop, or abbot—but . . . like a special daughter of the Roman church it would freely serve God alone and the Lord Pope."[18] The wording of this passage suggests that the author was attempting to provide a precedent for the status Marmoutier sought from Urban II at the end of the eleventh century. The abbey received exemption from episcopal jurisdiction and was granted special protection from Rome only in 1089.[19]

According to the author, however, Marmoutier's exempt status was not an innovation of the late eleventh century. Rather, it was based on a plan that Martin first drafted and the abbey's refounders redrafted, making a precise copy of Martin's original. When Maiolus attempted to assert Cluny's dominance over Marmoutier, which meant that the abbey could not elect its own abbot, the monks allegedly told him that Marmoutier's line of abbots had persisted "from the time of blessed Martin until the exile brought about by the Northmen and Danes." The implicit claims of this passage were twofold. First, the line of abbots epitomized the abbey's independence and the preservation of the tradition Martin had established; and second, the only break in the tradition of independence was caused by the Viking invaders. Abbot Maiolus, Marmoutier's historian asserted, responded favorably to both claims, granting the monks their right "to elect" and "to have" their own abbots.[20] In addition, like Count Robert in the tenth-century document, Maiolus acknowledged that Marmoutier derived its status and dignity from Martin and that any insult to Marmoutier would affect Martin as well: "I do not consider myself so great, neither would reason support that my rashness should dare to hinder the statutes of the lord pope, and that the place ever-loved by the blessed Archbishop Martin would lose the summit of its dignity through me."[21]

18. "Dantur insuper a praetaxato piae memoriae Papa Stephano, et a saepe dicto beatae recordationis rege Roberto privilegia firma et inconcussa, ne Majoris Monasterii ecclesia cuilibet vel personae archiepiscopi, episcopi, vel abbatis subjecta esset, sed tanquam specialis Romanae ecclesiae filia, deo soli, et domino tantum Papae libera deserviret" (*Narratio de commendatione*, 312, with slight corrections from Charleville 117, fol. 105v).

19. "Cenobium uestrum, quod Maius dicitur . . . in apostolice sedis tutelam specialiter protectionemque suscepimus" (Urban II, Bull of December 19, 1089, in *Papsturkunden in Frankreich*, n.s. 5, no. 21, p. 83. For further discussion of this document and the privileges of exemption it granted, see chapter 2 at note 29.

20. "In autenticis libris reperitur, a beati Martini temporibus usque ad facta a Normannis et Danis exitia, religione et strenuis abbatibus floruisse dinoscitur," "Statuo igitur et confirmo et sigilli mei auctoritate corroboro, ut Majus Monasterium a jugo et subjectione Cluniaci liberum et immune amodo et deinceps eligendi et habendi proprios abbates etiam a nobis libertate concessa, eidem monasterio pristinae dignitatis integritas illibata permaneat" (*Narratio de commendatione*, 313–14, with corrections from Charleville 117, fols. 106–106v).

21. "Non me tanti estimo, nec ratio suffragatur, ut meae parvitatis temeritas domini papae statutis obviare audeat, et locus beato archipraesuli Martino semper dilectus, dig-

Because he emphasized the tenth-century refoundation of Marmoutier, this late eleventh-century author was compelled to recognize the issue of Marmoutier's earlier decline into a house of canons and in so doing to acknowledge some discontinuity in the preservation of the tradition established by Saint Martin. He addressed this problem, first, by exonerating Marmoutier's monks of any responsibility for the decline, and second, by representing the abbey's history in both cyclical and linear terms, which served to bridge the gap created by the discontinuity.

An adjustment to the actual chronology of Marmoutier's transition from monks to canons freed the monks of responsibility for the abbey's decline. As the tenth-century interpolated charter might have suggested to this author (and the evidence suggests he probably knew the earlier document), Marmoutier had become a house of canons before the Viking attack of 903—and indeed, it may well be, before any of the Viking attacks on Tours. Certainly it already had a lay abbot before the first Viking attack.[22] Yet the eleventh-century author claimed that the religious life and succession of abbots continued uninterrupted from the time of Martin until the time of the Vikings, who rendered the abbey "unfit for inhabitants and for religion." After peace had once again been restored, the author continued, the king introduced canons to the abbey.[23]

---

nitatis antiquae per me culmen amittat" (*Narratio de commendatione*, 314, with corrections from Charleville 117, fol. 106v).

22. The interpolated document was still in use in the twelfth century: a long passage from it was incorporated into the *Deeds of the Counts of Anjou:* see Lévêque, "Trois actes faux," 56, 65, 300–301; *Chronica de gestis consulum Andegavorum* (MS. B), 152–53. The interpolated document was also included in at least one manuscript, along with the *Narratio de commendatione:* Bibliothèque Nationale, MS. lat. 13899, fols. 35, 51v. For more discussion of this manuscript, a fifteenth- or sixteenth-century copy of an earlier one from Marmoutier, see Source Appendix, I-B.

The transition from monks to canons—with particular mensa for particular offices—apparently took place at Marmoutier before 851, although there were still references to monks of Marmoutier in the 840s. Marmoutier was subjected to the lay abbot Vivien in 845. The earliest Viking attack at Marmoutier was in 853: see Lévêque, "Histoire de l'abbaye de Marmoutier," 96–98; Semmler, "Benedictus II," 15 n. 28; Lelong, "Etudes sur l'abbaye de Marmoutier," 283–84 (following Mabille); Gasnault, "Tombeau de Saint Martin et les invasions normandes," 54–55; Mabille, *Invasions normandes dans la Loire*, 25–26 (Mabille, however, put too much trust in a later martyrology that was apparently based on the account in the *Return from Burgundy* concerning the murder of Marmoutier's monks—the *Return from Burgundy* claimed 116 were murdered, the later martyrology, 126).

23. "Et habitatore et religione inhabile reddidit. Non multo vero tempore elapso, propitiae nutu divinitatis, et Rollo fidei, et pax ecclesiae redditur, et in Majori Monasterio regis cujus intererat imperio providentia canonicis regularibus restitutis, servitium divinum utcumque reformatur" (*Narratio de commendatione*, 306, 309–10, with corrections from Charleville 117, fols. 103–103v; in the manuscript, this is one continuous passage). The Charleville manuscript says the canons were regular canons; the later manuscripts edited by Salmon in the printed edition of the *Narratio* apparently said they were secular canons.

While freeing Marmoutier's monks of any responsibility for the decline in the abbey's religious life and autonomous status, the assertion that the Vikings caused a complete rupture in the abbey's history created a new sense of distance and exacerbated the need for continuity. The theme of typological—or mythic—repetition provided a means for overcoming this break: the history of the abbey after the time of the invasions, the author implied, was a recreation of its history before the invasions.

As table 3 demonstrates, the destruction of the abbey by the Vikings provided a midpoint in the author's narrative, which easily divides into two roughly equal parts, with four episodes in each. At several points the two halves of the abbey's history parallel each other. In both the period before the invasions and the one that follows a man associated with the abbey later becomes bishop of Bourges. Both before and after the invasions, the role of the abbot signifies the abbey's status and independence. And both halves begin with a double foundation: in the first half Martin's foundation improves and perfects the eremitical life set up by Gatien's followers; in the second half the installation of monks from Cluny improves upon and perfects the canonical way of life introduced by the king.

This division of Marmoutier's history into two mirrored halves bears striking resemblances to typological interpretations of the Bible. Like early medieval biblical commentators, this author drew parallels between two sets of events whose causal connections, he apparently assumed, existed not horizontally, through time, but vertically, through God's direct action. Just as a commentator on the Bible might argue that the Old Testament sacrifice of Isaac prefigured and found fulfillment in the New Testament sacrifice of Christ and that the two events were thus linked by God's meaningful plan for all of history, this typological representation of Marmoutier's past suggested that the earlier part of the abbey's history prefigured and found fulfillment in the later part and that the two were causally linked through God's plan for the abbey.[24]

While cyclical repetition helped the author leap across the gap in Marmoutier's continuous history, linear continuity helped narrow that gap. By providing a complete history of Marmoutier from the time of bishop Gatien until the time of Abbot Maiolus of Cluny, the author implied that he could account for all significant transitions and events in the abbey's past. The construction of a sequence—four

24. On figural or typological notions of causation in early medieval histories, see Auerbach, *Mimesis: The Representation of Reality in Western Literature*, 73–76.

TABLE 3   Eleventh-century history of Marmoutier

	Prologue: The preeminence of Marmoutier's monastic life.
A. Foundation 1	1. Christians who were converted by the first bishop of Tours left the secular world and began to live as hermits at the place now known as Marmoutier. They built a church, and their eremitical life continued until Saint Martin's coming.
B. Foundation 2	2. When Martin came, he became pastor and rector of the hermits.
C. Bishop of Bourges	3. After Martin's death, Sulpicius Severus (Martin's hagiographer) occupied the saint's cell as an heir until he became bishop of Bourges.
D. Abbot signifies status and independence of Marmoutier	4. The succession of abbots and religious zeal continued at Marmoutier until the time of the Viking invasions.
—Break—	5. The invaders destroyed the abbey, and it became uninhabited.
A. Refoundation 1	6. Not much later the king, who had jurisdiction over the abbey, installed canons there.
B. Refoundation 2	7. But the wife of Count Odo of Blois compelled her husband to reform the abbey after she found a concubine in its church. Odo agreed and convinced the king to transfer jurisdiction over Marmoutier to Odo's son
C. Bishop of Bourges	Hugh, who later became bishop of Bourges. 8. After gaining control of the abbey, Odo reformed it, bringing in thirteen monks from Cluny who attained grants of exemption from Pope Stephen and King Robert.
D. Abbot signifies status and independence of Marmoutier	9. Abbot Maiolus of Cluny wanted to assert Cluny's dominance over Marmoutier, but the monks convinced him to recognize both Marmoutier's grants of exemption and the glory of Saint Martin. Maiolus confirmed in writing that Marmoutier was free from Cluniac jurisdiction and that the monks had the right to elect their own abbots.

events preceding the invasions, the invasions themselves, and four events after the invasions—created an impression of continuity. The vagueness of the tenth-century charter, the "from the beginning" and "ever since," gave way to a more linear precision, a list of events that simultaneously highlighted temporal distance and provided continuity across that distance.

Especially in his account of the first half of the abbey's history, this author made efforts to describe continuity: from the time of Gatien "until the coming of Saint Martin," hermit-monks inhabited Marmoutier; and after the time of Saint Martin "both the vicarious succession of abbots, according to custom, and the daily augmentation of religion persisted until the time of [the Viking leaders] Hasting and Rollo."[25]

In his rudimentary attempts to account for Marmoutier's history in a linear fashion and to provide a sense of continuity through time, Marmoutier's first historian drew some inspiration from a very old genre, the *gesta episcoporum/gesta abbatum,* which had its roots in early Christian articulations of the idea of apostolic succession. It was not until the sixth century, however, that an anonymous author compiled the *Liber pontificalis,* a history of the bishops of Rome. In the same century, Gregory of Tours imitated that work by writing a short history of the bishops of Tours; and in the Carolingian period similar histories of various bishoprics and abbacies began to flourish. These episcopal and abbatial histories resembled later noble genealogies in several ways: they were arranged chronologially and sequentially according to a pattern provided by the list of individual bishops and abbots, and they even employed some family language.[26] But unlike the genealogies, which attributed continuity and causation to the natural biological inheritance of family traits, these earlier histories indicated that ecclesiastical continuity resulted from the transmission of divine grace from one prelate or abbot to another. God himself, imparting his special grace through the church, was thus the agent of continuity in the serial history of ecclesiastical institutions.[27]

Like the earlier gesta episcoporum/abbatum, Marmoutier's history, as well as the noble genealogies of the late eleventh and twelfth centuries, was arranged sequentially and served the purpose of legitimizing certain claims and aspirations to status in the present. An interest in the Viking invasions, however, distinguished the eleventh-century works—both monastic and noble—from the earlier gesta episcoporum/abbatum. The later authors approached the Viking era as a hazy period that needed to be brought into clearer focus. Monasteries turned to the invasions to explain their secularization or to

25. "Usque ad adventum beati Martini," "In praefato autem monasterio, et abbatum vicaria ex more successio, et vehemens religionis in dies augmentatio, usque ad Hastigni et Rollonis tempora perseveravit" (*Narratio de commendatione,* 303, 305).

26. Sot, *Gesta episcoporum;* Sot, "Historiographie épiscopale et modèle familial en Occident au IXᵉ siècle."

27. Gabrielle Spiegel has made a similar point concerning Sot's attempts to draw parallels between the *Gesta episcoporum* and the noble genealogies. Making a distinction between earlier typological histories and the genealogical histories of the eleventh century and later, she emphasized direct divine causation and nonlinear organization in the earlier works and biological causation together with linear organization in the later histories. By itself, of course, linearity was not the distinguishing feature of the genealogies, since the earlier *Gesta episcoporum* also had a linear organization: see Spiegel, "Genealogy: Form and Function in Medieval Historical Narrative," 43–53.

demonstrate, whether it was true or not, that they had been founded in the age before the invasions and that their links with the earlier period persisted despite the invasions. Nobles wished to establish that their families originated sometime during the Viking epoch, under the late Carolingians. The known surviving sources, however, did not lend much support to these claims, so both monks and nobles had to create the desired records for the Viking era.[28]

Marmoutier's eleventh-century history resembled noble genealogies in its use of the Viking era, yet it had more affinity with the gesta episcoporum/abbatum. A continuous transmission of grace apparently held together the chain of Marmoutier's abbots, which reached all the way back to the time of Saint Martin. Furthermore, it was God, by implication, who caused the second half of Marmoutier's history to recreate the first half of the abbey's history in a typological manner. Marmoutier's twelfth- and thirteenth-century histories, by contrast, would turn to more natural explanations for historical causation and continuity.

Unlike their tenth- and eleventh-century predecessors, Marmoutier's twelfth- and thirteenth-century authors were not immediately motivated by the need to promote or protect Marmoutier's institutional status. The abbey's most dramatic struggle for independence— the motivating force behind the eleventh-century history of the abbey—ceased to be a problem after the monks made their peace with Archbishop Gislebert sometime between 1118 and 1124.[29] Nevertheless, the reconstruction of the abbey's past continued to preoccupy the monks during the twelfth century and even into the thirteenth. Sometime between about 1137 and 1156 an anonymous monk at Marmoutier wrote the *Return from Burgundy*, which made the first attempt to account for the abbey's fate during the Viking invasions while at the same time reinforcing the monks' connection to Martin's relics. Another anonymous author, who probably completed his work before 1156 (and definitely before 1180), wrote the *Legend of the Seven Sleepers of Marmoutier*, which shed new light on the abbey's origins and its links to Saint Martin. And sometime around 1227 a third

28. On monastic history, relic legends, and the invasions, see Haenens, *Invasions normandes en Belgique*, 164–68; Wood, "Politics of Sanctity: The Thirteenth-Century Legal Dispute about St. Eloi's Relics," 91; Orderic Vitalis, *Historia ecclesiastica*, 4, 6:9, 6:10, ed. Chibnall, 2:244–49, 2:340–41, 3:276–77, 3:302–5. The third of Orderic's passages is especially relevant since, as Chibnall points out, Orderic asserted elsewhere that the monastery of Saint-Evroul was destroyed in the civil wars of the tenth century, but in this passage he blamed the Vikings for its decline and destruction.

29. See chapter 2.

anonymous author compiled the final version of the *Commendation of the Province of Touraine,* which included an interpolated version of the eleventh-century history of Marmoutier.[30]

Although some evidence in these works, as well as in others written at Marmoutier in the twelfth century, points to a sense of rivalry between Marmoutier and the abbey of Cluny (and we can assume that the monks were concerned about Cîteaux and Fontevrault as well), it appears that a central motivation for the continued attempt to reconstruct Marmoutier's past was not a pragmatic desire for status, but a need to overcome a sense of alienation from the past.[31] This sense of alienation arose in part from the monks' own historical reconstructions—they had brought to their own attention, and now they wanted to bridge, the distance in time and the break in continuity that separated them from Saint Martin. In part, however, their alienation was a response to the rapid growth that was transforming their own monastery as well as twelfth-century society in general.[32] The monks of Marmoutier perceived that their own role in society was changing, that the mounting complexity of society was tearing the fabric of the

30. *De reversione beati Martini; Historia septem dormientium; Narratio de commendatione* and *Chronicon abbatum Majoris monasterii* (these constituted a single text). See Source Appendix, I-A, I-B, I-E for discussions of these texts and their dates. For some useful discussion of the legend of the seven sleepers, see Oury, "Sept dormants de Marmoutier." Oury, however, mistakenly argued that the legend was written after 1180 (see Source Appendix, I-E).

31. Several manuscripts and works from Marmoutier point to a sense of rivalry with Cluny. Two manuscripts of the *De rebus gestis in Majori monasterio* (Charleville 117 and Bibliothèque Nationale MS. lat. 13899) opened with a famous passage borrowed from Ralph Glaber, in which Ralph's original praise of the unrivaled efficacy of Cluny's prayers for the dead was changed to apply, instead, to Marmoutier. (See Source Appendix, I-D, for further discussion of the manuscript evidence for the *De rebus,* and chapter 5 for discussion of the content of the text, which was written at Marmoutier in the twelfth century.) In one manuscript of Ralph Glaber's history (Bibliothèque Nationale, MS. lat. 6190), in the place where the name Cluny would have been written, a word was scratched out and Marmoutier was written in: see Ralph Glaber, *Historiarum libri quinque,* 5:1, ed. Prou, p. 125. The *De rebus* might also be seen as a collection whose purposes paralleled and even rivaled those of Peter the Venerable's *De miraculis,* which had many stories about Cluny: see chapter 5 at note 46. The implication, in the *Return from Burgundy,* that as a result of the Viking invasions Marmoutier was responsible for a transfer of culture from western Gaul to Burgundy (see below at note 49 ff.) paralleled Glaber's claim that adherence to the Benedictine *Rule* had traveled east from the abbey of Glanfeuil in the Loire valley to Cluny in Burgundy. Glanfeuil's monks, Glaber reported, fled the Vikings, carrying their *Rule* to Saint-Martin of Autun, and from there the *Rule* spread to Baume and then to Cluny: see Ralph Glaber, *Historiarum libri,* 3:5, ed. Prou, pp. 66–67. Finally, the eleventh-century history of Marmoutier made it clear that Abbot Maiolus of Cluny was compelled from the beginning to recognize Marmoutier's dignity: see above at note 21.

32. On historical writing and alienation in the twelfth century, see Southern, "Aspects of the European Tradition of Historical Writing 4: The Sense of the Past"; for a similar argument concerning the writing of autobiography, see Ferguson, "Autobiography as Therapy."

monastic community, and that cataclysmic historical events—symbolized by the Viking invasions—separated them from the past. They wrote history, then, to help themselves adjust to change and to map out their position in the new universe.

In their quest for connections with the past, the monks of Marmoutier began to employ, in some of their twelfth-century writings, organic metaphors of seasonal renewal and genealogical continuity. The introduction of these new metaphors into works about Marmoutier's past followed the development of noble genealogical literature, and in both cases we can detect a tendency to move toward natural, rather than providential, causation in history—that is to say, to an understanding that God may be the ultimate cause of events, but these events can also be explained within their own causal chain. Still, the monks never fully relinquished the idea that God directly intervened at various times to protect the abbey or to teach its monks a lesson. Also, their emphasis on organic continuity reflects not only the secularization of history but also a desire to reestablish a lost sense of connectedness, with each other as well as with the past.

The *Legend of the Seven Sleepers of Marmoutier* demonstrates how the idea of blood ties reinforced the perceived links between present and past, individual and community. According to the anonymous author of this work, which was attributed to Gregory of Tours, the monks who resided at Marmoutier in Saint Martin's day included seven men whose ties to Martin were both biological and spiritual: they were his first cousins, and Martin converted them to Christianity.

To establish the family relationship between the seven cousins and Saint Martin, the author created a genealogy for the saint that resembled those of noble families. Indeed, the contemporary preoccupation with high lineage and primogeniture was at the fore in this genealogy: the saint became the firstborn son of the firstborn son of the king of Hungary, who was himself the firstborn son of the preceding king of Hungary. And through the female line Martin was related to a Saxon king and a Roman emperor. The seven sleepers were the sons of two younger brothers of Martin's father—they were the saint's first cousins from the cadet lines on his paternal side (see table 4).[33]

This genealogy both linked Saint Martin organically to Marmoutier and enhanced the dignity of Martin himself. Earlier authors, following conventions introduced in Merovingian lives of saints, had made vague claims concerning Martin's noble birth, but this twelfth-

---

33. *Historia septem dormientium, PL* 71:1107–9.

TABLE 4 Martin's genealogy

Chut, king
of the Saxons   Amnarus, king of Hungary

Brichilde   =   Florus, king of Hungary   Martin, bishop   Amnarus, bishop

Sister of
Constantine
? ─────── =   Florus, tribune of Hungary   Hilgrinus = Hungarian   Amnarus = Hungarian
                         (born before his father's   noblewoman   noblewoman
                         kingdom falls)

                                                                                                        Twins

                         Florus (Martin)   Clemens Primus Laetus Theodorus   Gaudens Quiriacus Innocentius

                                                                      seven sleepers

century author now elevated Martin to membership in a specific royal line and, in accordance with contemporary concerns about primogeniture, gave him the most privileged position in the succession of firstborn sons within that line.[34] Indeed, even the timing of births distinguished Martin's own lineal descent from that of his seven cousins. According to the author, the Roman emperor Maximian conquered the kingdom of Martin's grandfather, King Florus, and compelled him to promise that his son, also named Florus, would rule Hungary as a tribune rather than as an independent king. But though Florus II, Martin's father, never ruled as king, his birth rooted him to his royal background in a way that distinguished him from his younger brothers, the fathers of the seven sleepers: Florus II was born in the heyday of his father's reign, before Maximian defeated him; his brothers were born only after Maximian's conquest of their father. And Martin himself was born while King Florus still lived; his cousins, only after the death of their grandfather.[35]

According to the secular standards of the twelfth century, Saint Martin, as the *Legend of the Seven Sleepers* represented him, was heir to the highest noble blood and held the most privileged position within his noble line. But Martin's inheritance from his family was not merely secular: his grandfather's generation endowed him with nobility of grace as well as birth. A double name symbolized this dual inheritance: Martin, like his father and grandfather, bore the name Florus until his baptism. Following his baptism he took the name Martin, after a great-uncle, a brother of King Florus, who was (along with a third brother) a Christian bishop, just as his great nephew would be in the future.[36] This dual relationship of royal blood and Christian grace characterized not only Martin's link to his grandfather's generation but also his link to the seven sleepers. The cousins

34. Alcuin mentioned the nobility of Martin's parents, and an anonymous eleventh-century *Life* claimed that Martin was from "the highest shoot of gentile blood": Alcuin, "De vita S. Martini Turonensis," *PL* 101:658–59; *Vita Sancti Martini di anonimo*, 6. By contrast, Sulpicius Severus merely claimed that Martin was not from a modest background, and Paulinus of Perigord (fifth century) said he was not from "humble stock": Sulpicius Severus, *Vita Sancti Martini*, 2:1, p. 254; Paulinus of Perigord, *De vita Sancti Martini . . . libri VI*, 1:12–15, p. 19. On the Merovingian convention that saints were from noble backgrounds, see Bosl, "'Adelsheilige'"; Gaiffier, "Mentalité de l'hagiographie médiévale d'après quelques travaux recents."

35. *Historia septem dormientium, PL* 71:1107–9.

36. *Historia septem dormientium, PL* 71:1107–9, 1110 n. f, 1113. The Florus-Martin naming pattern in this legend mirrored twelfth-century practice. Constance Brittain Bouchard has noted that in some noble families one given name was repeated among eldest sons—those destined to inherit their fathers' wealth and secular power—while younger sons who were expected to assume ecclesiastical positions would be given the names of uncles who already held such positions (*Sword, Miter, and Cloister*, 62).

shared the saint's royal blood and received from him the grace of Christian belief. Although Martin converted them, moreover, their great uncles, the two bishops, baptized them.[37]

Immediately after their baptism, the seven cousins practiced a communal and ascetic life in their home, and miraculous healings and conversions began to attest to their sanctity. Soon, however, they left Hungary, sought out Saint Martin at Tours, and received his formal blessing for a pilgrimage to Rome, Jerusalem, and Compostella. After this pilgrimage they returned to Marmoutier, where they began to lead an eremitical life, enclosed together in a tiny cell where they eventually died and were buried. They earned the name the seven sleepers during the period between their death and their burial, because their bodies remained miraculously peaceful and composed.[38]

When they settled at Marmoutier the cousins, who were already bound to Martin by ties of blood and conversion, entered into yet a third relationship with the saint, the one that joined the monks of Marmoutier to their founder and first abbot. Their new relationship to Martin transformed the link between Martin and his abbey: the first generation of Marmoutier's monks now included Martin's own blood relatives. Thus the connection between the abbey and its founder became, in more than just a metaphorical sense, a family tie.

This is not to say, however, that the legend's author ignored the relationship of grace that bound Marmoutier to its founder. Just as Martin's relationship with both the generation of his grandfather and that of his cousins was biological as well as spiritual, Marmoutier's tie to its founder involved both the biological link between the saint and his cousins and the spiritual link between the founder and the succession of abbots. Building on and transforming the information in the interpolated charter of the tenth century, which had claimed that Marmoutier's *first* abbot was named Walbert, the author of the *Seven Sleepers* connected the appointment of Walbert to the death of Martin, thereby indicating that Martin was the first abbot and Walbert the second. Unlike the tenth-century interpolator, this author was more interested in the idea of succession than in the separate jurisdictions of bishop and abbot: "having learned much earlier, through a revelation, about his own death . . . [Martin] called all the brothers of the monastery together, kissed each one, and blessed them. And he appointed one of the brothers from his place, named Walbert, and made him

37. *Historia septem dormientium, PL* 71:1107–9, 1110 n. f, 1113.
38. *Historia septem dormientium, PL* 71:1114–17.

abbot, confirming him with his benediction."[39] Martin, this author made clear, established a *traditio*, which he passed on as a spiritual inheritance to the abbot who succeeded him. This traditio continued after Walbert's death: the author gives the name of Walbert's successor and the number of years each of the two held the abbacy.[40] By creating a family link between Martin and Marmoutier's earliest monks and by lengthening the record of the traditio from Martin to the abbots who followed, the author doubly reinforced the sense of connection between the monks who inhabited Marmoutier in the twelfth century and Martin, who had founded their abbey in the fourth.

Indeed, the legend helped create a sense of connection in a third way: it enabled the monks to claim that they themselves possessed, within the boundaries of their own monastery, the physical remains of the seven cousins.[41] As early as the ninth century the bones that probably came to be identified with those of the seven sleepers were thought to belong to unnamed disciples of Saint Martin.[42] The *Legend of the Seven Sleepers* transformed those bones into saintly relics, the unnamed disciples into seven named cousins of Saint Martin, the dusty remnants of a hazily remembered past into tangible evidence that the past had never been lost or forgotten.

The overlapping relationship of blood and spirit that bound Martin to his seven cousins reinforced the perception that unbroken linear ties bound the monks to the founder, father, and patriarch of their abbey. Similarly, the unusual relationship among the seven cousins themselves served as a metaphor that simultaneously represented and

39. "Ipse quidem per revelationem obitum suum longe ante praenoscens . . . convocatisque omnibus monasterii fratribus, singulos osculatus est, atque benedixit, et praefecit eius unum ex fratribus loco suo, nomine Gualbertum, abbatemque constituit, et benedictione sua confirmavit" (*Historia septem dormientium*, PL 71:1115).

40. *Historia septem dormientium*, PL 71:1116.

41. The grotto of the seven sleepers was apparently identified as such by 1187, when Abbot Hervé of Villepreux retired to a life of reclusion in an oratory adjacent to that of "the sleepers": *Chronicon abbatum Majoris monasterii*, 324. Sometime before 1178, Stephen of Fougère indicated in his *Life* of William Firmat (ca. 1087–1104) that William and his mother had spent time as hermits at a place near Tours "that is called in the vulgar tongue, the seven brothers." This was probably a reference to the grotto of the seven sleepers: see Oury, "Erémitisme à Marmoutier," 322, 330–33; Stephen of Fougère, *Vita Guilielmi Firmati*, 335. By the time Péan Gatineau wrote his French life of Saint Martin (probably after 1229: see Source Appendix, II-C) the grotto of the seven sleepers had become the object of an annual pilgrimage: see Péan Gatineau, *Vie monseignor St. Martin*, lines 68–71, p. 4.

42. A charter of Abbot Vivien (+851) mentions a little place or crypt near the door of the monastery where "discipuli beati Martini in somno pacis quiescunt": see Mabillon, *Annales ordinis S. Benedicti*, vol. 2, appendixes, 76, 695; cited by Oury, "Sept dormants," 315.

reinforced the concept of monastic community. According to the legend, Hilgrinus and Amnarus, the fathers of the seven sleepers, were twins. This unusual relationship of birth both symbolized and inspired the unusual way the two men shared their inheritance. While living in the secular world, they provided their sons with an example for the cenobitic life: "Hilgrinus . . . and Amnarus did not divide their paternal inheritance as other brothers do. Rather, just as they were twins, brought forth during a single labor, thus they were content with a single house, a single estate, and one thing in common with their wives and sons."[43]

Hilgrinus and Amnarus, who converted to Christianity with their seven sons, died in the year of their conversion. The sons then sold the unified inheritance and gave the income to the poor. "Established in a garret without quarrel," they remained celibate, spent their time in sacred reading and prayer, preached the word of God, gave food to the poor, and performed miracles.[44]

The activities of the seven cousins were of course monastic activities, and their exemplary way of carrying them out attested to their sanctity. But underlying their spiritual grace was the unity they inherited through the special relationship of their twin fathers. By settling at Marmoutier, dying there on the same day, and being buried together on the abbey's premises the seven cousins passed on to the abbey, as a virtual inheritance, the special family unity that underlay their collective life. The kinship of blood that had united the seven cousins served as both metaphor and origin myth for the relationship of community that bound the monks together in a common life. The belief that Marmoutier's original monks were tied to Martin and to each other through links of blood gave the twelfth-century monks a sense that tangible realities underlay the abstract conceptual connec-

43. "Hilgrinus . . . et Amnarus, non sicut alii fratres paternam haereditatem dividentes, sed sicut uno ortu gemini nati sunt, sic una domo, uno fundo, una re communi cum uxoribus et filiis contenti sunt" (*Historia septem dormientium*, PL 71:1113–14).

44. "Coenaculo constituti sine querela" (*Historia septem dormientium*, PL 71:1114). Oury ("Sept dormants," 324) sees in this a parallel to the liturgy for Pentecost, according to which the Holy Spirit found the apostles "concorde caritate." See also, on the description of the harmony of believers in the book of Acts as a model for the spiritual and monastic life, Constable, "Renewal and Reform in Religious Life," 51; Leclercq, *Etudes sur le vocabulaire monastique du Moyen Age*, 38. There is a further parallel between ideas about the apostles and the seven sleepers in the fact that the theme of the "Holy Family" established blood links between Christ and some of the apostles, just as the *Legend of the Seven Sleepers* established blood links between Martin and the monks of Marmoutier: see Gaiffier, "Trinubium Annae." For further discussion of the influence of genealogical themes on hagiography, see Genicot, *Généalogies*, 39. Both the Merovingians and the Carolingians linked the royal families to saints, but since their kinship structure was not patrilineal, they would have perceived blood links in different ways.

tions—between present and past, self and other—which were invoked to strengthen and legitimize their community. This origin myth turned abstractions into historical events.

Figures of expression were not as tangible as origin myths, but they could extend and expand the implications of such myths. A collection of twelfth-century sermons, for example, claimed that Marmoutier's monks were Martin's "sons" and heirs and were therefore entitled to material and spiritual privileges. Marmoutier constituted a "patrimony" that "we possess almost by hereditary right, and bequeath . . . to ourselves like special sons."[45] Because they were Martin's sons, the monks could rely on special forms of intercession from the saint. Martin, Marmoutier's sermonist asserted, was the "patron" and "advocate" of everyone who lived a "good and faithful life," but his "care" and "solicitude" for his disciples and sons at Marmoutier were even greater.[46] If the monks lived up to this special relationship, they would receive their rewards: "Clearly, if we are wise and we imitate his wisdom . . . he will securely and most freely recognize on the Day of Judgment, before God and all his saints, both that he is our father and that we are his sons."[47] Because a spiritual lineage tied them to Saint Martin, the monks of Marmoutier benefited from the saint's paternal affection. And in turn they rendered special honor to him. One sermon claimed that Martin's feast on November 11 was Marmoutier's "Easter," because on that day the monks celebrated "the death of our father."[48]

In the *Seven Sleepers* and their twelfth-century sermons the monks of Marmoutier attempted to recapture a sense of connection to Saint Martin by employing the theme of genealogical continuity. But one detail in the abbey's history had the potential to obstruct their perception that its continuity had a basis in tangible and historical reality: as long as the monks believed that the Vikings had thoroughly destroyed

45. "Et locum habitationis.eius . . . quasi iure hereditario possidemus eiusque nobis patrimonium tanquam speciales filii vendicamus" ("De transitu S. Martini Sermo primus," Bibliothèque Nationale, MS. lat. 12412, fol. 154v).

46. "Omnium et maxime fidelium ac bonum viventium patronus et advocatus est. . . . Quod precipue de nobis debemus presumere, qui eius sumus spirituales discipuli. . . . Unde si dici fas est non modo discipulos sed . . . filios nos esse fateri possumus. . . . Id circo amplior est cura de nobis et maior sollicitudo" ("De transitu Sancti Martini Sermo secundus," ibid., fol. 155v).

47. "Si videlicet sapientes simus, et eius sapientiam imitemur, et se patrem nostrum et nos filios suos in die iudicii coram domino et omnibus sanctis eius . . . secure ac libentissime recognoscet" (ibid.).

48. "Hodie fratres pascha nostrum est quia transitum patris nostri hodie celebramus" ("De transitu Sancti Martini Sermo quartus," ibid., fol. 156).

their abbey, they could not claim direct organic links between Saint Martin's time and their own. The *Return from Burgundy* provided the solution to this problem. It claimed that although the Vikings attacked Marmoutier and murdered 116 of its monks, Abbot Herbern and 24 of the abbey's monks managed to survive. These survivors attained positions of prominence and helped carry the monastic life from west to east, into the region of Burgundy.[49]

According to the legend, Marmoutier's survivors initially received shelter at the basilica of Saint-Martin. When it became clear that the Vikings were going to strike again, however, the canons of the basilica decided that Abbot Herbern and the twenty-four monks, along with twelve canons of the basilica and twelve burghers from Châteauneuf—the walled town that surrounded the basilica—would carry Saint Martin's relics to more secure territory. Under the leadership of Herbern the party ended up in Burgundy, where the twenty-four monks became renowned for their piety and were elevated to abbatial and episcopal positions. When the Viking threat had subsided, Herbern called upon the twenty-four former monks to assist him in carrying Martin's relics back to Tours.[50]

The organic motif of genealogical continuity is only implicit in this legend, in the claims that the abbot of Marmoutier and twenty-four of its monks survived the incursions and that Marmoutier's religious life survived in Burgundy through the religious leadership of the twenty-four monks. Its author made no explicit connection between his claim that the monks survived and the need to establish linear organic continuity in the abbey's history, but a later author would employ the legend for precisely this purpose.

In addition to strengthening Marmoutier's organic links with its origins by implying that there was no break in the abbey's linear history, the *Return from Burgundy* reiterated the theme of divinely caused cyclical renewal. When Martin's relics returned to his parish, the legend claimed, "all the trees and bushes defied nature, turning green on that winter day . . . and in this way demonstrated just how exalted with merits was the return of the father to the fatherland."[51]

49. *De reversione beati Martini*, 21, 30.
50. *De reversione beati Martini*, 22–23, 30.
51. "Universae siquidem arbores et fruteta tempore brumali, repugnante licet natura . . . vernant et in sui ornatu quantae meritorum excellentiae sit pater patriae repatrians demonstrarunt" (*De reversione*, 33). This passage is strikingly similar to a passage in Theodoric of Amorbach's *Illatio Sancti Benedicti*, an early eleventh-century legend from Fleury about a struggle over the relics of Saint Benedict, which may have influenced the author of the *De reversione*. As I pointed out in chapter 2, however, the *De reversione* described a struggle between the clerics from Tours and an archbishop, whereas the *Illatio Sancti Benedicti* dealt with a struggle between two religious houses: see chapter 2 at notes 58 ff.

This theme of seasonal renewal was underscored by the date of the feast celebrating Martin's return from Burgundy—December 13. In the twelfth century that date virtually corresponded with the winter solstice, the day when the solar calendar turns around, offering hope for the coming of spring.[52] The legend and the feast day commemorating Saint Martin's return from Burgundy symbolically suggested that Martin's reentry into Tours marked the end of a period of death and destruction and the beginning of a period of rebirth. Marmoutier's refoundation was like the coming of spring; it was a divinely caused renewal—the natural recreation of the circumstances of an earlier season.

A new sense of contact with the relics of their founder provided the monks with yet another link to the past. The claim in the *Return from Burgundy* that during a time of crisis the canons of Saint-Martin relinquished the primary guardianship of Martin's relics to the monks of Marmoutier was highly unlikely, since the canons would not have risked losing exclusive rights to their most precious possession. But the idea behind this story was important for Marmoutier. Like the *Legend of the Seven Sleepers,* it gave the monks a tangible connection with physical remains from the time of their abbey's heroic origins.

The *Seven Sleepers* and the *Return for Burgundy* employed similar means to emphasize the links between Marmoutier's point of origin and its subsequent history. Both legends integrated natural explanations for historical change into more traditional emphases on divine causation, and both expanded Marmoutier's relationship with the relics of men who had participated in the abbey's foundation. And both were incorporated, sometime around 1227, into the section of the *Commendation of the Province of Touraine* that was devoted to the history of Marmoutier.

Like the *Legend of the Seven Sleepers* and the *Return from Burgundy,* this expanded version of the history of Marmoutier employed both natural and divine explanations for historical change. But the anonymous author of this work went further than the two earlier authors in his elaboration of natural themes, and he framed material from the *Return from Burgundy* in such a way that it provided the essential, organic link in an account of Marmoutier's continuous linear history.

The thirteenth-century history employed all four of the concepts that Marmoutier's earlier historians had used in their attempts to convey a sense of temporal continuity: the linear concepts of spiritual

52. For further discussion of the December feast day, see chapter 9 at notes 83 ff. The canons of Saint-Martin developed the liturgical theme of *periodic* seasonal renewal much more fully than did the monks of Marmoutier.

TABLE 5   Thirteenth-century history of Marmoutier

	Eleventh-century history	Thirteenth-century additions
A. Caves	1. (Original prologue, episodes 1 and 2): Settling at Marmoutier of first bishop's followers, *who lived in caves*; when Martin came, he was the leader.	
B. Monks Become Religious Leaders		2. Why it is called "Majus monasterium": Either because it is the greatest of Martin's three monastic foundations, or because the original hermits considered the main church the "greater monastery," or because Marmoutier *provided priests for churches and monasteries everywhere* and was thus known as the "greater monastery."
	3. (Original episodes 3–5): After Martin's death Sulpicius Serverus occupied his cell; the religious life continued at Marmoutier until the invasions.	
C. Gillebertus		4. List of abbots from *Gillebertus* to Herbern (abbot when Vikings came).
—Break—		5. Prologue to sections 6 and 7: Vikings destroyed Marmoutier, but those who returned there "seeded" and "planted" and attempted to restore its pristine rights.
A. Caves		6. Account from the *Return from Burgundy* of the destruction of Marmoutier and the survival of Abbot Herbern and twenty-four monks (*who hid in caves*); their trip to Burgundy with Martin's relics. Herbern's return.
B. Monks become religious leaders		7. Account (from *Deeds of the Counts of Anjou*/Miracles attributed to Herbern) of Abbot Herbern's elevation to the archbishopric of Tours. Abbot Herbern has the twenty-four monks, who have been *elevated to bishoprics*

TABLE 5–continued

	Eleventh-century history	Thirteenth-century additions
		and abbacies in Burgundy, accompany Martin's relics back to Tours.
	8. (Original episodes 6–9): the king installs canons, Odo of Blois reforms Marmoutier. The king, pope, and abbot of Cluny recognize its liberties.	
C. Gillebertus		9. Dedication of the new abbey church by Pope Urban II in 1096. Recognition of the abbey's autonomy by various popes. 10. List, with notices of their deeds, of abbots of Marmoutier from *Gillebertus* (II) to Hugh of Blois (d. 1227).

and biological continuity and the cyclical concepts of typological repetition and seasonal renewal. His use of the linear metaphor of spiritual continuity resembled that in the eleventh-century version of the abbey's history. Indeed, his interpolations brought the eleventh-century material into even greater conformity with the genre of gesta episcoporum/abbatum.

As the outline in table 5 illustrates, much of the new material in the thirteenth-century history consisted of two lists of abbots: those from Martin's time until the invasions (section 4) and those from the refounding to 1227 (section 10).[53] Even more than the eleventh-century history, this work constructed a sequence to represent temporal continuity, and this sequence had the appearance of a gesta abbatum.

Were it not for the destruction wrought by the Vikings, this author might have cobbled together a single list of all the abbots (real or invented) between the fourth and the thirteenth centuries. It appears that he actually wanted to do so, but to achieve his goal he had to add some tangential material to his list of abbots: he had to account for the abbey's fate during the Viking invasions, which according to the evidence in the abbey's earlier history had caused such extensive damage that Marmoutier's monastic life ceased.

53. *Narratio de commendatione,* 306; *Chronicon abbatum Majoris monasterii,* 318–26.

Drawing on but reshaping the *Return from Burgundy*, the author so arranged the earlier material that it conveyed one central theme: that Marmoutier's abbot and some of its monks survived the invasions and returned to Tours. Indeed (and here the author drew on an earlier text), Abbot Herbern even went on to become bishop of Tours.[54] Herbern provided the crucial link in Marmoutier's chain of abbots, and his story thus implied that Marmoutier benefited from the continuous transmission of spiritual grace from the time of Martin until the time when the author was writing.

But survival is more crucial to the concept of genealogical continuity than to the concept of spiritual continuity, and insofar as he emphasized survival, the author of this history superimposed a layer of natural causation onto that of direct divine causation, and his logic edged into that of a genealogy rather than a gesta abbatum. Genealogical continuity depends on direct links between generations—a father must physically engender his son. Episcopal or abbatial continuity, by contrast, can tolerate gaps between generations, since a bishop or abbot can receive spiritual grace, through the rite of consecration, from the bishop of another diocese. A gesta episcoporum/abbatum thus recorded vacancies in a prelacy; genealogies tried to avoid any mention of discontinuity.[55] Like the authors of genealogies, Marmoutier's historian avoided the issue of vacancies, especially during the period of the invasions. With the material from the *Return from Burgundy*, he made it clear that Herbern and the twenty-four monks survived. To that material he added an introduction suggesting that the refounders of the abbey may have included some survivors of the invasions, or at least their successors (*posteris*—the word can also mean descendants). The planting of new fields symbolized this refoundation, now portrayed as both continuation and rebirth:

> Finally . . . when . . . God brought back a certain light of security and peace to our country . . . as we should say simply, with the words of Scripture, having made the fruitful earth a desert because of the evil of those inhabiting it, He then resettled the hungering in the same place, and they constructed a city of habitation and seeded fields and planted vineyards and produced the fruit of birth. . . . [At that time] either the

---

54. *Narratio de commendatione*, 307, 309. The passage concerning Herbern's elevation to archbishop is printed in *PL* 129:1036, where it occurs in the *Miracula beati Martini* attributed to Archbishop Herbern. Halphen and Poupardin (*Chroniques des comtes d'Anjou*, 31 n. d) assumed that John of Marmoutier had borrowed the story from the Herbern collection, but it is possible that the borrowing was in the other direction. On the miracle collection, see chapter 9, note 30.

55. Sot, *Gesta episcoporum*, 33.

successors, that is, the posterity, or, if they survived, the same ones—whom that raging tempest of the barbarian hostility had disturbed from their pristine inhabitance—returned to their own seats.[56]

This passage demonstrates that while the author spliced together the two halves of the abbey's linear history, thus closing the gap wrought by the Viking invasions, he continued to employ cyclical metaphors as well. And indeed, as table 5 shows, he even elaborated the earlier author's use of the typological motif. Both halves of the abbey's history now included a first abbot named Gillebertus, and in both halves monks from the abbey became religious leaders—priests, bishops, and abbots—thus spreading the abbey's influence to other locations.[57]

Along with this typological plan, which implicitly pointed to divine causation, the author employed the language of seasonal renewal, which intermingled divine causation with natural or human causation. At the time of its original foundation, Marmoutier "extended the shoots of its religion to the sea" (Ps. 80:11); the Viking invasions, an expression of providential punishment, "thoroughly desolated" its possessions and reduced the "once flourishing region" to a "desert of empty waste and horrible solitude"; but God "resettled the hungering," and the monks themselves "seeded the fields and planted vineyards and produced the fruit of birth."[58]

The early thirteenth-century history of Marmoutier represents the culmination of Marmoutier's reinvention of the past. Like the earlier works from Marmoutier, this history is characteristic of a heightened sense of historical consciousness in the years around the twelfth century. In their historical writings the monks, like their contemporaries, demonstrated an awareness of change and of historical distance, and they began to enhance providential explanations for historical causation and continuity with more natural and human explanations.

---

56. "Cum . . . tandem . . . lucem quamdam nostrae revexisset patriae securitatis et pacis. . . . Dominus . . . ut Scripturae sanctae simpliciter verbis utamur, posuit terram fructiferam in salsuginem a malitia inhabitantium in ea. Ipse idem rursus ibidem collocavit esurientes et constituerunt civitatem habitationis et seminaverunt agros et plantaverunt vineam et fecerunt fructum nativitatis. . . . vel succedentibus scilicet posteris, vel eisdem, si qui supererant, redeuntibus in sedes proprias quos ab incolatu pristino deturbaverat illa barbaricae hostilitatis saeva tempestas" (*Narratio de commendatione*, 307).

57. *Narratio de commendatione*, 305, 306, 309; *Chronicon abbatum Majoris monasterii*, 318.

58. "Extendit usque ad mare religionis suae palmites," "regionum olim florentissimarum, partem . . . desertam vastitatis solitudinemque redegit horrendam," "desolata penitus" (*Narratio de commendatione*, 305, 306, 307, and above, note 55). For other examples of the Lord's vine as a metaphor for a monastic institution, see Orderic Vitalis, *Historia*, 3, ed. Chibnall, 2:4–5, and Peter the Venerable, *De miraculis*, PL 189:872.

The invention of the past, to adjust to new situations and to gain legitimacy and status within a changing social and political universe, was a typical twelfth-century response to change and controversy. Monks, canons, Gregorian reformers, and heretics appealed to golden-age models that they claimed, and often intensely desired, to recover. The themes of renewal, reform, and *renovatio* resound in twelfth-century writings, where they articulate an implicit, if unconscious, inclination toward change, which was masked and even perceived as a return to an earlier status quo. These themes both reflected and created a sense of historical distance—a perception that a period of decline and difference separated the golden age of the past from the present.[59]

A need to legitimize reform stimulated the search for or creation of texts. Texts provided archetypal models that were to supersede the customs that had come into existence during an intervening period. Indeed, neither the representation nor the perception of distance from the past would have been possible without written records: unwritten collective memory and custom, though extremely fluid in actual practice, perpetuate the notion of an unchanging, static past. The twelfth-century idea of the possibility of development—historical and personal—was closely related to the resurgence of literacy, of written records, and of written narrative.[60]

The theme of renewal and the construction of linear, sequential histories served the monks of Marmoutier in their simultaneous attempts to describe and overcome distance from the past. In turn, linear histories brought about an even greater awareness of change and distance. The increasingly detailed written record of sequential events made concrete the duration in time that separated the monks of Marmoutier from the time of Saint Martin. And again, the written medium both stimulated and made possible these changed perceptions.

As written documentation gained importance in the twelfth century, clarity and precision became necessary components of archival records and historical texts. Vague claims to continuity, such as that put forth in the tenth-century interpolated document, became less and less satisfactory. A more formalized judicial system favored pre-

59. Constable, "Renewal and Reform in the Religious Life," 38; Constable and Benson, "Introduction," in *Renaissance and Renewal*, xxv.

60. On the search for texts, see Stock, "Medieval Literacy, Linguistic Theory and Social Organization," 19. On unwritten custom, see Bloch, *Feudal Society*, 1:113. On connections between conceptions of self and historical consciousness, see Benton, "Consciousness of Self and Perceptions of Individuality," 284.

cise written evidence, and monks were especially inclined to accommodate the new requirements by producing the necessary documents, either from their archives or with their quills.[61]

But precision was not the only result of a shift from oral to written
records. Writing and texts bring with them psychological and perceptual changes. They transform an oral/aural universe into a visual
universe, a realm of simultaneity into a realm of sequentiality. The
sequential nature of genealogical works and of Marmoutier's histories
might be interpreted as one aspect of the perceptual change. These
works mirrored and expanded upon the sequential arrangement of
words and letters on a written page.[62]

Of course, as the evidence of the gesta episcoporum/abbatum at-
tests, written records and sequential thought had existed before the
twelfth century. But in volume and importance these earlier works
cannot match those of the twelfth century when, as the noble genealogies indicate, the effects of literacy spread beyond the realm of
clerics. The pattern at Marmoutier—six histories and legends concerning the abbey's past written between about 1090 and about 1227,
as opposed to a virtual absence of historical writings from the ninth,
tenth, and early eleventh centuries—conforms to a general pattern of
increased historical output in the period around the twelfth century.
And Marmoutier's authors were particularly adept at inventing their
past out of nothing—the sequential list of abbots from the fourth
through the tenth centuries was almost entirely the creation of its
author.[63]

In their implicit and explicit acknowledgment of historical change
and distance, twelfth-century historical writings demonstrated more
sophistication than did those of the early Middle Ages. This may also

61. On clarity, precision, and a formalized judicial system, see Dunbabin, *France in the
Making,* 277–86. On monks and the forged invention or reconstruction of history, see
Chibnall, *World of Orderic Vitalis,* 109–14; Southern, "Aspects of the European Tradition of
Historical Writing: 4. The Sense of the Past"; Guenée, *Histoire et culture historique,* 33–35;
Saxer, *Culte de Marie Madeleine en Occident;* and the response to that book by Silvestre,
"Problème des faux au Moyen Age."

62. On the perceptual differences between oral cultures and written cultures, and especially the emphasis on sequentiality and causality in written cultures, see Ong, *Presence of
the Word,* 91, 111 ff. On the impact of literacy in the eleventh and twelfth centuries, see
Stock, *Implications of Literacy.*

63. In addition to the four works discussed in this chapter, the monks wrote the legend
of the *Restoration of Marmoutier (Liber de restructione Majoris monasterii*—discussed in chapter
4) and the *Deeds of the Abbey of Marmoutier (De rebus gestis in Majori monasterio*—discussed in
chapter 5). The interpolated document from the end of the tenth century was one of several
forgeries the monks created at that time, but these were not works of history: see Lévêque,
"Trois actes faux," 54–82, 289–305. On what we know about actual abbots of Marmoutier
before 985, see Lévêque, "Histoire de l'abbaye de Marmoutier."

be true of their explanations for historical causality. An emphasis on direct divine intervention—on God not only as primary but also as secondary cause of historical events—sometimes gave way in the twelfth century to natural metaphors for development and to discussions of human causation.[64]

The transition from providential to biological explanations or metaphors is more evident in the noble genealogies than in the histories of Marmoutier. Nevertheless, in the monks' treatment of their past we can detect attempts to appropriate the idea of actual, as well as metaphorical, family connections, and we find some renewal metaphors that leave out providential intervention, thus allowing more room for the play of natural forces. But it was especially in their attention to the will of the individual—as discussed in chapters 3, 4, and 5—that the monks most clearly demonstrated a transition from otherworldly to this-worldly notions of causality: Henry II had to choose to recreate and renew the glory of his Angevin ancestors; Odo of Blois achieved his own salvation with his act of contrition; the interior will of every monk sustained Marmoutier's existence as a community.

There was much that was new, then, in the historical writings produced at Marmoutier between the end of the eleventh century and the beginning of the thirteenth. Its themes of renewal and genealogical continuity demonstrate a greater awareness of secular, or secondary, causation and of historical distance than one would have found in many of the historical writings of the early Middle Ages. Yet the monks of Marmoutier did not approach history in the same way we do. Rather, their attitude was backward-looking. Their theme of renewal represented a desire to recover the past, and their theme of genealogical continuity sprang from a desire to preserve a tradition. The idea of genealogical continuity, moreover, left even less room for change than did that of renewal, and it was genealogical continuity that the monks favored in their ultimate presentation of Marmoutier's past: although the thirteenth-century history of the abbey continued to use cyclical imagery, it emphasized continuity, arranging its account of the Viking invasions so that the message of preservation prevailed. On one level, this work implied, Marmoutier's inheritance from Saint Martin did not need to be recovered because it had never been completely lost.[65]

64. Hanning, *Vision of History in Early Britain,* 121 ff.; Spiegel, "Genealogy: Form and Function," 50.

65. Although we do not find it at Marmoutier, there is some evidence suggesting an idea of and affirmation of progress in the twelfth century: see Constable, "Renewal and Reform in the Religious Life," 38–39; Southern, "Aspects of the European Tradition of Historical Writing: 2. Hugh of St. Victor and the Idea of Historical Development."

The ritual for the election of a new abbot at Marmoutier reiterated this message. Indeed, the ritual suggested, each time a new abbot was chosen it was Saint Martin who did the choosing and who thus renewed the traditio he first established by appointing and blessing his successor, Walbert. According to Guibert of Gembloux (a Benedictine who visited Marmoutier in 1180–81), the monks of Marmoutier—including all the priors who were able to return to the mother house in time for the election—began their election process by fasting, giving away alms, and then making a solemn procession to Martin's tomb in Châteauneuf. There they celebrated masses and made supplications, asking "that the highest pastor permit them, in electing his vicarious pastor, neither to err nor to follow their own spirit but rather to follow his."[66] The monks then returned to their abbey, and while twenty or thirty brothers "of sounder council" conducted the election in a closed room, the other monks lay prostrate in the chapter room, performing a litany and saying prayers.

To Guibert of Gembloux this election process demonstrated the degree to which Marmoutier remained untainted by simony and by the influence of people in powerful secular or ecclesiastical positions. The monks of Marmoutier had fought and won a long series of battles to preserve the freedom of their abbots and of their abbatial elections. The procession from Marmoutier to Saint Martin's tomb thus served as a public reminder that the monks freely chose their own abbot, thereby protecting their tradition from corruptible outside influence. But the request that the monks made at Martin's tomb also demonstrated that the true force behind the election was not the fallible will of the monks, but the infallible will of Martin himself. Martin was the "highest pastor" of Marmoutier, and it was he who chose his own "vicar."[67] To question such a process, to attempt to change it in any way, would insult and offend the saintly protector of the abbey.

With both legend and ritual, then, the monks of Marmoutier communicated to others, and to themselves, the conviction that they

66. "Deprecans ut summus pastor in eligendo pastore sui vicario nec falli, nec suum, sed ipsius eos sequi permittat spiritum" (Guibert, Abbot of Gembloux, "Epistola," 609). On the date of Guibert's visit to Marmoutier, see Delehaye, "Guibert, Abbé de Florennes et de Gembloux."

67. It is not clear whether "highest priest" (*summus pastor*) refers to Martin or to Christ, and that confusion may have been deliberate. "Summus pontifex" could mean archbishop (Du Cange, *Glossarium*, s.v. "Summus," 7:655), and Martin was called "altissimus" and "optimus pastor": see "De cultu Sancti Martini apud Turonenses extremo saeculo XII," 241. The reference to "his vicarious pastor" would have been to Martin: just as the pope was the "vicarius Sancti Petri," the abbot of Marmoutier would have been the "vicarius Sancti Martini" (see Cowdrey, *Cluniacs and the Gregorian Reform*, 137).

preserved the distinctive qualities of an archetypal past. Their interest in such preservation arose in part from their aristocratic milieu: both noble families and monastic institutions, whose members were themselves from noble families, liked to believe that something enduring—the inherent and inherited qualities of a patriarch—set them apart. But Marmoutier's interest in preservation was also peculiarly monastic. Invented traditions, and the newly identified relics of the seven sleepers, demonstrated that the abbey had never lost anything.[68] Relics and histories served as the abbey's collective memory, as repositories of all moments from the abbey's past. They reinforced the perception that the cloister was a center of changelessness, and changelessness—immutability—was at the core of monastic spirituality because it was one of the attributes of eternity, or paradise.

Medieval Christianity's emphasis on the immutability of God and of the afterlife was in many ways in inheritance from Neoplatonism. Saint Augustine's writings, for instance, were saturated with Neoplatonism, and his language had a profound impact on monastic thought and literature.[69] Augustine's *Confessions* return again and again to the restless and "pulsating" nature of secular pursuits—of love for created things, in which "there is no peace or rest because they do not last." In contrast to these exhausting pursuits, Augustine portrayed, in language borrowed from the Psalms, the peace and repose to be found in concentrating all one's desire on love for the immutable God:

"In peace [*pace*] and friendliness I will sleep; I will take my rest" [Ps. 4:8] in the eternal God. Oh the joy of those words! . . . You truly are the eternal God, because in you there is no change and in you we find the rest [*requies*] that banishes all our labor.

O Lord God . . . grant us the peace of repose [*pacem quietis*], the peace of the Sabbath, the peace that has no evening. For this worldly order in all its beauty will pass away . . . . But the seventh day is without evening . . . for you have sanctified it and willed that it shall last forever.[70]

68. On relics as tangible connections with the past, see also Geary, "Ninth-Century Relic Trade: A Response to Popular Piety?" 19.

69. Leclercq, *Love of Learning*, 122–24; Leclercq, *Otia monastica: Etudes sur le vocabulaire de la contemplation au Moyen Age,* passim. The works of Augustine—especially the biblical commentaries and sermons—were standard monastic reading in the eleventh and twelfth centuries: see Hunt, *Cluny under Saint Hugh,* 116–17; *Antiquae consuetudines Majoris monasterii,* fol. 93. On the date (sometime after 1124) and identity of this customal, see Source Appendix, I-F.

70. Augustine of Hippo, *Confessionum libri XIII,* 9:4, 13:35, ed. Verheijen, 139–40, 272; trans. Pine-Coffin, 188, 346.

Descriptions of the monastic life resound with similar images of peace, rest, and repose—images conveying the impression that God's immutability, the Sabbath day of eternal rest, can be experienced in this life, within the walls of the cloister. "Our purpose," the monks of Marmoutier claimed when they protested the disturbance imposed on the abbey by their archbishop, "was monastic peace [*quies*] . . . it was forbidden that we should allow the paradise of our souls to be indecently trampled by wild weeds, and our peace [*quies*] to be disturbed, because God had sternly commanded that his Sabbath was to be guarded."[71]

Garden imagery and descriptions of perpetual spring also evoked the timeless, eternal, and paradisiacal qualities of the monastic life. The cloister, according to numerous writings, both recovered the garden of Eden and anticipated the place of eternal life.[72] It was an oasis of gentle cultivation, which contrasted with the harshness of untamed nature, the "wilderness" that threatened to overwhelm Marmoutier when the Vikings invaded and the archbishop attacked.[73]

Untamed nature, with its seasonal rhythms, climatic flux, and chaotic weeds, contrasted with the topos of the monastery as a cultivated garden of perpetual spring. Marmoutier, according to Guibert of Gembloux, smelled like an "orchard of pomegranates." It was a garden watered by the streams of Mount Lebanon . . . "and irrigated by celestial rains, which turn everything green and cause aromatic bushes, all kinds of flowers, and fruit trees to germinate."[74]

Marmoutier's garden, like those of other monasteries, knew no change of seasons, no rhythm. Its renewal did not recur annually. Rather, it had happened only once, after the Viking invasions. This timelessness, the absence of change, was also implicit in monastic liturgy. To be sure, monks celebrated a cycle of feasts, but their life of prayer, their liturgical observation, was virtually perpetual. Guibert

---

71. "Causa nostra erat quietem monasticam . . . pati non poteramus paradisum animarum nostrarum a feris harundineti indecenter conculcari, nec quietem perturbari; pro eo quod Dominus terribiliter praecipiat ut sabbata ejus custodiantur, nec servili opere, hoc est saeculari conversatione, ullatenus polluantur" (*Notitia seu libellus de tribulationibus . . . Majori-monasterio injuste illatis*, 93). On the themes of *otium, quies*, and *sabbatum* in monastic writings, see Leclercq, *Otia monastica*.

72. Constable, "Renewal and Reform in the Religious Life," 48–51.

73. See chapter 2 at note 38. For an excellent discussion of wilderness and garden imagery in early monasticism, and the links between this imagery and discussions of baptism, see Williams, *Wilderness and Paradise in Christian Thought*, 28–46.

74. "Emissiones ejus paradisus malorum punicorum," "Affluentiam vero salutarium aquarum salientium in vitam aeternam quae fluunt impetu de Libano probant areolae a peritissimis hortolanis . . . consitae, et coelestibus irrigatae imbribus, passim ibi vernantes, arbustaque aromata, et omnigenos virtutum flores, et fructus germinantes" (Guibert, Abbot of Gembloux, "Epistola," 610, 616).

of Gembloux declared that Marmoutier's monks praised God "perpetually—mixing, on lutes, tambourines and every instrument of spiritual music, the melody of their symphony with the supernal harmony of the blessed spirits!"[75]

The desire to represent and experience the monastery as a reflection of immutable eternal life provides one essential conceptual framework for approaching and understanding the reconstruction of the past at Marmoutier. Written history provided the monastery with its collective memory. And as Augustine had already suggested, it is memory that enables us not only to measure and perceive the existence of temporal duration, but also to deny the effects of time. In our minds, Augustine explained, we can simultaneously recall the past, experience the present, and anticipate the future, and for this reason our memories reflect, however remotely, the wisdom of God, for whom all time—past, present, and future—is eternally present, and for whom nothing changes.[76]

The histories and legends of Marmoutier, as well as the relics from its heroic age, indicated that, like the memory of the individual, the walls of the abbey preserved both the past and the present. Moreover, as the *Deeds of the Abbey of Marmoutier* stressed, those walls held an anticipation of the future as well. Visits from Saint Martin and from the ghosts of dead monks put the living monks in contact not only with the past but also with the future—with the life that awaited them beyond the threshold of death. The space of the monastery thus functioned like the space within our minds, providing its members with a reflection of the experience of eternity.

Monastic representations of the cloister as the experience of eternity provide one context for Marmoutier's preoccupation with establishing links between past, present, and future. But this preoccupation also points to a desire to reestablish a feeling of connection that could help the monks overcome alienation. Because they and their society were undergoing profound change and their world was becoming increasingly complex, the monks felt a need to recover an organic connection not only with each other—as I explained in chapter 5—but also with the past. They needed to convince both themselves and others that they still were, and always had been, a community of Saint Martin.

75. "Perpetuo non tacantes in cytharis et tympanis et omnibus spiritualis musicae instrumentis laudantes Deum, superne beatorum spirituum armoniae melodiam symphoniae suae immiscerent" (Guibert, Abbot of Gembloux, "Epistola," 617). On the concept of incessant monastic prayer, see Leclercq, *Etudes sur le vocabulaire monastique,* 129.

76. Augustine of Hippo, *Confessionum libri XIII,* 11:27–31, ed. Verheijen, 211–16, trans. Pine-Coffin, 275–80.

PART 3

The Chapter of Saint-Martin

Introduction

From the beginning and throughout its history, the religious community at the basilica of Saint-Martin was very different from that of Marmoutier. Its primary religious purpose was neither the ascetic quest for personal salvation nor the monastic intercessory function.[1] Rather, its members cared for the tomb of a major pilgrimage saint and performed the elaborate liturgy there. This religious function, which involved daily contact between the members of the community of Saint-Martin and the pilgrims who visited Martin's tomb, was not necessarily incompatible with Benedictine monasticism.[2] Nevertheless, efforts to maintain a cloistered life at Saint-Martin rarely succeeded. Its inhabitants were not disposed to a monastic renunciation of the world.

Columbanian reformers did manage to introduce monastic reforms at Saint-Martin in the mid-seventh century, but by the 770s the absence of monastic discipline there was drawing criticism. A few decades later, Charlemagne would complain that he could not tell whether Saint-Martin was a house of canons or a house of monks; and Alcuin, who was abbot there from 796 until 804, found it was easier to introduce the Benedictine *Rule* to the priory of Cormery, which was subordinated to Saint-Martin, than to reform Saint-Martin itself.[3]

1. Nevertheless, laypeople did make gifts to Saint-Martin for the sake of their souls, and both laypeople and canons of the chapter endowed anniversary masses there: see note 10 below and Mabille, *Pancarte noire de Saint-Martin*, 51, 54, pp. 91, 93 (anniversary for Charles the Bald founded in 878; gift for the souls of Count Heligaud's ancestors, in 813). In the Merovingian and Carolingian periods, Saint-Martin became one of the most richly endowed landed institutions in Francia: see Vaucelle, *Collégiale de Saint-Martin*, 110–12.

2. Vézelay and Saint-Foi of Conques were regular monastic communities with major pilgrimage shrines.

3. Chélini, "Alcuin, Charlemagne et Saint-Martin de Tours." On the seventh-century reform of Saint-Martin, see chapter 1 at note 43.

'Maison Dugnay de la Madeine.

Imp. Lemercier

ÉGLISE DE St MARTIN À TOURS TELLE QU'ELLE ÉTAIT EN 1700

PLATE 5. The basilica of Saint-Martin as it looked about 1700. The Gothic church of Saint-Martin was built about 1225–50 and destroyed

Sometime around 815 the ambiguous status of the religious life at Saint-Martin was resolved when the community officially became a house of canons.[4] After 817 members of canonical communities had the right to possess private property, and that concession led, in the course of the ninth and tenth centuries, to the establishment of private residences for individual canons and to the creation of individual prebends—either landed property or incomes from landed property—that were assigned to each canon.[5] There are references to private residences at Saint-Martin in sources that date back to 845 and to prebends there as early as 903.[6]

In describing and explaining the differences between the canons of Saint-Martin and the monks of Marmoutier, we must begin with these institutional arrangements. For though Benedictine monasteries were not collectively poor, each individual monk was symbolically poor because he was allowed no private possessions, not even the habit he wore. The canons of Saint-Martin, by contrast, lived in individual houses, ate at their own tables, and lived off the fruits of their own prebends. Moreover, the canons were not cloistered. Contemporary documents referring to the *claustrum*—the enclosed space within the defensive walls of Châteauneuf, built in 918—may lend the impression that Saint-Martin possessed a cloister,[7] but this was hardly a religious enclosure. Both within its walls and outside, the houses of canons and laypeople intermingled, and women were allowed to enter its boundaries.[8]

That the canons were not cloistered and that they did not practice individual poverty contributed to an ambiguous quality in their religious life—a tendency to blend in with their secular surroundings.

4. Semmler, "Benedictus II," 14–15.

5. Dereine, "Chanoines"; Edwards, *English Secular Cathedrals in the Middle Ages,* 1–7; Lesne, "Origines de la prébende." At Saint-Martin canons did not individually administer the estates their incomes were derived from. These were under the supervision of fifteen provosts: see Vaucelle, *Collégiale de Saint-Martin,* 210–11.

6. Mabille, *Pancarte noire de Saint-Martin,* 41, p. 86; *Recueil des historiens des Gaules,* 9:497; cited by Oury, "Idéal monastique dans la vie canoniale: Le bienheureux Hervé de Tours," 11–12 n. 32, 33.

7. Vaucelle, *Collégiale de Saint-Martin,* 273. A papal bull issued by Alexander III in 1179 distinguished Saint-Martin's possessions in the *claustrum* from those of the *castrum*—that part of Châteauneuf that extended from the exterior of the walls to the Loire: see *Papsturkunden in Frankreich,* n.s. 5, no. 143, p. 239.

8. On canons' houses outside the cloister, see Lévêque, "Trois actes faux ou interpolés . . . en faveur de l'abbaye de Marmoutier," 304–5. On burghers inside the cloister, see Mabille, *Pancarte noire de Saint-Martin,* catalog, 176, 186, 203, pp. 193, 195, 199; and Chevalier, "Cité de Tours et Châteauneuf," 242 (a merchant lives near the Church of Saint-Denis, which is inside the walls). On women entering the cloister, see Odo of Cluny, "Sermo de combustione basilicae beati Martini," *PL* 133:736 (for my argument that this really was by Odo of Cluny, see Source Appendix, II-A).

They were not even set apart by their relationship to the sacraments, since only a few of them (6 out of 150 in the thirteenth century) had to be priests: these were "ceremonial" rather than "sacramental" clergy.[9] Some of the canons, in addition, privately owned and rented residential and business properties in Châteauneuf, just like their merchant neighbors.[10] And like their burgher neighbors, all the canons derived their prosperity from the pilgrims who visited Martin's tomb.

This tendency for the canons of Saint-Martin to be drawn into the secular sphere was sometimes exacerbated by their relationship to their lay abbot. The abbacy of Saint-Martin, like that of many other monastic and canonical communities, became in the late ninth century a private possession that secular lords could give away to their subordinates or pass on to their sons. In 866 Robert the Strong became the lay abbot of both Saint-Martin and Marmoutier; from 888 until 987 the abbacy of Saint-Martin was the hereditary possession of the Robertians; and from 987 until 1789 it belonged to the kings of France.[11] In the ninth and tenth centuries the community of Saint-Martin struggled to protect its assets from the depredations of these lay abbots, and the internal governance of the chapter, as well as the disposition of its revenues, became the provenance of its dean and treasurer.[12] Still, the lay abbot continued to exercise a considerable

9. Six officers (dean, cantor, schoolmaster, subdean, almoner, and granger), plus the abbot of Cormery, had to be priests. The responsibilities of the basilica's priest of the week rotated among these seven men: see *Consuetudines ecclesiae beati Martini*, 116. Vaucelle, *Collégiale de Saint-Martin*, 193–94. It was also the case at cathedral chapters that only a few canons had to be priests: see Pycke, *Chapitre cathédral Nôtre-Dame de Tournai*, 243. Richard C. Trexler makes the useful distinction between ceremonial and sacramental clergy (*Public Life in Renaissance Florence*, 34).

10. In 1098 the canon Andrew gave the chapter half the wood and stone houses he possessed inside and outside the walls of Châteauneuf and the stall he owned near the drapers' shops in order to establish his anniversary; and about 1137 William, the cellarer of Saint-Martin, left Saint-Martin some houses in Châteauneuf with gardens and a vineyard across the Loire: see Bibliothèque Nationale, Collection Housseau, MS. 3, no. 1024 (Mabille, *Pancarte noire de Saint-Martin*, 203, p. 199); Tours, Archives d'Indre-et-Loire, vol. G381, p. 344; and (a second copy of the same) Bibliothèque Nationale, Collection Baluze, MS. 76, fol. 107. Péan Gatineau, the thirteenth-century canon from Saint-Martin who wrote *La vie monseignor Saint Martin de Tors*, was probably from a prominent burgher family in Châteauneuf: he shared a common name with one of the burghers who participated in the communes of 1180 and 1184, and the Gatineaux were still prominent in Tours in the fourteenth century: see Source Appendix, II-C, and chapter 9, note 14.

11. Boussard, "Trésorier de Saint-Martin," 71–72.

12. In 897, 930, and 941 the lay abbots restored to the mensa of Saint-Martin properties that they, or earlier lay abbots, had appropriated from the community; a forgery, dated 904, established that the abbots would give up the right of provision they had formerly demanded from new canons and that the dean (rather than the abbot) would nominate new canons; another forgery, dated 919, stated that the community had the right to maintain its possessions free from any intervention from the abbot: see Mabille, *Pancarte noire de Saint-*

amount of indirect control over the community: from at least the time of King Hugh Capet (987–96) on, the king/abbot had the right to appoint the dean and treasurer of Saint-Martin.[13]

Ninth- and tenth-century developments laid the foundations for the way the canons of Saint-Martin lived and behaved in the twelfth and thirteenth centuries. Nevertheless, it is important to recall that during this period a number of religious communities, including Marmoutier, evolved into houses of secular canons under the jurisdiction of lay abbots. For our purposes here, then, the significant differences between Saint-Martin and Marmoutier emerged in the late tenth and eleventh centuries when Saint-Martin, unlike Marmoutier, remained unaffected, first, by the wave of monastic reform that turned Marmoutier into a model Benedictine abbey and later, by the Gregorian reform, which managed to turn some houses of secular canons into communities of regular canons who held their property in common.[14]

The canons of Saint-Martin were certainly exposed to these reform movements. Odo of Cluny began his religious career at Saint-Martin and remained a lifetime devotee of its patron saint; Herveus, who was treasurer of Saint-Martin between 1001 and 1022, had been a student of the great defender of monasticism, Abbo of Fleury; and some of the canons of Saint-Martin left the chapter at the end of the eleventh century to found a house of regular canons on the island of Saint-Cosme, which became a place of spiritual refuge for those canons from Saint-Martin who felt a need for a more serious, or more cloistered, spiritual life.[15]

Martin, 55, 76, 111, 40, 7, pp. 94, 105, 125, 85, 58, and Vaucelle, *Collégiale de Saint-Martin*, 76, 81, 125, 198–201. On the forgeries attributed to Charles the Simple, see Gasnault, "Etude sur les chartes de Saint-Martin," 38. It seems that by the thirteenth century the canons themselves nominated new members: see Vaucelle, *Collégiale*, 186.

13. Griffiths, "Capetian Kings and St. Martin of Tours."

14. The historiography concerning canonical chapters in the period during and after the Gregorian reform has been dominated by studies of regular canons, even though most northern French cathedrals remained houses of secular canons. Three institutional studies of secular canons are Edwards, *English Secular Cathedrals;* Pycke, *Chapitre cathédral Nôtre-Dame de Tournai;* and Duggan, *Bishop and Chapter: The Governance of the Bishopric of Speyer to 1552.* These excellent studies are not concerned with the ritual life of the communities.

On the fact that northern French cathedrals and those of the low countries remained unreformed, see Dereine, "Chanoines," 379; Becquet, "Réforme des chapitres cathédraux en France aux XIe et XIIe siècles"; and Pycke, *Chapitre cathédral*, 111–12.

15. On Odo of Cluny, see Source Appendix, II-A. On Herveus, see Oury, "Idéal monastique dans la vie canoniale: Le bienheureux Hervé de Tours." On Saint-Cosme, see Oury, "Erémitisme dans l'ancien diocèse de Tours," 45; Mabille, *Pancarte noire de Saint-Martin*," catalog, 196, p. 198; Tours, Bibliothèque Municipale, MS. 1295, p. 605 (foundation charter); and chapter 7 at note 75.

Despite these influences, however, Saint-Martin remained a house of secular canons, and we can detect their more worldly orientation in the miracle stories they told about Saint Martin. Rather than assuring that Martin could assist sinners in attaining salvation or avoiding the punishments of purgatory, the canons recounted miracles that promoted the popularity of their pilgrimage shrine, indicating that Martin could restore physical health to those suffering from disease or injury. Other miracles, which I discuss in chapters 8 and 9, worked to support the canons' competitive interests, conveying the message that Martin's episcopal and judicial powers belonged to them.

Although the chapter of Saint-Martin was always inclined to merge with its secular surroundings, developments in the twelfth and thirteenth centuries introduced new problems for the community and its identity. As I explain in chapter 7, the most important of these attenuating forces was the king's right of collation over the offices of dean and treasurer of the chapter. After 1139 the Capetians began to grant these offices to their relatives, and by the early thirteenth century they were using the offices to remunerate members of the royal court.

Outside forces may have threatened the community of Saint Martin, but as I show in chapters 7, 8, and 9, the canons' response was to assert their collective rights vis-à-vis their king/abbot, their archbishop, and their burgher neighbors/subjects. In the course of defending those rights, I assert, the canons became even more aware of themselves as a collectivity. But to what degree did they see themselves as a community and, indeed, as a religious community with a religious vocation? This is the question I address in chapter 7. Our examination of Saint-Martin thus starts at the point where our examination of Marmoutier left off. The chapters in part 2 worked inward, from relations between Marmoutier and the outside world to relations among the monks themselves. With Saint-Martin, however, it seems more appropriate to begin with the group of canons themselves, because the very existence of that group appears problematic. Before we go on to discuss the interactions between the canons and other groups in society, we must establish in what ways the canons were aware of their identity as a religious community distinct both from a corporation of royal officials and from the secular society of Châteauneuf.

7

The Corporate Identity of the
Canons of Saint-Martin

[Just after the Viking incursion against Tours in 903] the sheep who had evaded the mouths of wolves—under the protection of their pious pastor [Saint Martin] and with the counsel and aid of the princes of France—took refuge and constructed this noble wall around the basilica, which had formerly stood nude, about 150 paces outside of the city. . . . And from then on, through the prayers of such a great intercessor, God strengthened the bolts of the doors of our Zion and blessed his sons in it and laid down peace within its boundaries. . . . Evidence of [Saint Martin's] protection toward us is in the books that recount how he frequently rescued us, our possessions, and even the city itself from enemies; evidence of his favor is in the multiple experiences by which . . . we feel his favor overflowing toward us; evidence is in the serenity of peace and the affluence of riches by which we rejoice that the city of Châteauneuf is strong. And testimony of our affection toward him—both our own and that of all the populace—lies in the fact that, unlike what is done in other churches, we do not appoint vicars—and indeed up until now no vicar has ever been allowed to enter the choir. Rather, day and night we ourselves serve both God and his saint.

—Philip and Renaud, dean and treasurer of the chapter
of Saint-Martin, Letters Written in 1180–81[1]

1. "Tunc sub pii pastoris protectione ovibus quae luporum dentes evaserant confugientibus, consilio et auxilio principum Franciae circa ejus templum antea nudum et ab urbe longo centum quinquaginta fere passuum interstitio distans, nobile hoc et multi decoris oppidum construentes. . . . Ex tunc et deinceps tanti intercessoris precibus confortavit Dominus seras portarum Syon nostrae et benedixit filiis ejus in ea et posuit fines ipsius pacem. . . . Protectionis ejus testes apud nos sunt libri in quibus refertur quomodo et nos et nostra, sed et urbem ipsam ab hostibus frequenter eruerit; testis multimoda experientia qua . . . ipsius erga nos favorem redundare sentimus; testis optatae serenitas pacis et divitiarum affluentia quibus castri nostri municipium pollere gaudemus. Affectionis autem nostrae et totius populi in eum praeclarum primo reddit testimonium quod non, ut in aliis fit ecclesiis, per vicarios (nec enim vicarios unquam aliquis hactenus chorum nostrum intrare permissus est), sed per nosmetipsos die noctuque servitio Dei et ejus assistimus" ("De cultu Sancti Martini apud Turonenses extremo saeculo XII," 226, 235). On the dates of the two letters that Philip and Renaud wrote during Guibert of Gembloux's visit to Tours between September 1180 and May 1181, see Delehaye, "Guibert, Abbé de Florennes et de Gembloux," 46–65.

On first consideration, the language in this passage conveys the impression that the religious and communal concerns of the canons of Saint-Martin resembled those of the monks of Marmoutier. Like the monks, who identified their monastic community with the chosen people of the Old Testament, Philip and Renaud represented their community as Zion, the home of the chosen people. Like the monks, the canons associated recovery from the Viking invasions with the physical and spiritual renewal of their community, and they attributed the continued well-being of their group to the protection of Saint Martin.

Yet one striking feature of this passage alerts us to differences between the canons' representations of their community and the monks' representations of Marmoutier: unlike the monks, the canons did not clearly distinguish the collective identity of their chapter from that of their secular neighbors. At times they used the first-person plural to refer to themselves. They took pride, for instance, in the fact that "we"—that is to say, the canons—did not appoint vicars to perform the liturgical offices at the basilica. At other times, however, Philip and Renaud's "we" referred to all the inhabitants of Châteauneuf. Thus, Philip and Renaud somehow associated the canons' act of devotion—the fact that they did not appoint vicars—with the populace at large. Along similar lines, they applied to the secular, urban space terms that the monks of Marmoutier used to describe their monastic community. They associated the "peace" God laid down in "Zion" with the city rather than with a religious community that was cloistered from the secular realm.

This Zion breathed the rhythms of secular time and commercial pursuits.[2] Philip and Renaud would claim that at least on certain days—such as Saint Martin's feast of May 12, which had become the urban patronal feast of Châteauneuf—the sacred took over, and the city resembled "the entrance of paradise."[3] When the day or week of a feast was over, however, the citizens of Châteauneuf turned their attention to profit and justice: "When the crowds of people [who attend the festivities for Martin's November feast] return to their own houses, the inhabitants [of Châteauneuf] drop everything and concern

---

2. For a similar depiction of urban catholic time, see Davis, "Sacred and the Body Social in Sixteenth-Century Lyon." Davis contrasts Catholic time with Protestant; I propose a similar distinction between monastic and urban time, as did Le Goff: see "Merchant's Time and Church's Time in the Middle Ages," in *Time, Work, and Culture in the Middle Ages,* 29–42.

3. "Ut plane videatur cunctis prae amoenitate et decore quasi quidam introitus paradisi" ("De cultu Sancti Martini," 236).

themselves exclusively with seeing that the law cases of the markets and inns satisfy with all integrity of devotion those who were injured during the solemnity."[4] Philip and Renaud obliquely alluded here to the fact that Châteauneuf's courts of high justice met each year for a number of days before and after Martin's November feast.[5] But perhaps despite themselves, they also indicated that even on sacred days, when Châteauneuf approximated the entrance to paradise, the canons and inhabitants of the town were preoccupied with profane concerns. Pilgrims poured into the town, especially during the November feast, bringing business and profit to the local shopkeepers and inns. There was money to be made, and there were disputes to be settled over who was to make it.[6]

Philip and Renaud's language points to the absence of any clearly articulated boundary separating the community of canons from the secular realm. The canons made no clear attempt to distinguish the identity of their religious community from that of the town of Châteauneuf. Their values, moreover, were blatantly secular: they associated Saint Martin's favor with "the affluence of riches" that blessed his town and its inhabitants. Indeed, they made a clear distinction between Marmoutier, in which religion and piety flourished, and Saint-Martin, which was renowned for its wealth: "In no city of the Christian world does any saint have two churches as noble and rich as . . . Marmoutier . . . and [Saint-Martin]. . . . That one is . . . incomparable in its religion and alms to the poor; this one, in the privilege of signs and the glory of riches."[7]

Along similar lines, the canons sometimes linked the interests and identity of their community with those of their lay abbots, the Capetian kings. There is no history of the chapter of Saint-Martin, no work that parallels the first and second versions of the *History of Marmoutier,* which reconstructed the history of the monastic community by accounting for the continuity of its inhabitants, emphasizing the collective rights and privileges that the monks themselves ob-

4. "Confluentium catervis populorum ad propria reversis, cives, aliis intermissis jam ad nil aliud vacant nisi ut causa nundinarum et causa hospitum injuriatae solemnitati omni cum integritate devotionis satisfaciant" ("De cultu Sancti Martini," 238–39).
5. Courts of Justice were held from November 1 to November 13 and from June 29 to July 4: see Accord between Philip Augustus and Richard the Lion-Hearted (1190) in *Recueil des actes de Philippe Auguste,* 1:441.
6. See chapter 9.
7. "In nulla urbe christiani orbis quilibet sanctorum unus tam divites et nobiles duas simul habeat ecclesias, quarum altera est Majus Monasterium . . . altera ista nostra . . . illa religione et pauperum eleemosynis, haec signorum privilegio et divitiarum gloria . . . incomparabilis" ("De cultu Sancti Martini," 225–26).

tained.[8] The only major historical work from Saint-Martin, the
Chronicle of Tours (written in or soon after 1225), was a history of
Francia, which provided one of the most innovative sources of pres-
tige for the Capetian kings.

According to the author of the chronicle, Hugh Capet's mother
was the granddaughter of the Carolingian king Louis the Child (who
had actually died childless), and thus Hugh's accession to the French
throne did not in any way represent a break in the Carolingian royal
line. Neither, according to this author, had the Carolingians represented a dynastic break, for Pipin, the first of the Carolingian line to
be crowned king, was a descendant of the Merovingian Childeric.
Thus the kings of France in the thirteenth century were part of a
single continuous Frankish royal bloodline.[9]

These claims were not entirely new. About the year 1200, Giles of
Paris had described a direct genealogical link between the Merovingians and the Carolingians. And he, as well as other propagan-
dists for Philip Augustus and Louis VIII, had made vague assertions
that there were links between the Carolingians and the Capetians.
Still, no one in French royal circles had previously established a specific link between Hugh Capet and the Carolingians.[10]

In their writings from the late twelfth and early thirteenth centuries, the canons of Saint-Martin tended to mesh their values and
identities with those of the town that surrounded them and of the
king who was their lay abbot. This was not a completely new situation. As I noted in the introduction to this section, the amorphous
qualities of the chapter of Saint-Martin can be traced back to the ninth
and early tenth centuries. Yet the sources indicate that, like other
houses of secular canons, the chapter of Saint-Martin experienced a
number of centrifugal forces in the twelfth and thirteenth centuries
that undermined even further whatever solidarity and religious character remained to the community.

First, the burghers of Châteauneuf rebelled against the canons'

---

8. The *Commendation of the Province of Touraine* did include a late twelfth-century
history of the basilica, but it was precisely that—an account of the various edifices that
housed Saint Martin's relics: see *Narratio de commendatione Turonicae provinciae*, 299–302. On
the dates and authorship of this section of the *Narratio* (probably about 1175 or soon
thereafter), see Source Appendix, I-B.

9. *Chronicon Turonense auctore anonymo*, 992–93, 948. For discussion by recent scholars
of the importance of this text to French royal historiography, see the following note.

10. Lewis, *Royal Succession in Capetian France*, 106–13; Lewis, "Dynastic Structures and
Capetian Throne-Right: The Views of Giles of Paris"; Brown, "Notion de la légitimité et la
prophétie à la cour de Philippe Auguste"; Baldwin, *Government of Philip Augustus*, 367–80.

seigneurial rights over their town. In chapter 9 I discuss at greater
length the canons' reactions to these rebellions. For now, however, let
me suggest that to assert their hierarchical authority over the burghers, the canons of Saint-Martin had to behave in worldly ways.

Much like their Italian counterparts, the burghers of Châteauneuf
were proud of the material possessions that were theirs to display:

> The men . . . of Châteauneuf are so illustrious that they walk about
> exuberantly purpled, with an abundance of gold and silver, grisling
> and vair, and a variety of splendors and glories from all over the world.
> They marvel, in rich affluence, at their doubled wealth. Their houses
> are all turreted; protected with fortifications, they reach to the sky. A
> daily and manifold splendor of dishes decorates their tables. Almost
> none of them ever drinks from a cup unless it is a gold or silver goblet.
> They play "wildcat" and dice, and they hunt with birds of the sky.
> Jovial and munificent receivers of guests, they greatly absolve their
> debts to God, to those who deserve honor, and to the poor. For their
> patron—that is, the blessed Martin—and for other saints as well, they
> build churches with wondrous stone floors and carved capitals. . . .
>
> So great is the beauty . . . of the women, so many the number of
> beauties, and so immense their beauty, that the truth of the matter
> seems to exceed trustworthiness. . . . Precious clothing of exceptional
> elegance adorns their beauty, and in certain cases, I should say, it in-
> creases it.[11]

As this description suggests, status and display were closely intertwined. If the canons of Saint-Martin were to rule the burghers of

11. "Castri Novi . . . cujus viri adeo illustres, ut auri et argenti, varii et grisii, div-
ersarum insuper specierum et totius mundialis gloriae copia exuberantes purpurati ince-
dunt. Duatricem pecuniam obstupescunt, affluentibus divitiis. Quorum domus fere omnes
turritae, munitae propugnaculis in coelum porriguntur. Quorum mensas quotidianus et
varius ferculorum splendor exornat. Nemo ferme ex eis in poculis scyphum nisi argenteum
et aureum novit. In catis, aleis et avibus coeli ludunt. Hilares et munifici, hospitum suscep-
tores, Deo, honorificentiae, pauperibus maxime debita in dies exsolvunt. Patroni sui beati
videlicet Martini, et aliorum sanctorum ecclesias mirifico tabulatu lapideo, et arcubus
caelatis construunt. . . .
    Feminarum vero . . . tanta est pulchritudo, tanta pulchrarum numerositas, tanta earum
pulchritudinis immensitas, ut veritas rei fidem excedere videatur. . . . Pretiosae etenim
vestis cultus eximius ipsam exornat pulchritudinem, et quaedam, ut ita dixerim, incrementa
ministrat" (*Narratio de commendatione,*" 298–99). By the late thirteenth century, sumptuary
laws began to prohibit burghers from wearing sumptuous furs and cloths, such as the vair
and grisling mentioned here: see Le Goff, "Apogée de la France urbaine médiévale," 397.
    For examples of Italian authors who praised the wealth of their cities and the people who
inhabited them in terms that resemble those of the *Narratio de commendatione,* see Hyde,
Society and Politics in Medieval Italy, 60–64, 153–58; Hyde, "Medieval Descriptions of Cities"; and Trexler, *Public Life in Renaissance Florence,* 328–30. See also William Fitz Stephen's
description of London, written about 1175, in *English Historical Documents,* 2:956–62.

Châteauneuf, they needed to prove that their status, and hence their power, was greater than that of the burghers.[12] To do so they needed to put on the appropriate display—to imitate noble habits of hunting and gaming, and perhaps to don secular hairstyles and dress as well.[13] Inverting the hierarchy and renouncing symbols of wealth may have been fine ideals for religious men who wished to withdraw from worldly involvement. But as Peter the Chanter, the Parisian theologian and fellow secular canon, made clear, churchmen who held positions of responsibility over others were dead wrong if they thought they would give up the material symbols that bolstered their authority: "I ought not to put aside my noble horses and precious ornaments . . . on account of the scandal [of others], for the truth of justice would be at risk. For if I were to take on a mean habit and conduct myself as if I were lowly and contemptible . . . my subjects would become disobedient and do evil things . . . and thus I would not be able to exercise justice [and] . . . they would have fuel for sin."[14]

12. Sumptuary legislation, which first became popular in the thirteenth century, represents a more coercive attempt on the part of those in power to bolster the hierarchy by limiting certain forms of ostentation to the upper and ruling classes: see Leriget, *Des lois et impôts somptuaires;* Rainey, "Sumptuary Legislation in Renaissance Florence," 42 ff. Some of the twelfth- and thirteenth-century church legislation concerning the dress of the clergy was similarly hierarchical: bishops did not want lower clergy to imitate them by wearing red and green: see the following two notes.

13. In 1180–81 Guibert of Gembloux complained that the canons of Saint-Martin were too busy "playing games of chance, sporting after birds of the sky, and hunting hares, roes, and deer with their dogs" to write down Saint Martin's miracles; in reform statutes of 1204, the canons were told to keep their heads tonsured and not to wear red or green vestments, sewn sleeves, silk shoes, or brooches; in reform statutes of 1208 they had to be reminded even more sternly that they were to be tonsured, and the penalty of excommunication was extended to all who wore sleeved mantles; in 1262 their participation in tournaments and military games was condemned and prohibited: see "De cultu Sancti Martini," 248; "Prima reformatio ecclesiae facta anno 1204," Tours, Bibliothèque Municipale, MS. 1295, 547–48; "Secunda ecclesiae reformatio anno 1208," ibid., 549; "Quarta reformatio facta anno 1262," ibid., 557.

The rules concerning dress were common prohibitions, repeated at the Fourth Lateran Council in 1215, chap. 16: *Sacrorum conciliorum nova et amplissima collectio,* 22:1003, 1006. Hence it is not clear that all the stipulations were actually being broken at Saint-Martin. But the statutes of 1208 make it clear that some canons were disobeying the earlier statute about wearing the tonsure.

14. "Nobiles equos et ornamenta pretiosa . . . non tamen debeo omittere propter scandalum eorum quia ueritas iustitie esset in periculo. Si enim essem in uili habitu et tamquam deiectus et contemptibilem me haberem . . . statim subditi fierent inobedientes et mala agerent, et ita non possem exercere iustitiam . . . ipsi haberent materiam peccandi" (Peter the Chanter, *Summa de sacramentis,* 319, ed. Dugauquier, 3:2a:377). I am grateful to Lauren Helm Jared for giving me this reference. Peter was the chanter of the cathedral chapter of Nôtre-Dame of Paris, and he held a nonresidentiary prebend at Reims: see Baldwin, *Masters, Princes and Merchants,* 1:6–7.

It is no wonder, then, that a number of twelfth- and thirteenth-century observers perceived that the canons of Saint-Martin were prone to worldly ostentation.[15] The canons' lavish behavior was fraught with symbolic significance. It was an essential part of their corporate identity and collective power.

In addition to challenges from the burghers of Châteauneuf, the canons of Saint-Martin faced an even greater threat to their corporate identity from their own abbot, the Capetian king. Although the Capetian kings had held proprietary rights and domain over the chapter of Saint-Martin since the time of Hugh Capet, the reign of Louis VII represents a major turning point in the pattern of effective intervention in the governing of Saint-Martin and its town of Châteauneuf.[16] The renewed relationship between the king and the chapter is best illustrated by the fact that in 1139 Louis appointed his brother Henri treasurer of Saint-Martin. This pattern of family ties would be repeated again and again: Philip Augustus appointed to the position of treasurer of Saint-Martin two royal cousins (including Renaud, the coauthor of the letters of 1180–81) and his own illegitimate son, Pierre Charlot.[17] From the time of Philip Augustus on, the Capetians relied on their right to appoint the dean and treasurer of Saint-Martin as a means of rewarding and remunerating members of their administrative government. In fact, as Quentin Griffiths recently argued, Saint-Martin was one of only three houses over which the Capetian kings had such close control of appointments and upon which they consistently drew to build up their administrative governments.

By the early thirteenth century, the men appointed by the king as dean and treasurer of Saint-Martin were serving regularly in the royal court.[18] And the Capetian court was not the only growing bureaucracy that threatened the integrity of the community of Saint-Martin. Beginning at the time of Innocent III, various popes claimed the right to give canonries at Saint-Martin to their close associates.[19]

15. See above, note 13.

16. Boussard, "Trésorier de Saint-Martin," 80.

17. Griffiths, "Capetian Kings and St. Martin of Tours," 127.

18. Griffiths, "Capetian Kings and St. Martin of Tours." Royal offices held by deans were as follows: Odo III Clement (dean 1211–16)—king's clerk in all but name, master of the Norman exchequer; Nicholas de Roye (dean 1217–28)—king's counselor in the curia (he held this office after he was dean); Aubry Cornut (dean 1229–36)—king's clerk, keeper of the seal, on the exchequer; Jean de La Cour d'Aubergenville (dean 1236–44)—king's clerk, on the exchequer, keeper of the seal. Treasurers holding offices were Pierre (treasurer 1190–1203)—possibly royal chamberlain; Simon de Brion (treasurer 1256–81)—keeper of the seal, member of Parlement, adviser to Charles of Anjou.

19. Vaucelle, *Collégiale de Saint-Martin,* 186–87. For examples of similar patterns of papal intervention at a cathedral chapter, see Pycke, *Chapitre cathédral Nôtre-Dame de Tournai,* 59. For a general discussion of the issue, see Barraclough, *Papal Provisions.*

Canonical prebends were convenient both in meeting the needs of rulers and in providing incomes for students and scholars in the newly emerging universities. For these reasons they contributed to the problem of absenteeism, which began to plague houses of secular canons in the twelfth century.[20] At Saint-Martin, the problem of enforcing residency was at the core of reform statutes that were issued by papally appointed commissions in 1204 and 1208. In 1204 the statutes established that an ordinary canon had to be in residence for seven lunar months. Absence for a single day during those seven months would deprive him of his prebend. A canon could not count himself present on any given day unless he attended matins, mass, and vespers. The 1204 statutes also stipulated that a fine of two sous was to be imposed on each priest of the week (the responsibility rotated among the six officers who were priests and the abbot of Cormery, which was subordinated to Saint-Martin) every day that he failed to perform the mass when it was his turn to officiate. Similarly, deacons were to pay seventeen deniers each time they missed a mass. The chapter general, which was convened three times each year, would be delayed no more than a month to await the arrival of absent priors of the house.[21] The statutes of 1208 returned to the issue of residency, this time dealing with the officers, or priors, of the chapter, who held liege prebends. Priors would be deprived of the fruits of their prebends if they failed to be in residence for six months.[22]

These two sets of statutes attempted to define a canon's responsibility to be in residence. Nevertheless, they left ample room for exceptions. Canons who had obtained permission from the chapter could hold their prebends while attending school, going on pilgrimage, or serving the church in an official capacity, and illness or bloodletting constituted legitimate excuses for absence from daily services.[23]

20. Edwards, *English Secular Cathedrals*, 35 ff.; Pycke, *Chapitre cathédral Nôtre-Dame de Tournai*, 69, 92, 102, 115–26.
21. "Prima reformatio," Tours, Bibliothèque Municipale, MS. 1295, 547–48. On priests of the week see introduction to part 3, note 9. The wars between Philip Augustus and Kings Richard and John of England exacerbated the disciplinary decline at Saint-Martin. At one point the canons were even expelled from the city: see Vaucelle, *Collégiale de Saint-Martin*, 176 ff.; "Prima reformatio," 547.
22. "Secunda reformatio," Tours, Bibliothèque Municipale, MS. 1295, 549.
23. "Prima reformatio," Tours, Bibliothèque Municipale, MS. 1295, 548. Similar exceptions applied at the cathedral chapter of Tournai: see Pycke, *Chapitre cathédral Nôtre-Dame de Tournai*, 116–17. Bloodletting was a regular, often seasonal, practice in religious houses. Those who had blood let rested for several days and were allowed to eat otherwise restricted foods; monks were allowed to break silence. For many the period of recuperation became an occasion for frivolity. See Gougaud, *Anciennes coutumes claustrales*, 49–68.

The more strictly defined residency requirements did not, then, eliminate the possibility of excessive absenteeism. Perhaps to ensure continued ceremonial display in the absence of a sufficient number of full resident canons, vicars choral were introduced at Saint-Martin in 1222.[24] In 1237 this measure was made official: the number of full canons was reduced from 150 to 50, 20 demi-prebends were established, 30 prebends were set aside for honorary canons—such as the count of Anjou and the abbot of Marmoutier—and 56 prebends were now designated for vicars choral, whose primary purpose was singing in the choir.[25] Vicars, who were not voting members of the chapter and were in positions of clear subordination to the canons, had the same residency requirements as ordinary canons—seven months, and they too could gain permission to attend school and go on pilgrimage. But no vicar who was away in such circumstances could draw from his daily benefice, and the chapter retained the right to revoke a vicar's permission to attend school if the need arose. Hence high absenteeism was less likely among the vicars than it was among simple canons and those holding liege prebends. Indeed, the problem of absenteeism was probably greatest among the high officers with liege prebends, and it did not disappear after 1237. In 1255 the pope issued an indulgence to the dean of Saint-Martin declaring that his presence anywhere on Saint-Martin's property (which extended as far as Lombardy) would count toward his required six months' residency for his prebend.[26] And in 1262 the fine against priests of the week who failed to perform the daily mass was raised from two sous to five for each mass they missed.[27]

Much of the twelfth- and thirteenth-century evidence thus seems to suggest that centrifugal forces were pulling the canons of Saint-Martin away from whatever sense of religious community their chapter had once known, submerging them in the ostentation and mate-

24. *Chronicon Turonense auctore anonymo*, 1063. The introduction of vicars choral at Saint-Martin fit a broader pattern: see Edwards, *English Secular Cathedrals*, 252–58. As the claim of Philip and Renaud in 1180–81 makes clear, however, many other houses introduced vicars at an earlier stage.
25. "Tertia ecclesiae reformatio anno 1237," Tours, Bibliothèque Municipale, MS. 1295, 550–51; Vaucelle, *Collégiale de Saint-Martin*, 184. That the number of full prebends was reduced from 150 to 50 is symptomatic of financial strains in the thirteenth century. See Vaucelle, *Collégiale*, 184, 301, on problems at Saint-Martin. On the general problem of inflation in the thirteenth century and how it affected seigneurial lords, see Duby, *Rural Economy and Country Life in the Medieval West*, 238–39; and Jordan, *From Servitude to Freedom: Manumission in the Sénonais in the Thirteenth Century*, 28 ff.
26. *Registres d'Alexandre IV*, 15:102, 109, nos. 342, 359; cited in Griffiths, "Capetian Kings and St. Martin of Tours," 102.
27. "Quarta reformatio," Tours, Bibliothèque Municipale, MS. 1295, p. 554.

rialism of urban life and drawing at least some of them into courtly circles. Like Marmoutier in the eleventh and twelfth centuries, Saint-Martin in the late twelfth and thirteenth centuries was being stretched out by the forces of social and political change.

Yet there was no literary work from Saint-Martin that paralleled, in sentiment and function, the *Deeds of the Abbey of Marmoutier*. None of the canons attempted to revive a sense of community and mutual responsibility among the brothers by appealing to conscience and affection. Indeed, I know of no literature from Saint-Martin that even deals with relations among the canons. When the issue of the canons' responsibility came up, as it did in the reform statutes, it was implicitly defined as the obligation to perform—to be present in the choir for the requisite liturgical hours—rather than the obligation to meet the needs of other individuals.

In their attempts to bolster responsible behavior, Saint-Martin's reformers made no appeal to conscience or to the emotions of individual canons. Rather, both the reformers and the initiators of the general customs of the basilica instituted a system of material rewards and punishments that would be meted out to canons who did or did not show up for the offices they were expected to perform. Canons who failed to fulfill their residency requirements—including daily attendance at matins, vespers, and mass—were deprived of their prebends; priests of the week who failed to perform the mass were fined; canons who neglected their responsibility to attend matins during the week of septuagesima were deprived of a part of the manual distributions of that week; and only those who were present at Sunday mass could get their share of the sales taxes collected that day.[28] Similarly, those who performed liturgical tasks that went beyond their minimal duties received material rewards: one-sixth of the oblations (up to two deniers each) for singing at mass on feasts of seven candelabras; two deniers for attending a weekly Sunday procession that was established in 1191; one hundred sous to be divided among those who attended the anniversary service established in 1212 for Josbert of Sainte-Maure; four lampreys for carrying the *Osanna* on Palm Sunday.[29]

A system of clearly defined exchanges provided the canons with

28. On the week of septuagesima, see Vaucelle, *Collégiale de Saint-Martin*, 192–93; on sales taxes, *Consuetudines ecclesiae beati Martini*, 152.

29. For singing at mass, see *Consuetudines ecclesiae beati Martini*, 155; for attending Sunday procession, Tours, Bibliothèque Municipale, MS. 1295, 602. For anniversary of Josbert of Sainte-Maure, see Bibliothèque Nationale, Collection Housseau, MS. 6, no. 2442; for lampreys on Palm Sunday, *Consuetudines ecclesiae beati Martini*, 51.

sufficient motivation to fulfill their liturgical responsibilities. There was no need for an appeal to conscience, since regulation and supervision were simple matters: each canon was required to be physically present in the choir of the basilica at certain designated times of the day and year; if he was absent, the entire chapter knew it and could thus take appropriate action. These rewards and punishments may themselves have worked to undermine the canons' sense of community by sending them a message that their relationship to the basilica was limited to a set of clearly circumscribed contractual obligations. Even when they underwent reform, the canons were encouraged to mirror the mentalities of their urban environment, to think in terms of credits and debits.

Protecting Corporate Interests

Nevertheless, despite the attenuating forces that worked to undermine their fraternal bonds and collective identity, the canons of Saint-Martin did not simply allow their community to dissipate. In fact we could argue the opposite—that challenges to their collective rights heightened the canons' sense of their corporate identity.

It would be wrong, for example, to conclude that the primary purpose of the *Chronicle of Tours* was to serve the interests of the French king. Rather, the author of this text directed a much greater portion of his writing to the corporate interests of Saint-Martin. In asserting those interests he was not alone—for the ceremonial life and administrative record of the canons focused repeatedly on the defense of their collective rights and privileges.

Through a selective use of earlier sources the author of the *Chronicle of Tours* not only gave disproportionate attention to Tours in his representation of French history, he also conveyed the impression that the kings of Francia had always favored Saint-Martin and graced it with numerous gifts. The implicit message to King Louis VIII and his successors was that they would do well to imitate Clovis, Charlemagne, Louis the Pious, Charles the Bald, Louis the Stammerer, and Charles the Simple, who had visited Saint-Martin, buried their family members there, and of course lavished gifts and privileges on the house.[30]

Such references to royal precedent did not simply hover in the

30. *Chronicon Turonense auctore anonymo*, 932, 933, 957, 962, 969, 973, 979.

literary realm. The canons were quick to remind the king, whenever the need arose, that his heritage obliged him to protect the interests of Saint-Martin and to honor its privileges:

> Since by the generous donations and charity of your fathers the church of Saint Martin is enriched, it is elevated to the noble summit of the churches of your realm, and it adheres to you especially as lord, father, patron and author, just as a member of the body adheres to its head. . . . Therefore we ask your royal majesty that for the love of the blessed Martin you warn [the count of Nevers—he was one of the honorary canons of Saint-Martin] as your loyal man to leave the possessions of the blessed Martin alone . . . since your precedessors, the kings and emperors . . . wanted [Saint-Martin] to be immune from all customs and exactions and thus privileged it with special liberties. And when those liberties inspire the envy of many, it is your role to protect and guard them.[31]

Not only through historical memory but also through ritual act, the canons reminded their king and abbot that his proper relationship to them was one of defense and protection. Thus, when they took their oaths as abbots and canons of the basilica, fifteen kings, from Louis VII in 1137 to Louis XIV in 1650, repeated the words that a twelfth-century canon of Saint-Martin had inscribed in a richly decorated Carolingian manuscript of the Gospels:

> I, N, with God's assent king of the Franks, abbot and canon of this church of the blessed Martin of Tours, swear to God and to the blessed Martin that among other things I will be the protector and defender of this church in all its necessities and uses, guarding and conserving the possessions, honors, rights, privileges, liberties, franchises, and immunities of the same church, insofar as I am able supported by divine assistance, with right and pure faith. May God thus help me and these holy words.[32]

31. "Cum de munifica donatione et eleemosyna patrum vestrorum locupletata sit ecclesia beati Martini, inter caeteras regni vestri generosum tollit apicem, vobis domino, patri, patrono, et auctori suo specialiter adhaerens, ut membrum capiti suo. . . . Rogamus igitur regiam majestatem vestram, quatinus pro amore beati Martini ipsum ut fidelem et hominem vestrum moneatis, ut parcat rebus beati Martini . . . quoniam Reges et Imperatores praedecessores vestri . . . aliorum omni prava consuetudine et exactione immunem esse voluerunt, et egregia libertate privilegiaverunt. Quae cum invidiam multorum moveat, vestrum est eam protegere et tutari" (Letter from the Chapter of Saint-Martin to King Louis VII [ca. 1164], in *Recueil des historiens des Gaules*, 16:100, no. 311). On the honorary prebend that the counts of Nevers held at Saint-Martin, see *Consuetudines ecclesiae beati Martini*, 135–36.

32. "Ego N., annuente Domino, Francorum rex, abbas et canonicus hujus ecclesie Beati Martini Turonensis, juro Deo et beato Martino me de cetero protectorem et defen-

Through appeal to memory and ritual action the canons of Saint-Martin voiced their own interests to the king, reminding him that Saint-Martin had played an important role in the history of the kingdom and that the king owed it his protection and defense. Their relationship with their royal patron thus paralleled Marmoutier's relationship with the Angevins. But Marmoutier does not provide the only significant parallel to the canons' use of the past. By the time the canon of Tours wrote his *Chronicle,* the monks of the abbey of Saint-Denis had taken on the role of royal historiographers. In endeavoring to write a history of the realm that both legitimized the French king and promoted the interests of his religious institution the canon from Tours may well have had in mind the historians from Saint-Denis— Suger, Odo of Deuil, and most especially, Rigord. Like Rigord, who completed his *Deeds of Philip Augustus* in 1196, the canon from Tours not only provided arguments supporting the view that the king came from a single royal line that stretched back to the first Merovingians, but he also placed his own house in a central position vis-à-vis that royal line.[33]

One striking difference distinguishes the historical work of the canon of Saint-Martin from the historical work of Rigord and other monks at Saint-Denis. The monks of Saint-Denis took great pains to remind their king that the supreme "patron and defender" of the realm was Denis, who constantly worked miracles to protect the members of the royal line. Rigord, for example, recounted how Philip Augustus recovered from a hunting accident after appealing to God, the Virgin, and Denis, and how his young son Louis recovered from a serious illness after Denis's relics, along with others from his abbey, were carried in procession through the streets of Paris.[34]

The author from Tours made no such claims on behalf of Saint Martin. Indeed, although a number of canons of Saint-Martin and observers of their basilica recorded Martin's most recent miracles in the twelfth and thirteenth centuries, none of these works described a

---

sorem fore hujus ecclesie in omnibus necessitatibus et utilitatibus suis, custodiendo et conservando possessiones, honores, jura, privilegia, libertates, franchisias et immunitates ejusdem ecclesie, quantum divino fultus adjutorio secundum posse meum, recta et pura fide. Sic me Deus adjuvet et hec sancta verba" (Tours, Bibliothèque Municipale, MS. 22, fol. 277; printed in *Catalogue général des manuscrits des bibliothèques publiques de France,* 37:1:17).

33. Rigord, *Gesta Philippi Augusti,* chaps. 38, 69 and passim, ed. Delaborde, 1:59, 60, 98, and passim. For general discussion of the historians of Saint-Denis, see Spiegel, *Chronicle Tradition of Saint Denis.* On the date of Rigord's first redaction, see Delaborde, 1:ix.

34. Rigord, *Gesta Philippi Augusti,* 3, 77, ed. Delaborde, 1:11, 111–12; Spiegel, "Cult of St. Denis and Capetian Kingship."

recent miracle that Martin had performed for the king.[35] The canons
still recounted the story about the assistance the Merovingian king
Clovis received from Martin before he defeated the Visigothic king in
507, but they did not draw out the potential implications concerning
the continued relationship between Martin and the royal line, and
they gave equal attention to Martin's role in assisting Count Geoffrey
of Anjou in his victory over Thibaud of Blois in 1044.[36] Concerning
their own era, the canons either were not interested in perpetuating
the theme of Martin's special role in the French realm or felt they
were no longer in a position to do so. The king was still the "protector and defender" of the house of Saint Martin, but the saint was not
the protector and defender of the king.

Certainly the tradition was there had the canons wanted to seize
upon it. Not only did the stories by Gregory of Tours (which the
author of the *Chronicle of Tours* appropriated) provide ample opportunity for portraying Martin as the "protector and defender" of the
realm, but the canons of Saint-Martin were still quite familiar with
the sermon of Radbod of Utrecht, which had appealed to Martin as
the potential savior of the Carolingian line. Moreover, Johannis
Beleth—one of the best-known liturgists of the twelfth century—had
recently recalled to people's minds the fact that the Frankish kings
once carried Martin's cape into battle.[37]

Apparently the canons of Saint-Martin did not offer up their saint
as the "patron and defender" of the Capetians and of the French realm
because they did not want to. To them—and their writings make this
abundantly clear—Martin was the "patron," "defender," "protector,"
and "possessor" of one community and only one: the chapter of
Saint-Martin and the walled town of Châteauneuf, which it ruled.[38]

---

35. "De cultu Sancti Martini," 229–35, 245–48; Péan Gatineau, *Vie monseignor Saint
Martin de Tors*, lines 9363–10289, 118–29; Herbernus (attributed), *Miracula beati Martini* (see
chap. 9, note 30, on date of this text—between ca. 1140 and 1185); "Ex codice MS.
monasterii S. Martini Tornacensis. For more discussion of some of these miracle collections, see chapter 9.

36. *Chronicon Turonense auctore anonymo*, 932, 1002.

37. Radbod's sermon was still used in the liturgy at Tours for Martin's feast of May 12,
which celebrated his delivery of the city in 903, and for the feast of December 13, which
celebrated the day his relics returned to Tours from Burgundy: see Tours, Bibliothèque
Municipale, MS. 1021, fols. 111v, 155v; Johannis Beleth (+1165), *Summa de ecclesiasticis
officiis*, chap. 163, ed. Douteil, 2:320–21.

38. For instance: "Tunc [that is, just after the Vikings attacked Tours] sub *pii pastoris
protectione* ovibus quae luporum dentes evaserant confugientibus, consilio et auxilio principum Franciae circa ejus templum antea nudum et ab urbe longo centem quinquaginta fere
passuum interstitio distans, nobile hoc et multi decoris oppidum construentes . . . ut,
temporalem *patroni* domum contra hostium visibilium impetus materialibus munientes

Of course the Capetian king was an indirect beneficiary of that patronage, since he was the lay abbot of the chapter of Saint-Martin and hence one of its members. It appears, however, that the canons of the chapter deliberately avoided identifying Martin's patronage and protection with the king and that they did so because the rights the king exercised as lay abbot were a threat to the corporate identity and integrity of the community.

A number of sources and incidents from the early thirteenth century suggest that most of the members of the chapter of Saint-Martin were not happy with the situation the king was imposing on them and that they frequently resented the officers they themselves could not elect. In 1206, for example, the canons struggled with their dean (the king's appointee) over the right to control the corporate seal of the chapter. After they had wrested control of the seal from the dean, they entrusted it to two officers they themselves elected.[39] In 1232 the canons struggled with the pope himself over the issue of absenteeism. Gregory IX granted permission to Pierre Charlot, the illegitimate son of Philip Augustus and treasurer of Saint-Martin, to stay away from the chapter. Ostensibly Pierre was granted this exemption from the chapter's rules in order to study theology, but the real reason was probably so he could be closer to the royal court in Paris. The canons resisted the pope's decision and gave in to his pressure only after they received the concession that the treasurer had to reside at the basilica at least one month each year.[40]

The use of aggressive rituals also points to tensions between the canons and their officers. According to the reform statutes of 1204, the canons could (and probably did) employ the powerful ritual of the clamor if relations with their officers broke down over the issue of residency. The chapter was to perform the clamor—a liturgical appeal for God's assistance against one's enemies—during the mass each day

---

obstaculis, spirituali ejus *defensione* ab infestationibus hostium invisibilium liberari" ("De cultu Sancti Martini," 226). See also ibid., 223, and chapter 8 at notes 3 and 16 ff.

39. Bibliothèque Nationale, Collection Baluze, MS. 77, fol. 248; *Consuetudines ecclesiae beati Martini*, 152; Vaucelle, *Collégiale de Saint-Martin*, 203. For discussion of various struggles between the dean (who was the internal head of the chapter) and the chapter, see Vaucelle, *Collégiale*, 216–17, and Griffiths, "Capetian Kings and St. Martin of Tours," 122 n. 19, 131 n. 16. On tensions between other chapters and their officers, see Edwards, *English Secular Cathedrals*, 145; Pycke, *Chapitre cathédral Nôtre-Dame de Tournai*, 132. See also Lawrence Duggan's discussion of the emergence of the chapter of the cathedral of Speyer as an autonomous corporate group (*Bishop and Chapter: The Governance of the Bishopric of Speyer*, 11–56).

40. *Registres de Grégoire IX*, 1:578–79, no. 982 (dated 1232), discussed in Vaucelle, *Collégiale de Saint-Martin*, 192. In 1234 the dean, Aubry Cornut, was given a dispensation by the pope to remain in Paris at the royal court: see *Registres*, 1:946–47, no. 1720.

for forty days or until the officer had complied with the chapter's rules. If he still failed to do so by the end of the forty days, his prebend and rights were to be taken away.[41]

The struggles within the chapter of Saint-Martin in the early years of the thirteenth century arose in large part as a result of the impositions of the Capetian kings on the internal governance of the community. As a rule, the canons of Saint-Martin were not *hostile* toward their Capetian lay abbot. After all, one of them provided the Capetians with the text portraying Hugh Capet as a descendant of the Carolingians. Moreover, the canons were eager to remind the king that he was the "protector and defender" of their house and that they adhered to him "just as a member of the body adheres to its head." Nevertheless, a lay patron who was not only king but also lay abbot (an extremely rare position in the High and late Middle Ages) and who exercised the right to appoint the most important officers of the community—such a friend and patron also had the potential to become a great danger to the integrity of the community. It was important to remind this patron that his duty was to protect and defend the house, and that *all* his predecessors had fulfilled their role in this way. But it was also important to withhold for the community itself a "patron and defender" who was above the king and who did not serve the king in the same way he served the community. This was the role Saint Martin played for the canons of Tours.

When Philip and Renaud recalled the role their saint had played during the Viking invasions, their theme was that Martin resided at *their* church and was *their* patron and defender. They did not ignore the stories Radbod of Utrecht and the monk of Marmoutier had already recorded, but they molded the earlier stories in a different way. Thus, though they did not go as far as the monk of Marmoutier had gone in portraying the Frankish king as a slothful and ineffective ruler, neither did they make any reference to Radbod of Utrecht's idea that Saint Martin was a special protector of the Frankish royal line.[42] Rather, Philip and Renaud pointed to the miracle of 903—when Martin's relics saved the city of Tours from the Vikings—as a shining example demonstrating that the saint continuously favored *his* com-

---

41. "Prima reformatio," Tours, Bibliothèque Municipale, MS. 1295, 548; the text of the lesser clamor is in *Consuetudines ecclesiae beati Martini*, 147; it is also in *De antiquis ecclesiae ritibus*, bk. 1, chap. 3, ordo 2, reprint edition, vol. 2, col. 899. For an excellent discussion of Saint-Martin's greater clamor—the humiliation of relics—see Geary, "Humiliation of Saints."

42. "De cultu Sancti Martini," 223, 240. See also *Chronicon Turonense auctore anonymo*, 965–66, 974.

munity—both the chapter of Saint-Martin and the city of Château-neuf that it ruled.

In their interactions with other individuals and groups the canons of Saint-Martin made manifest their own existence as a corporate group. Acting together at highly charged ritual moments, they called upon their king and abbot to protect them, and as I show in chapters 8 and 9, they reinforced their hierarchical claims vis-à-vis both the archbishops of Tours and the burghers of Châteauneuf.

It is one thing, however, to be able to say that the canons of Saint-Martin protected their common material interests by acting collectively; it is another to argue that they constituted a community. After all, legal rights and privileges in medieval France were granted corporately, and thus many people acted collectively to protect their interests.[43] But when they were not struggling with other groups, did such people consider themselves members of a community? Did they come together to express their common identity? And in the case of the chapter of Saint-Martin, whose canons were chastised so many times for their apparent failure to live up to certain standards of the clerical order, did that common identity extend beyond mere practical material interests?

Rituals of Community

It is impossible for us to know whether the canons of Saint-Martin *felt* themselves intensely bound to their chapter and its ceremonial religious functions. They have not left us their thoughts on these subjects. What we can analyze are their actions and most especially their incorporative rituals: entry ceremonies, ceremonial gifts, foot washings, and commemorations of the dead. What we find in these ceremonies is that the canons put considerable effort into reinforcing their collective bonds and, especially in their attention to the proper care of the dead and dying, that their preoccupations extended beyond the practical material concern of doing their job so as to receive remuneration. We also find that, like the language of the canons, their incorporative rituals hovered between monastic rituals, in which the solidarity of the group was clearly articulated, and the more fluid rituals of various groups in high medieval cities. And their corporate assistance to the dead and dying was not as intense, in the early thirteenth century, as was the assistance monks gave each other.

43. See, for example, Reynolds, *Kingdoms and Communities in Western Europe*.

Like houses of Benedictine monks, chapters of secular canons, including Saint-Martin, had entry rituals. These rituals involved an oath that established the new brother's obligation to the community, a ceremonial redressing—or redefining—of the new member, incorporative actions symbolizing the establishment of a new bond between the entrant and his brothers, and a liminal period when the status of the new brother was different from that of the others. There were, however, significant differences between the entry rituals of Benedictine monasteries and the entry ritual of Saint-Martin. Indeed, in its rituals Saint-Martin shared as many characteristics with urban guilds and confraternaties as with Benedictine monasticism.

A new Benedictine monk was marked for life, bound forever—at least in principle—to the community and its way of life. His entry into the monastic vocation was nearly as significant as the ceremony of baptism, and indeed the ritual symbols for entering a monastery paralleled those of baptism.[44] Hence the Benedictine *Rule* prescribed a lengthy liminal stage that *preceded* the ritual of incorporation. This stage, the novitiate, gave the novice time to consider the implications of the commitment he was soon to make and to back down while it was still possible to do so. The novitiate also enabled the new member to cleanse himself of secular pollutions before he fully joined the sacred and unpolluted community. When the new monk finally underwent the ritual of incorporation, the circumstances in which he made his solemn oath symbolized the gravity of his commitment: "When he is to be received, he comes before the whole community in the oratory and promises stability, fidelity to monastic life, and obedience. This is done in the presence of God and his saints to impress on the novice that if he ever acts otherwise, he will surely be condemned by the one he mocks."[45] After giving his promise orally, the professing monk then wrote it out and placed the document on the altar. Even if he later broke his oath and left the abbey, the monastery was to keep the document, which thus provided visible and tangible evidence that a covenant had been broken.[46]

The reclothing of the monk also symbolized that he was in his very essence permanently remade, just as was a neophyte Christian at the

44. See chapter 2, note 61.
45. *RB 1980: The Rule of St. Benedict*, 58:17–18, p. 117.
46. *RB 1980*, 58:29, p. 119. In later customals the novice first wrote out the profession, then read it in the choir: see Lanfranc, *Monastic Constitutions*, p. 108; Ulrich of Cluny, *Antiquiores consuetudines*, 2:27, *PL* 149:713. There is no discussion of the entry ceremony in Marmoutier's customal. In the eleventh and twelfth centuries some legalists did not consider the monastic novitiate to be probationary: Hourlier, *Age classique, 1140–1378: Les religieux*, 172–73.

time of baptism. In the oratory, the abbot stripped the incoming monk of his old clothing and dressed him in the monastic cowl, which (at least by the eleventh and twelfth centuries) had just been blessed and sprinkled with holy water.[47] As he undressed and then dressed the entrant, the abbot stated: "May the Lord strip thee of the old man with all his acts. . . . May the Lord clothe thee with the new man, who is created according to God in justice and the sanctity of truth."[48] After the entrant had been dressed, he was then incorporated into the entire community: each of the brothers kissed him.[49]

At Saint-Martin the ceremony of entry was different because the circumstances were different. The new canon was not marked for life, nor did he enter a community that was set apart from the pollutions of the secular realm. Rather, he entered into a set of well-defined obligations to a corporate group. Thus the essence of his oath was his promise to be "faithful in all the business and causes that pertain to the community of this church and to defend the liberty, honesty, and utility of the same church."[50]

The gravity of the entering canon's new obligations and the bonds of his new community were certainly not as intense as were those of a professing monk. Nevertheless, we should not minimize the effects of the entrance ceremony and the bonds it helped to form. The canon's entry promise was a solemn oath, and it was addressed not to an abstract corporation but to the men who made up the group and who depended on the loyal behavior of their brothers. This dependence was highlighted by the canon's promise that he would "not reveal to anyone those counsels of the chapter whence damage or shame might come to this church or to its persons."[51]

47. *RB 1980*, 58:26, p. 119; Lanfranc, *Monastic Constitutions*, p. 109; Ulrich of Cluny, *Antiquiores consuetudines*, 2:27, *PL* 149:713. The sprinkling with holy water may signify a change in the meaning of the redressing from the days of Benedict: for Benedict the emphasis was on the monk's having *nothing* that was his own, "not . . . even his own body" (*RB 1980*, 58:25, p. 119). In the *Life* of Odo of Cluny, however, the monastic habit has the qualities of a talisman, which protects the monk from the powers of the devil: see John of Salerno, "Vita Sancti Odonis," 3:6, *PL* 133:76–77; trans. Sitwell, 72–73.

48. Lanfranc, *Monastic Constitutions*, p. 109; Ulrich of Cluny, *Antiquiores consuetudines*, 2:27, *PL* 149:713.

49. Lanfranc, *Monastic Constitutions*, p. 109; Ulrich of Cluny, *Antiquiores consuetudines*, 2:27, *PL* 149:713. There is nothing about the kiss in the Benedictine *Rule*.

50. "In omnibus negociis et causis que pertinent ad communitatem hujus ecclesie fidelis ero, et ad tuendam libertatem et honestatem et utilitatem ejusdem ecclesie" (*Consuetudines ecclesiae beati Martini*, 95; printed in *De antiquis ecclesiae ritibus*, bk. 2, chap. 5, ordo 2, reprint ed. vol. 2, col. 513).

51. "Neque consilia capituli alicui relevabo unde dampnum vel dedecus ipsi ecclesie vel persone ejusdem possit provenire" (*Consuetudines ecclesiae beati Martini*, 95; printed in *De antiquis ecclesiae ritibus*, bk. 2, chap. 5, ordo 2, reprint ed. vol. 2, col. 513). The canon also had to promise to obey the reform statutes of 1204 and 1208.

An emphasis on the ceremonial function of the chapter, rather than on the remaking of the man, was made clear in that the new member was not ceremonially undressed and remade by a superior or a brother. Rather, at tierce, after he had taken his oath in the chapter, he was led to the choir, *already* dressed in the chapter's choir vestments. He himself took on his new clothing in private, rather than in a public ceremony. These were, moreover, vestments that he wore when he was in the choir. They were the uniform of his ceremonial function—that of performing the liturgy at Martin's tomb—not the mark of his complete remaking.

When the new canon arrived in his ceremonial garb at the door of the choir, he bowed to its four corners while the other canons bowed to him.[52] He was then placed in his new stall, where he proved his ability to carry out his new function by singing the responses at all the services on that day. In some circumstances, then—when an entering canon was already a member of the clerical order—the ritual of incorporation was not particularly intense. It required the new member of the choir to perform his singing function, but it did not involve any physical contact, which would highlight his new relationship with his brothers.

The ritual for new members who had never before been in clerical orders, however, required physical contact of a highly charged symbolic nature. At mass the new member was led to the altar, already dressed in his choir vestments, wearing a napkin around his neck. There the priest of the week began to make the new canon's *corona*, or crown, by cutting off a bit of hair from the top of his head. The priest then kissed him, and he was led in turn to the deacon, the subdeacon, the dean, the treasurer, and finally, to every other member of the chapter. Each member cut a bit of the new canon's hair and kissed him. Each of the brothers had a stake in the behavior and status of the new canon. Each therefore tangibly took part in remaking him into a member of the clerical order.[53] A number of abbeys had rituals for tonsuring a new member, but in most cases the abbot or a single priest did the honors. I know of no other case in which every member of the community participated in the ritual shearing.[54] In this cere-

---

52. *Consuetudines ecclesiae beati Martini*, 96; printed in *De antiquis ecclesiae ritibus*, bk. 2, chap. 5, ordo 2, reprint ed. vol. 2, col. 512. There are monastic parallels to this bowing ritual: see Lanfranc, *Monastic Constitutions*, p. 107.

53. *Consuetudines ecclesiae beati Martini*, 96–97; printed in *De antiquis ecclesiae ritibus*, bk. 2, chap. 5, ordo 2, reprint ed. vol. 2, cols. 512–13.

54. *De antiquis ecclesiae ritibus*, reprint ed. vol. 4, cols. 627–28. Martène gives indirect evidence that the abbot of Marmoutier performed the tonsuring: see *Histoire de l'abbaye de Marmoutier*, 1:447, 534; 2:225. I have found no discussion of a tonsuring ritual at other chapters of secular canons.

mony, and in others as well, Saint-Martin's ritual symbols stressed lateral bonds among the canons rather than hierarchical bonds between the individual canon and a superior.

The tonsuring rituals for new canons at religious houses that were subordinated to Saint-Martin stressed, by contrast, hierarchical relations. When a man became a canon at Léré, where Saint-Martin had "all spiritual and temporal jurisdiction," he had to be presented at Saint-Martin to swear his oath to the chapter and priors. If he had never been tonsured, the priest of the week tonsured him during the mass. The customal of Saint-Martin specifically stipulated that "he is not to be led among the canons in the choir to be tonsured, as if he were our canon."[55] Incorporative rituals were reserved for the canons of Saint-Martin alone.

As at other chapters of secular canons—and the same was true for lay confraternities in high medieval cities—the "liminal" stage of a new member of the chapter of Saint-Martin followed his ritual of entry rather than preceding it. Since he was not making an irrevocable commitment, or conversion, to a new way of life, the canon did not need to undergo a period of probation when he could still change his mind. And since the community was not ritually set apart from the pollutions of the world, he did not have to be cleansed before he could enter. But because the nature of a chapter of secular canons was fluid and somewhat amorphous (and this was generally true of lay confraternities as well), the new member did need to learn, through contact, what the community was. Hence new members of many secular chapters and lay confraternities were expected to observe a period of full participation in the group's activities.[56] At Saint-Martin, new canons had to meet strict residence requirements from Easter until the feast of Saint John, on December 27. This period of residency, which exceeded the seven months for ordinary canons (and for ordinary canons, those seven months did not have to be consecutive) and allowed for no exemptions, enabled the new member to get a feel for his community, its membership, and its liturgical rhythms. The requirement also ensured that the new member would be present for all four of Saint Martin's feasts (May 12, July 4, November 11, and December 13).[57]

---

55. "Si autem coronam non habeat, ad Missam facit ei coronam ebdomadarius solus, et non per canonicos in choro ducitur tonendus, sicut noster canonicus" (*Consuetudines ecclesiae beati Martini*, 145).

56. Edwards, *English Secular Cathedrals*, 51; Pycke, *Chapitre cathédral Nôtre-Dame de Tournai*, 119; Hautcoeur, *Histoire de l'église collégiale et du chapitre de Saint-Pierre de Lille*, 1:171; Weissman, *Ritual Brotherhood in Renaissance Florence*, 139–41.

57. *Consuetudines ecclesiae beati Martini*, 65. Canons who had not been in residence the previous year were also required to observe this period of residence.

Although Saint-Martin's ceremony of entry, and those of other secular chapters and lay confraternities as well, was not as intense as the Benedictine ceremony of profession, it served the purpose of consolidating bonds between a new canon and his brothers. Other incorporative ceremonies consolidated the bonds between a new treasurer or dean—the chapter's two most important officers—and the canons. In addition to undergoing an entry ceremony that paralleled that of a new canon, each new treasurer or dean had the right to eat at the houses of all the canons on the day of his entry.[58] Relations between the chapter and these two officers were frequently tense, in part because the officers held so much control over the chapter and in part because they were imposed on the chapter by the king.[59] Hence the obligatory meals served the function of symbolically establishing a desired friendship.[60] That the canons were *required* to feed their new officers, however, reinforced the relationship between superior and inferior. The right to visit the house of another and to demand nourishment there—the *droit de prise*—was the prerogative of the more powerful over the less powerful: the king held the droit de prise over various abbeys, the count of Blois held the droit de prise at Marmoutier's priories, Saint-Martin held the droit de prise at the religious houses that were subordinated to it, and the archbishop of Tours, as I have already discussed, had lost his droit de prise at Marmoutier and Saint-Martin. Hence the new officers' right to nourishment at the houses of the canons symbolically reinforced his position of authority. It was also a payment for the justice and administrative services these officers would provide.[61]

58. *Consuetudines ecclesiae beati Martini*, 99, 101.

59. On their powers, see *Consuetudines ecclesiae beati Martini*, 98–101; Vaucelle, *Collégiale de Saint-Martin*, 201 ff. The dean was the internal head of the chapter; the treasurer represented its civil power, including that over Châteauneuf.

60. The canons of Saint Paul's in London nicely articulated the role that a canon's entry meal (the new member gave the feast for his brothers and other dignitaries) played in forging friendships between the chapter and the powerful men who were invited: see Edwards, *English Secular Cathedrals*, 62. Fifteenth-century Florentines also had a strong sense of the role meals played in establishing bonds among men: see Weissman, *Ritual Brotherhood in Renaissance Florence*, 32–33.

61. Newman, *Domaine royal sous les premiers Capétiens*, 19; Robinet, "Conflit entre pouvoir civil et pouvoir ecclésiastique: Voies de faits et voies de droit entre comtes de Blois et abbés de Marmoutier" (the *droit de prise* of the count of Blois was part of his right to stay at the priories—the *droit de gîte*). On Saint-Martin's *droit de prise*, see *Consuetudines ecclesiae beati Martini*, 62 (on the second and third days after Easter the chapter visited the abbey of Beaumont and the priory of Saint-Cosme, where the boy clerics ate a meal and the bell ringers received wine, several loaves of bread, and four deniers. For more discussion of these visitations, see chapter 8). On the feast of the Innocents (December 28) the "officers" of the boy clerics (their bishop and cantor for the season) gave a feast for the other boys: see *Consuetudines ecclesiae beati Martini*, 35.

The meals also reinforced the bond between the canons and their officers, and that need was met as well by ceremonial exchanges of gifts that were repeated throughout the liturgical year. The gifts flowed in both directions and hence reminded both the canons and their officers that their relationship was one of mutual service: the chapter owed the dean three measures of wine "of the best quality"; and in exchange (the customal of the chapter made it very clear that the one gift was linked to the others) the dean was to provide each of the canons with spiced wine, which he delivered on Easter, Pentecost, and Saint Martin's feast of July 4.[62]

The entry meals for the dean and treasurer reinforced their authority and consolidated bonds of friendship. Nevertheless, as I have already indicated, the canons also had recourse to their own authority vis-à-vis these officers. When their officers failed to meet their obligations to the chapter the canons could, and apparently did, employ powerful rituals such as the clamor.

The relations between the officers of the chapter and its members were fraught with danger, and so there was a constant need to reinforce the hierarchical friendship. Yet, the customal of the chapter suggests that the most frequent ceremonies at Saint-Martin worked to reinforce the horizontal bonds of brotherhood. Some of these rituals, such as the periodic group tonsuring, resembled and probably were derived from monastic rituals. Others appear to have a greater affinity with the rituals of lay confraternities.

Saint-Martin's practices for Maundy Thursday, in which the canons reenacted the events of Christ's Last Supper, closely paralleled both monastic rituals and those of late medieval confraternities. Like their monastic peers, the canons imitated Christ by performing two maundies, or ritual foot washings: first each canon washed the feet of a "poor man" he himself had introduced into the chapter for that ceremony; and later in the day all the canons washed each other's feet. After the latter ceremony the canons engaged in a round of ceremonial wine drinking.[63] Both maundies were emotionally and symbolically intense, working to reinforce bonds between the chapter and the broader community and among the members of the chapter themselves. And both closely resembled the monastic ritual, except for three important differences.

First, though the canons certainly humbled themselves in washing each other's feet and the feet of the poor, they did not go to the

62. *Consuetudines ecclesiae beati Martini*, 91.
63. *Consuetudines ecclesiae beati Martini*, 52–55; partially printed in *De antiquis ecclesiae ritibus*, bk. 4, chap. 22, ordo 8, reprint ed. vol. 3, col. 281.

lengths of some monks, who bowed down and "worshiped Christ" in the poor before washing their feet and kissed their feet when the washing was done.[64] The canons, unlike the monks, had not embraced such humility as part of their calling. Moreover, they were intensely aware of symbols of status and hierarchy—too aware, in all likelihood, to kiss the feet of, or prostrate themselves before, the poor men of the city they ruled.

The second difference between the monastic ritual and that of Saint-Martin involved the way the poor men were chosen: in monasteries each monk had a poor man introduced for him by the almoner or an officer from the town.[65] At Saint-Martin, by contrast, each canon brought in his own poor man, thus highlighting the canons' daily contact with their secular surroundings and enhancing the possibility of forming patron-client relationships between individual canons and members of the urban community.[66]

The third difference between Saint-Martin's maundy and that of a Benedictine monastery involved the washing of the brothers' own feet: in monasteries, and in some cathedrals as well, it was the head of the community—the abbot, bishop, or dean—who took on the role Christ had played at the Last Supper by washing the feet of all his disciples.[67] At Saint-Martin, by contrast, the canons apparently washed each other's feet. The difference is striking: all the canons were ritually humbled by washing the feet of a poor man and of a brother; but all were simultaneously, and *equally*, exalted by playing the role of Christ. In all likelihood the canons would have considered it too much of a symbolic threat to allow any single officer to lord it over the others by exclusively playing the role of Christ. As in their tonsuring ceremony, the canons of Saint-Martin transformed a ritual

64. Lanfranc, *Monastic Constitutions*, p. 32.

65. Lanfranc, *Monastic Constitutions*, p. 30; Ulrich of Cluny, *Antiquiores consuetudines*, 1:12, PL 149:658. Marmoutier's customal does not give any details on how the maundies were carried out.

66. For a discussion of patron-client relations between confraternity members and the poor they sponsored, see Weissman, *Ritual Brotherhood in Renaissance Florence*, 130.

67. Lanfranc, *Monastic Constitutions*, pp. 35, 38; Ulrich of Cluny, *Antiquiores consuetudines*, PL 149:660 (the abbot had help in both of these cases, but the ideal was that he did it alone). At Rouen in the fifteenth century the maundy was performed by the bishop; at Hereford, it was done by the bishop or dean: see Bishop, *Liturgica Historica*, 294. The cathedral rites printed in Martène include hierarchical as well as nonhierarchical practices: see *De antiquis ecclesiae ritibus*, bk. 3, chap. 22, ordo 8, reprint ed. vol. 3, cols. pp. 279 ff. In several confraternities an elected officer performed the maundy, but the message may have been less hierarchical, because the offices frequently rotated among various members: see Weissman, *Ritual Brotherhood in Renaissance Florence*, 100; Gasté, "Drames liturgiques de la cathédrale de Rouen," 598 (citing the example of a confraternity initiated in 1374 at Saint-Patrice).

that usually stressed the hierarchical relations between the brothers and their superior into one that stressed the horizontal and collective ties of the brotherhood.

If the consolidation of a sense of brotherhood was one important outcome of Saint-Martin's entry and foot-washing rituals, it was an implicit prerequisite for the death rituals. Like the monastery of Marmoutier, and secular confraternities as well, Saint-Martin provided its members with an artificial family that enhanced or even replaced the natural family in providing spiritual assistance for the dead and dying. To be sure, the elaborate funeral processions for the canons of the basilica—which were attended by all the canons of Saint-Martin and all the monks, canons, and nuns of five religious houses that were subordinated to the basilica, as well as by the monks of the nearby monastery of Saint-Julian and ten monks of Marmoutier—helped enhance and reinforce the collective status of the chapter.[68] Still, there is no question but that the care given to the dying and the dead arose from the conviction that the dead needed help and that their spiritual brothers were the ones who should see that it was provided.

In this sense, then, there was no difference between the provisions for the death of a canon of Saint-Martin and those for the death of a Benedictine monk. And indeed the specific rituals at Saint-Martin paralleled those of a monastery. In both cases the entire community assembled at the bedside of a sick man; in both cases he was closely attended day and night by a few men who constantly prayed for him; in both cases the entire community gathered again at the moment of death and then for the funeral; in both cases proper remembrance involved almsgiving, commemorative meals, and commemorative masses—usually a cycle of thirty.[69] By the early thirteenth century, however, there was no specification, as there had been in the tenth century, that living canons of Saint-Martin would assist their dead brothers by completing the satisfaction for their sins.[70] Furthermore, a concern for status and formality and a hierarchical division of labor undermined the intimacy of the "fraternal" support provided to sick

68. *Consuetudines ecclesiae beati Martini*, 131–32.

69. *Consuetudines ecclesiae beati Martini*, 130–33; Lanfranc, *Monastic Constitutions*, pp. 120–32, 30, 32, 75; *Antiquae consuetudines Majoris monasterii*, chaps. 46, 48, fols. 109v–112; Ulrich of Cluny, *Antiquiores consuetudines*, 2:27–29, PL 149:769–75; *De rebus gestis in Majori monasterio*, 3, 16, pp. 396, 404.

70. In 922 it was established that all canons would assist at the thirty commemorative masses for each dead canon and that two or three of them would fast on bread and water during those thirty days to earn the forgiveness of that canon's sins: see Mabille, *Pancarte noire de Saint-Martin*, 144, pp. 144–45. The thirteenth-century customal mentioned only that a trental would begin on the day after the canon's death, without indicating what it would entail or who would perform it: see *Consuetudines ecclesiae beati Martini*, 133.

and dying canons. The chapter ensured that six "priests of charity" would watch each sick canon, praying for him and eating with him day and night until he either recovered or died. These six men also gathered for one last meal at the dead canon's house on the day he was buried. But these priests were not the social equals of the canons, nor were they full members of the chapter. Rather, they were employees of the chapter whose remuneration consisted of a fraction of a full canon's prebend plus the right to inherit the vestment of every canon when he died.[71]

In the early thirteenth century Saint-Martin thus provided for the "fraternal" assistance its canons needed at the time of death, but without the intimacy that characterized the assistance Benedictine monks gave each other.[72] There is also evidence that the canons' fraternal assistance for their dying and dead members was not always considered sufficient. Some canons gave substantial gifts to the chapter to endow special commemorations for their souls.[73] Others appar-

71. *Consuetudines ecclesiae beati Martini*, 121, 130, 131.

72. Ulrich of Cluny's customal (from the end of the eleventh century) may also point to some loss of intimacy. After he received extreme unction, a monk was to be watched by a "servant" (*famulus*) rather than by a "brother": *Antiquiores consuetudines*, 2:29, PL 149:771. Lanfranc and the *De rebus gestis in Majori monasterio* (written in the twelfth century) both specify that fellow monks kept the final watch: see *Monastic Constitutions*, p. 122; *De rebus*, 3, 16, pp. 396, 404. On confraternal assistance to the sick, dying, and dead, see Meersseman, *Ordo fraternitatis*, 1:143, 392; *Liberty, Charity, Fraternity: Lay Religious Confraternities at Bergamo in the Age of the Commune*, 117, 144–45, 187; Weissman, *Ritual Brotherhood in Renaissance Florence*, 87; *English Gilds: The Original Ordinances*, 26, 31, 35, 38, 41, 43, 56–57, etc. (most of these texts are from the fourteenth century); Coornaert, "Ghildes médiévales," 22–55, 208–43. Coornaert (p. 219) also notes an evolution from more intimate to less intimate corporate rituals: in the statutes of the confraternity of Valenciennes, a confraternal wake over the corpse of a dead confrater gave way to hiring clerics to perform this task.

73. In 1098 the canon Andrew gave the chapter half the wood and stone houses he possessed inside and outside the walls of Châteauneuf and the stall he owned near the drapers' shops to establish his anniversary. In 1203 Hamelin, the bishop of Le Mans (1190–1214) established anniversaries at Saint-Martin for two of its deans, Odo (ca. 1109–43) and Philip (1176–91), who were Hamelin's paternal uncle and brother. Hamelin established the anniversary with property that he and Philip had inherited from Odo. In 1212 Odo Clement, the dean of Saint-Martin (1211 to 1216–17), confirmed the establishment of an anniversary for William of Tallebourg, the cellarer of Saint-Martin, who had given a vineyard to the chapter as an endowment for this purpose: see Bibliothèque Nationale, Collection Housseau, MS. 3, 1024; Tours, Bibliothèque Municipale, MS. 1295, 590; Tours, Archives d'Indre-et-Loire, vol. G381, p. 279, no. 1.

By the thirteenth century some Benedictine monks were also endowing their own anniversaries. The cartulary of Saint-Julian of Tours provides a lively example of an annual anniversary meal that the abbot founded for himself in 1255. The monks were to eat warm pastries (*foliata*), to drink the best wine and spiced wine (*pigmentum*), and to have fish as their main course. After eating this meal the *convivii* were to sing together in a lusty voice (*voce non humile*): "May this father have peace / And rejoice with the saints in heaven, / Through whom we all rejoice today / With spendid food and drink!" ("Iste pater pacem possideat / Et cum sanctis in celis gaudeat, / Per quem cuncti letamur hodie, / Sic potati et pasti splendide!") (*Chartes de Saint-Julien de Tours*, 2:132–33).

ently chose to assume the monastic habit before their deaths.[74] Still others donned the habit of the Augustinian canons at the priory of Saint-Cosme. The residents of Saint-Martin believed this priory provided a "door to health," because it was "an apt place for doing penance." It was like "a terrestrial paradise from which souls that were cleansed by the bath of penitence" were "more easily transferred to the celestial paradise."[75]

There is no doubt, then, that the ceremonial life at Saint-Martin reinforced fraternal bonds among the canons and that the community came together to provide brotherly assistance for those making the critical passage from this life to the next. But the bonds of this community were not as intense as those of a monastery like Marmoutier, and the canons' collective identity was not as clearly set apart from its surrounding environment as those of Marmoutier and Saint-Cosme.

In their language and rituals, the canons of Saint-Martin assimilated the values and manners of their urban environment while at the same time preserving a sense of their collective identity and religious vocation. Among themselves, they were jealous defenders of lateral relations. When they interacted with other groups, however, they were intensely hierarchical. As I show in the following chapters, their orchestrations of the ceremonial rhythms of Châteauneuf marked the emerging city as subordinated to and defined by the lordship of Saint Martin and his house.

74. Herbernus (attributed), *Miracula beati Martini*, 3, *PL* 129:1041.
75. "Portus salutis est locus agendae paenitentiae aptus. . . . insulam videlicet sancti Cosmae . . . quasi quidam terrestris paradisus, inde animas per paenitentiae lavacrum purgatus ad caelestem paradisum facilius transmittens" (Charter of Theobald, the dean, and Peter, the treasurer, of Saint-Martin [1197], Bibliothèque Nationale, Collection Baluze, MS. 76, fol. 166).

8

Saint Martin's Diocese:
The Appropriation
of Episcopal Symbols

Saint Martin's Feast of July 4:
Divine Presence, Episcopal Authority

When Guibert of Gembloux made his pilgrimage to Tours in 1180–81 he brought with him a letter from Archbishop Philip of Cologne, who wished to clarify certain points about the way Saint Martin's cult was observed in Tours. The distance that separated him from Tours prevented Archbishop Philip from learning "your names"—those of the monks of Marmoutier and the canons of Saint-Martin, to whom he addressed his letter.[1] Nevertheless, news concerning the dramatic way the canons at Saint-Martin celebrated Saint Martin's July feast had reached Philip's ears. He found the practice so unusual that he wanted written confirmation of what he had heard:

> There are two matters especially that have been conveyed to us by rumor alone, which we vigorously entreat you to confirm in writing. . . . The second matter, if it is indeed true, is wondrous and incomparable in our view. For it is said that on the night of the ordination and translation of [Saint Martin] [July 4], after compline has been solemnly sung and the multitude of people turned out of the church, the doors of the church in which he corporally rests are carefully closed, all the instruments necessary for the mass are left on the altar, and no mortal is allowed to enter there until dawn. And the tradition accepted by most people—and held by yourselves to be confirmed by miracles—is that on that night and in that very church the divine office is celebrated by the blessed pontiff along with other saints. About this

---

1. "Itaque nomina vesta propter distantiam nobis quidem incognita" (excerpt from MS. 428–42, fols. 111r–112v, Bibliothèque Royale Albert I, Brussels, printed in *Catalogus codicum hagiographicorum . . . Bruxellensis*, 1:532–34 [the quoted passage is on p. 534]). There is a new edition of this letter in Guibert, Abbot of Gembloux, *Guiberti Gemblacensis epistolae*, 60–63. My references are to the old edition.

matter, which is so stupendous and unusual in everyone's eyes . . . we would like you to certify by which experience it is known, by which authors it has been publicized, and by what signs it has been proved.[2]

In their response to Archbishop Philip, Philip and Renaud, the dean and treasurer of Saint-Martin, assured him that much of what he had already heard was accurate. It was on the night of July 3, the vigil of Martin's July feast, that the canons at Saint-Martin observed the custom of emptying the basilica so that Martin and his saintly entourage could occupy it. The canons did not put out preparations for the mass, however, because "the spirits and souls of the saints have no need for those things." Still, Philip and Renaud left open the possibility that Martin may have dressed himself in his old liturgical vestments, since the canons still held these in their possession:

> After all the people, both citizens and pilgrims, have been sent outside with diligent care, we concede the same basilica, which is radiant with a number of torches and with candles that shine in coronas, to God and to its blessed possessor and to the other saints. And . . . the most notable members of our convent—the dean, treasurer, cantor, magister scholarum and cellarer—assign . . . two watchmen for each door of the temple, in addition to . . . [the six custodians who are always there]. In answer to your question, we put out on the altar no necessary preparations for the mass, because we know that the spirits and souls of the saints have no need for these things for the divine services. Nevertheless, we know that the sacred vestments that the great priest used in his days for the celebration of the sacraments are concealed in a secret place known to only a few, next to his tomb.[3]

2. "Duo maxime sunt, super quibus, cum ad nos ex sola fama perlata sint, ex scriptis vestris certificari obnixe exposcimus. . . . alterum, quod si verum est, mirabile immo incomparabile est in oculis nostris: siquidem fertur quod in nocte festi ordinationis seu translationis ejus, cantato solemniter completorio et conflua populi multitudine ejecta, januae omnes ecclesiae in qua corporetenus requiescit, diligenter claudantur, omnis missae necessarius altari apparatus adhibeatur, nullus mortalium usque ad ortum solis ingredi permittatur: eo quod et a majoribus traditum et etiam miraculis confirmatum apud vos teneatur, ipsa nocte in eadem ecclesia a beato pontifice sanctisque aliis divina celebrari. Super qua re tam stupenda cunctis et insolita, qua vobis experientia comperta, quibus auctoribus propalata, quibus signis comprobata sit . . . certificati fuerimus" (*Catalogus . . . Bruxellensis,* 1:240–41).
3. "Omnibus tam civibus quam peregrinis diligenti cura eliminatis, eamdem basilicam, cereis super coronas fulgentibus radiantem et pluribus coruscantem lampadibus, Deo beatoque ejus possessori et sanctis aliis concedimus, insignioribus personis conventus nostri, decano videlicet, thesaurario, archicantore, scholarum magistro et cellerario, singulis templi januis . . . duobus excubitoribus . . . assignantibus, praeter illos xii qui ex instituto seni et seni alternis vicibus perenniter templi ejusdem solvunt custodiam. Apparatum vero missae necessarium altari, ut quaeritis, nullum apponimus, spiritus et animas

This striking ritual was described again in the customal of Saint-Martin, written after 1226. Unlike Philip and Renaud, however, the customal specified that the canons *did* put out materials for the mass—bread, wine, a chalice, and a censer of incense.[4]

The ritual, and the supernatural presence it publicized, called attention to several themes discussed in chapter 7. First, like the celebration of the May feast—when Châteauneuf became a "paradise"—the July vigil suggested that at a particular time of year a particular place underwent a supernatural transformation. Saint Martin was always the "possessor" of the basilica where his relics resided, but on one day especially he and his entourage took possession of it. Like the city, the basilica underwent the alternation of secular times and sacred times, which corresponded in a predictable manner to certain feast days. This temporal emphasis was quite different from that of Marmoutier, where the rhythm of ghostly and saintly visitations corresponded to the rhythm of life and death rather than that of predictable calendrical times.[5]

The July ritual, and Philip and Renaud's recounting of it, also illustrated the importance the canons gave to material objects and display. When they relinquished the basilica to the saintly entourage, the canons left it shimmering with candles and coronas. They were proud that they still possessed Martin's vestments. More important, however, the supernatural visitation, the feast it celebrated, and the ritual that called attention to it all focused on the physical space of the basilica. The feast of July 4 celebrated, in part, the day Martin had been ordained into the priesthood, but it was primarily the celebration of two dedications when his relics were translated into the basilica. On July 4, in the fifth century, Perpetuus dedicated his new church over Martin's tomb, and again on that day in 1014 Herveus,

---

sanctorum in divinis obsequiis his scientes non indigere. Sacras tamen vestes quibus sacerdos magnus in diebus suis in celebratione sacramentorum utebatur, in loco secreto et paucis cognito juxta mausoleum ejus scimus esse reconditas" ("De cultu Sancti Martini apud Turonenses extremo saeculo XII," 227).

4. *Consuetudines ecclesiae beati Martini,* 78. (On the date of the customal, see Source Appendix, II-B.)

5. Most of the visions of Saint Martin in the "De rebus gestis in Majori monasterio" (see Source Appendix, I-D, and discussion in chapter 5) occurred at the time of an illness or death. The one exception (17, p. 405), which most resembles Saint-Martin's July visitation, was a vision on the night of All Saints', when a monk saw Martin, Saint Fulgentius, Saint Corentin, and the dead abbots and monks of Marmoutier. Although this story placed some emphasis on a calendrical date, there was no assertion that Martin visited every year at that time (only that he frequently visited), and the date itself made reference to the cycle of life and death and to the need for suffrages for the dead.

the treasurer of Saint-Martin, dedicated a newer basilica.[6] The feast of July 4 was really a dedication feast, and the fact that Martin took possession of his basilica by visiting it each year demonstrated the special success of the dedication.

On one level the emphasis on impressive display and the belief in Martin's presence in a particular place at a particular time demonstrates, once again, that the canons thought and behaved in ways that mirrored the secular rhythms, material values, and status orientations of their urban neighbors. But though these orientations lay beneath the surface of the July ceremony and the way it was represented, the more manifest message concerned the focused presence of divine—and episcopal—power. Martin's annual visitation, accounts of his occasional interactions with mortals who witnessed that visitation, and descriptions of what the witnesses saw served the purpose of illustrating, both to the ordinary laypeople who were ritually excluded from the church one night each year and to the archbishop of Tours, who was always excluded except on the day of his consecration, that divinely ordained episcopal power resided at the basilica. This power rubbed off on the canons, enhancing their claims to independence, dominance, and lordship.

In this chapter and the next I will examine the various ways the canons of Saint-Martin employed and manipulated the ritual calendar of Tours and the cult of Saint Martin to bolster their position vis-à-vis both their archbishop and the burghers of Châteauneuf. In both cases, the second half of the twelfth century and the early years of the thirteenth saw a resurgence of attempts to undermine the jurisdictional rights of the canons: the burghers attempted to form a commune and thus to escape the secular lordship of the canons, and the archbishop of Tours attempted to win back spiritual and temporal rights over religious houses that were subordinated to Saint-Martin.

Before turning in this chapter to the canons' struggles with the

6. On Perpetuus's church and the triple significance of the July feast (Martin's ordination, the dedication of the basilica, and the translation of his relics into it), see Gregory of Tours, *Historia francorum*, 2:14, p. 64. On the date of Herveus's dedication, see *Brevis historia Sancti Juliani Turonensis*, 229; *Narratio de commendatione Turonicae provinciae*, 301; Oury, "Idéal monastique dans la vie canoniale: Le bienheureux Hervé de Tours," 15.

Early medieval liturgical sources indicate that Martin's July feast was more important at Tours than elsewhere. By the eleventh century the octave of the July feast was observed at Tours with a dedication service: see Oury, "Messes de Saint Martin dans les sacramentaires," 82, 85; Oury, "Culte et liturgie de St. Martin"; Tours, Bibliothèque Municipale, MS. 184, fols. 78v–81, 230–34v, 269v; MS. 193, fols. 88v, 89, 91, 116–18; MS. 196, fols. 193v, 198v, 241, 245; MS. 198, fols. 80 ff., 97–97v; Treasury of Auxerre Cathedral, MS. 6, fols. 48v, 103v ff.; Bibliothèque Nationale, MS. lat. 9431, fols. 98, 130, 132v; MS. lat. 9434, fol. 201v; *Consuetudines ecclesiae beati Martini*, 79.

archbishop, I will analyze in greater detail the ritual of the July vigil and the stories about it. Again and again in their twelfth- and thirteenth-century accounts of the July visitations, the canons of the basilica eliminated all extraneous elements—spiritual edification, the welfare of souls—bringing their narratives around to a single message: the basilica possessed and was possessed by divine and episcopal power.

Philip and Renaud told several miracle stories to prove to Archbishop Philip of Cologne that Martin did indeed visit his church each year on the night of July 3. The first of those stories concerned a vision that the treasurer Herveus saw when he dedicated the basilica in 1014. Herveus's experience had been recounted by two eleventh-century authors—the Benedictine monk Ralph Glaber and an anonymous author who took the voice, in a dialogue, of Hugh, archdeacon of Saint-Martin. Both the differences between Hugh's and Ralph's accounts and the differences between the earlier and later versions of the event demonstrate the peculiar preoccupation of the canons of Saint-Martin and the evolution of their preoccupation between the early eleventh century and the late twelfth.[7]

According to Hugh's eleventh-century dialogue, the canons of Saint-Martin were bitterly disappointed in 1014 that Saint Martin did not bless the dedication of his new basilica with a miracle. The canons were looking for a material manifestation of divine presence in the form of a miraculous cure. But Herveus, who had been deeply influenced by Cluniac monasticism and who exceeded the piety of most monks with his private fasts and vigils, was better informed than his fellow canons. He learned that Martin did indeed bless the day of the dedication with a miracle but that it was a spiritual, rather than a material, miracle.[8]

Rapt outside himself, Herveus saw Saint Martin standing before the "highest judge" and requesting that in honor of the dedication God release from otherworldly punishment three deceased canons of Martin's basilica. Those canons were "held in the places of punishment for the fault of heedlessness," but Martin argued that they "used to perform my remembrance with a special vow."[9] God responded

7. "Hugonis Archidiaconi Turonensi dialogus," 213–17; Ralph Glaber, *Historiarum libri quinque,* 3:4, p. 64. For an earlier, and much briefer, comparison of the various versions of Herveus's vision, see Oury, "Idéal monastique dans la vie canoniale," 16–17. Oury was interested in monastic spirituality rather than the idea of focused power.

8. "Hugonis . . . dialogus," 214–15. On Herveus's connections with Cluniac monasticism, see Oury, "Idéal monastique dans la vie canoniale."

9. "Conspectum summi Judicis," "tres officiales Fratres pro culpa temeritatis locis poenalibus tenentur constricti, qui tamen quoad vivebant, mei memoriam speciali voto agere consueverant" ("Hugonis . . . dialogus," 215–16).

that because Martin cared more about the redemption of souls than the health of bodies, he would bring out of hell—*ab inferis*—not only the three for whom Martin had intervened, but also as many souls as there were people in attendance at the dedication of the new basilica. Hugh equated this miracle with the work of the Redeemer himself, implying that Martin performed a second harrowing—"a new plundering"—of hell.[10]

Hugh's story, with its stress on the possibility of release from otherworldly punishment, comes very close to the spiritual concerns of eleventh-century Benedictine monks. And indeed, it probably reflects how much Herveus's own spirituality temporarily affected the religious life at Saint-Martin.[11] Yet comparing this dialogue with Ralph Glaber's version of the story reveals significant differences between the concerns of black monks and those of the canons of Saint-Martin.

In Ralph Glaber's story, it was Herveus who asked for a miraculous sign on the day of the dedication. In answer to this request, Saint Martin visited Herveus and told him the miracles of former days would have to suffice because the gathering of the harvest was near at hand. Martin informed Herveus that everyone should pray for only one kind of cure, the "raising of souls," and said he himself had interceded especially for the canons of Saint-Martin, "who assiduously serve God in this church."[12] The spiritual message of Ralph's story thus resembled that of Hugh's, except that Ralph made no direct connection between Martin's intercession and the dedication of the basilica. Unlike Hugh—or whoever wrote with Hugh's voice—Ralph did not write as a propagandist for a sanctuary. He was not interested in Hugh's theme that Martin's power was focused at particular times and in one particular place—the basilica.

In one of the two letters they wrote to Archbishop Philip of Cologne in 1180–81, Philip and Renaud of Saint-Martin retold Ralph Glaber's version of the Herveus story, but they completely eliminated his monastic concern for the welfare of souls. Their preoccupation,

10. "Nova spoliatione" ("Hugonis . . . dialogus," 215–16).

11. Another text reflecting a concern for souls at Saint-Martin at the time Herveus was treasurer is an anonymous life of Saint Martin: *Vita Sancti Martini di anonimo.* Two references praising Herveus and his new church suggest this was written soon after the dedication, and several passages emphasize the Last Judgment and the need for intervention and repentance: 51, 53, 4, 5. For further discussion of this life, see my dissertation: "Societal Change and Religious Expression: Saint Martin's Cult at Tours, 1050–1200," 293–96.

12. "Tempori huic sufficere debent exibita dudum miracula, quoniam contiguum instat prius exsparsi seminis collecture messis. Sola enim animarum erigens medela exoranda est universis. . . . Nam et pro his noveris me apud Dominum precipue intervenire qui illi assidue in presenti serviunt ecclesia" (Ralph Glaber, *Historiarum libri,* 3:4, p. 64).

even more than in Hugh's dialogue, was to prove that Martin's power was focused in the basilica on the night of July 3. Herveus's story, Philip and Renaud proclaimed, was one of the "manifest signs and visions" proving that Martin did indeed visit his basilica during the vigil of his July feast.[13]

But Philip and Renaud knew an even better story, concerning an event that had taken place "most recently" and was still part of living memory. The canon Hildebert Paganus, who had accidentally witnessed the nocturnal visitation, described what he saw to a young canon who, in his old age, recounted the story to several canons who were still alive.[14] On the night he saw the visiting saint, Hildebert was among those canons who were assigned to keep watch at the various doors of the basilica. But he could not sleep because he had left his pillow in the locked sanctuary, and so he decided to enter the basilica in the middle of the night and retrieve the pillow. Hildebert had no problem entering the church, but as he turned to leave, he found that his route was blocked "by a long procession coming out of the choir and circling around to the altar and sepulcher [of Saint Martin]." That procession, "worthy of reverence" was made up "of archbishops and bishops shining beyond all estimation with the adornment of wondrous beauty."[15]

In recounting Hildebert's experience, Philip and Renaud stressed one thing: the awesome nature of supernatural presence. Hildebert had violated a fundamental taboo, and for that reason he was severely chastised:

> While [Hildebert] stood with his eyes fixed on the unaccustomed brightness, confused in mind and frozen in body, he was seized by someone who had diverged a little in his direction from the splendid procession. That one bitterly chastised him because with rash temerity he had presumed to intrude upon the sanctuary on the very night that . . . Martin, the lord and possessor of the place . . . visits his temple, along with his companions—citizens of the celestial fatherland.[16]

13. "Signis et visionibus manifestis" ("De cultu Sancti Martini," 228). On the dates of Philip and Renaud's two letters, see Delehaye, "Guibert, Abbé de Florennes et de Gembloux," 48–65. This letter was written during Peter of Pavia's sojourn in Tours in April–May 1181. The other letter was apparently written during Guibert's visit, which lasted from September 1180 to May 1181.

14. "Nuperrimis . . . diebus" ("De cultu Sancti Martini," 228, 230).

15. "Intermeantibus ad altare et sepulchrum pretiosi antistitis longae processionis ex chorea altari et sepulchro circumducta exeuntis, reverendo archipraesulum et episcoporum comitatu ultra omnem aestimationem mirae pulchritudinis ornatu fulgentium" ("De cultu Sancti Martini," 229).

16. "Qui dum oculis ad fulgorem insolitum mente consternatus et obrigescens corpore staret, ab uno ex illa processione praeclara ad ipsum paululum digrediente asperae invec-

Hildebert's critic went on to tell him that he had been allowed to witness the procession not because he deserved such a favor but because he would tell others what he had seen. When Hildebert found the courage to ask who was participating in the procession, his interlocutor replied that he himself was "Martin, the lord of that palace" and that the other participants included those who had succeeded him as bishop of Tours, the bishops of other cities, and Euvert of Orléans, who "though hardly known to the world, nevertheless has great merits with God." After warning Hildebert "with severe threats" that he should never again enter the basilica on the night of the July vigil, Martin returned to his saintly companions, and Hildebert found himself transported, "as if by the hair," into the chapter room.[17]

Philip and Renaud's claim that Martin returned to his church on the day of his feast was not unique—other saints did so too, at least on occasion.[18] But the liturgical practice of emptying and locking the church, which called attention to the saint's yearly presence, was at least unusual enough to arouse the curiosity of Archbishop Philip.[19] The miracle recounted by the canons resembled not only the accounts of saintly visitations, but also a more folkloric theme, which Alexander Krappe designated the "perilous chapel" or "the mass of the dead."[20] These stories about supernatural nocturnal church services stressed the breaking of a taboo—the violation of the boundary separating the living from the dead. Martin's reproaches to Hildebert were mild compared with the folkloric accounts, in which the intruders sometimes died. Yet the effect of Philip and Renaud's legend was similar to the folkloric stories. It provided no spiritual or moral edi-

tionis increpatione correptus est, quod ausu temerario praesumpsisset sanctuarium irrumpere, ea praesertim nocte qua . . . dominum et possessorem loci Martinum . . . cum consortibus suis, coelestis patriae civibus, visitare templum suum" ("De cultu Sancti Martini," 229).

17. "Martinum illius aulae dominum," "quamvis mundo non valde cognitum, magni tamen meriti apud Deum," "Severaque interminatione," "quasi per capillos" ("De cultu Sancti Martini," 229).

18. Gregory of Tours told a story describing how Saint Martin went to Tours to celebrate his feast (this was cited by Philip and Renaud as further evidence of the July visitations); Saint Febronia was seen every year on the night of her feast praying in the place where she had formerly sung psalms; and Saint Benedict revealed that he was present at Saint-Benôit-sur-Loire for his feast of July 9: see *Liber in gloria confessorum*, 94, pp. 358–59; "De cultu Sancti Martini," 228; Thomais, *Vita et martyrium S. Febroniae*, 33; *Miracles de Saint Benôit*, 1:40, pp. 83–86.

19. The door of Saint Foi's church at Conques was closed on the vigil of her feast because the clerics did not want the local devotees to disturb the office: see Bernard of Angers, *Liber miraculorum Sancte Fidis*, 2:12, pp. 120–21.

20. Krappe, "Squire's Adventure in *Perlesvaus*." Examples include Gregory of Tours, *Liber in gloria confessorum*, 72, pp. 340–41; Thietmar of Merseberg, *Chronicon* 1:7, p. 738. See also Thompson, *Motif-Index of Folk Literature*, vol. 2, no. E492.

fication, since the only personal lesson one could deduce from it was
to avoid entering Saint-Martin's church on the night of July 3. The
story focused instead on eliciting fearful respect for supernatural presence. Its purpose was to demonstrate that Martin was indeed the
spiritual *possessor* of the place that housed his relics, that his *power* was
focused both in place and in time.[21]

The distinctive focus of the canons' various accounts of the July
visitation can be highlighted, once again, by comparing their stories
with a monastic version, recounted by a twelfth-century Cluniac
named Walter in a small, and very early, collection of miracles of the
Virgin. In some ways Walter's Martin resembled the Virgin—he was
kind, gentle, and willing to bend the rules, and he offered hope for
the spiritual welfare of the canon who witnessed the saintly visitation.

Walter's Martin differed from Philip and Renaud's Martin, and
indeed, so did his canon. He was old, pious, and ready to die:

> This one about whom we speak had been a righteous canon since his
> boyhood, leading an honest life without complaint in the same church.
> And when he was already truly decrepit, he distributed everything
> whatever that he was able to own to the church of the blessed Martin.
> And as we indicated above, since he now had nothing and felt his death
> to be near, he remained in the church on the night of the vigil of the
> translation of Saint Martin, after the people and the clergy had
> withdrawn.[22]

Unlike Philip and Renaud, Walter implied that the merits of this
canon earned him the right to witness the procession. The guardians
of the church responded favorably when he requested permission to
stay in the church. Similarly, when one of Saint Martin's entourage

21. One thirteenth-century story about the July vigil, by a canon of Saint-Martin,
reiterated the same message: Péan Gatineau, *Vie monseignor Saint Martin de Tors,* lines 9393–
9464, pp. 118–19. For my argument that Péan's *Life* was written after 1229, see Source
Appendix, II-C.

22. "Hic autem, de quo loquimur canonicus a pueritia iustus in eadem ecclesia hon-
estam et sine querela vitam duxerat, cum vero jam decrepitae esset aetatis omnia quaecun-
que habere potuit in ecclesia beati Martini distribuit, et cum iam nil penitus haberet,
mortemque sibi sentiret adesse praesentem, ut jam praemisimus, vigilia translationis beati
Martini, populo cum clero recedente, in supradicta remansit ecclesia" (Walter of Cluny,
"De miraculis beatae Virginis Mariae," 654). This edition (by Labbe) of Walter's collection is
in *PL* 173:1379–86, but the Martin miracle is not included. There is a variant of the text in
the *Catalogus codicum hagiographicorum . . . parisiensi,* 1:19–21, but I will refer only to the
Labbe text. The *Histoire littéraire de la France,* 12:491–92, attributed this collection to Walter
of Compiègne, a monk from Marmoutier, but as Halphen and Poupardin pointed out
(*Chroniques des comtes d'Anjou,* xlii), the author identified himself (Labbe, 650) as "Gualterius
Cluniacensis monachus," which suggests he was some other monk.

pointed out to the saint that a living cleric was in the basilica, Martin replied, "Let . . . him stay, for he has come here with good intentions."[23]

But when Saint Nicholas entered the basilica, red bearded and accompanied by a retinue of one hundred bishops, he insisted that the canon not remain, "because he has not yet obtained our fellowship from the Lord."[24] Thus prodded, Martin gently escorted the canon to the locked door of the basilica, opened it without a key, and suggested that he remain just outside the door to listen to the divine service. As he departed, the canon tearfully asked Martin to seek pardon for his sins, and Martin responded by predicting his imminent death and assuring him that he could take hope in Christ's clemency. He also told the canon that Saint Euvert, who was among the saints present that evening, had so much merit before God "that as long as the present world lasts, God frees, each day, one soul from the place of punishment because of his grace."[25] Philip and Renaud had made no connection between Euvert's merits and the easing of the punishment of sinners.

Like Philip and Renaud, Walter emphasized that Martin was present at his basilica on his feast day, and he depicted a boundary separating the realm of the living from that of the dead. Walter's boundary, however, was more permeable: Martin, at least, was willing to bend the rules and to pay heed to the canon's good intentions. And unlike Philip and Renaud, Walter was less interested in the theme of divine presence than in the salvation of souls and the possibility that interactions between the living and the dead could incur spiritual benefit for those who still needed help in cleansing themselves of their sins.

The ritual of the July vigil and the miracle stories the canons told about it spread the message that divine power dwelt at Saint-Martin's basilica. In itself this message was not unusual. Saints were supposed to perform miracles wherever their relics resided, thus demonstrating both their own holiness and the power of God. But the July miracles, or visitations, focused in a peculiar way on the issue of divine presence. They involved neither physical healing nor the welfare of souls.

23. "Permittite . . . eum ibi manere, quia bona intentione huc advenit" (Walter of Cluny, "De miraculis beatae Virginis," 654).
24. "Quia necdum nostram societatem impetravit a Domino" (Walter of Cluny, "De miraculis beatae Virginis," 654).
25. "Ut quandiu praesens seculum duraverit, omni die animam unam a loco poenarum Dominus ob illius gratiam liberat" (Walter of Cluny, "De miraculis beatae Virginis," 654).

On first consideration it might appear that the theatrical display of the July vigil was meant to impress pilgrims. Summer, after all, was the great season for pilgrimage, and the July feast might have caught some of the stragglers making their way to Compostella (Saint James's feast was on July 24). If indeed the stories about the July vigil were meant to impress pilgrims, the reason may have been that the rest of the world had forgotten Martin's July feast. The *Guide of the Pilgrim of Compostella* mentioned only Martin's feast of November 11, and Philip and Renaud acknowledged that it was the autumn feast that was known to all the world.[26]

It seems, however, that the July vigil and its legends were intended for a more local audience. The theme of divine presence would have been relevant to the canons in their relations both with their archbishop and with the burghers of Tours, because it indicated that the basilica possessed a very special kind of power. Indeed, Philip and Renaud's account contained one theme that could have displeased the archbishop of Tours: Martin, they claimed, visited the basilica in the company of every deceased pontiff of Tours. On the night of July 3, then, the cumulative weight and power of the episcopal tradition of Tours resided not at the cathedral, but at the basilica. This message— that episcopal power was concentrated at the basilica—was conveyed by other legends and rituals of Saint-Martin as well.

Saint Martin and the Theban Martyrs: Appropriating the Cathedral's Cult

In its underlying theme, Philip and Renaud's account of the July vigil resembled another story they told in response to the letter of Archbishop Philip of Cologne, who had heard "that it is said that while he was still living, [Martin], the holy priest, prayed at the place where the Theban martyrs were martyred, and in so doing he elicited out of the earth's dry bosom . . . some of the blood of those martyrs, many years after their passion."[27]

Philip and Renaud confirmed the rumors that had reached Archbishop Philip and provided him with a full written version of the

---

26. *Guide du pèlerin de Saint-Jacques de Compostelle,* chap. 8, p. 61; "De cultu Sancti Martini," 227, 236–39. See above at note 6 concerning the greater importance of the July feast in the early Middle Ages.

27. "Quod dicitur sanctus sacerdos adhuc vivens sanguinem martyrum Thebaeorum post multos passionis eorum annos, cum in loco martyrii eorum oraret ex arido terrae sinu, quo receptus fuerat, elicuisse" (*Catalogus . . . Bruxellensis,* 1:240).

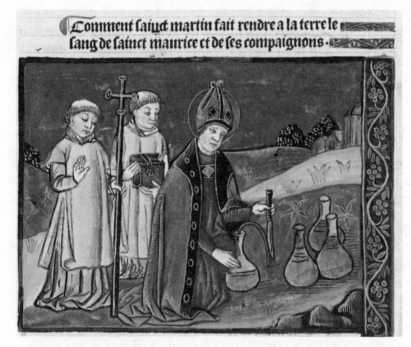

PLATE 6. Saint Martin and the Theban relics. According to the late twelfth-century legend recounted by the dean and treasurer of Saint-Martin, Saint Martin went to the place where the Theban legion had been martyred and cut the earth with a knife, causing a dense shower of blood to pour forth. This painted woodcut was one of several late medieval illustrations of the legend (*Vie et les miracles de monseigneur Saint Martin,* Diiii). Photograph courtesy Bibliothèque Nationale.

legend, which they associated with Martin's feast of May 12. While returning from a trip to Rome, they claimed, Martin decided to pray at the spot where Saint Maurice and his Theban legion had shed their blood. At the monastery of Agaune, now in Switzerland, he asked the monks for some of the Thebans' relics, but because they did not know Martin, the monks refused his request. Martin, however, learned from the local inhabitants precisely where the martyrs had died. After praying there, he cut the earth with a knife, releasing "a dense . . . shower of abundant blood." Martin filled some vessels with the blood and started for home, but before he could leave God compelled him to return to the monastery "so that Martin, rejected, would appear as Martin, God's chosen pontiff" (see plate 6). Martin gave some of the martyrs' blood, along with the knife he had used to cut the turf, to the monks of Agaune; and upon returning to Tours he gave more blood to the cathedral of Tours and to that of Anjou, which he consecrated to Saint Maurice and his companions.[28]

Philip and Renaud went on to explain that on May 12 they celebrated both this translation of Maurice's relics and Tours's deliverance from the Vikings (in 903). But their statements suggest that their legend concerning Martin's translation of the Thebans' blood was of recent origin. Martin, they claimed, was so devoted to the martyrs that he always carried an ampulla of their blood with him, and he even asked to be buried with it. "Only in our times" had that ampulla been discovered, in a hidden place near Martin's relics. "Almost all of us saw it brought forth, and we exhibited it for a long time, so that it could be revered and kissed by the people."[29] It was also in recent years that some canons from Agaune (there were no longer monks there) had come to Saint-Martin seeking alms after their church burned. At that time the canons of Saint-Martin asked the canons of Agaune to affirm the authenticity of their relics and of the legend about how Martin brought the blood to Tours from Agaune.[30]

Liturgical manuscripts from Tours indicate that in the eleventh century the monks of Marmoutier already honored Saint Maurice on May 12.[31] But there is no way to be sure that the eleventh-century liturgical calendars referred to this legend. And indeed, the probable date for the origin of the legend is the time of the "discovery" of the relics, which had taken place in the living memory of Philip and Renaud, who were writing in 1180–81.

It is most likely, therefore, that this legend, which represents a significant infringement by Martin's cult on the cult of the cathedral of Tours originated in the second half of the twelfth century. Since the

28. "Locum roseo quondam cruore purpuratum," "Dominatorem vitae et mortis oravit . . . densus . . . copiosi sanguinis imber," "ut Martinus abjectus, Martinus electus Dei pontifex appareret" (*Traditio Turonensium de sanguine sanctorum Thebaeorum,* 384–85). This text of the legend was excerpted by the Bollandists from one of the letters that Philip and Renaud wrote in 1180–81, and indeed, the only way to read the complete legend in this edition is to intersperse the text in the *Acta sanctorum* with the corrections and additions in the edited text of the letters: see "De cultu Sancti Martini," 223. The legend is now edited integrally in Guibert, Abbot of Gembloux, *Guiberti Gemblacensis epistolae,* 73–75. I have followed one slight variation from the old edition ("dominatorem vitae" rather than "dominatorem terrae" in the newer edition, p. 73).

29. "Hanc nostris modo temporibus ex occulto secretario quod sub arca corporis ejus est, inventam . . . prolatam omnes pene vidimus, populis salutandam et osculandam longo tempore exhibuimus" ("De cultu Sancti Martini," 223).

30. "De cultu Sancti Martini," 224. I can find no reference to this fire at the chapter of Agaune, which would provide a terminus ad quem for the discovery of the relics.

31. Tours, Bibliothèque Municipale, Missal from the Petit-Séminaire; Rouen, Bibliothèque Municipale, MS. 243. Both were from Marmoutier. See Bosseboeuf, "Missel de Marmoutier du XIᵉ s."; Leroquais, *Bréviaires manuscrits des bibliothèques publiques de France,* 4:115.

sixth century, when Bishop Gregory of Tours found some relics of the Theban martyrs in the crypt of Saint-Martin's basilica and translated them to the cathedral, the cathedral had been dedicated to Saint Maurice.[32] The twelfth-century legend emphasized in a new way that the cathedral owed its relationship with its patron saint to the basilica, and to Saint Martin in particular. It asserted, moreover, that the basilica of Saint-Martin possessed a major portion of those relics. Like the story of Hildebert's vision during Martin's July feast, the story about the translation of the Theban relics suggested that some of the episcopal authority of Tours resided at the basilica. Martin, the patron saint of the basilica, first gave the cathedral the relics of its patron. But Martin had also reserved some of those relics for himself and his tomb, thus endowing the basilica with a portion of the cathedral's patronal relics.

Visual Representations of Episcopal Authority

Philip and Renaud's stories about the Theban relics and the July vigil drew particular attention to Saint Martin's attributes as priest and bishop. Martin was "God's chosen pontiff"; he appeared on July 3—the vigil of the feast that celebrated his ordination into the priesthood—with an entire retinue of bishops and archbishops; and during that visitation he performed the divine office.[33] This attention to Martin's sacerdotal and episcopal attributes appears as well in a missal from Saint-Martin (Tours, MS. 193) that was copied and illuminated about the time Philip and Renaud wrote their letters.[34]

The offices for all four of Saint Martin's feasts are included in this missal, which was one of the basilica's most precious liturgical objects. The text for three of those four offices opens with a decorated letter depicting a scene from Martin's life. The illumination for the

32. Gregory of Tours, *Historia Francorum*, 10:31, pp. 534–35.

33. The phrase "God's chosen pontiff" had apparently been used to describe Martin in an inscription that was known to Alcuin: see Alcuin, "Sermo de transitu S. Martini," *PL* 101:662.

34. Tours, Bibliothèque Municipale, MS. 193. For a description of the manuscript and its date, see *Catalogue général des manuscrits des bibliothèques publiques de France*, 37:1, pp. 135–39. Collon, the editor of this volume, based his date of about 1175–80 on the paleography of the manuscript and on the fact that the name of Saint Thomas (Becket) was a later addition, implying that the manuscript was copied before Thomas's feast was widely celebrated. Garand, Grand, and Muzerelle basically agree with Collon, arguing that though the manuscript follows the calendar of Saint-Martin, the paleography suggests it was probably copied at Marmoutier during the abbacy of Herveus of Villepreux (1177–87): *Catalogue des manuscrits en écriture latine portant des indications de date*, 7:535.

PLATE 7. Saint Martin and the pagan tree. In this late twelfth-century illumination for Martin's feast of May 12, Martin wears full episcopal regalia, including the miter, even though he is outdoors, in a nonliturgical setting. As I note in chapter 9, the illumination does not depict the events that were actually celebrated on May 12—the routing of the Vikings by Martin's relics in 903. Rather, it depicts another of Martin's victories over pagans, taken from his *Life:* according to Sulpicius Severus, Martin proved the truth of the Christian faith by standing under a tree while pagans who worshiped the tree cut it down. The tree fell away from Martin, and the pagans converted to Christianity. Tours, Bibliothèque Municipale, MS. 193, fol. 78v. Photograph courtesy Tours, Bibliothèque Municipale.

PLATE 8. Saint Martin's ordination as bishop. In this illumination for Martin's feast of July 4 it is Martin, rather than the bishop who ordains him, who has a gray beard and gray hair. Tours, Bibliothèque Municipale, MS. 193, fol. 89 (late twelfth century). Photograph courtesy Institut de Recherche et d'Histoire des Textes, Centre Augustin Thierry, Orléans.

May feast (fol. 78v; plate 7), when Martin's relics saved Tours from invading pagan Vikings, depicts an earlier hostile encounter between the saint and pagans, when Martin proved the superiority of his God by standing under a sacred pine tree as the pagans cut it down. The illumination for the July feast (fol. 89; plate 8) depicts Martin's ordination as bishop; and that for the November feast (fol. 117; see plate 1 above)—the date of the saint's death—depicts not the pious moment when Martin died, but the nocturnal translation of his relics when the men of Tours passed his body out a window in Candes,

PLATE 9. Saint Martin's apostolic dignity. *Left:* The dove of the Holy Spirit descends on Saint Florent when Saint Martin ordains him: illumination for the feast of Saint Florent, Tours, Bibliothèque Municipale, MS. 193, fol. 109. *Right:* The dove of the Holy Spirit descends on the apostles: illumination for the feast of Pentecost, Tours, Bibliothèque Municipale, MS. 193, fol. 56v. Like Saint Peter in the illumination on the right, Martin has gray hair and a gray beard; like the apostles, Martin is associated with the dove of the Holy Spirit. Photographs courtesy Institut de Recherche et d'Histoire des Textes, Centre Augustin Thierry, Orléans.

thus stealing it away from the men of Poitiers. Additionally, a fourth
illuminated letter (fol. 109; plate 9), at the beginning of the office for
the feast of Saint Florent, depicts Martin ordaining the other saint. As
Martin extends his hand over Florent, the dove of the Holy Spirit
descends upon the new priest. In all these illuminations Martin wears
full liturgical vestments and a bishop's miter. In all but the one depicting the translation of his body, he carries a bishop's staff. And two of
the illustrations focus on a moment of ordination: Martin's own and
that of Saint Florent.

These four illuminated letters are the only ones in the manuscript that represent post-apostolic saints. With the exception of one letter depicting Saint Michael the Archangel and one for All Saints' Day, all the other illuminated letters concern scenes from the lives of Christ and of Mary and episodes in the history of the apostolic church. Additionally, two full-page and two half-page illuminations depict Christ on the cross, Christ in majesty, Christ extending a blessing, and personifications of the church and the synagogue.[35]

Parallels between the illuminations of Martin and those of the apostles draw attention to Martin's dignity and apostolic nature. Martin, like Saint Peter in several other illuminations in the manuscript, has gray hair and a gray beard.[36] This depiction of a patronal saint as an "elder" may have been a topos, but the parallel between Saint Martin and Saint Peter is striking. The uniqueness of the resemblance is highlighted, moreover, in that the bishop who ordains Martin has brown hair and a brown beard.

A second parallel linking Martin's miniatures to those of the apostles was the depiction of the dove of the Holy Spirit in the miniature for Florent's ordination. In a miniature for the feast of Pentecost (fol. 56v; plate 9) the dove also appeared, descending on all the apostles. The visual image for Florent's feast thus called attention to the concept of apostolic succession and to the idea that through the rite of ordination bishops preserved and transmitted the church's inheritance from the apostles.[37]

In contrast to the eleventh-century illuminations in another manuscript from Saint-Martin (Tours, MS. 1018), these late twelfth-century illuminations persistently focus on Martin's ecclesiastical dignity and liturgical functions. The persistent representation, in the twelfth-century manuscript, of Martin in a bishop's miter reflects the fact that the use of the miter, which began to spread in the late eleventh century, had become widespread by the end of the twelfth. Furthermore, that Martin was depicted in the miter even in the outdoor encounter with the sacred pine calls attention to the liturgical emphasis of the illuminations: the miter was part of a bishop's liturgical costume.[38]

35. Tours, Bibliothèque Municipale, MS. 193, fols. 17, 21v, 48v, 54, 56v, 59, 69v, 70, 71, 71v, 86, 98, 110v, 115. For descriptions, see Dorange, *Catalogue descriptif et raisonné des manuscrits de la bibliothèque de Tours,* 104–6.

36. Tours, Bibliothèque Municipale, MS. 193, fol. 86, for the feast of Saints Peter and Paul; fol. 54 for the feast of Christ's ascension; fol. 56v for Pentecost; and fol. 98 for the feast of the Assumption of the Virgin.

37. On Florent's ordination by Saint Martin, see "Acta S. Florentii dubiae fidei auctore anonymo seculo IX scripta," 429.

38. Dix, *Shape of the Liturgy,* 405–7.

The visual and legendary focus on Martin's priestly and episcopal functions, as well as on the splendor that signified the dignity of his hierarchical position, was not unique to the canons of his basilica. The general influence of the Gregorian reform had highlighted the authority and sacramental power of the priesthood. And in the face of the challenge of lay religious movements, more and more clerical authors began to stress the laity's necessary dependence on and obedience to the priestly hierarchy. Some clerical authors went so far as to insist that precious ornaments and noble horses were necessary possessions for a person holding ecclesiastical office, because such outward trappings instilled obedience in one's subjects.[39]

These hierarchical concerns heightened clerical interest, not only in Tours but in other religious centers as well, in Saint Martin's episcopal and priestly attributes and in the dignity of his position. Toward the middle of the thirteenth century, Jacob of Voragine echoed the new concerns when he described Saint Martin in the *Golden Legend*. Voragine's descriptions of the saint diverged significantly from those of Sulpicius Severus's fourth-century *Life of Saint Martin*.

Sulpicius had emphasized that *despite* his accession to episcopal office Martin maintained his monastic virtues, "the same humility in his heart, the same poverty in his dress." For Sulpicius the monastic state was superior to the episcopal, and indeed, as bishop Martin did not have "that fullness of miraculous power" that he had as a monk. After he became bishop, Sulpicius pointed out, Martin resuscitated only one dead man; before he became bishop, he had resuscitated two.[40] In contrast to Sulpicius, Jacob of Voragine depicted Martin's accession to episcopal office as an increase in dignity over his monastic state, and he did not mention Martin's continued observance of monastic poverty and humility once he became bishop. Also, because the episcopate represented the superior state, Jacob transferred all Martin's resuscitations to that period in his life.[41]

The most blatant example of Martin's new function as exemplar of priestly and episcopal dignity is the theme of the "mass of Saint

39. See chapter 7, note 14.

40. Sulpicius Severus, *Vita Sancti Martini*, 10, p. 272; Sulpicius Severus, *Dialogi*, 2:4, p. 184. Translations by Peebles, 117, 206.

41. Reames, "Saint Martin of Tours in the *Legenda Aurea* and Before"; and Reames, *Legenda Aurea: A Reexamination of Its Paradoxical History*, 107–13. See also Alain Boureau's discussion of Voragine's classification of saints into three hierarchical categories: witnesses (those, like monks, who are perfect but not active); defenders (bishops and confessors especially—those who protect the Christian community and fight the devil); and preachers ("Structures narratives de la *Legenda aurea*," 68 ff.).

Martin," which the liturgist Johannis Beleth first fully articulated about 1160. Beleth developed this theme to explain why Saint Martin deserved the unique epithet "equal to the apostles." When Saint Odo of Cluny gave Martin that title in the tenth century, he explained that it was because Martin had resuscitated three dead men. Beleth argued that this explanation could not work, because the achievement of raising the dead was not unique to Martin. Rather, Beleth suggested, Martin deserved to be called "equal to the apostles" because he had his own Pentecost. Before he went to celebrate mass one day, Martin gave his tunic to a poor man and replaced it with a vile one that was too short and had sleeves that reached only to his elbows. Martin went on to perform the mass wearing this undignified garment under his vestments. As he began to recite the preface to the mass, he raised his arms and the loose sleeves of his vestments fell back, exposing his bare arms. At that moment, however, "gold rings miraculously came forth and decently covered his arms, and a globe of fire appeared above his head, through which it was demonstrated that, with respect to authority, the Holy Spirit descended on him just as it did on the apostles on the day of Pentecost."[42] In telling this story, Beleth distorted Sulpicius Severus's original account. Sulpicius made no mention of the length of the garment and the problem of the bare arms; nor did he connect the globe of fire over Martin's head with the Holy Spirit and Pentecost. Rather, his main concern was the charitable indifference with which Martin approached the dignity of his priestly office.[43]

Beleth singled out this event and molded it so that it fit a genre of priestly eucharistic miracles that had been gaining prominence in the

42. "Miraculose proueniunt aurei torques ipsaque decenter operiunt, et globus igneus apparuit super caput eius, per quod demonstratum est Spiritum Sanctum super eum descendisse ad robur, sicut super apostolos in Pentecoste" (Johannis Beleth, Summa de ecclesiasticis officiis, chap. 163, ed. Douteil, 2:320–21). Odo of Cluny first called Martin "par apostolis" in his hymn "De S. Martino Turonorum archiepiscopo," PL 133:515. Sulpicius Severus associated Martin with the terms "apostle" and "apostolic" without calling him "equal to the apostles"; Fortunatus had called Martin "conpar apostolis": Sulpicius Severus, Vita Sancti Martini, 7:7, 20:1, pp. 268, 294; Sulpicius Severus, Epistolae, 1:5, 2:8, pp. 318, 328; Sulpicius Severus, Chronica, 2:50:4, p. 103; Sulpicius Severus, Dialogi, 2:5:2, p. 183; Fortunatus, Vita Sancti Martini, 2:460, p. 329. On the phrase "par apostolis," see Du Cange, Glossarium, 6:147.
43. Sulpicius Severus, Dialogi, 2:1–2, pp. 180–82. Sulpicius describes only flames over Martin's head. In describing the gold rings that covered Martin's arms, Beleth borrowed from and transformed another passage in Sulpicius's dialogues, in which a certain Arborius claimed that "once, when Martin was offering the sacrifice, he saw the saint's hands, decked as it were with precious jewels," Dialogi, 3:10, p. 208; trans. Peebles, 238. Again, Sulpicius made no mention of bare arms.

twelfth century.[44] His theme also supported an idea that clerics were emphasizing in the face of popular religious movements and heresies: that apostolic grace belonged exclusively to the priesthood and was passed on from one generation to another by the bishops. "The bishop," Hugh of Rouen declared, "is the foundation of the church, because through the bishop the church has the Holy Spirit."[45]

Probably for these reasons, Beleth's account of the "mass of Saint Martin" was incorporated into the *Golden Legend,* William Durand's treatise on the divine office, and a number of widely disseminated collections of sermons and exempla.[46] Beleth's story also became the basis for a number of iconographic representations of Saint Martin, and we find that in some depictions the miracle occurred not when Martin raised his arms for the preface, but when he raised the chalice or the host at the moment of consecration. The seal of Aubry Cornut, dean of Saint-Martin from 1229 to 1236, for instance, depicts Martin raising the chalice while flames—the flames of the Holy Spirit— descend upon his head (see plate 10).[47] The ritual moment of consecration, which highlighted the priest's power to bring Christ's flesh and blood into the world, was the subject of much theological discussion in the twelfth century. One preacher declared in a sermon addressed to priests that God had caused Christ's incarnation only once, through the Virgin's womb, but "you do it daily, at the altar."[48] The visual representations of the mass of Saint Martin reinforced this idea.

---

44. Dumoutet, *Corpus Domini: Aux sources de la piété eucharistique médiévale,* 117–26; Browe, *Eucharistischen Wunder des Mittelalters,* esp. 16–20; and Bynum, *Holy Feast and Holy Fast,* 51.

45. "Est episcopus ecclesiae fundamentum, quia per episcopum habit ecclesia Spiritum Sanctum" (Hugh of Rouen, "Contra haereticos libri tres," 2:1, *PL* 192:1275).

46. Jacob of Voragine, *Legenda aurea,* chap. 166,pp. 746–47 (mentions that Johannis Beleth added the part about the arms not being covered); William Durand, *Rationale divinorum officiorum,* 708–9 (very close to Beleth's text); Maurice of Sully, "Homilie pour la fête de St. Martin" (no mention of charity); Caesarius of Heisterbach, *Dialogus miraculorum,* 9:31, ed. Strange, 2:188–89 (no mention of charity); *Alphabet of Tales,* 323; Adam of Perseigne (a monk of Marmoutier, writing ca. 1180–81 for Guibert of Gembloux), "Epistola ad S. Martini cultores," *PL* 211:668–72 (gives Beleth's arguments as well as those of Odo of Cluny and others); Péan Gatineau (a canon of Saint-Martin, writing ca. 1229), *Vie monseignor Saint Martin de Tors,* lines 421–56, 1019–84, pp. 8, 15–16.

47. Archives Nationales, Service des Sceaux, D. 7599. On Aubrey's dates, see Griffiths, "Capetian Kings and St. Martin of Tours," 117. A fifteenth-century woodcut from Tours shows Martin raising the host while the angels cover his arms and flames descend on his head: see *Vie et les miracles de monseigneur Saint Martin,* ciiii.

48. "Hoc opus [Deus] fecit semel in uirgine, uos in altari cotidie" (Peter Comestor, "Sermo ad sacerdotes," 213). On the twelfth-century emphasis on the sacramental power of the priesthood and the priest's ability to incarnate Christ, see Kennedy, "Moment of Consecration and Elevation of the Host," 121–50; Dumoutet, *Corpus Domini;* and Bynum, *Holy Feast and Holy Fast,* 57.

PLATE 10. The mass of Saint Martin. The seal of Aubry Cornut, who was dean of Saint-Martin between 1229 and 1236, depicts the flames of the Holy Spirit descending on Martin while he lifts the chalice during the mass. In Johannis Beleth's twelfth-century account of this event the flames—which made Martin "equal to the apostles"—descended on the saint as he lifted his arms during the preface to the mass. Beleth's story, and the visual elaborations of it, point to a high and late medieval interest in the apostolic grace that belonged exclusively to the priesthood. Paris, Archives Nationales, Service des Sceaux, D.7599. Photograph courtesy Archives Nationales.

Struggles over Episcopal Prerogatives: Saint-Martin's Rituals of Dominance

The attention that the canons of Saint-Martin were paying, about the year 1180, to Martin's priestly, sacramental, and episcopal attributes is thus representative of a general clerical interest in the power of the priesthood and the hierarchical authority of bishops. Nevertheless, this general context provides only a partial explanation for the visual and legendary products of the canons of Saint-Martin or for their ritual behavior. In the context of their own diocese, the canons were more interested in appropriating episcopal authority for them-

selves than in supporting the hierarchical authority of their archbishop. Their interest in this appropriation had been accelerating since
the late 1150s, when the archbishop of Tours began a campaign to
win back and expand his jurisdictional prerogatives within his diocese.[49] In their confrontations with Saint-Martin, the archbishops'
attention focused on the religious houses that were subordinated to
the basilica. By the early thirteenth century, some of those subordinate houses took the initiative in trying to gain greater independence
from the domination of the basilica.

Sometime after 1226, and before the struggles with the archbishop
and the subordinate houses had all been resolved, one of the canons of
Saint-Martin put into writing the liturgical customs of the basilica.
Although the customal described a number of legal rights and rituals
that had arisen at earlier dates, it seems that its author's central purpose was to bolster, and perhaps extend, the canons' symbolic power.
The customal described a system of rituals that called attention to
Saint-Martin's rights of lordship. Many of these rituals were formal
expressions of jurisdiction over a religious community. Others, however, served the broader function of defining the basilica as the hub of
an ecclesiastical community. Unlike Philip and Renaud's legends and
the images in the twelfth-century missal, which suggested only that
episcopal dignity resided *at* the basilica, the rituals in the customal
demonstrated that episcopal dignity and authority emanated *from* the
basilica.

The basilica's ritualized expressions of dominance focused primarily on five religious communities in and around Châteauneuf. Just
outside the walls of Châteauneuf were the tiny secular chapters of
Saint-Pierre-le-Puellier and Saint-Venant. To the southwest, about
one kilometer away, stood Beaumont, a house of nuns founded in
1007 by Saint-Martin's treasurer, Herveus. About three kilometers to
the west stood Saint-Cosme, a priory of regular canons founded by
canons from Saint-Martin in 1092. And finally, about seventeen kilo-

49. The *Chronicon Turonense auctore anonymo,* written by a canon of Saint-Martin, sin-
gles out Joscius (1157–74), Geoffrey du Lude (1206–8), and John de Faye (1208–29) as the
aggressive archbishops. It explicitly states that Bartholemy of Vendôme (1174–1206) was
not an aggressor, but a struggle in 1176 over the election of the abbot of Cormery (see
below at note 61) suggests that he too was engaged in the more aggressive archiepiscopal
politics: see *Chronicon Turonense,* 1020, 1042. The charters of Saint-Julian of Tours indicate
that jurisdictional struggles between the cathedral and that abbey also accelerated at the time
of Archbishop Joscius and continued into the second quarter of the thirteenth century: see
Chartes de Saint-Julien de Tours, 1:129–30, 2:9–10, 12–17. Martène claimed that the abbot
who was elected at Saint-Julian in 1150 refused to take an oath of obedience to the archbishop of Tours. I do not know Martène's source: see *Histoire de l'abbaye de Marmoutier,*
1:553.

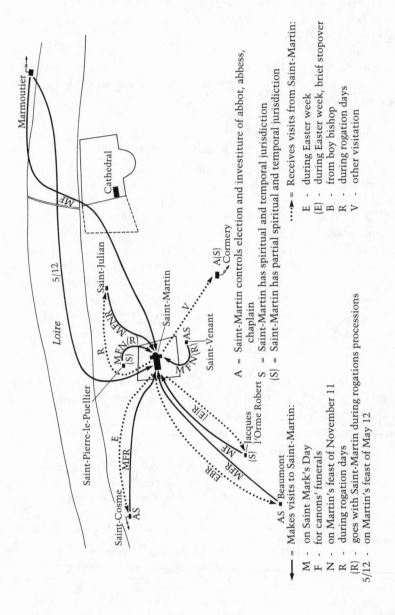

MAP 6. Saint-Martin's processional diocese.

→ = Makes visits to Saint-Martin:

M - on Saint Mark's Day
F - for canons' funerals
N - on Martin's feast of November 11
R - during rogation days
(R) - goes with Saint-Martin during rogations processions
5/12 - on Martin's feast of May 12

A = Saint-Martin controls election and investiture of abbot, abbess, chaplain
S = Saint-Martin has spiritual and temporal jurisdiction
(S) = Saint-Martin has partial spiritual and temporal jurisdiction

···► = Receives visits from Saint-Martin:

E - during Easter week
(E) - during Easter week, brief stopover
B - from boy bishop
R - during rogation days
V - other visitation

meters to the southeast there was Cormery, founded by Abbot Ithier of Saint-Martin in the ninth century and transformed into a Benedictine monastery by Ithier's successor, Alcuin of York (see map 6).[50] Between 1163 and the time when the customal was written, each of these five communities became the focus of struggles between Saint-Martin and the archbishop of Tours. The communities of Saint-Venant and Cormery also made a number of attempts to enhance their independence.

According to Saint-Martin's customal, the canons exercised some kind of jurisdiction over these five houses. The customal claimed "all spiritual and temporal jurisdiction" over three of the houses—Saint-Venant, Saint-Cosme, and Beaumont.[51] It is reasonable to assume, however, that before the mid-twelfth century, when the bishop began to win back some spiritual rights, the canons had claimed similar rights over Saint-Pierre-le-Puellier and Cormery.

By virtue of their partial and total jurisdiction over these five communities, the canons of Saint-Martin assumed the right to engage in certain rituals of domination that were denied to the archbishop in his relations with exempt houses, such as Saint-Martin and Marmoutier. First, according to the customal, the canons partially controlled the process of electing and investing spiritual leaders. Saint-Martin was involved in both the election and the investiture of every new prior, abbess, and abbot of Saint-Cosme, Beaumont, and Cormery. At Saint-Venant, which did not have an abbot or a prior, Saint-Martin was involved in the investiture of the community's chaplain. Only in the case of Saint-Pierre-le-Puellier were the canons of the basilica excluded from the process of electing and investing a spiritual leader. It is possible, however, that before 1163, when Pope Alexander III intervened in favor of the archbishop's jurisdiction over Saint-Pierre, Saint-Martin's spiritual lordship over that house had been more extensive.[52]

50. On the foundation of Saint-Cosme, see the introduction to part 3 at note 15; on the foundation of Beaumont, see Oury, "Idéal monastique dans la vie canoniale," 21; and *Gallia Christiana,* vol. 14, Instrumenta, 63–64; on Cormery, see *Cartulaire de Cormery,* v–xxiv, 3–8; Chélini, "Alcuin, Charlemagne, et Saint-Martin de Tours," 40.

51. *Consuetudines ecclesiae beati Martini,* 140–41.

52. Alexander III's summary of the arguments presented to him by the archbishop of Tours and the canons of Saint-Martin reported that the archbishop had always exercised the right of conferring the holy oil and chrism to the priests of Saint-Pierre-le-Puellier (this was in contrast to Beaumont, where the canons of Saint-Martin conferred these elements to the abbess). It seems, however, that the canons did claim the right of presentation: "De clericis uero beati Petri ad ordines promouendis testes hinc inde producti sunt, qui super hoc capitulo diuersa et uaria proponebant." Alexander decided that the archbishop would always confer the chrism and that only in some cases would the canons of Saint-Martin have

The communities of Cormery, Saint-Cosme, and Beaumont had to seek permission before they could elect a new abbot, prior, or abbess; all three houses had to defer a disputed election to Saint-Martin; and all three had to send their leader to the basilica to swear an oath of fidelity and obedience to Saint-Martin before being invested by the canons of the basilica with the *cura animarum*. After the canons of Saint-Martin invested a new spiritual leader, that candidate—like the abbot-elect of Marmoutier—still needed to be consecrated by a bishop. Unlike Saint-Martin's subordinate houses, however, Marmoutier gained the right in 1089 to go to any bishop for consecration if the archbishop of Tours did not wish to cooperate.[53]

In the case of Cormery, spiritual investiture involved an elaborate ritual established by Urban II in 1096. Whenever an abbot died his pastoral staff was given back to the canons of Saint-Martin, who placed it on the tomb of Saint Martin. After a new abbot of Cormery had sworn his oath of obedience, the canons took him to the tomb and invested him with the pastoral staff.[54]

According to the thirteenth-century customal, the canons of Saint-Martin could refuse to invest abbatial and prioral candidates from Cormery and Saint-Cosme.[55] This claim suggests that Saint-Martin had expanded its rights over Saint-Cosme since its foundation in 1092: the foundation charter had stipulated that if the priory became large enough to constitute a regular community, its members could elect their own priors and present them to the chapter of Saint-Martin, which could not refuse those candidates.[56]

The chapter of Saint-Venant did not have a prior or dean, but the canons there did elect a chaplain who was invested at Saint-Martin with the cura animarum. Furthermore, Saint-Venant's dependence on Saint-Martin was such that the canons there were not allowed to have

---

the right of presentation: "De representatione autem clericorum Sancti Petri, qui ad ordines fuerint promouendi . . . clerici sancti Petri, qui canonici sancti Mart(ini) uel sancti Uenanti fuerint, a capitulo sancti Martini debeant archiepiscopo presentari; alii uero, qui clerici sancti Petri tantum existunt, a clericis eiusdem ecclesie archiepiscopo, cum ordinandi fuerint, presententur" (Letter of Alexander III to Archbishop Joscius of Tours [1163], in *Papsturkunden in Frankreich*, n.s. 5, no. 123, pp. 216–17).

53. *Consuetudines ecclesiae beati Martini*, 138–41; Bull of Urban II, in *Papsturkunden in Frankreich*, n.s. 5, no. 21, p. 84.

54. *Consuetudines ecclesiae beati Martini*, 138; *Gallia Christiana*, vol. 14, Instrumenta, 74; *Cartulaire de Cormery*, 44, pp. 88–90. Urban II had to intervene in the relations between Saint-Martin and Cormery because the count of Anjou was attempting to extract the abbey from Saint-Martin's control: Guillot, *Comte d'Anjou*, 1:167–73.

55. *Consuetudines ecclesiae beati Martini*, 138, 141.

56. Vaucelle, *Collégiale de Saint-Martin*, 262; Foundation charter of Saint-Cosme, Tours, Bibliothèque Municipale, MS. 1295, p. 605.

their own seal, and they could not confirm any legal act without getting the canons of Saint-Martin to apply their seal to it. Concerning Saint-Pierre-le-Puellier, the customal indicated that Saint-Martin held all the same rights there that it held at Saint-Venant except that of parochial cura animarum. This suggests that Saint-Martin did not invest the chaplain of that house but that the canons of Saint-Pierre, like those of Saint-Venant, could not have their own seal.[57]

Certain rituals reinforced the blurring of the legal identities of Saint-Venant and Saint-Pierre with that of Saint-Martin. The two subordinate houses joined Saint-Martin in its processions but were not allowed to carry a cross, which would have symbolized their separate corporate identities. In the funeral procession for a canon of Saint-Martin, the canons of Saint-Venant and Saint-Pierre walked with the canons of Saint-Martin rather than separately, as did the monks of Marmoutier and Saint-Julian, the nuns of Beaumont, and the canons of Saint-Cosme. And during rogations, Saint-Martin did not visit Saint-Venant and Saint-Pierre. Rather, the canons of those two houses accompanied the canons of Saint-Martin in a procession to Saint-Julian.[58]

Saint-Martin's jurisdiction over elections and investitures at Saint-Cosme, Beaumont, Cormery, and Saint-Venant represented one aspect of its spiritual lordship, which rivaled the archbishop's within the confines of his own diocese. Indeed, it is not surprising that many of the jurisdictional struggles between the archbishop and Saint-Martin concerned either the process of making a new spiritual leader or the lordship that control over that process symbolized.

On three occasions in the second half of the twelfth century Saint-Martin's rights over the abbot of Cormery became the focus of a struggle with the archbishop. Sometime between 1157 and 1174, Archbishop Joscius demanded that the new abbot of Cormery take on oath of obedience, which the canons and the abbey protested.[59] In 1174, however, two arbitrating bishops who had been appointed by the pope decided that new abbots of Cormery were indeed to make an oral promise of "obedience, subjection, and reverence" to the arch-

---

57. *Consuetudines ecclesiae beati Martini*, 140–41.

58. *Consuetudines ecclesiae beati Martini*, 140–41, 133, 67. It seems that the rogation procession went by Saint-Pierre but did not enter it. In 1163 the canons of Saint-Martin attempted to use some of these rituals as evidence of their jurisdiction over Saint-Pierre: see Letter of Alexander III to Archbishop Joscius, in *Papsturkunden in Frankreich*, n.s. 5, no. 123, pp. 215–16.

59. *Cartulaire de Cormery*, 63, p. 124 (the editor mistakenly dates this 1147, but Joscius was not bishop until 1157); letters of Alexander III and Lucius III, in *Papsturkunden in Frankreich*, n.s. 5, nos. 167, 183, pp. 260–61, 276.

bishop and that the archbishop had the right to depose culpable abbots of Cormery. It was probably for this reason that Saint-Martin's
customal did not claim all "spiritual and temporal rights" over the
abbey.[60]

In 1176 the archbishop addressed the way Cormery's abbot-elect
was presented to him for consecration. Because the canons of Saint-
Martin, rather than the monks of Cormery, claimed the right to
present the abbot, the archbishop refused to consecrate him. The
canons insisted there were many precedents for their action; the archbishop argued that the previous abbot had been presented to him by
the monks of Cormery. A papal legate ruled that for the sake of the
community of Cormery the archbishop should go ahead with the
consecration, but he did not indicate how this dispute should be
resolved in the future.[61]

In 1213 Innocent III responded to a dispute between the archbishop
of Tours and Saint-Martin involving spiritual rights over Beaumont.
The archbishop claimed he held the spiritual rights because one abbess had given an oath of obedience, reverence, and submission when
he blessed her. The canons of Saint-Martin, claiming spiritual jurisdiction for themselves, replied that the nuns sought permission from
the canons whenever they needed to elect a new abbess; that the
canons of Saint-Martin installed the newly elected abbess; that they
received, "in French," her oath of obedience, subjection, and reverence; and that they gave the abbess her pastoral staff, as well as holy
oil, chrism, and the fire that was blessed on Easter. Innocent III's
response was not sufficiently precise to resolve the dispute. Finally, in
1238 two arbitrators decided that Beaumont was under Saint-Martin's
jurisdiction. From then on the abbess was to be blessed by the archbishop without any inquest into her election or morals and without
any oath of obedience. If he refused to cooperate, she could receive
her blessing from another archbishop. In 1243 the pope approved this
arrangement.[62]

Jurisdictional struggles between the archbishop and Saint-Martin
over Saint-Pierre-le-Puellier, Saint-Cosme, and Saint-Venant tended
to concern spiritual jurisdiction over the parishes belonging to those

60. Cartulaire de Cormery, 66, pp. 127–30.
61. Letter of Peter of Grisogonus, in Papsturkunden in Frankreich, n.s. 5, no. 162, pp.
254–55.
62. Innocent III, "Regestorum sive epistolarum liber duodecimus," 15:229, PL
216:764–66; Cartulaire de l'archevêché de Tours, 1:71–72; Bibliothèque Nationale, Collection
Baluze, MS. 76, fols. 189–189v (1238 arbitration); Vaucelle, Collégiale de Saint-Martin, 259–
60; Grandmaison, Chronique de l'abbaye de Beaumont-lez-Tours, 11–17 (Grandmaison cites
the sources, but his narrative is confusing).

houses. Also, with regard to spiritual jurisdiction over its parishes rather than over the monastery itself, the archbishop was able to regain some territory at Beaumont. In 1163 Archbishop Joscius asserted his "authority" and "rights" over Saint-Pierre-le-Puellier. He gained approval of his claims from the pope, but when the archbishop went to Saint-Pierre to make good his claims, the canons of Saint-Martin locked him out. Nevertheless, the customal of Saint-Martin suggests that the canons were not able to persist in their resistance.[63] Similarly, the canons could not resist the archbishop's assertion of parochial rights at Beaumont. In 1211 the archbishop gained parochial rights over the parish belonging to that abbey. The settlement stipulated that the abbess, or one of her priests, was to present to the archbishop, or one of his officers, the curate of the parish, who would swear obedience to the archbishop and receive from him or his representative the chrism and holy oil. In 1238, when Saint-Martin gained recognition of its full spiritual rights over the nuns of Beaumont, the archbishop's rights over Beaumont's parishes were reaffirmed.[64] The canons of Saint-Martin were apparently more successful in retaining parochial rights at Saint-Cosme and Saint-Venant. In 1211 the archbishop conceded to them the rights over the parishes of those two houses.[65]

The process of electing and investing new spiritual leaders, and the implications of that process, also constituted a focus of strife between Saint-Martin and the subordinate communities themselves. In 1211, as a result of an internal struggle with his own monks, the abbot of Cormery was compelled to acknowledge in writing that all disputes in his abbey, as well as disputed abbatial elections, had to be deferred to Saint-Martin. In 1212 a panel of external ecclesiastical judges determined that the canons of Saint-Martin did not have the right to prevent the monks of the abbey from holding an election. In 1217 the two communities were again engaged in a struggle, though it is not clear that it involved abbatial elections. The abbot of Cormery had failed to respond to the canons' request that he appear before them, so

63. Vaucelle, *Collégiale de Saint-Martin*, 254; Joscius, archbishop of Tours, two letters to King Louis VII (1163), *Recueil des historiens des Gaules*, 16:49–50; Letter of Alexander III to Archbishop Joscius (1163), in *Papsturkunden in Frankreich*, n.s. 5, no. 123, pp. 214–17; *Consuetudines ecclesiae beati Martini*, 140–41.

64. *Cartulaire de l'archevêché de Tours*, no. 35, 1:73–75; Bibliothèque Nationale, Collection Baluze, MS. 76, fols. 213–14 (1211), fols. 189–189v (1238); Grandmaison, *Chronique de l'abbaye de Beaumont*, 11–12; Vaucelle, *Collégiale de Saint-Martin*, 259–60.

65. Vaucelle, *Collégiale de Saint-Martin*, 253; Tours, Bibliothèque Municipale, MS. 1294, p. 50; Mabille, *Pancarte noire de Saint-Martin*, 148, p. 464. *Chronicon Turonense auctore anonymo*, 1042.

the canons, as was their right, seized all the property of the monastery.[66] In 1214 the canons of Saint-Venant also failed to appear when summoned to Saint-Martin, which was demanding reprisals because Saint-Venant had attempted to carry out a legal action without the permission of the canons at the basilica. The canons of Saint-Venant were finally forced to submit when Saint-Martin placed them under interdict and withheld the benefice they normally received from the basilica.[67]

In addition to controlling elections, investiture, and the right to take legal action, Saint-Martin exercised the right to be received in processions at several of the subordinate houses and to be given food, lodging, or both. These processions served to define geographical space and to remind the local community that Saint-Martin had jurisdiction over its subordinate houses.

Probably because it was too far from Tours, the abbey of Cormery did not play a regular role in Saint-Martin's annual processional calendar as we know it from the thirteenth-century customal. But that customal shows that the monks of Cormery were obliged to receive the dean of Saint-Martin with a procession the first time he visited there after his accession to office and whenever he returned from Rome. On those occasions, the monks owed procuration to the dean; that is, they were obliged to feed him and give him shelter. The dean's right to a procession at Cormery paralleled the archbishop of Tours's right to a procession at Saint-Martin on the day of his consecration. The archbishop, however, was limited to one procession at Saint-Martin, and he did not have the right to any procuration.[68]

Saint-Martin's ritual involvement with Beaumont and Saint-Cosme was more intense that its involvement with Cormery. One aspect of that involvement occurred during the week after Easter, when the canons of the basilica went in procession to each of those two houses. On the occasion of those processions, the two houses owed procuration to the boy clerics and bell ringers of Saint-Martin: on the Monday after Easter, when the chapter visited Beaumont, the boy clerics ate a meal and the bell ringers received four deniers, four

---

66. Vaucelle, *Collégiale de Saint-Martin*, 257 n, 258 n; Bibliothèque Nationale, Collection Housseau, MS. 6, 2309, 2310 (1211); *Cartulaire de Cormery*, 77, pp. 144–45 (1212); Tours, Bibliothèque Municipale, MS. 1294, p. 125 (1217); Bibliothèque Nationale, Collection Housseau, MS. 6, 2444. On Saint-Martin's right to seize the property, see *Consuetudines ecclesiae beati Martini*, 138.

67. Vaucelle, *Collégiale de Saint-Martin*, 253; Bibliothèque Nationale, Collection Baluze, MS. 77, fol. 428.

68. *Consuetudines ecclesiae beati Martini*, 138, 148.

loaves of bread, and a serving of wine; on Tuesday, at Saint-Cosme, the boys ate a meal and the bell ringers received four deniers, twelve loaves of bread, and a serving of wine.[69]

The episcopal symbolism of the canons' Easter visitations is striking. The week after Easter was a traditional time for bishops to make processions to religious institutions in their dioceses. Indeed, it was the archbishop of Tours's Easter visitation to Marmoutier that had given rise, in the eleventh century, to the exemption struggle between the monastery and the archbishop. The canons of Saint-Martin, who had also gained rights of exemption, demonstrated through their Easter procession and their right of procuration that their spiritual lordship over Beaumont and Saint-Cosme (two of the three houses over which they had full spiritual lordship) exceeded that of the archbishop over themselves.[70]

Saint-Martin's practices during the Christmas season also involved a visit by the boy clerics to Beaumont, and again the visit entailed episcopal symbolism, though it was masked by the playfulness of traditional observances of the Christmas season. On the feasts of Saint Stephen (December 26), Saint John (December 27), and the Holy Innocents (December 28), the chapter of Saint-Martin, performed, as did a number of cathedral chapters, a series of ritual inversions. At vespers on the evening preceding each of the feasts, the canons sang the line from the *Magnificat*—"He has put down the powerful from their seats, and he has exalted the humble"—and the baculus of the cantor was passed to the members of one of the lower orders, who took over the canons' stalls for the next twenty-four hours. On Saint Stephen's Day the deacons took over; on Saint John's Day, the presbyters; and on Innocents', the boy clerics.[71]

---

69. *Consuetudines ecclesiae beati Martini*, 61–62.

70. On the Easter visitation to Marmoutier, see chapter 2, notes 9 ff. Arnulf, the archbishop who made the visit to Marmoutier that ignited the violence at that abbey, also observed the custom of making an "episcopal station" at Saint-Julian each year on the second day after Easter: see *Chartes de Saint-Julien*, 12 (1034), p. 18. Saint-Julian never became an exempt house, and the archbishop continued to exercise rights of procuration there into the thirteenth century. In 1231, however, the monks gave some properties to the archbishop so that he would give up the right of procuration, including the right he had demanded when he visited the abbey each year on the vigil and feast of Saint Julian: see *Chartes de Saint-Julien*, 2:9–10, 12–17. It was also in 1231 that the monks of Cormery contested the archbishop's right of procuration at some of their priories and settled the matter with a financial exchange: see *Cartulaire de Cormery*, 84, pp. 153–54.

71. At many houses the subdeacons took over the stalls and performed the rowdy feast of fools on New Year's Day. Saint-Martin's customal gives no evidence for this, though statutes from the late thirteenth century condemning the potential "scandal" and "shame" of the Christmas octave suggest that perhaps there was a feast of fools there: see *Consuetudines ecclesiae beati Martini*, 33–40 (parts of this passage were printed in *De antiquis*

At Saint-Martin, as elsewhere, the feast of the Innocents was more elaborate than the feasts of Saints Stephen and John. Unlike the other lower orders, the boy clerics had their own bishop and cantor, who had been appointed on Saint Martin's feast of December 13.[72] Moreover, the boys' festivities lasted more than just one day. On the day preceding the feast of the Innocents, the boys made a procession on horseback to the abbey of Beaumont, where they installed their bishop in his *cathedra*. After he was installed, the boy bishop changed into silk vestments and made his first benediction over the nuns. Back at Saint-Martin, the boy bishop was raised in his cathedra at one of the doors of the basilica and carried to Martin's tomb, where a prayer was said and he made another benediction, over "the people." On Innocents' Day, when the boys took over the choir, their bishop read the seventh lession at matins and provided a meal for the other boys. On New Year's Day the boy bishop came last in a procession and made another benediction.

Although most of these arrangements for the boy bishop resemble those at cathedral chapters in other towns, the rituals at Saint-Martin had special significance, because the basilica was not a cathedral and because the boy bishop made a visitation to one of Saint-Martin's subject houses. The practice of electing or appointing a boy bishop usually occurred in cathedral chapters. When the boys of a cathedral took over the stalls of the choir, they inverted the usual hierarchy within their religious community by miming their elders and superiors—both the canons of the chapter and the bishop.[73] At Saint-Martin, by contrast, the boys could invert only half of this hierarchy, by miming the canons. In appointing a boy bishop (he was not elected by the boys themselves), the senior members of the chapter of the basilica appropriated a symbol that did not belong to them.

The visitation of Saint-Martin's boy bishop to Beaumont was not unique—other boy bishops made visitations too.[74] But in most cases

---

ecclesiae ritibus, bk. 4, chap. 13, reprint edition, vol. 3, cols. 107–8; "Quarta ecclesiae reformatio anno 1262" (Tours, Bibliothèque Municipale, MS. 1295, p. 557). For a general discussion of the ritual inversions of the Christmas octave, see Chambers, *Medieval Stage*, 1:249–371, 2:279–89. On the New Year's feast, see chapter 9 at notes 94 ff.

72. *Consuetudines ecclesiae beati Martini*, 27–30. For further analysis of the feast of December 13, see chapter 9 at notes 82 ff.

73. Chambers does cite examples of monasteries that elected boy bishops, but most of the evidence seems to be late: see *Medieval Stage*, 1:360–361. For an excellent discussion of ritual inversion and misrule, see Davis, *Society and Culture in Early Modern France*, 97–123.

74. Thirteenth-century service book from Padua, published in Young, *Drama of the Medieval Church*, 1:108. Chambers, *Medieval Stage*, 1:347–48, citing Du Cange, *Glossarium*, s.v. "Kalendae," 4:481–85, who quotes the fifteenth-century statutes of Toul.

a visitation from the boy clerics of a cathedral chapter would have reinforced the claims of their bishop. This visitation, by contrast, served as a reminder that the chapter of Saint-Martin exercised certain ecclesiastical powers over Beaumont, powers that the archbishop of Tours was still trying to reclaim at the time Saint-Martin's customal was written. And the boys themselves were a direct reminder of the chapter's jurisdictional rights over the nunnery, since during the Easter visitation they were the major beneficiaries of the chapter's rights of procuration.

The most blatant aspect of the appropriation of episcopal symbolism for Saint-Martin was the way the ceremony of the boy bishop's installation paralleled the installation of the archbishop of Tours. On the day of his consecration, the archbishop was consecrated at the abbey of Saint-Julian, then he came to Saint-Martin in procession. He was led to the tomb of Saint Martin, and after a prayer was said he made his benediction over the people. Then the archbishop was led to the choir and placed in his cathedra, and the barons carried him back to the cathedral.[75]

In the ceremony of the boy bishop's installation, the geographical relation between Beaumont and Saint-Martin paralleled the relation between Saint-Martin and the cathedral during the archbishop's installation. At Beaumont the boy bishop was raised up in his cathedra and made his first benediction, and from there he returned in procession to his mother church, or "cathedral." But one difference distinguished the boy's ceremony from that of the archbishop: the boy bishop of Saint-Martin had the right to visit Beaumont every year and to demand procuration along with the other boy clerics; the archbishop of Tours exhausted his rights to visit Saint-Martin on the day of his consecration.

It is possible that the boy bishop of Saint-Martin was installed at Beaumont precisely because that house was the only focus of continued disagreement between the archbishop and Saint-Martin at the time the customal was written. The sources do not indicate just when this custom arose, however, and there may have been other reasons for installing the boy bishop at Beaumont. Just as the custom of having the boy clerics receive a meal at Beaumont may have drawn out or symbolized the potential nurturing relationship between the women and the boys, the custom of installing the boy bishop there may have encouraged a playful encounter between the women and the children.

75. *Consuetudines ecclesiae beati Martini,* 148.

In addition to engaging in rituals that symbolized their lordship over Cormery, Beaumont, Saint-Cosme, Saint-Venant, and Saint-Pierre-le-Puellier, the canons of Saint-Martin joined with these and other local houses in an exchange of ritual obligations that did not symbolize hierarchical dominance. Saint-Martin exchanged funeral obligations not only with the four subordinate houses that were close enough to be involved (all, that is, except Cormery), but also with the abbeys of Saint-Julian and Marmoutier and with the priory of Saint-Jacques-l'Orme-Robert. Saint-Julian and Marmoutier were not at all subordinate to Saint-Martin, and Saint-Jacques was a priory of Saint-Florent of Saumur, though it had once belonged to Saint-Martin, which still maintained some rights over it, including the right to stop there during the Easter procession to Beaumont.[76]

Rogation processions, which took place during the week before Ascension Sunday, were also more representative of spiritual exchange than of domination. Saint-Julian and Beaumont exchanged rogation processions with Saint-Martin, the canons of Saint-Cosme made a rogation procession to Saint-Martin, and the monks of Saint-Jacques received a rogation procession. The canons of Saint-Venant and Saint-Pierre processed with the canons of Saint-Martin to Saint-Julian.[77]

In themselves, Saint-Martin's exchanges of rogations and funeral obligations with these seven houses did not undercut the authority or dignity of the archbishop of Tours. Indeed, the canons of Saint-Martin also attended the funerals of the archbishop; and Saint-Julian made rogation processions to the cathedral as well as to Saint-Martin.[78] Nevertheless, the cumulative effect of Saint-Martin's exchanges enhanced the dignity of the basilica. First, the visual impact of the ritual exchanges was uneven: whereas all the members of the seven proximate houses, except for the monks of Marmoutier, attended all the

---

76. *Consuetudines ecclesiae beati Martini*, 61, 137–45. Saint-Martin's liturgical relations with Marmoutier originated with the charter of 1115 (see chapter 2 at note 41 ff.). Liturgical relations between Saint-Martin and Saint-Julian originated about 935 when Archbishop Theotolus refounded Saint-Julian. Theotolus established that Saint-Julian would celebrate matins at the basilica on Saint Martin's feast of November 11. That practice was still observed when the customal was written: see *Brevis historia Sancti Juliani Turonensis*, 226; *Consuetudines ecclesiae beati Martini*, 145.

77. *Consuetudines ecclesiae beati Martini*, 67–68.

78. Concerning Saint-Martin's attendance at the funerals of archbishops, see Letter of Alexander III (1163), in *Papsturkunden in Frankreich*, n.s. 5, no. 123, p. 215. Attendance at these funerals is not mentioned in Saint-Martin's customal. Concerning Saint-Julian's rogation processions, see Treasury of the Cathedral of Auxerre, MS. 6, fols. 74v (Monday after the fourth Sunday after the octave of Easter—procession to Saint-Martin); 75v (Tuesday—to Saint-Maurice); 77v (Wednesday—to a church of the convent's choice; the manuscript mentions certain liturgical arrangements if the monks choose to go to Saint-Loup, one of the abbey's possessions).

funerals at Saint-Martin, the canons of the basilica attended only some of the funerals at the other houses. Thus, at the time of the funeral of one it its canons, Saint-Martin appeared as the hub of an impressive ecclesiastical community, one that included not only the houses subordinate to it, but also the monks of Saint-Julian and Saint-Jacques and at least some of the monks of Marmoutier.[79] The absence of the archbishop from these funerals enhanced the dignity of the basilica, since the archbishop could not present himself as a rival to its authority. The absence of the cathedral chapter was also notable, because it was the only major religious institution in the city and its immediate surroundings that was not represented at these funerals.

Although the funerals of the archbishops of Tours may have matched those of the canons of Saint-Martin in solemnity, the cathedral chapter could not match Saint-Martin's observances on the feast of the Major Litany, which took place on April 25, the feast of Saint Mark. On that day the nuns of Beaumont, the canons of Saint-Cosme, Saint-Venant, and Saint-Pierre, the monks of Saint-Julian and Saint-Jacques, and thirty of the monks of Marmoutier all made solemn processions to Saint-Martin. There each of the seven visiting communities took its place at a different door of the basilica, where they waited for the canons of the basilica to complete their own procession back from the church of Saint-Hilary. The eight religious communities then entered the basilica and took up positions at different altars. Once in place, they began to recite the litany—a general supplication for divine assistance and favor.[80]

That seven neighboring religious communities converged on Saint-Martin during the Major Litany was significant. The canons of Saint-Martin were superimposing on their observation of the litany for April 25 the format of a litany that had been instituted by Pope Gregory the Great for the Lenten season of 590, when Rome was besieged by a plague. Indeed, the conflation of the two litanies was explicit: in the foundation charter of the priory of Saint-Cosme (1092) the canons of Saint-Martin stipulated that as soon as the members of the new house numbered twelve or more they would be obliged to attend the "Gregorian litanies" at Saint-Martin.[81]

---

79. *Consuetudines ecclesiae beati Martini,* 131–33, 137, 139–42, 145. The section on the burial of a canon of Saint-Martin mentions that the "monks" of Saint-Jacques came to the burial of every canon, but the section on Saint-Jacques mentions only that the prior of Saint-Jacques attended Saint-Martin's funerals. All the monks of Marmoutier attended the burial of one of Saint-Martin's priors; only ten came to the burial of an ordinary canon.

80. *Consuetudines ecclesiae beati Martini,* 69–71.

81. "Si vero in duodecim et amplius numerus eorum pullulaverit deinceps Gregorianas rogationes in ecclesia B. Martini praesentiae suae frequentiae conventus ille decorabit" (Foundation Charter of Saint-Cosme, Tours, Bibliothèque Municipale, MS, 1295, p. 605).

Gregory the Great had arranged that all the people of Rome, who
were divided into seven groups according to their stations in life, were
to process from seven different churches to the Church of Saint-
Mary.[82] At Tours the seven religious communities that converged on
the basilica from all directions also symbolically represented the entire urban area. In this representation of the city, the archbishop was
once again noticeably absent, while Saint-Martin was clearly at the
center. Whatever the archbishop attempted to do on this day, he was
limited by the fact that all the major religious houses of the town and
its immediate vicinity were obliged to participate in the litany at
Saint-Martin. During the Major Litany, when the people appealed to
God to bestow his grace and favor on their community, the basilica of
Saint-Martin clearly represented the center of the community of
Tours.

The appropriation of symbols of ecclesiastical power and dominance at Saint-Martin is representative, in part, of a concern with
hierarchy and status that seems to have heightened about the time of
Philip Augustus. Like the canons of Saint-Martin, the monks of Marmoutier, and most especially their abbots, began toward the end of
the twelfth century to display the symbols of their status. Abbot
Robert of Blois (1165–76) built a separate bedchamber and chapel for
himself and his successors; Abbot Hugh of Rochecorbon (1210–27)
or one of his immediate predecessors assumed or attained the right to
wear a bishop's miter. When the archbishop of Tours protested this
practice, Hugh stopped wearing the miter, but he constructed a gate
to the abbey that was known as the gate of the miter. Hugh also
initiated the construction of Marmoutier's elaborate Gothic church,
and his funeral was carried out "more solemnly" than those of earlier
abbots.[83]

Yet chronological developments alone do not account for the preoccupation at Saint-Martin with power and prestige. On the one
hand, we can trace Saint-Martin's grandiose style back to the days of

82. For general discussions of the Major Litany and Gregory the Great's "septiform
litany," see Cabrol, "Litanies," and Leclercq, "Marc (Procession de Saint)." See also Weiser,
Handbook of Christian Feasts and Customs, 38–45. Weiser mentions that in some places rogation observances are still reminiscent of the septiform litany.

83. Hugh's brother was William de Roches, the seneschal of Anjou who turned against
the Angevins and sided with Philip Augustus in 1203. After 1204 royal registers listed
Marmoutier as a royal abbey; however, John Baldwin found no royal charters of protection
for Marmoutier, and it was not until 1259 that the king replaced the count of Anjou as the
lay protector of Marmoutier: see Martène, *Histoire de l'abbaye de Marmoutier,* 2:188, 199–
200; Baldwin, *Government of Philip Augustus,* 233–39, 413, 445, 448; *Chronicon abbatum
Majoris monasterii,* 321, 325–26; my Conclusion, at note 7.

Odo of Cluny, if not before.[84] And on the other hand, the abbey of
Marmoutier still retained, at the end of the twelfth century, spiritual
concerns that distinguished its monks from the canons of the basilica.
Guibert of Gembloux wrote his description of Marmoutier in 1181 or
1182, and the second legend about Odo of Blois and his wife Ermengard was probably written sometime in the second half of the
twelfth century or the early years of the thirteenth. These sources
indicate that suffrages for the dead, concern for the welfare of souls,
penance, and a need to remain separate from the secular world remained central themes at Marmoutier at least until the very end of the
twelfth century.

The abbey of Marmoutier ruled a large empire of priories and
daughter houses, but for the monks, unlike the canons, domination
was not an articulated theme, nor does domination appear in the
records of the abbey's rituals. Indeed, most of Marmoutier's priories
were inhabited by members of the mother abbey. Those monks did
not undergo, as did the canons of Saint-Martin's priory of Léré, an
entry ceremony that symbolized their separate and subordinate
status.[85]

On one level, the different purposes and corporate structures of
Saint-Martin and Marmoutier help to explain the greater concern for
status and power at the basilica. The canons, as I argued in the introduction to part 3, were much more openly entangled than were the
monks of Marmoutier in the secular affairs and values of the world
around them. They were also much more involved in the city of
Tours itself—and this involvement led, especially after 1150, to frequent jurisdictional disputes between the basilica and the archbishop
of Tours. Although the monks of Marmoutier also engaged in jurisdictional disputes with bishops and archbishops, those disputes were

84. Odo of Cluny, "Sermo de combustione basilicae beati Martini," *PL* 133:736. Odo
also told a story involving the ostentatious dress of an earlier generation of canons at Saint-
Martin: see John of Salerno, "Vita Sancti Odonis," 3:1, *PL* 133:75. Odo's description of the
earlier generation seems to be confirmed by a depiction of the canons of Saint-Martin in the
Vivien Bible: Bibliothèque Nationale, MS. lat. 1, fol. 423 (illumination depicting the presentation of the Bible to Charles the Bald).
85. The customal of Marmoutier does not mention any processions with outside communities. This is somewhat misleading, since we know the monks went to Saint-Martin on
April 25 and May 12: *Antiquae consuetudines Majoris monasterii* (see Source Appendix, I-F, on
the date, sometime after 1124). Evidence that the monks in the priories were considered
monks of Marmoutier is in the following: *De rebus gestis in Majori monasterio* (see Source
Appendix, I-D, on the date of the text—after 1137); Guibert, Abbot of Gembloux, "Epistola," 609 (the priors of the priories helped elect Marmoutier's new abbot); Letter of Urban
III (1186–87), in *Papsturkunden in Frankreich*, n.s. 5, no. 227, p. 321; Odo Rigaldus, *Register of
Eudes of Rouen* (1248–69), 96, 102, 524. On the entry ceremony of the canons of Léré, see
chapter 7 at note 55.

much more dispersed than were those of Saint-Martin.[86] The abbey did not enter into a new period of conflicts with the archbishop of Tours in the second half of the twelfth century.

In the face of local opposition to their dominance over the urban community of Tours, the canons became increasingly preoccupied with symbols of power and hierarchy. Just as they wished to maintain their domination over subordinate religious communities, the canons wished to maintain their domination over the lay community of Châteauneuf. Their struggles with that lay community are the subject of the next chapter.

86. *Papsturkunden in Frankreich*, n.s. 5, nos. 27, 34, 69, 234, pp. 90–91, 98–99, 148–49, 327–28.

9

Martin's New Town: Dominance and Resistance in Châteauneuf

Between 1122 and 1305 the burghers of Châteauneuf attempted on numerous occasions to extract themselves from the seigneurial lordship of the canons of Saint-Martin. They resorted to various tactics—both legal and violent—and they persisted in their attempts for over 150 years, even though they gained a number of rights and concessions from the king of France.[1]

In 1122 the basilica of Saint-Martin and Châteauneuf were burned "because of the war that took place between the rebellious burghers and the canons."[2] In 1141 the townspeople paid 500 silver marks to King Louis VII and 200 livres of Anjou to the treasurer of Saint-Martin (a total of 10,650 sous) in exchange for new limitations on Saint-Martin's rights over the taverns and the sale of wine in the city. In return for this cash payment, Louis VII also dismissed a grievance that he and the treasurer of Saint-Martin had against the inhabitants of Châteauneuf because they had begun to build their houses on the city walls, in its ditches, and on its roads. He promised, moreover, that he would observe the rights and customs of the people of Châteauneuf, except in the case of three men—two of them named Renaud Fremaud.[3] In 1143 the burghers paid 30,000 sous to Louis VII, who exempted them from his taxes and promised that he would never pursue them for practicing usury or "multiplying" money in any other way. The king also gave assurances that he would never "oppress" the burghers of Châteauneuf for any grievance he might have as long as they would answer to him in the "house" of the treasurer of

---

1. The narrative on the following pages draws heavily on Giry, *Etablissements de Rouen*, 1:178–209, but I have consulted all the primary sources myself.

2. "Propter guerram quae inter burgenses rebelles et canonicos fuit" (*Chronicon Petri filii Bechini*, 62).

3. Bibliothèque Nationale, Collection Housseau, MS. 5, no. 1640; *Layettes du trésor des chartes*, 1:53, no. 76.

Saint-Martin, who was in charge of secular justice in Châteauneuf.[4] In 1164 the townspeople rallied behind the cause of a Nicolas Fremaud, possibly the son of one of the earlier Fremauds. The sources do not reveal the nature of this dispute, but one letter from the canons of Saint-Martin to the king mentions with disdain the swearing of an oath and the townspeople's attempt to free themselves from the "justice" of the canons.[5]

In 1180 the burghers were caught making another oath among themselves—a secret oath known as a commune. The pope sent John of Salisbury, the aged bishop of Chartres, as a judge delegate to investigate the event. When John arrived the leading townspeople attempted to appeal their case. Indeed, it was probably on this occasion that they produced a false document indicating that Louis VII had granted them permission to come together and form bonds among themselves. John of Salisbury refused to hear the appeal and instead excommunicated the inhabitants of Châteauneuf, singling out thirty men who had instigated the commune. One of those thirty was named Fremaud or Fromaud. After the inhabitants of Châteauneuf took their appeal to Rome, the excommunication was lifted and John granted the burghers the right to designate one hundred representatives whom he and the archdeacon of Tours ceremonially absolved at Marmoutier and the cathedral of Tours.[6] The absolution took place in September 1180.

Sometime between April and October of the following year, King Philip Augustus granted a limited form of self-government to the lay inhabitants of Châteauneuf. They had the right to hold annual elections to select ten men who would take care of collecting money for the expenses of the town. Every inhabitant of Châteauneuf was to swear an oath to these men promising to abide by their decisions concerning the "needs" and "expenses" of the city.[7] But Philip's concession did not satisfy the men who had agitated in 1180—in 1184 they were again caught attempting to form a commune. After receiv-

4. Bibliothèque Nationale, Collection Housseau, MS. 5, no. 1699; partially quoted by Giry, *Etablissements de Rouen*, 1:190 n. 1.

5. "Per hoc enim exemplum tam ipse praedictus N. quam ejusdem castri burgenses omnes, siquidem tanto sacrilegio conjurati, capituli nostri justitiam vestrique dominii jugum a se repellere contumaciter machinantur" (Letter of G., treasurer of Saint-Martin to King Louis, in *Recueil des historiens des Gaules*, 16:95, no. 291). Other letters concerning this dispute are in vol. 16, nos. 290, 293, and 295, pp. 95, 96, and vol. 15, nos. 140, 144, 145, pp. 820, 822.

6. Giry, *Etablissements de Rouen*, 1:194–96; Letter of John of Salisbury, in *Recueil des historiens des Gaules*, 16:624–25, no. 104; Bibliothèque Nationale, Collection Housseau, MS. 5, no. 1938.

7. "De misis et necessitatibus" (*Recueil des actes de Philippe Auguste*, 1:41–42, no. 30).

ing an appeal from the canons of Saint-Martin, the pope dissolved the commune and granted the canons the right to excommunicate the oath swearers if they did not abjure. The canons then pronounced an excommunication, and this, combined with papal and royal pressure as well as some class resentment, convinced the more modest inhabitants of the town to submit. When the archbishop of Reims and Abbot Herveus of Marmoutier came to Châteauneuf as papal judge delegates, the modest burghers told them they had been forced to take part in the oath and to help finance its goals. They then abjured, and the abandoned leaders of the commune were soon forced to abjure as well. The canons of Saint-Martin took advantage of this victory, gaining permission from the pope to destroy certain change tables and stalls that the merchants of Châteauneuf had erected without their permission.[8]

In 1212, apparently in response to further agitations from the burghers, Philip Augustus dissolved the limited form of self-government he had granted to the inhabitants of Châteauneuf in 1181.[9] Then in 1231, eleven townsmen, whom the canons claimed had acted with the complicity of the other inhabitants of Châteauneuf, attacked the house of the treasurer of Saint-Martin. The penalty for this deed was a payment of 300 silver marks plus 100 livres of Tours (a total of about 6,000 sous) to the chapter of Saint-Martin.[10]

Even after 1231, the discontented burghers continued to agitate against the canons.[11] In 1247 they refused to pay an annual tax to maintain the lights of Saint-Martin, and in 1251 they claimed that only the king could exercise high justice in Châteauneuf.[12] Finally, in 1305 the formation of the pious confraternity of Saint Eloi provided them with the opportunity to come together, to arm themselves, and to take a solemn oath. They proclaimed the reestablishment of the commune and attacked the cloister of Saint-Martin, killing a canon and a cleric. During their attack they also burned one of the doors of the cloister and broke into the prison. For several days they managed to place the canons and their associates under siege, forbidding anyone to provide them with food and other necessities. Despite this

---

8. Letters of Lucius III, in *Papsturkunden in Frankreich*, n.s. 5, nos. 193, 194, 213, 214, pp. 282–87, 302–5; *PL* 201:1321–22. Letters of Archbishop William of Reims and Abbot Herveus of Marmoutier, in *Gallia Christiana*, vol. 14, Instrumenta, 86–87; *Recueil des historiens des Gaules*, 18:291–92 n. a. Letter of Philip Augustus to the burghers of Châteauneuf, in *Recueil des actes de Philippe Auguste*, 1:150–51, no. 122.

9. Giry, *Etablissements de Rouen*, 2:101–3 (*preuves*, no. 20).

10. Giry, *Etablissements de Rouen*, 2:104–5 (*preuves*, no. 21).

11. Giry, *Etablissements de Rouen*, 1:204–6.

12. Giry, *Etablissements de Rouen*, 1:204–5.

organized effort, however, the burghers again failed to establish their commune, and as reparations for their insurrection they had to pay 10,000 livres (200,000 sous), one-third of which went to the basilica while the other two-thirds went to the king. This was a staggering sum, and indeed, after this date the burghers of Châteauneuf never again attempted to evade the lordship of the basilica.[13]

The men at the center of these agitations were the most prominent lay inhabitants of Châteauneuf and, indeed, of the entire urban conglomerate of Tours. The repetition of a number of surnames in the twelfth-century accounts of the burgher agitations, as well as in fourteenth-century sources, shows that these men came from a core group of elite burgher families that passed on their status and grievances from one generation to the next. The core group numbered about thirty in a town—Châteauneuf, that is—of about three thousand.[14]

These were merchants, money changers, and tavern owners—commercial men who made their living primarily by providing goods and services for the pilgrims who visited Saint-Martin's tomb (see map 3 in chap. 1, which shows the market centers of Châteauneuf). They especially resented the canons' monopoly on some commercial enterprises in Châteauneuf and their right to extract a percentage from the burghers' commercial enterprises.[15] Even after the concessions of 1141, the canons had a monopoly on the sale of wine in Châteauneuf for a total of forty-one days each year, though they apparently could not practice that monopoly on major feast days, including Saint Martin's November and July feasts. The canons received the bridge and gate tolls paid by travelers to the town. They charged rent on the stalls and change tables that the merchants set up

13. Giry, *Etablissements de Rouen*, 2:107–9 (*preuves*, no. 23). The burghers of Reims were compelled to pay this sum after they attacked the cathedral and its men in 1233–36: see Branner, "Historical Aspects of the Reconstruction of Reims Cathedral, 1210–1241," 32–37. See also Abou-El-Haj, "Urban Setting for Late Medieval Church Building." I am grateful to Professor Abou-El-Haj for allowing me to read this article before it appeared in print.

14. On the prominence of the leaders of the commune, see the letters of Archbishop William and Abbot Herveus, who called them "potentiores burgenses," see *Gallia Christiana*, vol. 14, Instrumenta, 87. In the twelfth century the repetition of names involved not only the Fremauds, mentioned above, but also the four men singled out in 1184, who had already been mentioned in 1180: see ibid., 87; Letter of John of Salisbury, in *Recueil des historiens des Gaules*, 16:624. It was John of Salisbury who listed thirty men as the principal instigators of the commune of 1180. Three families whose members participated in the communal movement of the 1180s—the Fremauds, the Gatineaux, and the de Fourques (de Fulchis)—were among the prominent financial families in fourteenth-century Tours: see Chevalier, *Tours, ville royale*, 186–87. On the population of Châteauneuf in the twelfth century, see Chevalier, "Cité de Tours et Châteauneuf," 243.

15. Chevalier, "Cité de Tours et Châteauneuf," 243–45.

in Châteauneuf, and they destroyed unauthorized stalls, tables, and shops. Moreover, the canons could reinforce their advantages and enhance their profits through their control of the courts of justice.[16]

The accounts of the struggles in Châteauneuf mention again and again the burghers' attempts to circumvent or bring to an end these seigneurial rights—rights to extract payments, to charge rent, to control major sources of income, and to administer justice. The prominent townspeople were willing to pay dearly to escape these seigneurial prerogatives, but they never attained all they desired. The reasons for their failure were several. First, as Bernard Chevalier has pointed out, their town was much smaller than those of Italy, southern France, and the Low Countries, where the urban inhabitants did succeed in overthrowing their immediate seigneurial lords and forming communal governments. Because Châteauneuf was small, the number of prominent burghers who constituted a potential patriciate was also small. Of course there were other wealthy laypeople in the other sections of the urban conglomerate of Tours, especially in the suburb of Saint-Symphorian, near Marmoutier, but their numbers were relatively insignificant. Châteauneuf was the most highly developed commercial area of Tours, and so most of the prominent merchants lived there. In the period preceding 1204, moreover, the inhabitants of the other sections of Tours did not share common goals with those of Châteauneuf because they were subject to the political jurisdiction of the Angevins, the archbishop of Tours, and Marmoutier rather than that of the Capetians and Saint-Martin.[17] The inhabitants of the other parts of Tours never rebelled against their seigneurial lords.

Another obstacle to the extension of urban liberties at Châteauneuf was the Capetian king's close alliance with the canons of Saint-Martin. Those French towns that succeeded in forming communes usually gained the backing of the Capetian kings, who tended to use the recognition of urban liberties to extend their own influence and power. At Châteauneuf the king had nothing to gain in recognizing a commune, which would undermine the authority of Saint-Martin,

16. Concerning the monopoly on the sale of wine, see *Consuetudines ecclesiae beati Martini,* 100, 103, 152. On bridge and gate tolls and the canons' monopoly on justice, see Agreement of Philip Augustus and Richard the Lion-Hearted (1190), in *Recueil des actes de Philippe Auguste,* 1:440–43, and above at note 4. On rents on the stalls, see Mabille, *Pancarte noire de Saint-Martin,* catalog, 176, p. 193 (Bibliothèque Nationale, Collection Baluze, MS. 76, p. 168). In 1067–70 the dean and treasurer sold some land at the Place Saint-Martin to some merchants who were going to establish stalls there. They would pay an annual rent to the chapter and its treasurer. On the destruction of stalls, see text above at note 8.

17. Chevalier, "Cité de Tours et Châteauneuf," 241, 245–46.

where he held the office of lay abbot and cultivated a close alliance. Indeed, the treasurer whose house was attacked in 1231 was Pierre Charlot, the illegitimate son of Philip Augustus.[18]

Rituals of Dominance: Excommunication and Abjuration

In the long run, the political and social contexts were probably the most important obstacles preventing the burghers of Châteauneuf from attaining their goals. Yet it would distort the picture if we failed to consider the role that cult and ritual played in reinforcing the power and authority of the canons of Saint-Martin. In 1180 and again in 1184, the only two occasions before 1305 when the burghers were formally accused of forming a commune, the canons of Saint-Martin and their ecclesiastical allies resorted to the sentence of excommunication. In 1184 the excommunication apparently helped convince the modest burghers to submit to the ecclesiastical authorities. And on both occasions the prominent inhabitants, or at least most of them, finally abjured their oath, presumably because they did not wish to suffer the social and spiritual isolation of excommunicants.[19]

The themes of ecclesiastical, juridical, and spiritual power that were central both to the ritual of excommunication and to that of absolution were clearly conveyed to all the burghers of Châteauneuf. The ceremony of excommunication emphasized both the political authority of the ecclesiastical hierarchy and its ability to invoke divine vengeance.[20] When the canons of Saint-Martin excommunicated the burghers in 1184 they were exercising juridical power, a power that the inhabitants of Châteauneuf resented. The sentence was probably repeated daily. When he excommunicated the burghers in 1180, John of Salisbury instructed the canons to incorporate the excommunica-

18. Petit-Dutaillis, *French Communes in the Middle Ages*, 63–85; Baldwin, *Government of Philip Augustus*, 59–64. On Pierre Charlot, see Griffiths, "Capetian Kings and St. Martin of Tours," 127, 131 n. 17.

19. The stipulations concerning who was and was not allowed to associate with excommunicants were complex, and of course it is difficult to gauge how effective such stipulations were: see Vodola, *Excommunication in the Middle Ages*, 44–69. Barbara Abou-El-Haj discussed a case at Reims paralleling that in Tours, in which the rituals of excommunication and penance brought the rebellious burghers to submission: see "Urban Setting for Late Medieval Church Building."

20. Vodola makes the important point, however, that by the early thirteenth century the form of excommunication used in the ecclesiastical courts, which was often extended by court members who were not priests, affected one's purgatorial status rather than one's salvation. Nevertheless, a sentence of anathema, which turned the individual into a sinner, could follow upon the original excommunication if the guilty party did not submit (*Excommunication in the Middle Ages*, 36, 41–46).

tion into their divine offices. The priests of the minor altars were to read the sentence of excommunication, singling out by name those individuals who were considered the instigators of the crime. Once the names of the excommunicants had been pronounced in public, good Christians were supposed to shun them.[21]

Even belief in miracles and the cult of the saints—in particular that of Saint Martin—served to establish the canons' position of dominance. In 1184 Archbishop William of Reims and Abbot Herveus of Marmoutier wrote that a virtual miracle occurred when they came to Châteauneuf. After they had failed to make any progress in establishing peace between the instigators of the insurrection and the canons, a multitude of people— "miraculously" and "beyond our hopes"—entered the chapter claiming they had been forced to support the commune. Because the crowd was so large, the archbishop and abbot led them outside. There the judge delegates enhanced the impact of the group assembly by employing the cult of the saints. Claiming that "God directed our footsteps," they moved to a spot where Saint Martin's relics had once resided. They also placed the relics of some other saints in front of themselves, thus visually and spatially enhancing their authority. After reading the crowd letters from Pope Lucius III and King Philip Augustus condemning the commune, they released the people from the obligations of the oath and enjoined them not to provide any further support for the commune. The people then raised their hands toward the relics and abjured the commune.[22]

The blatant uses of cult and ritual to support the dominance of the canons over the inhabitants of Châteauneuf, and the fact that the burghers' grievances centered on the profits from the pilgrimage to Martin's tomb, suggest that the relationship between the inhabitants of Châteauneuf and the cult of their city's patron saint was complex. This relationship was rendered even more so by the way the canons molded Saint Martin's image and rituals to support their claims to power. It was during the period of the greatest civil strife at Châteauneuf—1180 to about 1251—that the canons of Saint-Martin produced most of their literary works. Philip and Renaud wrote their

---

21. Vodola, *Excommunication in the Middle Ages*, 50. John of Salisbury's instructions to the canons are in his letter of 1180 in *Recueil des historiens des Gaules*, 16:624–25.

22. "Miraculose," "praeter spem nostram," "Deo . . . gressus nostros dirigente," "coram nobis" (Letter of Archbishop William of Reims and Abbot Herveus of Marmoutier, in *Recueil des historiens des Gaules*, 18:291–92 n. a. I am grateful to Geoffrey Koziol for pointing out the significance of the phrase "coram nobis." If the authors had emphasized that the relics stood "between" themselves and the people, they would have been highlighting the mediating role of the relics. Instead they emphasized an alliance of power between themselves and the saints.

letters to Archbishop Philip of Cologne in 1180–81. The *Chronicle of Tours* was written in or soon after 1225. The customal of the basilica was written between 1226 and 1237. And Péan Gatineau wrote his French *Life* of Saint Martin sometime between 1229 and about 1250 (see Source Appendix, II-B and II-C). It thus appears—and indeed I argue in the following pages—that the message of power in a number of these works was directed not only at the archbishops of Tours but also at the burghers of Châteauneuf.

Still, an analysis of the relationship between the townspeople and the cult of Saint Martin must begin with an understanding that cult and ritual lent themselves to complex and even contradictory possibilities. The theme of contested power was not the only aspect of the burghers' relationship to the cult of Saint Martin. Thus, before I discuss the canons' use of Saint Martin's cult to enhance their hierarchical dominance over the burghers of Châteauneuf, I must first depict the burghers' willing participation in the cult of their urban patron.

The Townspeople and the Cult of Saint Martin: Income, Salvation, and Health

To be sure, the prominent leaders of Châteauneuf were probably all too aware that sacraments, relics, cult, and liturgy were used against them, but they were also aware that their own financial advantages stemmed from the pious devotion that pilgrims held for Saint Martin. In 1175 they apparently cooperated in financing the revaulting of the nave of the basilica, which was finished about 1180. And in 1176 they formed a pious confraternity with the canons, establishing perpetual candles, an altar, a priest, and commemorative services.[23]

A need for funds for the building project probably provided one stimulus for the foundation of this confraternity, which included an

23. *Narratio de commendatione Turonicae provinciae*, 302; Notice of Philip, the dean, and Geoffrey, the treasurer, of Saint-Martin (1176), in *Papsturkunden in Frankreich*, n.s. 5, no. 161, pp. 252–54. On the date of the completion of the Gothic vaults of the nave, see Mussat, *Style gothique de l'ouest de la France*, 153 ff., citing "De cultu Sancti Martini," 243–44. As Geoffrey Koziol pointed out to me, however, it is possible that the agreement for the confraternity in 1176 served as a resolution for conflicts that had already arisen. See, for example, *Chartes de Saint-Julien de Tours*, 1:49–50, no. 35. The charter, dated 1080, resolved a dispute between the canons of Saint-Martin and the monks of Saint-Julian regarding certain burghers who had built their houses on Saint-Martin's land. It was agreed that although the monks were quit of all responsibility for the houses constructed up to that date, no more houses would be built, and "for the sake of peace" the monks would celebrate a mass each year after Saint Martin's summer feast for the dead brothers of Saint-Martin.

endowment to support the observances.[24] But there was another concern as well: care for the dead and dying. Burial at Saint-Martin was an obligation for the adult male inhabitants of Châteauneuf, as well as for their wives and eldest sons, unless they received permission from the chapter to be buried elsewhere or entered a religious institution. Thus, as the charter establishing the confraternity makes clear, it was in the burghers' spiritual interest to enhance their friendship with Saint Martin and his priests.[25]

The charter established that two candles were to burn continuously at Saint Martin's sepulcher for the souls of the members of the confraternity and that a priest at the altar of Saint Julian in the basilica was to be set aside to perform commemorative services for the deceased members of the confraternity. Each year a series of commemorative services was also to be celebrated for the dead lay brothers, during the days immediately preceding Saint Martin's feast of May 12.[26]

May 12 was an appropriate date for these commemorations. It had evolved into Châteauneuf's urban patronal feast, and it was thus logical that the inhabitants of the town should be involved in its celebration and derive spiritual benefit from its practices. The November feast was not appropriate for local celebrations because it was oriented toward pilgrims. Similarly, the July feast focused on the themes of the dedication of the basilica and the presence of supernatural power. The May feast, as I will argue later in this chapter, centered on the town of Châteauneuf itself. This was also an appropriate time for commemorating the dead because such commemorations, as well as confraternal banquets, frequently took place in May or early June, during the week after Pentecost. In fact, before the feasts of All Saints and All Souls were established in the ninth and tenth centuries, May had been the dominant month for commemorations, and vestiges of that tradition still existed.[27]

The burghers of Châteauneuf and the canons of Saint-Martin founded their confraternity during a period (1164–80) of relative peace between their two groups. Unfortunately we do not know what

24. On confraternities and the funding of churches, see Graham, "Appeal, about 1175 for the Building Fund of St. Paul's Cathedral Church."

25. On required burial at Saint-Martin, see *Consuetudines ecclesiae beati Martini*, 134. The charter of confraternity indicated that the burghers acted "deuotione et amore beati Martini," "pro animabus suis et suorum" (Notice by Philip, the dean, and Geoffrey, the treasurer, of Saint-Martin, in *Papsturkunden in Frankreich*, n.s. 5, no. 161, p. 253.

26. Notice by Philip, the dean, and Geoffrey, the treasurer, of Saint-Martin, in *Papsturkunden in Frankreich*, n.s. 5; no. 161, pp. 253–54.

27. James, *Seasonal Feasts and Festivals*, 227; Leclercq, "Quatre-temps"; Ulrich of Cluny, *Antiquiores consuetudines*, PL 149:688–89; Molinier, *Obituaires français au Moyen Age*, 27–28.

happened to the confraternity after the insurrections of 1180 and 1184, but it is perhaps significant that at least one name in the notice for the confraternity recurs in the list of instigators of the 1180 commune. Furthermore, there is no mention of the confraternity or of the special commemorative services in the early thirteenth-century customary of the basilica.[28] Perhaps, then, the communal strife brought the confraternal arrangements to an end. Nevertheless, six years after the insurrection of 1184 a Nicolas Engelardus—probably the same Nicolas Engelardus who had been a leader of the 1180 and 1184 communes—gave 5,000 sous of Anjou to Saint-Martin to endow a weekly Sunday procession there. He endowed this procession "for the salvation of his soul, and those of his mother and father and of all deceased believers."[29] Whatever his relationship to the communes of 1180 and 1184, in 1191 this burgher was concerned for the welfare of his soul. That concern, and his proclaimed desire to show honor to Saint Martin, suggest that the relationship between the burghers and the cult of Saint Martin was not limited to financial and political practicalities. They considered Saint Martin an important ally in their personal quest for a comfortable afterlife.

Accounts of Saint Martin's miracles also suggest that the saint's cult served the interests not only of the canons of Saint-Martin but also of the townspeople of Châteauneuf. Three collections of miracle stories date from the twelfth or early thirteenth century.[30] By enhancing

28. Philip and Geoffrey's notice for the formation of the confraternity mentioned among the elected individuals who would maintain the candles the laymen Hugh of Furcis and Ralph of Furcis. It was probably the same Ralph Fulchis or Furchis who in 1185 sold a stone house in Châteauneuf to several laymen and their wives. The document recording this transaction (which suggests that Ralph was relatively prosperous) stated that Ralph's father's name was Hugh: see Tours, Archives d'Indre-et-Loire, G381, p. 480. John of Salisbury's letter concerning the commune of 1180 mentioned Ralph of Fulchis and Fulbert of Fulchis: see *Papsturkunden in Frankreich*, n.s. 5, no. 161, p. 254; *Recueil des historiens des Gaules*, 16:624. The custumal could have mentioned the confraternity in the sections concerning the feast of May 12, the burial of burghers, laymen who had confraternal relations with the chapter, or suffrages for the dead. It did not do so: see *Consuetudines ecclesiae beati Martini*, 71, 134, 135–36, 117.

29. "Pro salute animae suae patris quoque et matris suae et omnium fidelium defunctorum" (Notice by Philip, the dean, and Pierre, the treasurer, of Saint-Martin, Tours, Bibliothèque Municipale, MS. 1295, p. 602. On Nicholas's involvement in 1180 and 1184, see Letter of John of Salisbury, in *Recueil des historiens des Gaules*, 16:624; Letter of Archbishop William and Abbot Herveus, ibid., 18:292 n. a.

30. "Ex codice MS. monasterii S. Martini Tornacensis" (this collection from 1141 concerns the miracles Martin performed along with Saint Agnes and Saint Fare when the relics of the two female saints were brought to the basilica); "De cultu Sancti Martini apud Turonenses extremo saeculo XII," 231–35 (these are miracles reported by Philip and Renaud, the dean and treasurer of Saint-Martin, in one of their letters to Archbishop Philip of Cologne in 1180–81); Herbernus (attributed), *Miracula beati Martini*, PL 129:1032–52, re-edited in Van der Straeten, *Manuscrits hagiographiques d'Orléans, Tours et Angers*, 163–84

Martin's fame and prestige, the stories served the financial interests of both canons and burghers.[31] But those stories also demonstrate that Martin's power was available to meet the needs of sick and distressed individuals and that those individuals interacted with the relics in various private rituals. More than half of the people who sought Martin's assistance, these miracle collections suggest, were either local townspeople or inhabitants of nearby villages and towns.[32]

People from virtually every level of society came to Martin, and they sometimes stayed days or even weeks awaiting their cures.[33] At

---

(collection probably compiled between 1140 and 1185—see below). Except where corrections from Van der Straeten's edition are noted, all references to the Herbernus collection are to the *PL* edition.

Both the Agnes collection ("Ex codice . . .") and the False Herbern collection are included in an extensive thirteenth-century compendium of "Martinelli" from the abbey of Gembloux (Brussels, Bibliothèque Royale, MS. 5397–5407, fols. 100v–110v, 111r–113r). It was Guibert of Gembloux who brought back extensive materials concerning Saint Martin after his pilgrimage to Tours in 1180–81 and perhaps again after his pilgrimage of 1185. It thus seems reasonable to assume that the False Herbern collection was written before 1185. Its terminus a quo is established by its borrowing a story written after 1140: see below, note 42. On the Brussels manuscript, see *Catalogus codicum hagiographicorum . . . Bruxellensis,* 1:506–15. On Guibert's pilgrimages to Tours, see Delehaye, "Guibert, Abbé de Florennes et de Gembloux," 46–65.

31. Although the miracle collections were in Latin, it seems reasonable to assume that the canons used their knowledge of the stories to enhance Martin's prestige. The miracles attributed to Abbot Herbern were copied into a number of manuscripts: see Van der Straeten, "Recueil de miracles de S. Martin attribué à Herberne." Van der Straeten's provisional list included twelve manuscripts from the thirteenth century through the sixteenth. Additionally, one twelfth-century manuscript (Charleville 117) included miracles 1–3 plus twenty-two from the Herbernus collection, and Péan Gatineau (*Vie monseigneur Saint Martin de Tors*) translated a number of the miracles into French: for example, lines 9261–62 (pp. 117–18) was an elaborate retelling of Herbernus, *Miracula,* no. 3, *PL* 129:1040–41. The miracles sent to Archbishop Philip of Cologne had the immediate effect of enhancing Martin's prestige. Finally, a concern with Martin's prestige also emerged in the collection about the miracles he performed with Saint Agnes and Saint Fare: "Credulitas nostra est, ut quia S. Agnes B. Martini visitationi interfuit, eam B. Martinus in Ecclesia sua per effectum multiplicis miraculi esse voluerit venerandam" ("Ex codice . . . Sancti Martini Tornacensis," 39).

32. The miracles from Saint-Martin identify fifty-three places of origin for beneficiaries of Martin's miracles. Of those, I (or Van der Straeten, in his edition of the Herbernus collection) was able to identify forty-three places. Ten of the forty-three beneficiaries were from Tours, seven traveled less than thirty kilometers, eight traveled between thirty and fifty-nine kilometers, and eighteen traveled sixty kilometers or more. Hence, 58.1 percent traveled less than sixty kilometers, and 41.9 percent traveled sixty kilometers or more. Pierre-André Sigal noted that 44.5 percent of the identifiable pilgrims in the miracle collections he studied traveled over sixty kilometers to the saints' tombs: see *Homme et le miracle dans la France médiévale,* 295.

33. The stories give or imply the class background of nineteen beneficiaries of Martin's miracles. The breakdown is as follows: seven noble or upper-class beneficiaries, four clerics (including one bishop and one abbess), four peasants/agricultural workers, three artisans, and one prosperous burgher. The male/female ratio is about even, as is the adult/child ratio.

times the stories of their afflictions offer glimpses into the emotional
and physical conditions of domestic life and work in the twelfth and
thirteenth centuries. A husband's violence left his wife Maria unable
to walk for three years. The parents of a demented young man from
the knightly class (he was thought to be possessed by a demon) led
him in chains to Martin's tomb. A mason who fell while working on
the walls of the cathedral of Tours suffered such extensive physical
damage that he could not stand, walk, or sit. A boy of ten had "no
bones" in his shins and feet. His mother, who normally secured the
useless limbs to the boy's waist, skillfully helped him make his way to
the tomb on his knees.[34] Even the rich and powerful could not escape
the ravages of debilitating disease. The flesh of the bishop of Liège
was devoured by the disease called lupus. "His only solace" came
twice each day when two freshly eviscerated and plucked chickens
were applied to the itching places where his flesh should have been.
He and his retinue spent seven days and nights at Martin's tomb
awaiting a cure.[35]

Accounts of people's powerlessness against crippling and disabling
diseases illustrate how prominent were the physical realities of pain
and suffering in the Middle Ages. Yet, these stories also demonstrate
that disease was—and is—as much a matter of cultural interpretation
as of physical condition. A girl's hands became paralyzed after her
angry mother cursed her. The devil caused Maria's husband to injure
her. An old peasant was invaded by a demon while he worked in the
fields—he began to vomit, spit, rage, and roar; he stopped eating and
lost the ability to speak.[36] Another peasant, a girl who was helping
with the harvest, was stuck dumb when she witnessed a troop of
spirits that apparently conformed to the folkloric motif of the wild
hunt: "A girl by the name of Menolde from the *castrum* of Mont-
richard was resting in the fields with the reapers on a certain summer
night. Suddenly she saw the most terrible spirits in the form of armed
knights running over her and violently crushing her. Terrified by that
dreadful experience, and almost driven insane, she lost her ability to
speak in that very hour."[37]

34. Herbernus, *Miracula*, nos. 10, 3, *PL* 129:1042, 1040; "De cultu Sancti Martini,"
231, 233–34.
35. "Solumque solatium" (Herbernus, *Miracula*, no. 1, *PL* 129:1036). This cure may
have involved a form of sympathetic magic, but it is also possible that the chicken flesh
actually provided relief.
36. Herbernus, *Miracula*, nos. 39, 10, 22, *PL* 129:1047, 1042, 1044.
37. "Puella nomine Menoldis de castro quem Montricardum nominant, quadam nocte
estivo tempore dum cum messoribus in area quiesceret, repente conspexit teterrimos spiritus in specie militum armatorum super se discurrere et se vehementer opprimere. Qua

To some extent individual devotees were free to engage in personal rituals in their encounters with Saint Martin. The structure of the pilgrimage church at Tours, like those of other pilgrimage churches, lent itself to an intimacy of access. Visitors could enter the sanctuary and walk up the side aisles without disturbing the services in the main sanctuary or the side altars, and they could circle around to the apse where a rear opening offered direct access to Martin's tomb, which was at ground level rather than in an underground crypt.[38] Devotees slept at Martin's tomb; they walked back and forth between Martin's tomb and that of Saint Brice, who had succeeded Martin as bishop of Tours; they cried; they prostrated themselves on the floor; they kissed and embraced the tomb; they left gifts.[39] When Martin cured the woman who had been crippled by her husband, she ran home to fetch a kettle, which she then left at the basilica as a votive offering. Another cripple who was blessed with a miraculous recovery left his crutch suspended on a beam of the church. The bishop of Liège sent silk vestments and gold and silver liturgical vessels. The marquis of Montferrat, whom Martin had helped to pay off a debt, returned to Italy, where both he and his creditor founded churches in honor of the saint. At least one devotee converted to the religious life after Martin cured her.[40]

Miracles and Power

Martin's generosity touched people at almost all levels of society, and his tomb was the scene of a cacophony of pious practices. Yet the stories about his miracles suggest that even at this most basic level of pious encounter, the canons manipulated the behavior of the devout. In their written accounts, moreover, the canons conveyed certain messages about the social hierarchy and about social tensions; and

horrenda visione exterrita et pene amens effecta, eadem hora usum loquendi amisit. Cum vero post trium septimanarum circulum ad tumulum sancti a suis deducta fuisset, mox in laudes Christi et famuli sui Martini os aperuit, quod sibi daemonum terribilis effigies divina permissione concluserat" (Herbernus, *Miracula*, no. 45, *PL* 129:1048; with corrections from Van der Straeten, *Manuscrits hagiographiques d'Orléans, Tours et Angers*, 180). On the wild hunt, see Thompson, *Motif-Index of Folk Literature*, vol. 2, nos. E501–E501.20.3.

38. The accessibility of the saint's relics or reliquary was an important aspect of most popular saints' tombs: see Sigal, *Homme et le miracle*, 35–40. On Saint Martin's reliquary, see Vieillard-Troiekouroff, "Tombeau retrouvé en 1860," 172.

39. See examples cited in the next several pages.

40. Herbernus, *Miracula*, no. 10, 9, 1, 2, *PL* 129:1042, 1038, 1039–40; "Ex codice . . . S. Martini Tornacensis," 37. For a general discussion of these kinds of rituals, see Sigal, *Homme et le miracle*, 126–34, 138–44, 147–51.

they reinforced the theme that Martin and his basilica were privileged with certain powers.

The stories described a set of social expectations concerning obligations to the saint. If one made a vow to visit Martin or to give him a gift, that vow should not be broken.[41] It was customary to reciprocate Martin's gift of health or well-being with a gift to him and his basilica. A poor woman might give a candle or a kettle; a rich man might donate a church or gold and silver vessels. Several of the stories recounted miraculous visions in which Martin or some other celestial being encouraged or enabled the fulfillment of an obligation to the saint. When the abbess of Beaumont forgot her vow to give some wax tapers to Saint Martin, he appeared to her servant and instructed him to remind her of the promise. A poor woman who had just been cured returned home to get a candle for Martin, but she found she had nothing to buy it with. An "angelic" monk then appeared to her and gave her the necessary coin.[42]

In addition to suggesting how devotees should carry out their pious obligations to the saint, Martin's miracle stories reinforced the canons' claims to power while presenting their vision of the social and ecclesiastical hierarchy. Descriptions of the miracles at Martin's tomb emphasized Martin's hierarchical role as bishop and priest rather than his life as a humble and ascetic monk. Because Martin's relics belonged to the basilica, and because he continued to make appearances there when he cured people, these episcopal themes reinforced the canons' own claims to episcopal powers. The written accounts of Martin's appearances to devotees frequently described him as wearing episcopal vestments.[43] Before healing a sick person, he might exercise his hierarchical authority by instructing or reprimanding the supplicant. A lame man who was sleeping near Martin's tomb suddenly saw the saint dressed in full liturgical and episcopal regalia—alb, stole, and pallium—and carrying a pastoral staff. Martin touched the lame man and made him well. Before doing so,

41. For general discussion of vows and votive offerings, see Sigal, *Homme et le miracle,* 79–116.

42. Herbernus, *Miracula,* no. 30, 5, *PL* 129:1045–46, 1041–42. The story about the abbess of Beaumont was borrowed from the "Miracula S. Girardi" (*Acta sanctorum,* November, vol. 2, part 1, p. 505a), in which the abbess concerned was Abbess Theophany of Ronceray (active around 1140): see Oury, "Idéal monastique dans la vie canoniale," 10 n. 28.

43. Six miracle stories (out of a total of eighty-one) describe appearances by Saint Martin. In three of the six Martin wore episcopal vestments; in a fourth he wore "sacerdotal" garments; the other two did not describe his dress: see Herbernus, *Miracula,* no. 1, 2, 30, *PL* 129:1037, 1039, 1045–46; "Ex codice . . . S. Martini Tornacensis," 38; "De cultu Sancti Martini," 232, 234.

however, he chastised him for wearing his hair too long and ordered him to get it cut.[44]

This hierarchical encounter between the bishop-saint and the layman is brought into relief by the more fraternal approach that Martin took with the bishop of Liège. This time, too, Martin appeared dressed in episcopal garments, and he was accompanied by his fellow bishop Saint Brice. "Does it not seem just to you," Martin asked Brice, "that this sick man, who so devoutly came to our tomb from so far away should regain his health?" Brice replied that indeed it was just, especially since "he is a man of our order, one whose life does not disfigure that order" (see plate 11).[45]

Saint Martin assisted both nobles and peasants, he cured bishops and artisans, and he relieved the suffering of women and children who were both rich and humble in background. Notably absent from the accounts of miraculous assistance, however, are wealthy burghers—people like the rebellious inhabitants of Châteauneuf, who made their living from commerce and trade.[46] Only two times in the three collections of miracles (a total of eighty-one stories) was there any mention of men who engaged in commerce, and in both cases these men either functioned as mundane background or had created the unpleasant circumstance. The story about the marquis of Montferrat indicated that his unpaid debt to an Italian "burgher" caused him considerable fear and consternation. The story about the woman who received a coin from an "angelic" monk mentioned the money changers of Châteauneuf as part of the background. The worldly concerns of those money changers neutralized the beauty of the miraculous encounter between the woman and the angelic individual. The changers took the woman's miraculous coin, which had a "shine of the purest quality," and reduced it to the value of three halfpennies.[47]

During his stay at Tours between September 1180 and May of 1181, Guibert of Gembloux heard an independent miracle story that blatantly criticized the burghers of Châteauneuf. Indeed, the story dealt with civic strife, which had just erupted in Châteauneuf in 1180.

44. "Pontificis insignia" ("Ex codice . . . S. Martini Tornacensis," 38).
45. "Iustumne tibi videtur ut eger hic optatam recipiat sanitatem, qui tam devotus ex tam longis partibus ad nostrum venit tumulum . . . ?" "presertim homo nostri ordinis, et cuius vita ordinem non deturpat" (Herbernus, *Miracula*, no. 1, PL 129:1037; with minor corrections from Van der Straeten, *Manuscrits hagiographiques d'Orléans, Tours et Angers*, 167).
46. Sigal found a general underrepresentation of merchants and wealthy townspeople in the miracle collections, but he did not explain it: see *Homme et le miracle*, 298–99.
47. "Purissimi candoris" (Herbernus, *Miracula*, no. 5, 2, PL 129:1041, 1038–39).

PLATE 11. Saint Martin and Saint Brice cure the bishop of Liège. The miracle story from the twelfth-century collection attributed to Herbernus was retold and illustrated in *Vie et les miracles de monseigneur Saint Martin,* Liv. The painted woodcuts in this book give us some indication of what Martin's reliquary looked like in the late fifteenth century (see Lelong, *Basilique,* 105, who refers to some early sixteenth-century wood-cuts that were probably copied from the ones in this book.) Photograph courtesy Bibliothèque Nationale.

Guibert was told that one day an enormous dispute arose among some of the townspeople at the time the conventual mass was commencing at the basilica. Because their special role was to "make peace" and to act as "legates of peace," all the clerics who were attending the mass rushed outside to calm the "sedition," thinking that if they did not intervene the situation would escalate into bloodshed, with detrimental effects for the entire city.[48]

The priest who was performing the mass did not know he had been left alone. He continued with the words that preceded the preface to the mass, and miraculously, at the moment when a response

48. "Omnes qui missae mysteriis astabant et maxime clerici quibus etiam inter extraneaos, nedum inter proprios, utpote legatis pacis, pacem reformare incumbit," "seditionem" ("De cultu Sancti Martini," 247).

was required, the "citizens of heaven" spoke all the words. Again, when the priest completed the preface, the celestial voices recited the Sanctus "with such resounding" that all the people outside were astonished and filled with "terror because of the presence of the celestial crowd." Everyone rushed into the church, and after the mass, when the priest told them what had happened, the peace that had been broken was easily restored.[49]

This story represented the canons of Saint-Martin as the protectors of the peace in Châteauneuf. Their seigneurial lordship and their control over the courts of justice, both deeply resented by the prominent burghers, were thus idealized. Peace was a major prerequisite for the commerce and profit that merchants sought. In this story, however, the townspeople themselves threatened that peace, and hence the well-being of the city. The miraculous intervention of the celestial voices not only restored order but also proved that the canons' role as peacekeepers—their judicial power—was divinely ordained.

Another twelfth-century legend pursued the same themes, borrowing its narrative line from the *Return from Burgundy*. The legend asserted that because of "a certain sedition" in Tours, the townspeople feared for the body of Saint Martin, so they translated it to Poitiers. There Martin worked many miracles, but the Poitevins gave credit to Saint Hilary and thus refused to share any of the alms with the prelates and canons who had accompanied Saint Martin. By employing the same experiment described in the *Return from Burgundy*, however, the people of Tours were able to prove that Martin was responsible for the miracles. This was a mixed blessing, for once they learned that Martin was performing the miracles, the Poitevins decided they did not want to give him up. When the sedition in Tours had been "pacified," Martin's guardians had to seek the assistance of armed men to return to their town with their saint.[50]

This story, which had no basis in fact, ended with a return to the status quo ante. Its weak dramatic theme, adapted from the *Return from Burgundy*, focused on the threat of losing both the income from Martin's miracles and the saint's relics. The apparent lesson for anyone who might contemplate stirring up "sedition" in Tours or Châteauneuf was that civic strife could bring the loss of the city's patron saint and of the income he provided for the city's inhabitants.

49. "Coeli cives," "tanta sonoritate," "prae terrore praesentium coelestium agminum" ("De cultu Sancti Martini," 247–48).

50. "Seditione quadam," "pacificata seditione" ("Quatre miracles de Saint Martin de Tours," 47–48). The Bollandists found this miracle story in MS. 12131–50, fols. 167–167v of the Bibliothèque Royale in Brussels. It was copied in the twelfth century. There is no direct evidence that the story originated in Tours.

Anticommunal Rhetoric: Saint Martin's Peace,
Saint Martin's Justice, Saint Martin's Prosperity

In their miracle stories, the canons of Saint-Martin reiterated a number of themes that reinforced their authority over the lay inhabitants of Châteauneuf. The stories emphasized the hierarchical relationship between the laypeople and Martin, the sainted bishop whose relics the canons possessed. They emphasized Martin's right to discipline the laity and to draw them into his system of justice. They served as a warning to seditious townspeople, they represented the canons as the guardians of peace in Châteauneuf, and they indicated that prosperity in Tours depended on maintaining the right relationship with its saint.

Similar themes come up in other texts that the canons produced in the twelfth and early thirteenth centuries, including the letters of Philip and Renaud, the dean and treasurer of the chapter. A superficial examination of Philip and Renaud's letters might lead one to conclude that they were not interested in the political strife that had become, just days or months before they wrote their letters, a central issue in their town. Philip and Renaud avoided any mention of conflict in Châteauneuf, and their incorporative language obscured the differences between their own perspectives and those of the townspeople. By obscuring different perspectives, however, the canons exercised textual power, since they thus denied the existence of the townspeople's independent interests and concerns. In discussing Saint Martin's peace and justice, moreover, Philip and Renaud lent divine legitimacy to the claim that the canons were the providers of peace and justice in Châteauneuf.

Philip and Renaud asserted, for example—in the passages I quoted at the beginning of chapter 7—that God and Saint Martin were the ultimate sources of the peace of Châteauneuf. Divine sanctions, then, strengthened and legitimized the peacemaking role of the canons. Along similar lines, Philip and Renaud argued that because Saint Martin had been second to none "in devotion, faith and works," he sat in the "hall of the eternal king" and qualified for the highest judicial role—the one that would be exercised at the Last Judgment.[51]

---

51. "Sedit in aula regis aeterni cum principibus, et solium gloriae tenuit. Nec enim dubitandum est arcem judiciariae sedis competere, cum devotione, fide et opere nullo eorum inferior appareat quibus laborum aequus appensor et mercedis justus redditor Christus pollicetur dicens: *Amen dico vobis quod vos qui secuti estis me, in regeneratione, cum sederit Filius hominis in sede majestatis suae, sedebitis et vos super sedes XII, judicantes XII tribus Israel*" ("De cultu Sancti Martini," 237).

Philip and Renaud described Martin's role as a divine judge in the midst of their discussion of the saint's November feast day. The feast, they explained, celebrated the day of the saint's death, and it was on that day that he attained his place in the hall of justice. After making this argument concerning Martin's place in the divine court, Philip and Renaud then gave a brief account of the special joy the people of Martin's town felt when they celebrated their patron's feast. Next they turned from the discussion of heavenly courts to one concerning earthly courts. After the octave of the November feast, they asserted, "the inhabitants [of Châteauneuf] drop everything and concern themselves exclusively with seeing that the law cases of the markets and inns satisfy with all integrity of devotion those who were injured during the solemnity."[52] Such cases could be settled only in the court of the treasurer of Saint-Martin's basilica. By sliding from Martin's role as divine judge to their own roles as secular judges, and by idealizing the devout nature of the townspeople's participation in the secular judicial process, Philip and Renaud obscured the differences between their own judicial functions in the secular realm and the judicial functions of Saint Martin in the spiritual realm.

It was in the interest of the canons of Saint-Martin to blur distinctions between their secular powers and their spiritual power and to associate Saint Martin's divine functions with their own mundane ones. The canons, like Saint Martin, had the power to judge the townspeople of Châteauneuf. Like Saint Martin, they were the guardians of the peace in that city. Any affront to the policing and judging role of the canons was, by implication, an affront to Saint Martin himself.

In his vernacular *Life* of Saint Martin, which he completed between 1229 and about 1250, Péan Gatineau recounted another story that linked Martin's supernatural powers to the secular judicial process. This story differed from most of the others in Péan's *Life* because Péan did not copy it from an earlier written text. It is possible that an oral tradition—perhaps originating in Italy—lay behind Péan's story.[53] At any rate, the emphasis on justice and the way the story centered on the selfishness of innkeepers—the type of urban dwellers who prospered in Tours—suggest that Péan had in mind the

52. "Cives, aliis intermissis jam ad nil aliud vacant nisi ut causa nundinarum et causa hospitum injuriatae solemnitati omni cum integritate devotionis satisfaciant" ("De cultu Sancti Martini," 238–39).
53. Péan states at the beginning of the story, "Un conte rai ici escrit, / Mes onc nou trovai en escrit" (Péan Gatineau, *Vie monseignor Saint Martin de Tors*, lines 1881–82, p. 26). The entire text of the story is at lines 1881–2096, pp. 26–28. On the date of Péan's *Life*, see Source Appendix, II-C.

local audience of Châteauneuf when he rendered the legend into writing.

Péan claimed that during his childhood Saint Martin lived for a while near the city of Pavia, in northern Italy, with a certain innkeeper named Meinarz and his wife Persois, who acted as surrogate parents. Persois, on the one hand, was indulgent, nurturing, and protective. She loved Martin with a mother's love. Indeed, "she was crazy [fole] about him, as if she had carried him herself."[54] Meinarz, on the other hand, was a stern authority figure who, like the father of Saint Francis, took care to protect his property from the carelessness of the child saint who was under his tutelage.[55] Indeed, on a practical level, Meinarz's possessions needed to be protected from young Martin, who was in the habit of giving away his clothing and shoes whenever he met a poor man on the road.[56]

Persois tended to supply the young saint with new clothing every time he gave it away, but Meinarz told her "she was a fool [sote]" to provision him so easily.[57] Finally, when Meinarz learned from his neighbors that Martin was distributing his grain supply to every poor man he encountered, Meinarz, again like Saint Francis's father, scolded his wife. He told her she should chastise Martin, who, after all, was not the steward of their kitchen. Persois defended the boy and pointed out that their supplies were actually increasing, but Meinarz replied that "it is foolishness [folie] to put so much faith in a child."[58]

When Martin learned of Meinarz's complaints, he decided to leave the inn, despite Persois's protests. He stole away secretly, but Persois followed close behind, and when she finally caught sight of him on the open road she called out with the distress of a mother who has lost her child:

54. "Cele, qui de lui estoit fole / Ausi com s'el l'ëust porté" (Péan Gatineau, Vie . . . Saint Martin, lines 1960–61, p. 27).

55. On Francis's father, see Thomas of Celano, Vita prima S. Francisci, 1:4–6, pp. 13–19. For my arguments concerning the similarities between Péan's story and Celano's Life of St. Francis, see Source Appendix, II-C.

56. "Mes quant aucun povre esgardoit / Qui n'avoit de quoi soi vestir, / Tantost li donnoit son vestir / Et a l'autre sa chaucemente" (Péan, Vie . . . Saint Martin, lines 1916–19, p. 26).

57. "Meinarz li disoit qu'ele iert sote / De lui si tost robe baillier" (Péan, Vie . . . Saint Martin, lines 1922–23, p. 26).

58. "Persöis dit que cil est lierres / Qui li a dit tel felonie, / C'onques, par la Virge Marie, / Ne vit nul enfant plus leal / N'en totes choses plus feal. / Par sommet s'est aperceüe / Qu'el a plus de sa cruce ëue / Que devant, puis qu'il le garda. / Menarz Persöis esgarda. / Si li a dit que c'est folie / Don tant en .i. se fie" (Péan, Vie . . . Saint Martin, lines 1944–54, pp. 26–27). On Saint Francis's father scolding his mother, see Thomas of Celano, Vita prima, 1:6, p. 17.

Good son, do not ever leave me!
Good son, come here! Good son, return!
You leave me so pensive and mournful,
Good son, and you do not care at all about me.
Well have I lost the nourishment
That I had from you for so long.[59]

A miraculous fire enabled Martin to escape Persois,[60] but before he left her the saint promised she would see him again when "the dead man speaks to the living." Persois did not think this could occur before Judgment Day,[61] but Martin's prophecy came to fruition when Meinarz was accused of a murder he did not commit. Meinarz had been framed by a neighbor, a fellow innkeeper, who murdered a man in the middle of the night. Partly because he was jealous that Meinarz had more guests than he did, the neighbor attempted to escape punishment and to harm Meinarz by hiding his victim in Meinarz's stable. When the body was discovered, Meinarz was imprisoned. The following day he was put on trial, and Saint Martin, who suddenly appeared at the trial, saved Meinarz's life by asking God to reveal the identity of the murderer. In answer to Martin's prayer, the dead man spoke up, naming the man who had killed him.[62]

The murderer's primary motive for hiding his crime was to escape the arm of justice. Martin's intervention at Meinarz's trial precluded this escape and thus served to remind the inhabitants of Châteaneuf that divine sanctions—and the prayers of Saint Martin himself— could reinforce the efficacy of the secular courts of law. Laypeople who wished to resist or circumvent the justice of the saint were setting themselves up against a formidable opponent. Martin, whose saintliness qualified him to serve as a judge at the Last Judgment, could also enhance the system of justice in this world. When she doubted that the dead could speak to the living before the Last Judg-

59. "Beaus filz, ne me laissier tu mie! / Beaus filz, ça vien! beaus fils, retorne! / Molt me laisses pensive et morne; / Beaus filz, et tu n'as de mei cure; / Bien ai perdu la norreture / Que j'ai fait en toi longuement" (Péan, *Vie . . . Saint Martin*, lines 2002–7, p. 27). In his account of Martin's secret departure Péan may have drawn on Saint Augustine, who described in his *Confessions* how he secretly sailed away for Rome, leaving his mother behind in North Africa: see Augustine, *Confessionum libri XIII*, 5:8, pp. 64–67.

60. Péan, *Vie . . . Saint Martin*, lines 2023–36, p. 27. The fire explained the name of a church in Italy—Terra Arsa—that belonged to Saint-Martin: Bibliothèque Nationale, Collection Baluze, MS. 76, fol. 15.

61. "Quant ce sera / Que li morz au vif parlera" (Péan, *Vie . . . Saint Martin*, lines 1979–80, p. 27). Persois's response to this assertion was: "Que, quant mes, dont li vendra / Que li jöices avendra, / Qu'avant nus morz ne parlereit" (lines 1983–85, p. 27).

62. Péan, *Vie . . . Saint Martin*, lines 2027–96, pp. 27–28.

ment, Persois had erroneously assumed that divine power was some-how separate from the ordinary realm of events. The outcome of the narrative demonstrated that she was wrong.

In a second story, concerning an adulterous wife who attempted to hide her offense, Péan Gatineau reiterated the theme that divine inter-vention and the power of Saint Martin would expose the truth, thus enhancing the pursuit of worldly justice. According to Péan's story, a baron who returned home after serving the king began to hear ru-mors of his wife's infidelity. Desiring to establish the truth of the matter, the baron had his wife swear, in every church in the city of Reims, that the accusations against her were lies. In all the churches of the city itself, the woman uttered her oath without any mishap. Just as they were leaving the city, however, the baron spotted an old church dedicated to Saint Martin, and he decided that if his wife could successfully swear her oath in that holy place, the affair would be closed. The woman swore her oath, asking God, the Holy Spirit, and Saint Martin to help her expose the lie of those who accused her. This time, however, divine vengeance stepped in to expose *her* lie. God and Saint Martin caused her to give birth to a child—which no one had known she was carrying—and she and the child fell dead on the floor.[63]

In these stories Péan provided negative responses to at least two of the demands of the rebellious burghers of Châteauneuf. First, by asserting that it was impossible to escape Saint Martin's justice, he showed that the burghers erred in their attempts to gain exemption from the courts administered by the canons of Saint-Martin. Péan's stories resembled a number of High and late medieval exempla in which perjurers and adulteresses were punished for their secret sins. But many of the exempla did not identify a particular saint as the agent of divine justice.[64] Péan's stories thus adapted the more general theme of his day, redirecting attention to the glory and power of the patron saint of his chapter and basilica. As a canon of Saint-Martin, Péan wished to associate the abstract forces of justice with the power of his patron saint. Individual citizens should rest assured that justice would prevail: adultery would be exposed, and innocent men would not suffer from false accusations. Nevertheless, the citizens of Châteauneuf should also acknowledge that in their town the pre-

63. Péan, *Vie . . . Saint Martin,* lines 9675–9825, pp. 122–23.
64. See, for example, the following stories in Tubach's index: nos. 56, 59 (adulteress exposed by iron ordeal; adulterer in flames); 3702, 3704, 3709 (perjurer bursts, perjurer's hand shrinks, perjurer drops dead). To be sure, however, there were just as many exempla emphasizing that justice would prevail only in the next life: see Tubach, *Index Exemplorum.*

rogatives of justice—indeed, the judicial institutions themselves—belonged to Saint Martin. The canons' right to control those institutions was wrapped in the aura of their saint's miraculous ability to ensure that justice would prevail, even on this side of the grave.[65]

The second issue Péan addressed was the burghers' resistance to the financial prerogatives of the chapter of Saint-Martin. In the example of Meinarz, Péan demonstrated that calculating and entrepreneurial selfishness would result only in loss. As a result of Meinarz's complaints, Martin abandoned Persois and her husband. Unlike Persois, Meinarz did not recognize that generosity toward the charitable child saint had resulted—both literally and metaphorically—in his being "nourished" in return. Meinarz's worldly eyes were capable only of perceiving that provisions were leaving his storeroom. He did not realize that he too was a beneficiary of Martin's miraculous generosity. For this reason Meinarz ultimately deprived both himself and his wife of Martin's presence. Meinarz's murderous neighbor provided a second, more sinister, example of a calculating innkeeper, one whose sense of commercial rivalry contributed to his criminal behavior. Péan was careful to point out that the murderer's motives in framing Meinarz included his calculating jealousy because Meinarz had more guests than he did.

From the perspective of the canons of Saint-Martin it was Persois's attitude, rather than that of Meinarz and his sinister neighbor, that should apply to the relationship between the townspeople of Châteauneuf and Martin and his church. The townspeople—and indeed, it seems from the records of the various insurrections, the town's men more than its women—were far too concerned that the canons of Martin's church extracted some of their wealth by taxing them. For Péan and his fellow canons there was no distinction between Martin and his church. The burghers needed to realize that only if Martin and his church were generously provisioned and appreciated would the saint enhance the prosperity of his town by bringing it pilgrims and commerce. Selfishness toward the saint (or toward his canons), this

65. Like the exempla and Péan's stories, eleventh-century monastic vengeance miracles often involved judicial processes. In the eleventh-century monastic miracles, however, saints' punishments usually worked in a much more concrete way to protect the corporate interests (property rights, etc.) of the monastery itself. In Péan's stories, Martin protected the abstract principle of justice (wives should tell the truth, murderers should be punished for their crimes), which was attached to the corporate prerogatives of Saint-Martin only in the more attenuated sense that Saint-Martin had the right to administer secular justice in Châteauneuf. On the earlier vengeance miracles, see Head, "Andrew of Fleury and the Peace League of Bourges," 520–21; Sigal, "Aspect du culte des saints"; Southern, *Making of the Middle Ages,* 138.

story suggested, might cause him to leave town, thus depriving everyone of basic nourishment.

In his portrait of Persois, Péan suggested that the marginal behavior of a "foolish" woman was ultimately more rational (or at least wiser) than the calculating behavior of tradesmen. Martin's town would prosper only if its inhabitants imitated Persois and acted as "fools." Maternal "foolishness" and feminine indulgence were, Péan suggested, the models for imitation. Like the monks of Marmoutier, who presented Countess Ermengard as a model for imitation, Péan presented a woman and her feminine generosity as an example of the proper attitude and behavior to assume in interacting with Saint Martin and, by implication, with his church.

Space, Time, and Hierarchy: The Ritual Description of Châteauneuf

In legends about Saint Martin and his cult, the canons of his basilica enhanced their legitimacy and claims to seigneurial lordship by portraying their patron saint as the guarantor of peace, justice, and prosperity in his town and by demonstrating that laypeople stood below the saint in a hierarchical relationship. Their rituals and processions helped convey the same message. Indeed, the rituals probably had more impact, since they were regularly performed in the theater of the urban space and involved the people, sometimes as active participants and always as participant-observers. Through these urban rituals the canons of Saint-Martin defined the space and time of Châteauneuf as Martin's space and Martin's time and represented their own vision of the hierarchical ordering of the town. Yet since rituals, like all symbols, are polyvalent, we cannot assume that the burghers of Châteauneuf chose to interpret the rituals in the same ways the canons did.

As the discussion in chapter 8 has already shown, the processions that took place on some of Martin's feast days, on rogation days, during funerals, and on April 25 represented the basilica of Saint-Martin as the hub of the urban space of Tours. But it was especially Saint Martin's feast of May 12 that helped to define Châteauneuf as Martin's town. In one of their letters of 1180–81, Philip and Renaud reported that on May 12 Châteauneuf was decorated with herbs, flowers, incense pots, tapestries, and silk coverlets "so that indeed it plainly seems to all, because of the pleasantness and decor, like the entrance of paradise."[66] None of Martin's other three feasts involved similar decoration of the entire walled town. Only on May 12 did Châteauneuf dress up to honor its saint, thus becoming Martin's space.

Celebrations for the May feast also defined Châteauneuf as Martin's territory by excluding the archbishop's town from the ritual space and by pointing to the basilica, rather than the cathedral, as the ritual center of Tours. This was a significant redefinition of the urban space of Tours. The May feast commemorated the time in 903 when Martin's relics delivered the walled *cathedral* town from the Viking invaders. The feast commemorating that event, however, took place in Châteauneuf, and indeed, the procession of the monks of Marmoutier from their abbey to Saint-Martin completely circumvented the cathedral town, thus excluding it from the ritually defined community that was bound together by its ties to Saint Martin.[67]

Perhaps the most important way the May feast marked Châteauneuf as Saint Martin's possession was that it commemorated the genesis of the town as a separate entity and suggested the town's origin was divinely sanctioned. Philip and Renaud reported that the Viking raid of 903 had given birth to Châteauneuf, and they suggested that both the delivery of the town from the Vikings and its continued safety were linked to Saint Martin's holy power. Martin had delivered the town in 903 and had sanctioned its new walls by reinforcing the material defenses with his own spiritual defense:

> [Just after the Viking incursion against Tours in 903] the sheep who had evaded the mouths of wolves—under the protection of their pious patron [Saint Martin] and with the counsel and aid of the princes of France—took refuge and constructed this noble wall around the basilica, which had formerly stood nude, about 150 paces outside the city. . . . And so, providing the temporal house of their patron with material obstacles against visible enemies, they thus merited by his spiritual defense to be freed from the infestations of invisible enemies and to be received in the halls of heaven by God.[68]

66. "Ut plane videatur cunctis prae amoenitate et decore quasi quidam introitus paradisi" ("De cultu Sancti Martini," 236). Tapestries on the walls, flowers on the streets, and the idea that the city became a "paradise" also marked the fifteenth-century celebrations of Florence's patronal feast, that of John the Baptist. See Trexler, *Public Life in Renaissance Florence,* 247, 249, 266.

67. See chapter 2 at notes 42 ff.

68. "Tunc sub pii pastoris protectione ovibus quae luporum dentes evaserant confugientibus, consilio ex auxilio principum Franciae circa ejus templum antea nudum et ab

In the minds of Philip and Renaud, the very existence of Châteauneuf as a separate urban space was thus the outcome of Martin's general favor and of the specific events of May 12, 903. Similarly, both Martin and the events of 903 stood behind Châteauneuf's urban peace. Until the time of the Viking incursion of 903, the suburb around the basilica stood unprotected. After the events of 903—after the canons and inhabitants of the suburb built their walls—God and Martin "laid down peace within its boundaries" and "strengthened the bolts of the doors of our Zion."[69] The memory of the events of 903 thus invoked for Philip and Renaud the idea that the space of Châteauneuf owed its well-being and prosperity to the fact that Martin, and by implication his canons, was the guarantor of peace within its walls: "Evidence of [Saint Martin's] protection toward us is in the books recounting how he frequently rescued us, our possessions, and even the city itself from enemies; evidence of his favor is in the multiple experiences by which . . . we feel his favor overflowing toward us; evidence is in the serenity of peace and the affluence of riches by which we rejoice that the city within our walls is strong."[70] Philip and Renaud left unspoken in this passage that keeping the peace was one aspect of legal and political power. Such power, they implied, belonged to Saint Martin and thus to his canons. The May feast both commemorated the birth of Châteauneuf and legitimized the political arrangements that perpetuated its "peace."

In addition to defining the space of Châteauneuf as subject to Martin's jurisdiction, the May feast conveyed the message that within the walls of Châteauneuf the rhythms of the seasons belonged to the saint. This was the significance of the feast's incorporating a number of elements and symbols—flowers, references to battle, tapestries, commemorations of the dead—that recurred in the spring celebrations of other towns and villages in the High and late Middle Ages. In some towns or villages the celebrations occurred on May 1, Ascension Day, or Pentecost—secular and ecclesiastical occasions for the observance of the May cycle. In others, such as Florence, the celebrations were held both during the May cycle and on the spring feast day of the local patron saint. In the successful commune of Florence,

---

urbe longo centum quinquaginta fere passuum interstitio distans, nobile hoc et multi decoris oppidum construentes . . . ut, temporalem patroni domum contra hostium visibilium impetus materialibus munientes obstaculis, spirituali ejus defensione ab infestationibus hostium invisibilium liberari et in aula coelesti a Deo recipi mererentur" ("De cultu Sancti Martini," 226).

69. "Confortavit Dominus seras portarum Syon nostrae . . . et posuit fines ipsius pacem" ("De cultu Sancti Martini," 226).

70. "De cultu Sancti Martini," 235. For Latin, see chapter 7, note 1.

however, secular groups—private families and the commune—vied for control of the celebration of the city's patronal feast. In Châteauneuf the canons of Saint-Martin controlled the spring cycle.[71]

The dubbings, jousts, commemorations of the dead, flowers, and tapestries that marked the urban spring celebrations at Tours and other medieval towns highlighted the interlocking experiences of birth and death that were logically associated with the advent of spring and, traditionally, with the month of May. On the one hand, the season ushered in the rebirth of nature; on the other, it provided the warm weather that enabled warriors to resume their battles.

In Châteauneuf the remembrance of the Viking battle and the floral decorations for the May feast linked the cosmic cycles of birth, death, and rebirth to the cult of Saint Martin. These connections were strengthened by the legend of the Theban martyrs. As Philip and Renaud's letter to Philip of Cologne proclaimed, it was on May 12 that Saint Martin had returned to Tours with the blood of Saint Maurice and the other Theban martyrs. Since the Thebans had been soldiers in the Roman army, their association with the May feast further enhanced its noble and military qualities. Indeed, the name of Saint Maurice, head of the Theban legion, was included in the ceremony for arming a knight, which frequently took place during the May cycle, on the day of Pentecost.[72]

By the fifteenth century, and perhaps as early as 1262, ceremonial jousting and tournaments emphasized the military and chivalric aspects of Martin's May feast, just as the palio marked Saint John's Day in Florence.[73] At Châteauneuf, then, all the powerful imagery of

71. For general discussions of the May cycle and of the festivals that coincided with it, see Chambers, *Medieval Stage*, 1:116–45, 160–81; Van Gennep, *Manuel de folklore français*, vol. 1, part 4; Schmitt, "Jeunes et danse de chevaux de bois: Le folklore méridional dans la littérature des exempla." On May Day and the feast of Saint John the Baptist in Florence, see Trexler, *Public Life in Renaissance Florence*, 215–18. On the secular political role of patronal feasts in Venice, see Muir, *Civic Ritual in Renaissance Venice*. On urban festivals in general, see Heers, *Fêtes, jeux et joutes dans les sociétés d'Occident à la fin du Moyen Age*, 57–64, 112–13.

72. Andrieu, *Ordines romani du Haut Moyen Age*, 1:112–113, 188, 509; Franz, *Kirchlichen Benediktionen im Mittelalter*, 2:295–97. At least two counts of Anjou—Fulk Rechin and Geoffrey the Fair—were dubbed knights on Pentecost: see Fulk Rechin, *Fragmentum historiae Andegavensis*, 236, and John of Marmoutier, *Historia Gaufredi*, 178. For general discussion, see Duby, *Three Orders*, 296–301; Gautier, *Chevalerie*, 250–52.

73. The chapter register for the years 1443 and 1446 mentioned granting permission to ride horses in honor of Saint Martin's May feast: Bibliothèque Nationale, Collection Baluze, MS. 77, fols. 351v, 353. Prohibitions against jousting and tournaments in the fourth reform of Saint-Martin, which took place in 1262, may have been directed against tournaments that took place on May 12: "Quarta reformatio facta anno 1262," Tours, Bibliothèque Municipale, MS. 1295, 557. On the palio in Florence, see Trexler, *Public Life in Renaissance Florence*, 262–63.

spring, with its references to human, cosmic, and Christian cycles of birth and death, converged on the cult of Saint Martin.[74] Within the walls of Châteauneuf Saint Martin controlled not only space but also cosmic time and the forces of nature.

An illuminated initial in a late twelfth-century manuscript from Saint-Martin—one of their most precious liturgical objects—provided visual reinforcement for the idea that on May 12 Martin controlled both cosmic time and the forces of nature (see plate 7 in chap. 8).[75] The letter occurred at the beginning of the office for the May feast, but it did not depict Martin's victory over the pagan Vikings in 903. Rather, it represented a story from Sulpicius Severus's *Life of Saint Martin,* in which Martin proved the truth of his religion by standing under a sacred pine tree while several worshipers of the tree chopped it down. The tree would have fallen on Martin, but when he made the sign of the cross it fell the other way, and the assembled pagans then converted to Christianity.[76]

The illuminator of this manuscript may have chosen to depict this scene rather than the events of 903 because it represented an accomplishment of the living saint. There was an appropriate parallel between the two events, since in both cases Martin's miraculous powers triumphed over pagans. Yet the artist could have chosen any one of a number of Martin's encounters with pagans. What made this story unique, and thus may have drawn the illuminator to it, was its vegetative and natural imagery. In the initial itself, Martin made his sign of the cross while the pagans chopped away at the tree. Thus the saint's triumph over paganism was visually associated with his control over natural forces. But the illumination also suggested a connection between Martin and one particular vegetative symbol of the May cycle—the Maypole or May tree.[77]

In addition to highlighting Martin's power over nature, the illumination clearly depicted all the symbols of Martin's hierarchical role as bishop. Even though this was not a liturgical setting, Martin

74. Of course there were other spring ceremonies at Saint-Martin as well. The canons performed some kind of ritualized battle with a dragon banner on the feast of the Ascension, and they had flowers and birds scattered in the church during the Pentecost ceremonies: see *Consuetudines ecclesiae beati Martini,* 68–69, 73. For other examples of the use of birds and flowers on Pentecost, see Du Cange, *Glossarium,* s.v. "Pascha rosata," and "Nebula," 6:191, 5:582; Chambers, *Medieval Stage,* 2:66; Young, *Drama of the Medieval Church,* 1:489–91.

75. Tours, Bibliothèque Municipale, MS. 193, fol. 78v.

76. Sulpicius Severus, *Vita Sancti Martini,* 13, pp. 280–83.

77. For medieval references to the Maypole and May tree, see *Monasticon Anglicanum,* vol. 6, part 2, p. 907, col. 2, lines 81–83 (charter of Richard II for Cokersand Abbey); Du Cange, *Glossarium,* s.v. "Maius" and "Maium," 5:189; Chambers, *Medieval Stage,* 1:180.

wore the full liturgical garb of a priest and bishop—stole, alb, miter—and carried a pastoral staff. Thus his hierarchical authority as bishop, an authority that the canons of Saint-Martin claimed for themselves, was visually associated with his miraculous power over paganism and over nature.

The messages concerning the subordination of time and space to Saint Martin indirectly reinforced the canons' hierarchical vision of the social and political relations within their town. But the May feast also involved more direct hierarchical messages. The very way the laypeople participated in the celebration of their urban patronal feast set them up in a relationship of subordination to the canons. Their participation was passive: while the canons of Saint-Martin and the monks of Marmoutier performed the rituals, the laypeople watched.[78]

Even the confraternal arrangements between the canons of the basilica and the burghers placed the burghers in a passive relationship to the clergy of the basilica. The charter establishing the confraternity carefully described the commemorative rituals that were to be performed just before Martin's May feast, but it mentioned no banquets or potations, occasions when the lay members themselves would both express their solidarity and commemorate their fraternal dead. Rather, the canons were to read the names of the dead members in their chapter meeting on the third day before the May feast, a vigil was to be performed on the same evening—presumably by some clerics in the basilica—and a mass was to be celebrated the next day. Moreover, on each day of the year (except Christmas, Good Friday, Holy Saturday, Easter, Pentecost, and All Saints' Day) a priest appointed to the altar of Saint Julian was to perform a vigil and a mass and to sing all the hours in honor of the dead members of the confraternity.[79] Thus the arrangements for the confraternity stressed the dependence of the laity on the sacramental intervention of the canons and priests at Saint-Martin. The confraternal arrangements for May 12 ritually involved the burghers in the patronal feast of Châteauneuf, but that feast remained under the control of the seigneurial lords of the town rather than that of the people themselves.

Although the May feast was unique in the way it defined the space of Châteauneuf, its temporal and hierarchical messages recurred in Martin's other feasts as well. The exclusion of the people from the basilica on the night before July 4 reinforced a message about Martin's hierarchical authority.[80] And the fact that the treasurer assembled his

78. "De cultu Sancti Martini," 236.
79. See above, at notes 25 and 26.
80. See chapter 8 at note 1 ff.

courts of justice on July 4 and November 11 reinforced the association of Martin's saintly authority with the canons' seigneurial authority.[81]

But it was especially the feast of December 13 that reinforced, and even reduplicated, the seasonal, temporal, and hierarchical messages of the May feast. Like the May feast, the December feast commemorated an event associated with the Viking invasions: the return of Martin's relics from Burgundy.[82] The May and December feasts, moreover, employed the same liturgy, and they marked off that half of the liturgical year—from Pentecost to Advent—that was dedicated to particular commemorations and to pilgrimage.[83] The period between Advent and Pentecost was dominated by the two liturgical cycles associated with the story of redemption: Christmas and Easter. The other half was left free for more particular commemorations, and at Châteauneuf, commemorations of Saint Martin predominated. Martin's May and December feasts marked off that half of the year; his July and November feasts occurred within that half; and as the customal of Saint-Martin specified, a special mass for him was performed every Thursday between May 12 and the beginning of Advent.[84]

Like the May 12 feast, Martin's December feast was imbued with the imagery of renewal and rebirth. For the canons of Saint-Martin the feast marked the beginning of the Christmas season—the season of the birth of the Redeemer—and it was associated with the winter solstice, which began to fall, toward the end of the twelfth century, on December 14.[85]

81. See chapter 7, note 5.

82. The calendars of four eleventh-century liturgical manuscripts from Tours refer to the December 13 feast as the "exceptio Sancti Martini a Burgundio" or the "reversio Sancti Martini": see Tours, Bibliothèque Municipale, Missal from the Petit Séminaire; Tours, Bibliothèque Municipale, MS. 196; Rouen, Bibliothèque Municipale, MS. 243; Bibliothèque Nationale, MS. lat. 9434. Two of those manuscripts (Tours 196 and Bibliothèque Nationale 9434) have indications for a commemoration of Saint Martin on May 12, but the note in Bibliothèque Nationale 9434 is in a later hand. No special prayers for the May 12 feast appeared until the twelfth century. One eleventh-century manuscript from Marmoutier has special prayers for Saint Maurice on May 12: Rouen, Bibliothèque Municipale MS. 243, fol. 190. For a more complete discussion of the manuscript evidence for the May and December feasts, see my dissertation, "Societal Change and Religious Expression: Saint Martin's Cult at Tours," 163–66.

83. Notations in Tours, Bibliothèque Municipale, MS. 193, fol. 78v, and MS. 1021, fol. 155, indicate that the December feast (which was older than the May feast, as the manuscript evidence in the previous note suggests) provided the model for the liturgy of the May feast. On the season from Pentecost to Advent, see Johannis Beleth, *Summa de ecclesiasticis officiis*, 56, ed. Douteil, 2:102; and Le Roy Ladurie, *Montaillou*, 279.

84. *Consuetudines ecclesiae beati Martini*, 72. From May 3 (the feast of the Discovery of the True Cross) until Advent, a mass for the cross was to be performed on Fridays and one for the Virgin on Saturdays: *Consuetudines ecclesiae beati Martini*, 71.

85. On the slippage of the Julian calendar, see Giry, *Manuel de diplomatique*, 1:160–62.

Several elections and appointments that took place on December 13 suggest that that feast marked the beginning of the Christmas and New Year's season at Saint-Martin. It was on that day that the subprecentor of the chapter appointed the boy bishop and boy cantor, who would perform their duties during the week between Christmas and New Year's, especially during the feast of the Innocents. Other chapters of canons frequently appointed or elected their boy bishop on Saint Nicholas's Day, which fell on December 6.[86] Thus in Châteauneuf the cult of Saint Martin appropriated the seasonal role that frequently belonged to Saint Nicholas.

It was also on December 13 that the canons elected the two *crupitores,* whose major responsibility was to administer the illuminations for the New Year's feast. After this election, the canon or deacon who was to be the special cantor of the New Year's feast performed his first duty by leading the chapter in singing *Laetemur gaudiis.* This hymn, which would be sung again at the opening of the feast of January 1, brought the December 13 feast to a close.[87]

The election of the crupitores and the initiation of the cantor of the New Year (who was, appropriately, either the newest canon or the newest subdeacon) highlighted the fact that Martin's December feast marked the beginning of the Christmas season. The season reached its peak during the week beginning on Christmas Day and ending on New Year's Day, although in some places it ended on January 6, the feast of Epiphany. There were twelve days from December 13 to Christmas Day and twelve days from Christmas Day to Epiphany.[88] The anticipation of January 1 on December 13 also served as a symbolic reminder that both the winter solstice (which the canons linked to the December 13 feast) and New Year's Day marked the renewal of solar or calendric time and thus pointed to the Christian themes of rebirth and renewal.

Rebirth, renewal, and light were central elements in the legends about the December 13 feast as well as in its decorations. According to the author of the *Return from Burgundy,* the original return of Mar-

86. *Consuetudines ecclesiae beati Martini,* 29–30, 35. On Saint Nicholas's Day, see Chambers, *Medieval Stage,* 1:369–70; on Nicholas's relation to the boy bishop, as well as his role in the winter cycle, see Jones, *Saint Nicholas of Myra, Bari, and Manhattan,* 292–306.

87. *Consuetudines ecclesiae beati Martini,* 29–30, 36–37. "Crupitores," or possibly "erupitores," is not in Du Cange. Edmond Martène defined the word as "ministers of the church who light the candles." His only source for the term was the customal of Saint-Martin: *De antiquis ecclesiae ritibus,* appendix to vol. 3, "Nomenclator exoticarum vocum," reprint ed. vol. 3, unpaginated end pages.

88. In asserting that the cantor of the New Year was the youngest canon or deacon, I am giving my own reading to an ambiguous passage: see below at note 94. Epiphany was not a particularly festive feast at Saint-Martin, and there were no impressive arrangements for January 2–6: see *Consuetudines ecclesiae beati Martini,* 36–41.

tin's relics to Tours on December 13 had caused candles to ignite spontaneously and trees to burst into bloom.[89] And as both the author of the *Return* and Philip and Renaud pointed out, this efflorescence was particularly striking because it happened at the time of the winter solstice: "The harshness of winter in the middle of December began to grow warm, the sky to become milder, boreas to change to zephyr, and the air, at the time of the winter solstice, to breathe green charm."[90]

The winter solstice marked the point in the year when darkness prevailed but the hours of daylight began to wax once again. Thus it was a time of hope, and it symbolized the ultimate triumph of the forces of light over darkness. On a more microcosmic level, it was associated with vision, both spiritual and physical. Significantly, a thirteenth-century hymn, written at Saint-Martin especially for Martin's December feast, opened with a reference to the time when Saint Martin restored the eyesight of Paulinus of Nola:

> Let us rejoice and be glad in the feast of Martin
> Who with prayers, not salve, gave light to Paulinus.[91]

The decorations for the feast of December 13 reinforced its associations with light symbolism. According to a financial note in the customal of Saint-Martin, which concerned the purses that paid for the candles of various feasts throughout the year, the lighting for the December 13 feast—"when the choir of the church is so extensively provisioned"—was more elaborate than for most other major feasts.[92] The exceptional illumination recalled the candles that had once spontaneously ignited on that day, but it also represented the renewal of solar light at the winter solstice.

Martin's cult was not the only one that associated light imagery and the restoration of vision with December 13. According to a tenth-century legend, Saint Odilia of Hohenbourg, whose feast fell

---

89. *De reversione beati Martini*, 33.

90. "Asperitas hiemis medio Decembri tepescere, coelum clementius fieri, boreas commutari in zephyrum, et aer vernas in bruma coepit spirare blanditias" ("De cultu Sancti Martini," 241). The *Return from Burgundy* read: "Universae siquidem arbores et fruteta tempore brumali, repugnante licet natura, redivivis vestita foliis vernant" (*De reversione beati Martini*, 33).

91. "Exultemus et laetemur Martini solemnio / Qui Paulino lucem dedit prece non collirio" (Tours, Bibliothèque Municipale, MS. 1021, fol. 154v, edited by Keane, "Martin Hymns of the Middle Ages," 160). The hymn is listed in Chevalier, *Repertorium hymnologicum*, no. 5757. The story about Paulinus's eyes is in Sulpicius Severus, *Vita Sancti Martini*, 19:3, pp. 293–95. Fontaine argued (*Sulpice Sévère*, 2:885) that Paulinus probably had cataracts.

92. "In quo caput ecclesie paratur tantum" (*Consuetudines ecclesiae beati Martini*, 90).

on December 13, had been born blind but gained her sight when she was baptized. She was the object of special invocations by people with eye diseases. Similarly, the feast of Saint Lucy, whose name meant light, fell on December 13, and at the end of the thirteenth century Dante referred to her beautiful shining eyes. At least as early as the fourteenth century, a legend claimed that Lucy had torn out her eyes because they attracted the attentions of a suitor. From the fourteenth century on, artistic representations tended to show Lucy holding her eyes on a plate, and she, like Odilia, was invoked by people with eye diseases. About the time that Lucy's new legend and iconography first emerged, the winter solstice, which had been slipping back one day every 128 years, began to fall on December 13. In Sicily and Scandinavia Lucy's cult became the occasion for a festival of lights, and this association persisted even after the solstice no longer fell on December 13.[93]

But popular practice and religious belief were not rigidly bound by precise astronomical timing. Odilia's legend predated the concurrence of December 13 with the winter solstice, and Dante may have already been familiar with some legend about Lucy's eyes. Already in the first half of the twelfth century, the *Return from Burgundy* associated light imagery, as well as the solstice, with Martin's December 13 feast. At Tours, Martin's cult could incorporate important seasonal imagery even when the timing was off by two days.

The themes of rebirth, renewal, and light that predominated in the December 13 feast were repeated on January 1. And just as the December 13 feast anticipated New Year's Day, the New Year's feast included a number of references to Saint Martin and his December feast. According to the thirteenth-century customal of Saint-Martin, the canons there did not celebrate on January 1 the feast of fools—a bawdy ritual of inversion when subdeacons took over the choir stalls. Some elements of this ritual inversion were evident in the ceremonies for the evening hours of January 1, but most of the day involved the joyous, yet serious, commemoration of the Virgin, the performance of miracle and prophet plays, and the use of the symbol of light.[94]

93. Van Doren and Raggi, "Odilia"; Amore and Celletti, "Lucia di Siracusa"; Amore, Battisti, and Toschi, "Lucia"; Dante, *Inferno*, 2:116, *Purgatorio*, 9:62, cited by Kretzenbacher, *Santa Lucia und die Lutzelfrau*, 14. In many places Saint Lucy's Day opened the Christmas season: Amore, Battisti, and Toschi, "Lucia," col. 1622.

94. *Consuetudines ecclesiae beati Martini*, 36–40. There is some discussion of the New Year's ceremonies at Saint-Martin in Chambers, *Medieval Stage*, 1:309, and Young, *Drama of the Medieval Church*, 2:153. Martène printed the January ceremonies of Saint-Martin: see *De antiquis ecclesiae ritibus*, bk. 4, chap. 13, no. 17, reprint edition, 3:116–18. For a general discussion of the feast of fools, see Chambers, *Medieval Stage*, 1:274–335.

At Saint-Martin the ritual inversions on January 1 consisted of the following: during the

These themes suited the idea that New Year's was the octave of
Christmas, a season of renewal and light when the Virgin gave birth
to the Redeemer. In the early Christian era December 25 had corresponded with the winter solstice, and since the early Middle Ages the
octave of Christmas had been specially dedicated to the Virgin.[95]

During their January 1 ceremonies the canons of Saint-Martin honored the Virgin with the hymns "Ave regina" and "O regina Vir-
ginum" and with the sequence "Ave Maria," and they emphasized
light imagery with the hymns "Lumen patris" and "O Nazarene, lux
Bethleem." At matins and again at vespers they performed a miracle
play and a "procession of prophets" in which several clerics who
posed as Old Testament prophets foretold the coming of the Redeemer and the role of the Virgin Mary in that story.[96] Another
impressive aspect of the January 1 ceremonies was the splendor of the
visual decorations. During the New Year's feast the crupitores used all
the wax from Saint Martin's major feast day of November 11, the
missive candles from every day between December 13 and January 1,
and a large candle given to them by the boys of the choir. These
specifications, as well as directives for lighting candles, lamps, can-
delabra, and coronas, show that New Year's was one of the most
brilliantly illuminated feasts of the year, and the actual candles used
provided a tangible link between Saint Martin's November and De-

<hr>

vespers service, if there was someone to take up the baculus, the cantor mounted his bench
and sang the hymn *Deposuit* ("He has put down the mighty") three times, while he handed
over his baculus to the other person, though this did not always happen ("post levat se
cantor super formam, capam habens super humeros, et incipit antiphon et dicit ter *Deposuit*,
baculum tenens; et si baculum capitur, *Te deum laudamus* incipitur"). Later, at compline, the
treasurer of the chapter was beaten with sticks while the "cantor of the feast" and the
crupitores looked on. After the service the "new cantor," if there was one, sang "The word
was made flesh" and was then escorted back to his house, while clerics of the basilica struck
the walls with sticks: *Consuetudines ecclesiae beati Martini,* 36–40. There is some discussion of
this passage in Chambers, *Medieval Stage,* 1:309.

There is some confusion in the references to cantors here. One of the two cantors—
either the "cantor of the feast" or the "new cantor"—was supposed to be the newest canon
or the newest deacon ("In hoc festo tenet baculum ille qui facit formam vel qui ultimo
fecerit, vel aliquis ex subdiaconibus simplicibus qui facit capam"). My own reading of the
sense of the passage would be that the "cantor of the feast" was the youngest canon or
deacon and that he presided throughout the day on January 1. In the evening he handed over
the baculus to the new cantor of the chapter, if there was a new cantor that year.

95. Duchesne, *Origines du culte chrétien,* 289–90.

96. *Consuetudines ecclesiae beati Martini,* 36–40. The hymns "Lumen patris" and "O
Nazarene" are in Chevalier, *Repertorium hymnologicum,* nos. 38731 and 73303. The "O
Nazarene" sometimes read "Dux Bethleem." It was by Prudentius. On the "Ordo proph-
etarum," see Young, *Drama of the Medieval Church,* 2:125–71. He argued (p. 153) that the
performance at Tours probably resembled the Laon performance, for which he gave the text
on pp. 145–50.

cember feasts and the New Year's feast. The singing of a number of antiphons and responses in honor of Saint Martin further underscored these links.[97]

The symbolic connections between the New Year's feast and Martin's December feast and the use of the imagery of the winter solstice during the feast of December 13 reinforced the message of the May 12 feast: that at Châteauneuf Saint Martin controlled calendric and cosmic time. Similarly, the election on December 13 of the boy bishop, whose duties during Christmas week included extending his episcopal blessing over the people, reinforced another message of the May feast: that Saint Martin and the basilica possessed hierarchical authority over the people of Châteauneuf.[98]

As the canons of Saint-Martin interpreted and performed them, the feasts of their patron saint symbolized the subjection of Châteauneuf and its laypeople to the hierarchical authority of Saint Martin and his basilica. But how did the burghers receive those messages? The communal struggles in Châteauneuf show that the definition of the community was a contested issue. It is thus possible—and even probable—that the meanings of Martin's feasts, and especially the patronal feast of May 12, were also contested or resisted. There is no reason to believe that simply because they participated in the May feast all the lay inhabitants of Châteaneuf accepted the canons' definition of the community. Nor is it necessarily true that all the laypeople willingly cooperated in the rituals all the time.

Although the voices of the burghers can no longer be heard, we can surmise that a number of the lay inhabitants of the town did indeed cooperate in the celebration of the May festivities. Some of them must have helped dress up the town by decorating their houses. Others went to meet the monks of Marmoutier at the banks of the Loire. Still others, according to Péan Gatineau's thirteenth-century *Life* of Saint Martin, gathered to see and hear the performance of the monks of Marmoutier and the canons of Saint-Martin.[99]

Nevertheless, though some of the lay residents of Châteauneuf clearly cooperated in the May celebrations, it is highly probable that others did not. Indeed, that the customal of Saint-Martin includes no discussion of the burghers' confraternity of 1176 suggests that one important element of the May feast—the commemoration of deceased burghers—had disappeared by the time the customal was

97. *Consuetudines ecclesiae beati Martini*, 29–30, 36–40.
98. *Consuetudines ecclesiae beati Martini*, 29–30, 34, 36–40.
99. Péan Gatineau, *Vie . . . Saint Martin*, lines 9464–72, p. 119.

written down in the early thirteenth century. One reasonable explanation for this disappearance is that the political strife of the 1180s provoked either the burghers or the canons to sever their collective ritual relations with their rivals.

Despite its silence concerning the confraternity of the burghers of Châteauneuf, the customal of Saint-Martin does note that on some occasions the burghers continued to engage, as active participants, in the ritual life of the basilica. At mass on the day of Pentecost, for instance, boys from town scattered birds and flowers in the choir.[100] More important, a number of laypeople participated in the candlelight procession that took place in February 2, the feast of the Purification of the Virgin:

> All the knights and sworn servants of Saint-Martin who are present at the procession [of February 2], as well as their wives, will have candles. And the same is true for the external clerics and servants of the canons, and the butchers and fishmongers of Châteauneuf, and the provost of the town and his wife, and servants of the fabric of the church, and the master stonemason, and the master carpenter and the woodworker, with their wives, and the guardians of the gate of the town, and the sacristans and priests of charity.[101]

Do these examples necessarily mean that at the time the customal was written, between 1226 and 1237, all the burghers of Châteauneuf enjoyed peaceful relations with the canons? Probably not. The boys of Châteauneuf were paid for their duties on Pentecost. And the participants in the February 2 procession did not represent all the lay inhabitants of Châteauneuf: there is no mention of merchants or money changers or tavern keepers. Indeed, it appears that all the people who were given candles on February 2 were in some way or other servants of the chapter. The knights were listed as a subgroup of the "sworn servants" of the chapter; the provost was an urban official who answered to the chapter; and the master stonemason, carpenter, and woodworker were probably closely affiliated with the "servants of the fabric" of the basilica.

But what of the fishmongers and butchers? Apparently their rela-

---

100. *Consuetudines ecclesiae beati Martini*, 73. For a general discussion of such practices, see Young, *Drama of the Medieval Church*, 1:489–91.

101. "Milites omnes et servientes jurati Beati Martini cum uxoribus eorum qui ad processionem serviunt, habent candelas et clerici extranei et servientes canonicorum et carnifices et piscatores Castrinovi et prepositus civitatis et uxor ejus et servientes operis et magister cementarius et magister carpentarius et faber cum uxoribus eorum et custos porte civitatis et matricularii et elemosinarii" (*Consuetudines ecclesiae beati Martini*, 41–42).

tionship to the chapter was more intimate than that of other artisans and tradespeople, perhaps because they were, or had once been, members of the *familia* of the chapter.[102] Thus, whereas the customal made no mention of the taxes owed by other burghers in Châteauneuf, it went into great detail concerning the taxes that the fishmongers and butchers owed for every fish they caught and every animal they slaughtered. Also, the customal noted that the candles given to the fishmongers and butchers on February 2 constituted part of an elaborate symbolic exchange. On Palm Sunday the fishmongers and butchers owed a lamprey to each of the canons of the basilica and four lampreys to the deacons who carried the "Hosanna." In return for the lampreys, these tradespeople each received a pennyworth of bread, a measure of wine, and the candles they carried on February 2. The donation of the lampreys also qualified the fishmongers and butchers for exemption from the customary rights of the treasurer.[103] A document drawn up by Philip Augustus and Richard the Lion-Hearted indicates that in 1190 the fishmongers and butchers of the cathedral town also participated in the exchange of lampreys for wine, bread, and candles. This document also reports, though the customal does not, that the fishmongers and butchers of both parts of town were *obligated* to participate in the procession on February 2.[104] There is no mention of the fishmongers and butchers of the cathedral town in the thirteenth-century customal, but the procession on February 2 probably continued to be obligatory for the fishmongers and butchers of Châteauneuf itself.

Although the procession on February 2 included only a small portion of the laypeople in Châteauneuf, it still represented the community as a corporate and organic whole. Like Philip and Renaud's letters, which tended to blur distinctions between the canons and the town, and like the miracle collections from the basilica, which conveyed the impression that Martin's miraculous power was available to everyone who sought it, the procession on February 2 suggested that the people in Châteauneuf were united in their devotion and in their collective identity under the hierarchical authority of their patron saint.

Such representations of organic unity did not correspond to reality.

102. Many early guilds grew out of the *familia* of the seigneurial lords of towns: see Brentano, "Preliminary Essay on the History and Development of Gilds," cxiv–cxv.

103. *Consuetudines ecclesiae beati Martini*, 51–52.

104. Act of Philip Augustus and Richard the Lion-Hearted confirming the respective rights of the French king (and Saint-Martin) and the Angevin count in Tours, in *Recueil des actes de Philippe Auguste*, 1:440, no. 361.

Indeed, closer inspection of the miracle stories and of the February procession reveals that the most prominent, and resistant, burghers of Châteauneuf are not to be found in these representations of the united community of devotees. The canons of Saint-Martin wished to represent the town of Châteauneuf as a united corporate whole, but to do so they had to cut out part of the picture. Their legends and rituals served the purpose of masking and legitimizing their own seigneurial power. Until the beginning of the fourteenth century, however, the most prominent members of the town continued to resist that power.

Conclusion

Soon after he became king in 1322, King Charles IV, the last of the Capetian kings (he died without a male heir in 1328) obtained permission from Pope John XXII to separate Saint Martin's head from the rest of his body and translate it to a new gold reliquary. The translation, which took place on December 1, 1323, marks the first time in the history of Tours that any of Martin's relics was placed on display for the veneration of the faithful (see plate 12).[1] From then on Martin's "chief" (the new reliquary, which had the shape of a mitered bust) was exhibited two times each year, and it was carried in times of crisis from Martin's basilica to the cathedral of Tours.[2] In 1356 Saint Martin and Saint Gatien (the first bishop of Tours, who was now the patron saint of the cathedral) were thought to have assisted the people of Tours in delivering their town from the Black Prince, the heir to the English throne who managed in that year to take King John of France prisoner.[3]

In the course of the fourteenth and fifteenth centuries, Saint Martin recovered some of his earlier luster as a patron saint of the French monarchy. This was especially true after 1444, when the royal court came to reside at Tours. King Charles VII sponsored yet another new reliquary for Saint Martin, and his son was buried at Martin's basilica. King Louis XI, who declared that Martin was a "special tutor of the realm" and credited him with a victory at Perpignan, commissioned a genealogy of the saint (based largely on the *Legend of the Seven Sleepers*) and gave some windows to Saint-Martin that recalled King

---

1. Vaucelle, *Collégiale de Saint-Martin*, 165–66; Mesnard, "Collégiale de Saint-Martin à l'époque des Valois," 90.
2. Vaucelle, *Collégiale de Saint-Martin*, 166; Chevalier, *Tours, ville royale*, 198.
3. Tours, Bibliothèque Municipale, MS. 156 (fourteenth-century lectionary from the cathedral), fol. 61v. The passage is reproduced in *Catalogue général des manuscrits des bibliothèques publiques de France*, 37:1:111–12.

PLATE 12. Translation of Saint Martin's head, December 1, 1323. In the top half of this illuminated S for the feast of December 1, the bishop of Chartres removes Martin's skull from his old reliquary, while another cleric lifts the miter from the top of the new reliquary. In the bottom half, King Charles IV and his queen pray at an altar. Tours, Bibliothèque Municipale, MS. 1023, fol. 101. Photograph courtesy Tours, Bibliothèque Municipale.

Clovis's devotion for Martin.[4] During an illness, Louis also had himself anointed with oil from an ampulla that the Virgin had allegedly given to Saint Martin.[5] In 1496 Charles VIII was presented with one of the first printed books from Tours—a prose version of the life and miracles of Saint Martin. The woodcuts in the book depicted several stories that the monks of Marmoutier and the canons of Saint-Martin had invented in the twelfth century (see plates 2, 6, and 11).[6]

Local religion and the cult of relics continued to thrive in late medieval Tours, although the basilica of Saint-Martin declined as a center for pilgrimage. I emphasize this point because broad narratives of twelfth- and thirteenth-century history sometimes leave the impression that the concrete, collective, and highly localized religion of the early and central Middle Ages ultimately gave way to the universal cult of the Virgin, the growth of centralized governments, and the emergence of mendicant saints and female mystics.

Nevertheless, the late medieval "communities of Saint Martin" differed from those of the eleventh, twelfth, and early thirteenth centuries. Indeed, it almost seems that at the end of the Middle Ages Martin became the patron and protector of the same communities he had served in the fifth and sixth centuries. Once again his saintly favors graced the entire urban community of Tours—including its prominent laypeople and its cathedral; once again he was a major protector of the royal line and the French realm. What, then, had happened to the developments of the eleventh, twelfth, and thirteenth centuries? What had become of the rivalries between the archbishop and the canons of Saint-Martin, between the monks of Marmoutier (or at least their noble patrons) and the Capetian kings, between the burghers of Châteauneuf and the chapter of Saint-Martin?

The growth of centralized authority—to some extent papal, but most especially royal—played the greatest role in reshaping the late medieval community of Saint Martin. After Philip Augustus's victory

4. Chevalier, *Tours, ville royale,* 203, 222 ff.; Mesnard, "Collégiale de Saint-Martin à l'époque des Valois," 93–97; Beaune, *Naissance de la nation France,* 173; Lecoy de la Marche, *Saint Martin,* 70–71 (he gives an extensive description of Tours, Archives d'Indre-et-Loire G365—the genealogy of Martin that was commissioned by Louis XI). Louis XI also commissioned two statues of Saint Martin: see Robin, "Chapelles seigneuriales et royales françaises au temps de Louis XI," 238.
5. Gasnault, "Sainte ampoule de Marmoutier." There is no record of this ampulla from before 1318. In 1594 King Henry IV's royal anointing was performed with this oil.
6. *Vie et les miracles de monseigneur Saint Martin.* One of the guard pages of the Bibliothèque Nationale's copy of this incunabulum has a note ("Au Roy K: au Plessis") indicating that the volume was given to the king. See Omont, "Deux incunables imprimé à Tours," 154.

at Bouvines in 1214, the era of powerful local magnates, who had provided Benedictine monks with their raison d'être, came to a close. In the case of Marmoutier, the end of that era is best illustrated by the violent struggle between the abbey and the counts of Blois, which began in 1230 when the county passed into the hands of the house of Châtillon. In 1259 the monks paid King Louis IX 3,500 livres so that he would replace the count as the abbey's lay protector and bring the struggle to a close.[7] The episode left Marmoutier in spiritual and financial disarray. In the fourteenth century the Avignon popes would cause the further decline of the abbey by appointing their own relatives as its abbots.[8]

The Hundred Years' War between the French and English monarchs (itself a symptom of the growth of centralized power) provided the major impetus for the political, topographical, and religious transformation of the town of Tours. About 1354 the war compelled the inhabitants of the town to begin building a wall that encompassed both Châteauneuf and the cathedral town, which had retained their separate identities and fortifications since the tenth century. In 1356 King John II established a local committee to organize the defense of the town, and in 1385 Charles VI transformed that committee into an oligarchic urban government. The ruling group, which regularly elected two officials to manage the city's affairs, included at least one royal officer, up to forty local notables, and three canons who represented the archbishop, the cathedral chapter, and the chapter of Saint-Martin.[9] It was this group—or its elected officers—that now had the authority to decide when Saint Martin's relics would be carried through the town, on a route that symbolically united the basilica and the cathedral.[10] Decisions about more major translations of Martin's relics—to new reliquaries, for example—apparently involved the king and the pope.[11]

The rise of royal and papal power had also affected the community of Tours in the years between 1050 and 1250, but the earlier period represents a unique transitional stage in the history of medieval France. In the eleventh and twelfth centuries the immediate beneficiaries of the growth of centralized power were local magnates and

7. Robinet, "Conflit entre pouvoir civil et pouvoir ecclésiastique." The struggle actually dragged on for several years after 1259.

8. Martène, *Histoire de l'abbaye de Marmoutier,* 2:219–39, 287, 292.

9. Chevalier, *Tours, ville royale,* 59, 79–90.

10. Chevalier, *Tours, ville royale,* 197–98.

11. Vaucelle, *Collégiale de Saint-Martin,* 165–66; Gasnault, "Sainte ampoule de Marmoutier," 250.

religious communities. The road to centralized and sophisticated government was paved, for the Capetians, by comital and ducal houses such as those of Anjou and Blois. Similarly, monastic reforms preceded papal reform, and when the popes and kings began to wield their influence in France, monasteries and chapters like Marmoutier and Saint-Martin enhanced their local positions—vis-à-vis both archbishops and burghers—by turning to the pope or the king for support.

A heightened consciousness of collective identities was symptomatic of this transitional stage when older local collectivities and the new centralizing powers were both competing with each other and working together. In the eleventh, twelfth, and early thirteenth centuries, the monks of Marmoutier and the canons of Saint-Martin enhanced their prestige in the eyes of counts, popes, and kings, and strengthened their own collective cohesiveness as well, by calling attention to their close links with Saint Martin. After the mid-thirteenth century, however, royal and papal power overwhelmed, absorbed, or transformed Saint Martin's communities. In the late Middle Ages the saint remained an important symbol of group identity, but the nature of his constituency had changed.

Source Appendix

Most of the narrative and liturgical sources discussed in this book are anonymous, and several present rather thorny dating problems. In attempting to identify the dates and authors of the texts, I have drawn heavily on the work of earlier scholars. Nevertheless, for most of the texts discussed below I have provided my own emendations, hypotheses, or corrections.

I. Sources from Marmoutier

I-A. *Saint Martin's Return from Burgundy (De reversione beati Martini a Burgundia tractatus)*

Attributed to: Odo of Cluny (879–942).
Author: Anonymous monk of Marmoutier, ca. 1137–56.
Edition: André Salmon, *Supplément aux chroniques de Touraine* (Tours: Guilland-Verger, 1856), 14–34.
Manuscript Evidence: Metz, Bibliothèque Municipale, MS. 1183, destroyed in 1944.
References: Gasnault, "La 'Narratio in reversione beati Martini a Burgundia'"; *Chronicon Petri filii Bechini; Chartes de Saint-Julien de Tours (1002–1300)*, 1:49; William of Malmesbury, *De gestis regum Anglorum*, 2:121, ed. Stubbs, 1:127–28; chapters 2 and 5 above.

Pierre Gasnault based his argument for the terminus ad quem of the *Return from Burgundy* on its inclusion in MS. 1183 from Metz, which was copied in 1156. He also pointed out that about 1140 William of Malmesbury apparently borrowed a vignette from the *Return from Burgundy*. The story concerned the contest in Auxerre in which a leper lay for one night between the relics of Saint Martin and those of Saint Germanus. On the following morning the leper had been cured only on the side that was closer to Martin, thus proving that Martin was performing all the recent miracles in Auxerre.

Gasnault argued for a terminus a quo in that Peter Bechin, who wrote a chronicle in 1137, apparently did not know the legend. Bechin, who was probably a canon of Saint-Martin, dwelt extensively on the history of Saint-Martin. He gave an account of the Viking attack on Tours when Martin's relics saved the town, and he referred to the peregrinations of Martin's relics in Burgundy, but his account contained none of the material that originated with the *Return from Burgundy*. Gasnault thus made the reasonable assumption that Bechin did not know the text. Gasnault attempted to provide further evidence for the terminus a quo by pointing out that the *Return from Burgundy* used the word *burgenses,* a term, he maintained, that was not used in Tours until after the first communal revolt of 1122. The word was already in use in Tours in 1080, however; it occurs in a charter resolving a conflict between Saint-Julian of Tours and Saint-Martin.

The assertion that the author of the *Return from Burgundy* was a monk of Marmoutier is my own, based on the evidence I give in chapters 2 (at notes 53 ff.) and 6 (at notes 49 ff.) that the author clearly had the perspective of one of Marmoutier's monks rather than of a canon of Saint-Martin.

I-B. Eleventh- and thirteenth-century histories of Marmoutier (untitled in original texts)

Authors: Eleventh-century redaction—anonymous monk of Marmoutier, probably before 1095; Thirteenth-century redaction—anonymous monk of Marmoutier, sometime after 1227.
Edition: *Narratio de commendatione Turonicae provinciae* and *Chronicon abbatum Majoris monasterii* (the eleventh-century sections on Marmoutier are on pp. 302–3, 305–6, and 309–14; the thirteenth-century history of Marmoutier is on pp. 302–26).
Manuscript evidence: Charleville, Bibliothèque Municipale, MS. 117 (twelfth-century), fols. 102–106v; Bibliothèque Nationale, MS. lat. 15067 (fourteenth-century, from Marmoutier), fols. 15–36; Bibliothèque Nationale MS. lat. 13899 (fifteenth- or sixteenth-century copy of an earlier manuscript from Marmoutier, which begins with an inscription saying it was copied in 1187 but contains later material as well), fols. 35–47v.
References: Van der Straeten, "Recueil de miracles de S. Martin dans le manuscrit 117 de Charleville"; *Chroniques des comtes d'An-*

jou, xlv–lvi, liv n. 1, lxix; Tricard, "Touraine d'un Tourangeau au XIIᵉ siècle"; *Recueil de chroniques de Touraine,* Salmon's introduction, lxxxvii–cxvi (must be read with caution); Mussat, *Style gothique de l'ouest de la France,* 152–56; Lelong, *Basilique Saint-Martin de Tours,* 79–84; chapter 6 above.

Until recently, the only known manuscripts of the *Commendation of the Province of Touraine* were Latin manuscripts 15067 and 13899 of the Bibliothèque Nationale. In both of these manuscripts the *Commendation* and the *Chronicle of Abbots of Marmoutier* occur as a single text, although Salmon published them separately. In these two manuscripts the *Commendation* consists of (a) a commendation of the Province of Touraine (or actually of the town of Tours); (b) a *gesta* of the bishops and archbishops of Tours, which draws heavily for the early centuries on Gregory of Tours (book 10 of the *History of the Franks*); (c) a commendation of Châteauneuf and a history of the basilica of Saint-Martin; and (d) a history of Marmoutier, from its original foundation until 1227 (MS. lat. 13899, the later of the two manuscripts, has a continuation to 1426).

Halphen and Poupardin argued in 1913 that the *Commendation of the Province of Touraine* as it appears in these late manuscripts (fourteenth and fifteenth/sixteenth centuries) was a thirteenth-century composite of earlier texts, and that part d, the history of Marmoutier, originally ended with the account of Urban II's dedication of the new abbey church of Marmoutier in 1096. Recent scholarship has proved that Halphen and Poupardin were basically correct. Jean Tricard has argued convincingly that part a of the *Commendation* was written by a twelfth-century monk of Marmoutier; and Joseph van der Straeten's examination of Charleville MS. 117 has brought to light a twelfth-century version of part d—the history of Marmoutier—that ends just before the account of the dedication in 1096, with the story of Marmoutier's refoundation in the tenth century (see chap. 6 for tables showing the contents of the eleventh- and thirteenth-century histories).

The version of the history of Marmoutier that occurs in the Charleville manuscript contains exaggerated claims concerning the history of the abbey's independent status (see chap. 6). I thus argue that one motivation for writing this original version of the history of Marmoutier (although the Ermengard story—discussed in chap. 4—suggests there were probably others) was to bolster the abbey's claims to exemption from the jurisdiction of the archbishop of Tours. Pope Urban II granted the abbey its first bull of exemption in 1089. The archbishop of Tours continued to assert his claims vis-à-vis Marmoutier, however, and the case was not resolved until the Council of Clermont in 1095 (see chap. 2). The motivating circumstances for inventing claims to earlier liberties persisted until 1095, and I thus propose that date as a terminus ad quem.

In the fourteenth-century manuscript of the *Commendation of the Province of Touraine* the history of Marmoutier includes a list of abbots that ends with Abbot Hugh, who died in 1227. In the fifteenth/sixteenth-century manuscript that list continues through the death of Abbot Guy de Lure in 1426. It thus seems reasonable to assume that the longer history of the abbey was written about 1227 and that the list of abbots was extended at a later date.

Since both the fourteenth- and the fifteenth/sixteenth-century manuscripts containing the *Commendation of the Province of Touraine* are from Marmoutier, it also seems reasonable to surmise that the thirteenth-century compiler of the *Commendation* may have been a monk from Marmoutier, possibly the same one who wrote the longer version of the history of Marmoutier (part d of the *Commendation*). In any case, all four parts of the *Commendation* were apparently written before or near 1227: part a dates from the twelfth century; the list of archbishops in part b ends with John de Faye, who became archbishop in 1208; and part c, the section on Saint-Martin and Châteauneuf was apparently written in or soon after 1175: it mentions the beginning of a building campaign in 1175 (when the nave of the basilica was revaulted), but it does not mention the end of that campaign, about 1180 (see Mussat and Lelong).

I-C. *The Restoration of Marmoutier* (*Liber de restructione Majoris monasterii*—twelfth and later twelfth- or thirteenth-century versions)

Authors: Anonymous monks from Marmoutier.
Edition: *Recueil de chroniques de Touraine,* 343–73 (this is the later version; those parts of the published edition that are in the earlier version are described by Van der Straeten).
Manuscript evidence: Charleville, Bibliothèque Municipale, MS. 117 (twelfth-century), fols. 124v–128; Bibliothèque Nationale, MS. lat. 15067, fols. 36–56; MS. lat. 13899, fols. 31–35 (see above, section I-B).
References: Van der Straeten, "Recueil . . . de Charleville," 92–93; *Recueil de chroniques de Touraine,* Salmon's introduction, cii–civ, cxx–cxxx (must be read with caution); *Catalogus codicum hagiographicorum Bibliothecae regiae Bruxellensis,* 1:233–49, 484–509, 529–

57 (MS. 428–42, fifteenth century, from Cologne, contains Guibert of Gembloux's correspondence with Archbishop Philip of Cologne; MS. 5387–96, thirteenth century, from Guibert's monastery of Gembloux; MS. 5527–34, thirteenth century, edited by Guibert himself); chapter 4 above.

The earlier version of the *Restoration* is in the twelfth-century manuscript Charleville 117. I place the authorship of the earlier version of this legend in the twelfth century, rather than before, because it discusses contrition, confession, mercy, and purgation (see chap. 4 at notes 22 ff.). Unlike Van der Straeten, I believe the text in Charleville 117 is an original that was interpolated by a later author, whose text is in MS. lat. 15067 and 13899 at the Bibliothèque Nationale, the two manuscripts on which Salmon based his edition.

I suggest that there were two different authors, rather than a longer and an excerpted version of the same text, because the portions of the *Restoration* that occur only in the longer version employ a different language and address different concerns than the portions that are in Charleville 117. The longer, interpolated text, for example, uses words referring to mercy a total of twenty-seven times; only two of those usages occur in the portions that appear in Charleville 117. See chapter 4, note 31, and the discussion in text that begins at note 30.

Unfortunately, there are no sound clues for dating the later, interpolated text, which occurs only in the fourteenth- and fifteenth/ sixteenth-century manuscripts at the Bibliothèque Nationale. Salmon thought it must have been written about the time Guibert if Gembloux visited Marmoutier in 1180–81 because MS. 13899 begins with a note saying it was copied in 1187 and the text of the *Restoration* in MS. 15067 begins with a letter from "G" to "R" asking him to recount the story. As Salmon well knew, however, MS. 13899 contained a number of texts written after 1187; morever, that manuscript does not include the letter from "G," and there is no reason to assume that the letter was always associated with the longer version of the *Restoration*. More important, I have found no indication that the *Restoration* ended up in any of the extensive manuscripts dedicated to Saint Martin that Guibert of Gembloux either edited or inspired at his home monastery. Since Guibert was exceedingly thorough in his search for written texts concerning Martin, it is reasonable to assume that, had he been exposed to the *Restoration* during his visit to Marmoutier, he would have taken a copy back to Gembloux. On the manuscripts concerning Saint Martin that bear the imprint of Guibert's quest for Martinian materials, see *Catalogus . . . Bruxellensis*.

I-D. *The Deeds of the Abbey of Marmoutier in the Eleventh Century (De rebus gestis in Majori monasterio saeculo XI)*

Author: Anonymous monk of Marmoutier, twelfth century, after 1137.
Edition: Jean Mabillon and Luc d'Archery, *Acta sanctorum ordinis Sancti Benedicti* (Venice, 1733–38), saec. vi, pt. 2, 395–405.
Manuscript evidence: Charleville 117, fols. 108v–124v.
References: *Chroniques des comtes d'Anjou,* xliii; Van der Straeten, "Recueil . . . de Charleville," 89–92.

The *Deeds of the Abbey of Marmoutier* is included in Charleville 117, so it definitely dates from the twelfth century. It mentions Abbot Garnier (p. 398), who became abbot in 1137, so that marks the terminus a quo. The fifteenth paragraph in Mabillon's edition (p. 403) is not in the Charleville manuscript.

I-E. *The Seven Sleepers of Marmoutier (Historia septem dormientium [Majoris monasterii])*

Attributed to: Gregory of Tours.
Author: Anonymous twelfth-century monk(s) of Marmoutier, one of them writing before 1181 and possibly before 1156.
Edition: *PL* 71:1105–18.
Manuscript evidence: Metz, Bibliothèque Municipale, MS. 1183 (destroyed in 1944); Brussels, Bibliothèque Royale, MS. 5387–96, fols. 1r–8v; Charleville, Bibliothèque Municipale, MS. 117, fols. 128–39v.
References: Oury, "Septs dormants de Marmoutier"; "De cultu Sancti Martini apud Turonenses extremo saeculo XII," 218; Delehaye, "Guibert, Abbé de Florennes et de Gembloux," 48–65; *Catalogue général des manuscrits des bibliothèques publiques de France,* 48:403; *Catalogus codicum hagiographicorum . . . Bruxellensis,* 1:484–85.

As Oury pointed out in his article, this legend had both shorter and longer versions. In the *Patrologia* edition (copied from an earlier one by Ruinart) the passages that occur only in the longer redaction are marked off with brackets. Oury also argued convincingly that the longer version was an interpolation of the shorter version: the bracketed passages consistently stress monastic themes such as humility, obedience, and poverty.

Concerning the shorter redaction, Oury argued that the chivalresque content points to a twelfth-century author rather than one who came before. Oury was not aware, however, that this twelfth-century author had to have written before 1181: in a letter he wrote to the archbishop of Cologne during Guibert of Gembloux's visit to Tours, Abbot Herveus of Marmoutier referred to the legend ("De cultu Sancti Martini"; and see Delehaye on the dates of Guibert's visit to Tours); and parts of the legend made their way into Guibert's *Life* of Saint Martin (*Catalogus . . . Bruxellensis*). There is also some evidence that the legend was written before 1156: the description of manuscript 1183 of the Bibliothèque Municipale of Metz in the *Catalogue général* indicates that the manuscript, which was transcribed in 1156, included a work entitled "Gregorii Turonensis vita septem dormientium." Since the entire manuscript concerned the life and miracles of Saint Martin, this legend was probably the one about the seven sleepers of Marmoutier rather than the seven sleepers of Ephesus.

Concerning the longer version of the legend, Oury surmised that it may have been written about 1239, but the longer version of the legend is included in MS. 117 from Charleville, which was copied in the twelfth century.

I-F. Customal of Marmoutier (*Antiquae consuetudines Majoris monasterii prope Turones*)

Author: Anonymous monk of Marmoutier, sometime after 1124.
Edition: In progress.
Manuscript evidence: Tours, Bibliothèque Municipale, MS. 1393 (mid-thirteenth-century manuscript destroyed in 1940); Bibliothèque Nationale, MS. lat. 12879 (late seventeenth or early eighteenth century; Edmond Martène's handwritten *preuves* for his *Histoire de l'abbaye de Marmoutier*), fols. 86–118v.
References: *Catalogue général des manuscrits des bibliothèques publiques de la France*, 37:2:941–42; Martène, *Histoire de l'abbaye de Marmoutier*, 2:87; Martimort, *Documentation liturgique de Dom Edmond Martène*, 445.

Most recent scholars, including Martimort, have assumed that the customal of Marmoutier was completely lost when the library at Tours burned in 1940. But Martène's copy of the Marmoutier customal corresponds almost exactly with Collon's description of the thirteenth-century manuscript in the *Catalogue général:*

—Collon's incipit, which reads "Sabbato primo de advento Do-
minis ante vesperas chorus et altaria ornentur," is the same as
Martène's incipit at fol. 86.

—The passage Collon cited to date the customal ("Tamen vidi
Annunciationem dominicam quod evenerit in feriam quintam dominice cene, quam transtulimus in v feriam post infra octabas
Pasche, ad octavum videlicet ejus festivitatis diem. Alia vice evenit
die eodem dominice cene, anticipavimusque eam, quarta feria cele-
brantes. Item alia vice evenit similiter, sed nichil egimus") is in
Martène at fol. 89v.

Collon surmised that the manuscript was written after 1193 by a
monk who was already at Marmoutier in 1171. It was definitely
written after 1124 (it mentioned Abbot Odo, who took office in
1124), and its author was apparently at Marmoutier on three occasions when the feast of the Annunciation (March 25) fell on Maundy
Thursday (when Easter was on March 28). Between the time of Odo's
accession, Collon maintained, and the mid-thirteenth century (when
the manuscript was copied), this happened in 1171, 1182, and 1193.
But it is also possible (and I think more likely) that the author was
referring to the three occasions *before* 1124 when Easter fell on March
28: in 1087, 1092, and 1098. I have not yet located the reference in
Martène's transcription to Abbot Odo, but I have found a reference to
Odo's predecessor, Abbot William (1104–24; fol. 108v). Martène was
relatively certain the customal was written during the tenure of Abbot
Odo (1124–37).

I-G. Statutes of the priories of Marmoutier

Author: Twelfth- or thirteenth-century monk of Marmoutier,
with later continuations.
Edition: "Statuts des prieurés de Marmoutier," ed. Guy Oury,
Revue Mabillon 60 (1981): 1–16.
Manuscript evidence: Tours, Bibliothèque Municipale, MS. 94
(collection of texts begun before 1375), fols. 37–39v [T]; Nantes,
Musée Dobrée, Pontifical of Saint-Serge of Angers (after 1389),
fols. 230 ff. [D]; Bibliothèque Nationale, Collection Housseau,
MS. 28, part 1, p. 102 (eighteenth-century copy of a third version
of the statutes) [H].
References: Oury, "Statuts"; Martène, *Histoire de l'abbaye de Mar-
moutier,* 2:260–63.

Oury based his edition of the statutes for Marmoutier's priories on three manuscripts; two of them were also available to Edmond Martène, and the third, H, is apparently a copy of the third manuscript Martène saw.

Oury has proposed that version H was based on a set of the statutes written not long after 1261, since the text mentioned Pope Alexander IV "of saintly memory," and Alexander died in 1261. Version D, Oury argued, was written after 1312 because the last entry mentioned an Abbot Odo "of good memory." Marmoutier had an Abbot Odo who died in 1312. Finally, Oury proposed that T, which was much shorter than D and H, represented the latest version of the statutes, and he suggested the possible date of 1354, when Abbot Pierre du Puy wrote some statutes.

Oury's reasoning for D and H seems sound, but I suggest that version T could well represent an earlier version of the statutes that may have been written in the twelfth century. T consistently lacks passages in D and H that can be dated to the thirteenth century— references to Pope Alexander IV and to the Franciscans and Dominicans (Oury, "Statuts," p. 11, chap. 13; p. 16, chap. 21). T also has stricter dietary rules than do D and H (D and H forbid meat eating only on the fourth day of the week and during Advent, T forbids meat eating on the second and fourth days and during Advent and Septuagesima; T also has an additional statute restricting serving fish with sauces—Oury, "Statuts," p. 10, chap. 10; Tours 94, fols. 38v– 39). It is reasonable to assume that thirteenth- and fourteenth-century dietary rules were less strict than those of the twelfth century. Indeed, like version T of the statutes, Marmoutier's twelfth-century customal (see I-F above) also indicates that the monks were not to eat meat during Septuagesima (*Antiquae consuetudines Majoris monasterii*, fol. 103v, chap. 35: "De septuagesima . . . His duabus hebdomadis casus [cuttings?] et ova comedentur").

II. Sources from or about the Chapter of Saint-Martin

II-A. "Sermon on the Burning of the Basilica of Saint-Martin" ("Sermo de combustione basilicae beati Martini")

Author: Odo of Cluny (879–942).
Edition: *PL* 133:729–49.
References: Martène and Durand, *Thesaurus novus anecdotorum*

(Paris, 1717; reprint New York, 1968), 5:617; Mabille, *Invasions normandes dans la Loire*, 43 n. 2; Plat, *Art de bâtir en France des Romains à l'an 1100;* Vieillard-Troiekouroff, "Tombeau de S. Martin retrouvé en 1860," 160–61; John of Salerno, "Vita Sancti Odonis," *PL* 133:43–86; Odo of Cluny, *Hymni quatuor, PL* 133: 514–15; Odo of Cluny, *Sermones quinque, PL* 133:709–52.

Martène and Durand's edition of the "Sermo de combustione" begins with a rubric attributing the sermon to Odo of Cluny: "Sanctae et egregriae recordationis Odonis sermo nuper orante Theotheloneo episcopo, de adiustione B. Martini Turonensis ecclesiae editus." It is plausible that Odo would have written such a sermon, given that he began his religious career at Saint-Martin and had a close relationship with Bishop Theotolus of Tours (see John of Salerno, *Vita*, 1:11–17, and Odo, "Hymnus . . . in extremis").

Nevertheless, Mabille argued that Odo could not have written the "Sermo de combustione" because it mentioned a fire at Saint-Martial of Limoges that took place in 952, ten years after Odo's death. He went on to suggest that the most probable date for the "Sermo de combustione" was soon after a fire that destroyed Saint-Martin in 997.

More recently, Gabriel Plat argued that the "Sermo de combustione" must have been written before 997 and that Odo of Cluny may well have been its author: the sermon mentioned a recent fire at Saint-Martin, which Plat assumes to have been that of 903—no longer recent in 997; the author associated new abuses with the building of the walls of Châteauneuf, which were completed in 918, so he probably wrote soon after 918; and he stated that he knew very old canons who could remember the gilded roof of the basilica. The gilded roof was probably that of Perpetuus's basilica, which was destroyed in 853; thus the author would probably have been writing before the end of the second quarter of the tenth century. Although she did not concur with all Plat's arguments concerning the archaeological evidence of the basilica, Vieillard-Troiekouroff also believed the reference in the sermon to a recent fire was to that of 903.

In general, Plat's arguments make sense. And I would add the observation that the theological content of the "Sermo de combustione" is consistent with the theological content of other works by Odo of Cluny: an emphasis on the saints' work in bringing people to salvation and repentance, rather than on their ability to work miracles, occurs again in Odo's "Sermon for the Feast of Saint Benedict"; an emphasis on repentance (*PL* 133:735) occurs again in Odo's "Sermon for Saint Martin's Feast" (*PL* 133:749); and in two of his hymns Odo, like the author of the "Sermo de combustione" (*PL* 133:748–49), transformed the story about Martin's giving away half his cape to a beggar into a metaphor for the protection the saint could give to sinners at the Last Judgment.

II-B. Customal of Saint-Martin (*Consuetudines ecclesiae beati Martini Turonensis*)

Author: Thirteenth-century canon of Saint-Martin, between 1226 and 1237.
Edition: A. Fl[euret], *Rituel de Saint-Martin de Tours (XIIIᵉ siècle)*, Documents et Manuscrits (Paris, 1899–1901).
Manuscript evidence: Tours, Bibliothèque Municipale, MS. 1508 (thirteenth century, destroyed in 1940); Tours, MS. 1295, pp. 451–521.
References: Vaucelle, *Collégiale de Saint-Martin de Tours*, xxviii–xxix, 222; fifteenth-century register of the chapter of Saint-Martin, Bibliothèque Nationale, Collection Baluze, MS. 77, fol. 367v; *Catalogue général des manuscrits des bibliothèques publiques de France*, 37:2:900–901; "Prima reformatio ecclesiae facta anno 1204," "Secunda ecclesiae reformatio anno 1208," "Tertia ecclesiae reformatio anno 1237," in Tours, MS. 1295, pp. 547–53.

A tradition from the chapter of Saint-Martin that goes back to at least 1459 (Baluze 77, 367v) claims that Péan Gatineau wrote the thirteenth-century customal of Saint-Martin. The text itself does not give any indication of authorship, however, and the only clear evidence for its date is that the customal, which was copied in the thirteenth century, referred to a confraternal arrangement with Mayence, renewed in 1226 (Vaucelle, *Collégiale*, 333; *Consuetudines*, 143), and that it referred directly to the reforms that took place at Saint-Martin in 1204 and 1208 (*Consuetudines*, 121–30) but not to the third reform of 1237. See the next section for a discussion of the name Péan Gatineau and the difficulties of ascribing a date to any text bearing that name.

II-C. *La vie monseignor Saint Martin de Tors*

Author: Péan Gatineau, canon of Saint-Martin, ca. 1229–50.
Edition: Söderhjelm, *Das altfranzösische Martinsleben des Péan*

Gatineau aus Tours, neue nach der Handschrift revidierte Ausgabe.
Manuscript evidence: Bibliothèque Nationale, MS. fr. 1043.
References: Söderhjelm, *Leben und Wunderthaten des heiligen Martin, altfranzösisches Gedicht aus dem Anfang des XIII Jahrhunderts von Péan Gatineau;* Letter of John of Salisbury (1180), in *Recueil des historiens des Gaules,* 16:624; Letter of Archbishop William and Abbot Herveus (1184), in *Gallia Christiana,* vol. 14, Instrumenta, 87; Moorman, *History of the Franciscan Order,* 67; *Chronicon Turonense auctore anonymo,* 1065; Brooke, "Lives of St. Francis of Assisi," 181–83; Weinstein and Bell, *Saints and Society,* 23–72, esp. 59; and Herlihy, *Medieval Households,* 120–21.

There is no question that someone named "Péan Gatineau" wrote this vernacular life of Saint Martin: the author tells us his name at the end of the poem (line 10291, p. 129). But this signature is about all we know of the man, except that he must have been a canon from Saint-Martin and was probably a native of Tours: the author of the poem knew very well some of the administrative details of the chapter, and he told a story about a cousin of his who attended Martin's May feast (lines 9464 ff., p. 119).

In his marginal note concerning the customal of Saint-Martin (Tours, MS. 1295, p. 451), Michel Vincent stated that someone named "Paganus Gastinelli" founded his own anniversary in the year 1227. Nevertheless, the language and paleography of the only surviving manuscript of the *Vie* point to the mid-thirteenth century. Moreover, there is no reason to believe there was only one Péan Gatineau in the history of medieval Tours. There was a regular pattern of name repetition in medieval families, and indeed, one of the burghers of Châteauneuf who participated in the communes of 1180 and 1184 was named "Paganus Gastinelli" (See *Gallia Christiana,* 14:87, and *Recueil des historiens des Gaules,* 16:624). Finally, I argue that the author of the *Vie* was still working after 1229.

My primary reason for suggesting that the author of the poem continued to work after 1229 is the content of the story about Persois and Meinarz (see chap. 9), which seems to have been influenced by Thomas of Celano's first *Life* of Saint Francis, completed in 1229 (see Brooke). Although there are no direct textual borrowings in Péan's account of Persois and Meinarz, there are a number of striking parallels with Celano's *Life* of Francis: the tension between the father or father figure and the saint over the saint's squandering the father/father figure's wealth; the father/father figure's activity in the commercial realm; the mediating mother/mother figure who is scolded by her husband for protecting or assisting the holy boy; an emphasis on pious folly or craziness (that of Persois, that of Francis himself); the idea that the saint accepted his own clothing from the wealthy and then redistributed it to the poor (on Francis's frequent distributions of cloaks that he received from the wealthy, see Thomas of Celano, *Vita*, bk. 1, chap. 28, p. 80).

It is possible that after the Franciscans founded their convent in Tours in 1224 (see Moorman, *History of the Franciscan Order*, and *Chronicon Turonense auctore anonymo*) Péan Gatineau began to hear stories about Saint Francis's charity, his struggle with his father, and the mediating role of his mother. Another possibility would be that both Celano and Péan reflected a general cultural interest in generational conflict between fathers and sons and in the mediating role of mothers: the themes of saintly discomfort with inherited wealth and position and stories about family tension in which a mother backed her son who was at odd with his father were gaining prominence in the twelfth and thirteenth centuries (see Weinstein and Bell and also Herlihy). Nevertheless, the overlap between Celano's *Vita* and Péan's *Vie* extended beyond generational conflict, and I suspect that a number of the texts mentioned by Weinstein and Bell and by Herlihy were inspired by the *Life* of Saint Francis.

Abbreviations

Acta sanctorum
   Acta sanctorum quotquot toto orbe coluntur. Edited by Society of Bollandists.
   New ed. Vols. 1–. Paris: V. Palmé, etc., 1863–19–.

Chroniques des comtes d'Anjou
   Chroniques des comtes d'Anjou et des seigneurs d'Amboise. Edited by Louis
   Halphen and René Poupardin. Collection de Textes pour Servir à l'Étude
   et à l'Enseignement de l'Histoire. Paris: Auguste Picard, 1913.

J.-L.
   *Regesta pontificum romanorum ab condita ecclesia ad annum post Christum natum
   MCXCVIII.* Edited by Philippus Jaffe, 2d corrected ed. by S. Loewenfeld
   et al. Leipzig: Veit, 1885–88.

MGH, AA
   *Monumenta Germaniae historica inde ab anno Christi quingentesimo usque ad
   annum millesimum et quingentesimum: Auctorum antiquissimorum,* vols. 1–15.
   Berlin: Weidmann, 1877–1919.

MGH, Scr. rer. mer.
   *Monumenta Germaniae historica inde ab anno Christi quingentesimo usque ad
   annum millesimum et quingentesimum: Scriptorum rerum Merovingicarum,* vols.
   1–7. Hannover: Hansche Buchhandlung, 1885–1919.

MGH, SS
   *Monumenta Germaniae historica inde ab anno Christi quingentesimo usque ad
   annum millesimum et quingentesimum: Scriptorum,* vols. 1–32. Hannover,
   Leipzig: Hansche Buchhandlung, 1826–1934.

PL
   Patrologiae cursus completus, series Latina. Edited by J. P. Migne. 221 vols.
   Paris: Migne, 1844–64.

Recueil de chroniques de Touraine
    Recueil de chroniques de Touraine. Edited by André Salmon. Tours: Ladevèze, 1854.
Recueil des historiens des Gaules
    Recueil des historiens des Gaules et de la France. Edited by M. Bouquet et al. 24 vols. Paris: Aux dépens des Libraires Associés, 1738–1904.

Bibliography

Manuscript Sources

Antiquae consuetudines Majoris monasterii prope Turones. See Paris, Bibliothèque Nationale, MS. lat. 12879.

Auxerre, Treasury of the Cathedral
   MS. 6—Missal from Saint-Julian of Tours, copied in the second half of the thirteenth century.

Charleville, Bibliothèque Municipale
   MS. 117—Twelfth-century collection from the Cistercian abbey of Signy. Fols. 79–128 constitute a collection concerning the cult of Saint Martin and the Abbey of Marmoutier. It includes the *De reversione beati Martini a Burgundia,* four miracles from the collection attributed to Herbernus, sections of the *De commendatione Turonicae provinciae* dealing with the history of Marmoutier, the *De rebus gestis in Majori monasterio,* and the *Liber de restructione Majoris monasterii.* Under a different rubric, but immediately following this section (fols. 128–39ᵛ), is the *Historia septem dormientium (Majoris monasterii).* (See Source Appendix, I-B, I-C, I-D, I-E.)

Paris, Archives Nationale
   Le Service des Sceaux, D. 7599—Seal of Aubrey Cornut, dean of Saint-Martin 1229–36.

Paris, Bibliothèque Nationale
   MS. lat. 1—The Vivien Bible, ninth century.
   MS. lat. 9431—Sacramentary from Marmoutier, copied after 1096.
   MS. lat. 9434—Eleventh-century missal from Saint-Martin of Tours.
   MS. lat. 12412—Late twelfth-century collection of sermons from Marmoutier.
   MS. lat. 12875—Contains (at fol. 607) original parchment of charter written in 1115 establishing ceremonial ties between Marmoutier and Saint-Martin.
   MS. lat. 12878–79—Dom Edmond Martène's *preuves* for his *Histoire de l'abbaye de Marmoutier.* Includes (12979, fols. 86–118ᵛ) the only surviving copy of the *Antiquae consuetudines Majoris monasterii,* as well as copies of other documents that have been lost. Early eighteenth century.

MS. lat. 13899—Fifteenth- or early sixteenth-century copy of an earlier manuscript from Marmoutier, which began with an inscription saying it was copied in 1187. Nevertheless, this manuscript contains later material as well.

MS. lat. 15067—Fourteenth-century collection from Marmoutier.

Collection Baluze

MS. 76—Extracts from the archives of Saint-Martin of Tours, copied primarily by Etienne Baluze in the late seventeenth and early eighteenth centuries. Includes copies of medieval originals that have been lost.

MS. 77—Extracts from cartularies of Marmoutier and Saint-Martin, copied primarily by Etienne Baluze. Includes copies of medieval originals that have been lost.

Collection Housseau (or Touraine)

Late seventeenth- and early eighteenth-century collection completed by Dom Housseau, which includes copies of medieval documents that have been lost. MS. 3, 4, 5, 6, 20.

Rouen, Bibliothèque Municipale

MS. 243—Eleventh-century breviary from Marmoutier.

Tours, Archives d'Indre-et-Loire

G381—Eighteenth-century inventory of property rights containing summaries of medieval documents, many of which are now lost.

Tours, Bibliothèque Municipale

Missal from the Petit Séminaire—Eleventh-century missal from Marmoutier.

MS. 94—Collection of texts copied in the late fourteenth century, primarily by Laurent de la Faye. Includes, at fols. 37–39^v, the Statutes of the Priories of Marmoutier.

MS. 153—Early thirteenth-century breviary used at Marmoutier.

MS. 184—Parts of several sacramentaries from Tours that were copied in the late ninth and tenth centuries.

MS. 193—Missal, copied about 1177–87 for Saint-Martin of Tours.

MS. 196—Eleventh-century sacramentary from Saint-Martin, used at Marmoutier.

MS. 198—Missal from Villeloin in Touraine, copied in the second half of the thirteenth century.

MS. 1018—Eleventh-century lectionary from Saint-Martin, concerning Saint Martin and his cult.

MS. 1021—Thirteenth-century lectionary from Saint-Martin, concerning Saint Martin and his cult.

MS. 1023—Fifteenth-century collection from Saint-Martin, primarily concerning Saint Martin and his cult.

MS. 1294–95—*Celeberrimae Sancti Martini ecclesiae historia.* Originally printed by Raoul Monsnyer, then augmented with handwritten additions by Michel Vincent in the early eighteenth century. Contains copies of medieval documents that are now lost.

Primary Sources

Abbo, Monk of Saint Germain. "De bello Parisiaco." Edited and translated by Henri Waquet. In *Le siège de Paris par les Normands*. Paris: Belles Lettres, 1942.

Abbo of Fleury. *Epistolae. PL* 139:417–62.

Acta S. Florentii dubiae fidei auctore anonymo seculo IX scripta. In *Acta sanctorum,* September, 6:428–32.

Adam of Perseigne. *Correspondance d'Adam, Abbé de Perseigne.* Edited by Jean Bouvet. Archives historiques du Maine, 13. Le Mans: Société Historique de la Province du Maine, 1951–62.

———. *Epistolae. PL* 211:579–694.

———. *Lettres.* Edited and translated by Jean Bouvet. Sources Chrétiennes 66. Paris: Cerf, 1960.

Alcuin. "De vita S. Martini Turonensis." *PL* 101:657–62.

———. "Sermo de transitu S. Martini." *PL* 101:662–64.

An Alphabet of Tales: An English Fifteenth-Century Translation of the Alphabetum Narrationum of Etienne de Besançon. Edited by M. M. Banks. Early English Text Society 126. London: K. Paul, Trench, Truber, 1904–5.

"Analekten zur Geschichte des Reformpapsttums und der Cluniazenser." Edited by Johannes Ramackers. *Quellen und Forschungen aus Italienischen Archiven und Bibliotheken, Herausgegeben von Preussischen Historischen Institut in Rom* 23(1931–32): 22–52.

Anonymous of Pavia. *Liber de laudibus civitatis Ticinensis.* Edited by L. Muratori. In *Rerum Italicarum scriptores,* vol. 11, part 1. 32 vols. in 119. New revised edition, under the direction of Giosuè Carducci, Vitorio Fiorini. Città di Castello: S. Lapi, 1900–1975.

Arnulphus, Archbishop of Tours. "Decretum." Edited by Joannes Maan. In *Sancta et metropolitana ecclesia Turonensis sacrorum pontificum suorum ornata virtutibus et sanctissimis conciliorum institutis decorata,* 248–49. Tours, 1667.

Augustine of Hippo. *Sancti Augustini Confessionum libri XIII.* Edited by Lucas Verheijen. Corpus Christianorum, Series Latina 27. Turnhout: Brepols, 1981. Translated by R. S. Pine-Coffin. Harmondsworth, England: Penguin Books, 1961.

Baudry of Bourgueil. *Les oeuvres poétiques de Baudri de Bourgueil, 1046–1130.* Edited by Phyllis Abrahams. Paris: H. Champion, 1926.

Bernard of Angers. *Liber miraculorum Sancte Fidis.* Edited by Auguste Bouillet. Paris: A. Picard, 1897.

Bibliotheca rerum Germanicarum. Edited by P. Jaffé, Wilhelm Wattenbach, and Ernst Ludwig Dümmler. 6 vols. Berlin: Weidmann, 1864–73.

Brevis historia Sancti Juliani Turonensis. In *Recueil de chroniques de Touraine,* 220–34.

Caesarius of Heisterbach. *Dialogus miraculorum.* Edited by Joseph Strange. 2 vols. Cologne: J. M. Herberle (H. Lempertz), 1851.

Cartulaire de Cormery. Edited by J.-J. Bourassé. Mémoires de la Société Arch-éologique de Touraine 12. Tours: Guilland-Verger, 1861.

Cartulaire de l'abbaye de St. Aubin d'Angers. Edited by Arthur Bertrand de Brous-sillon. Paris: R. Picard, 1903.

Cartulaire de l'archevêché de Tours. Edited by Louis de Grandmaison. 2 vols. Mémoires de la Société Archéologique de Touraine, 37–38. Tours: Péricat, 1892–94.

Cartulaire de Marmoutier pour le Dunois. Edited by Emile Mabille. Chateaudon: H. Lecesne, 1874.

Cartulaire de Marmoutier pour le Perche. Edited by M. Barret. Documents sur la Province du Perche, 3d ser., 2. Mortagne: G. Meaux, 1894.

Cartulaire de Marmoutier pour le Vendômois. Edited by M. de Trémault. Paris: Alphonse Picard, 1893.

Chartes de Saint-Julien de Tours (1002–1300). Edited by L.-J. Denis. 2 vols. Ar-chives Historiques du Mans 12. Le Mans: Société des Archives Historiques du Maine, 1912–13.

Chronica de gestis consulum Andegavorum. In *Chroniques des comtes d'Anjou,* 25–73, 135–71.

Chronicon abbatum Majoris monasterii. In *Recueil de chroniques de Touraine,* 318–37.

Chronicon Petri filii Bechini. In *Recueil de chroniques de Touraine,* 1–63.

Chronicon rhythmicum Sancti Juliani Turonensis. In *Recueil de chroniques de Touraine,* 235–56.

Chronicon Turonense abbreviatum. In *Recueil de chroniques de Touraine,* 162–200.

Chronicon Turonense auctore anonymo canonico Turonensi S. Martini. Edited by Ed-mond Martène and U. Durand. In *Veterum scriptorum et monumentorum histor-icorum, dogmaticorum, moralium, amplissima collectio,* 5:917–1072. 9 vols. Paris: Montalant, 1724–33. Reprint New York: Burt Franklin, 1968.

Consuetudines ecclesiae beati Martini Turonensis. Edited by A. Fl[euret]. *Rituel de Saint Martin de Tours.* Documents et Manuscrits. Paris: Firmin-Didot, 1899–1901.

Le couronnement de Louis: Chanson de geste du XIIᵉ siècle. Edited by E. Langlois. Paris: Firmin-Didot, 1888.

De antiquis ecclesiae ritibus. Edited by Edmond Martène. 2d ed. 4 vols. Antwerp: Joannis Baptistae de la Bry, 1736–38. Reprint Hildesheim: Georg Olms, 1967–69.

"De cultu Sancti Martini apud Turonenses extremo saeculo XII epistolae quatuor." *Analecta Bollandiana* 3(1884): 217–57. Reedited in Guibert, Abbot of Gembloux, *Guiberti Gemblacensis epistolae,* 64–102, 128–57.

"De professionibus abbatum." Edited by Jean Leclercq. "Un traité sur la 'profes-sion des abbés' au XIIᵉ siècle." *Studia Anselmiana* 50(1962): 182–91.

De rebus gestis in Majori monasterio saeculo XI. Edited by Jean Mabillon and Luc d'Archery. In *Acta sanctorum ordinis Sancti Benedicti,* saec. 6, part 2, 395–405. 9 vols. Venice: Coletti and J. Bettinelli, 1733–38.

De reversione beati Martini a Burgundia tranctatus. Edited by André Salmon. In *Supplement aux chroniques de Touraine,* 14–34. Tours: Guilland-Verger, 1856.

Eadmer. *The Life of Saint Anselm, Archbishop of Canterbury.* Edited by Sir Richard Southern. London: T. Nelson, 1962.

English Gilds: The Original Ordinances of More Than One Hundred Early English Gilds. Edited by Toulmin Smith. Early English Text Society 40. London: Oxford University Press, 1870. Reprint, 1963.

English Historical Documents. 2d ed. London: E. Methuen, 1981.

"Ex codice MS. monasterii S. Martini Tornacensis." Edited by Michel Toussaint Chrétien du Plessis. In *Histoire de l'église de Meaux,* 2:36–39. 2 vols. Paris: Julien-Michel Gandouin et Pierre-François Giffart, 1731.

Exordium magnum ordinis Cisterciensis. PL 185:2:993–1198.

Fortunatus, Venantius. *Carminum, epistularum, expositionum libri undecim.* Edited by F. Leo. In *MGH, AA,* 4:1:7–270.

————. *Vita Sancti Martini.* Edited by F. Leo. In *MGH, AA,* 4:1:293–370.

Fulk Rechin. *Fragmentum historiae Andegavensis.* In *Chroniques des comtes d'Anjou,* 232–38.

Genealogiae comitum Andegavensium. In *Chroniques des comtes d'Anjou,* 247–50.

Gerbert. *Epistolae. PL* 139:201–68.

Gesta episcoporum Cameracensis. Edited by L. C. Bethmann. In *MGH, SS,* 7:402–89.

Gregory of Tours. *De virtutibus beati Martini episcopi.* Edited by B. Krusch. In *MGH, Scr. rer. mer.,* 1:2:584–661.

————. *Historia Francorum.* Edited by W. Arndt. In *MGH, Scr. rer. mer.,* 1:1. Translated by Lewis Thorpe as *History of the Franks.* Harmondsworth, England: Penguin Books, 1974.

————. *Liber in gloria confessorum.* Edited by B. Krusch. In *MGH, Scr. rer. mer.,* 1:2:744–820.

Gregory the Great. *Dialogues.* Translated by O. J. Zimmerman. New York: Fathers of the Church, 1959.

Gregory VII. "Trois lettres de Grégoire VII." Edited by Léopold Delisle. *Bibliothèque de l'Ecole des Chartes* 26(1865):556–61.

Guibert. *Vita Leonis IX papae.* In *Acta sanctorum,* April, 2:648–65.

Guibert, Abbot of Gembloux. "Epistola ad Philippum, archiepiscopum Coloniensem." Edited by Edmond Martène and U. Durand. In *Thesaurus novus anecdotorum,* 1:606–18. 5 vols. Paris: F. Delaulne, 1717. Reprint New York: Burt Franklin, 1968. Reedited in *Guiberti Gemblacensis epistolae,* 111–27.

————. *Guiberti Gemblacensis epistolae.* Edited by Albert Derolez. Corpus Christianorum, Continuatio Mediaevalis 66. Turnhout: Brepols, 1988.

Guibert of Nogent. *De vita sua.* Edited by John Benton. Translated by C. C. Swinton Bland as *Self and Society in Medieval France.* New York: Harper and Row, 1970.

Le guide du pèlerin de Saint-Jacques de Compostelle. Edited by Jeanne Vielliard. 3d ed. Macon: Protat Frères, 1963.

Guigo of La Grande Chartreuse. "Consuetudines." *PL* 153:631–760.

Herbernus, Archbishop of Tours (attributed). *Miracula beati Martini. PL* 129:1035–52.

Hildebert of Lavardin. *Carmina miscellanea. PL* 171:1381–1448.

––––––. *Vita S. Hugonis Abbatis Cluniacensis.* In *Recueil des historiens des Gaules,* 14:70–71.

Historia Sancti Florenti Salmurensis. Edited by Paul Marchegay and Emile Mabille. In *Chroniques des églises d'Anjou,* 2:217–328. 2 vols. Paris: Mme Vᵉ J. Renouard, 1869.

Historia septem dormientium (Majoris monasterii). PL 71:1105–18.

Hugh of Fleury. *Historia ecclesiastica.* Edited by G. Pertz. In *MGH, SS,* 9:349–53.

Hugh of Rouen. "Contra haereticos libri tres." *PL* 192:1255–98.

"Hugonis Archidiaconi Turonensi dialogus ad Fulbertum amicum suum de quodam miraculo, quod contigit in translatione Sancti Martini." Edited by Jean Mabillon and Luc d'Archery. In *Vetera analecta,* 213–17. Paris: Montalant, 1723.

Innocent III. "Regestorum sive epistolarum liber duodecimus." *PL* 216:9–194.

Ivo of Chartres. *Epistolae. PL* 162:11–290.

Jacob of Voragine. *Legenda aurea.* Edited by Th. Graesse. Reprint from 3d ed. (1890). Osnabrück: Otto Zeller, 1965.

Johannis Beleth. *Summa de ecclesiasticis officiis.* Edited by Herbert Douteil. 2 vols. Corpus Christianorum, Continuatio Mediaevalis 41–41A. Turnhout: Brepols, 1976.

John of Marmoutier. *Historia Gaufredi ducis Normannorum et comitis Andegavorum.* In *Chroniques des comtes d'Anjou,* 172–231.

John of Salerno. "Vita Sancti Odonis." *PL* 133:43–86. Translated by Gerald Sitwell as *St. Odo of Cluny.* New York: Sheed and Ward, 1958.

Lanfranc. *The Monastic Constitutions.* Edited and translated by David Knowles. London: Thomas Nelson, 1951.

Layettes du trésor des chartes. Edited by Alexandre Teulet, Joseph de Laborde, Elie Berger, and H. François Delaborde. 5 vols. Inventaire et Documents Publiés par la Direction des Archives. Paris: Plon-Nurrit, 1863–1909.

Liber de restructione Majoris monasterii. In *Recueil de chroniques de Touraine,* 343–73.

Liberty, Charity, Fraternity: Lay Religious Confraternities at Bergamo in the Age of the Commune. Introduction by Lester K. Little. Texts edited by Sandro Buzzetti. Smith College Studies in History 51. Northampton, Mass.: Smith College, 1988.

Marmoutier, Cartulaire Blésois. Edited by Charles Métais. Blois: E. Moreau, 1889–91.

Maurice of Sully. "Homilie pour la fête de St. Martin." Edited by Albert Lecoy de la Marche. In *Saint Martin*, 693–94. Tours: Alfred Mame, 1881.

Les miracles de Saint Benôit, écrits par Adrevald Aimoin, André, Raoul Tortaire et Hughes de Sainte Marie, moines de Fleury. Edited by E. de Certain. Paris: Mme Vᶜ J. Renouard, 1858.

Monasticon Anglicanum. Edited by Sir William Dugdale. New edition by John Caley, Henry Ellis, and the Rev. Bulkley Bandinel. 6 vols. in 9. London: Longman, Hurst, Rees, Orme and Brown, 1817–30.

Narratio controversiae inter capitulum S. Martini Turonensis et Radulphum ejusdem urbis archiepiscopum. In *Recueil des historiens des Gaules*, 12:459–61.

Narratio de commendatione Turonicae provinciae. In *Recueil de chroniques de Touraine*, 294–317.

Notitia seu libellus de tribulationibus, et angustiis, et persecutionibus Majori-monasterio injuste illatis ab archiepiscopis et clericis S. Mauricii Turonensis. In *Recueil des historiens des Gaules*, 14:93–98.

Odo of Cluny. *Hymni quatuor. PL* 133:513–16.

———. *Sermones quinque. PL* 133:709–52.

Odo Rigaldus, Archbishop of Rouen. *The Register of Eudes of Rouen.* Translated by Sydney M. Brown. Edited by Jeremiah F. O'Sullivan. Records of Civilization, Sources and Studies 72. New York: Columbia University Press, 1964.

Orderic Vitalis. *Historia ecclesiastica.* Edited and translated by Marjorie Chibnall. In *The Ecclesiastical History of Orderic Vitalis.* 6 vols. Oxford: Clarendon Press, 1969–80.

Othloh of Saint Emmerman. "Liber visionum tum suarum, tum aliorum." *PL* 146:341–88.

Papsturkunden in Frankreich. n.s., vol. 5. Edited by Johannes Ramackers. Abhandlungen der Akademie der Wissenschaften in Göttingen, Philologisch-Historische Klasse. 3d ser., 35. Göttingen: Vandenhoeck und Rupreckt, 1956.

Paulinus of Perigord. *De vita Sancti Martini episcopi libri VI.* Edited by M. Petschenig. In *Poetae Christiani minores*, 1:17–159. 2 vols. Corpus Scriptorum Ecclesiasticorum Latinorum 16. Vienna: F. Tempsky, 1888.

Péan Gatineau. *La vie monseignor Saint Martin de Tors.* Edited by Werner Söderhjelm. In *Das altfranzösische Martinsleben des Péan Gatineau aus Tours, neue nach der Handschrift revidierte Ausgabe.* Helsingfors: Wentzel Hagelstam, 1899. An earlier edition by Söderhjelm is less accurate but has a better introduction: *Leben und Wunderthaten des heiligen Martin: Altfranzösisches Gedicht aus dem Anfang des XIII Jahrhunderts von Péan Gatineau aus Tours.* Tübingen: Literarischer Verein in Stuttgart, 1896.

Peter Abelard. *Epistolae. PL* 178:113–380.

Peter Comestor. "Sermo ad sacerdotes." Edited by J. P. Bonnes. "Un des plus grands prédicateurs du XIIᶜ siècle, Geoffroy du Loroux dit Geoffroy Babion." *Revue Bénédictine* 56(1945–46): 174–215.

Peter Damian. *Epistolae. PL* 144:205–498.

Peter the Chanter. *Summa de sacramentis et animae consiliis.* Edited by Jean-Albert Dugauquier. 3 vols. in 5. Analecta Mediaevalia Namurcensia, 4, 11, 16, 21. Louvain, Lille: Nauwelaerts, 1954–67.

Peter the Venerable. *De miraculis libri duo. PL* 189:851–954.

———. "Dispositio rei familiaris Cluniacensis." *PL* 189:1047–54.

———. *The Letters of Peter the Venerable.* Edited by Giles Constable. 2 vols. Cambridge: Harvard University Press, 1967.

———. *Statuta Petri Venerabilis.* Edited by Giles Constable, with J. D. Brady and D. C. Waddell. In *Consuetudines Benedictinae variae,* edited by Giles Constable, 19–106. Corpus Consuetudinum Monasticarum 6. Sieburg: Franciscum Schmitt, 1975.

"Les prieurés de Marmoutier en Anjou, inventaire des titres et supplements aux chartes des XIᵉ et XIIᵉ siècles." Edited by Paul Marchegay. *Archives d'Anjou* 2(1853): i–xlviii, 1–90.

"Quatre miracles de Saint Martin de Tours." Edited by Hippolyte Delehaye. *Analecta Bollandiana* 55(1937): 29–48.

Radbod of Utrecht. *Carmina.* Edited by P. de Winterfeld. In *Monumenta Germaniae historica, Poetae Latini medii aevi,* 4:1:160–73. Vols. 1–. Berlin: Weidmann, 1880–19–.

———. *Libellus de miraculo S. Martini.* Edited by O. Holder-Egger. In *MGH, SS,* 15:2:1239–44.

Ralph Glaber. *Historiarum libri quinque.* Edited by Maurice Prou. In *Raoul Glaber, les cinq livres de ses histoires (900–1044).* Paris: Alphonse Picard, 1886.

RB 1980: The Rule of Saint Benedict in Latin and English with Notes and Thematic Index. Edited by Timothy Fry. Abridged ed. Collegeville, Minn.: Liturgical Press, 1981.

Recueil des actes de Philippe Auguste, roi de France. Edited by Elie Berger, H.-François Delaborde, et al. 4 vols. Chartes et diplomes relatifs à l'histoire de France. Paris: Imprimerie Nationale, 1916–79.

Les registres de Grégoire IX. Edited by Lucien Auvray et al. 4 vols. Bibliothèque des Ecoles Français d'Athènes et de Rome. Paris: Albert Fontemoing, Boccard, 1896–1955.

Rigord. *Gesta Philippi Augusti.* Edited by H.-François Delaborde. In *Oeuvres de Rigord et de Guillaume le Breton.* 2 vols. Paris: Librairie Renouard, 1882, 1885.

Rouleaux des morts du IXᵉ au XVᵉ siècle. Edited by Léopold Delisle. Paris: Mme Vᵉ J. Renouard, 1866.

Sacrorum conciliorum nova et amplissima collectio. Edited by J. D. Mansi. 31 vols. Florence, etc.: A. Zatta, etc., 1759–98.

Select Historical Documents of the Middle Ages. Edited by E. F. Henderson. London: George Bell, 1892.

Sidonius Apollinaris. *Poems and Letters.* Edited by W. B. Anderson. 2 vols. Cambridge: Harvard University Press, 1956, 1965.

"Statuts des prieurés de Marmoutier (XIIIᵉ–XIVᵉ siècles)." Edited by Guy Oury. *Revue Mabillon* 60(1981): 1–16.

Stephen of Fougère. *Vita Guilielmi Firmati.* In *Acta sanctorum*, April, 3:334–42.

Sulpicius Severus. *Chronica.* Edited by C. Halm. In *Sulpicii Severi libri qui supersunt*, 1–105. Corpus Scriptorum Ecclesiasticorum Latinorum 1. Vienna: C. Geroldi Filium, 1866.

————. *Dialogi.* Edited by C. Halm. In *Sulpicii Severi libri*, 152–216. Translated by Bernard Peebles in *Niceta of Remesiana, Writings, Sulpicius Severus, Writings, Vincent of Lérins, Commonitories, Prosper of Aquitaine, Grace and Free Will*, 161–251. Fathers of the Church 7. New York: Fathers of the Church, 1949.

————. *Epistolae.* Edited by Jacques Fontaine. In *Sulpice Sévère: Vie de Saint Martin*, 1:316–44. 3 vols. Sources Chrétiennes 133–35. Paris: Cerf, 1967–69. Translated by Peebles, 141–60 (see above).

————. *Vita Sancti Martini.* Edited by Fontaine, 1:248–316. Translated by Peebles, 101–40 (see above).

Textus de dedicatione ecclesiae Majoris monasterii. In *Recueil de chroniques de Touraine*, 338–42.

Theodoric of Amorbach. *Illatio Sancti Benedicti.* Edited by Jean Mabillon and Luc d'Archery. In *Acta sanctorum ordinis Sancti Benedicti*, saec. 4, part 2, 362–67. 9 vols. Venice: Coletti and J. Bettinelli, 1733–38.

Thietmar of Merseberg. *Chronicon.* Edited by Georg Pertz. In *MGH, SS*, 3:733–871.

Thomais. *Vita et martyrium S. Febroniae.* In *Acta sanctorum*, June, 5:17–34.

Thomas of Celano. *Vita prima S. Francisci Assisiensis.* Edited by College of Saint Bonaventura. Analecta Franciscana 10. Quaracchi, Italy: Typographia Collegii S. Bonaventurae, 1926.

Thomas of Chobham. *Summa confessorum.* Edited by F. Broomfield. Analecta Mediaevalia Namurcensia 25. Louvain: Nauwelaerts, 1968.

Traditio Turonensium de sanguine sanctorum Thebaeorum. In *Acta sanctorum*, September, 6:384–86. Reedited in Guibert, Abbot of Gembloux, *Guiberti Gemblacensis epistolae*, 73–75.

Ulrich of Cluny. *Antiquiores consuetudines Cluniacensis monasterii.* PL 149:643–778.

La vie et les miracles de monseigneur Saint Martin. Tours: Mathieu Latheron, 1496. Paris, Bibliothèque Nationale. La Réserve, vélin 1159.

Vita Radbodi. Edited by O. Holder-Egger. In *MGH, SS*, 15:1:568–71.

Vita Sancti Martini di anonimo. Edited by Gianvita Resta. Padua: Antenore, 1964.

Walter of Cluny. "De miraculis beatae Virginis Mariae." Edited by Philip Labbe. In *Novae bibliothecae manuscript: Librorum tomus primus.* Paris: Sebastianum Cramoisy et Gabrielem Cramoisy, 1657.

William Durand (or Durantis). *Rationale divinorum officiorum.* Naples: J. Dura, 1859.

William of Malmesbury. *De gestis regum Anglorum libri quinque.* Edited by William Stubbs. 2 vols. Rolls Series. London: Eyre and Spottiswoode, 1887–89.

Secondary Sources

Abou-El-Haj, Barbara. "The Urban Setting for Late Medieval Church Building: Reims and Its Cathedral between 1210 and 1240." *Art History* 11 (1988): 17–41.

Amore, Agostino, Eugenio Battisti, and Paolo Toschi. "Lucia." In *Enciclopedia Cattolica,* 8:1618–23. 12 vols. Vatican City: Ente per l'Enciclopedia Cattolica e per il Libro Cattolico, 1949–54.

Amore, Agostino, and Maria Chiara Celletti. "Lucia di Siracusa." In *Bibliotheca sanctorum,* 8:241–57. 13 vols. Rome: Istituto Giovanni XXIII della Pontificia Università Lateranense, 1961–69.

Anciaux, Paul. *La théologie du sacrement de pénitence au XIIe siècle.* Universitas Catholica Lovaniensis, Dissertationes ad Gradum Magistri in Facultate Theologica vel in Facultate Iuris Canonici Consequendum Conscriptae. 2d ser. 41. Louvain: Nauwelaerts, 1949.

Andrieu, M. *Les ordines romani du Haut Moyen Age.* 5 vols. Louvain: "Spicilegium Sacrum Lovaniense" Bureaux, 1931–61.

Anonymous monk of La Grande-Chartreuse. "La doctrine monastique des coutumes de Guigues." *Théologie de la Vie Monastique* 49(1961): 485–501.

Arbois de Jubainville, H. d'. *Histoire des ducs et des comtes de Champagne depuis le VIe siècle jusqu'a la fin du XIe.* 6 vols. in 7. Paris: A. Durand, 1859–66.

Auerbach, Erich. *Mimesis: The Representation of Reality in Western Literature.* Translated by Willard R. Trask, 1953. Reprint Princeton: Princeton University Press, 1968.

Bachrach, Bernard S. "The Angevin Stategy of Castle Building in the Reign of Fulk Nerra, 987–1040." *American Historical Review* 88(1983): 533–60.

———. "Geoffrey Greymantle, Count of the Angevins, 960–987: A Study in French Politics." *Studies in Medieval and Renaissance History* [old series 17] 7(1985): 3–67.

Baldwin, John W. *The Government of Philip Augustus.* Berkeley: University of California Press, 1986.

———. *Masters, Princes and Merchants: The Social Views of Peter the Chanter and His Circle.* 2 vols. Princeton: Princeton University Press, 1970.

Baron, Hans. *The Crisis of the Early Italian Renaissance.* 2 vols. Princeton: Princeton University Press, 1955.

Barraclough, Geoffrey. *Papal Provisions: Aspects of Church History Constitutional, Legal and Administrative in the Later Middle Ages.* Oxford: Basil Blackwell, 1935.

Bartlett, Robert. *Trial by Fire and Water: The Medieval Judicial Ordeal.* New York: Oxford University Press, 1986.

Beaune, Colette. *Naissance de la nation France.* Paris: Gallimard, 1985.

Becker, Marvin. *Medieval Italy: Constraints and Creativity.* Bloomington: Indiana University Press, 1981.

Becquet, Jean. "La réforme des chapitres cathédraux en France aux XIᵉ et XIIᵉ siècles." *Bulletin Philologique et Historique (jusqu'a 1610) du Comité des Travaux Historiques et Scientifigues,* 1977 for 1975, 31–41.

Benedict, Ruth. *The Chrysanthemum and the Sword: Patterns of Japanese Culture.* Boston: Houghton Mifflin, 1946.

Benson, Robert. *The Bishop-Elect: A Study in Medieval Ecclesiastical Office.* Princeton: Princeton University Press, 1968.

———. "Political *Renovatio:* Two Models from Roman Antiquity." In *Renaissance and Renewal in the Twelfth Century,* edited by Giles Constable and Robert L. Benson, 339–86. Cambridge: Harvard University Press, 1982.

Benton, John F. "Consciousness of Self and Perceptions of Individuality." In *Renaissance and Renewal in the Twelfth Century,* edited by Giles Constable and Robert L. Benson, 263–95. Cambridge: Harvard University Press, 1982.

Berlière, Ursmer. "L'exercice du ministère paroissial par les moines dans le Haut Moyen-Age." *Révue Bénédictine* 39(1927): 227–50.

———. "Le nombre des moines dans les anciens monastères." *Révue Bénédictine* 41(1929); 231–61; 42(1930): 19–42.

Bernstein, Alan. Review of *La naissance du purgatoire,* by Jacques Le Goff. *Speculum* 59(1984): 179–83.

Bezzola, R. "De Roland à Raoul de Cambrai." In *Mélanges de philologie romane et de littérature médiévale offerts à Ernest Hoepffner par ses élèves et ses amis,* 195–213. Publications de la Faculté de l'Université de Strasbourg 113. Paris: Belles Lettres, 1949.

———. *Les origines et la formation de la littérature courtoise en Occident (500–1200).* Paris: Honoré Champion, 1960.

Bienvenu, Jean-Marc. "La réforme grégorienne dans l'archidiocèse de Tours." In *Histoire religieuse de la Touraine,* edited by Guy-Marie Oury, 77–91. Chambray: C. L. D. Normand, 1975.

Bishop, Edmund. *Liturgica Historica: Papers on the Liturgy and Religious Life of the Western Church.* Oxford: Clarendon Press, 1918. Reprint, 1962.

Bloch, Marc. *Feudal Society.* Translated by L. A. Manyon. 2 vols. Chicago: University of Chicago Press, 1961.

Bloch, R. Howard. *Etymologies and Genealogies: A Literary Anthropology of the French Middle Ages.* Chicago: University of Chicago Press, 1983.

———. *Medieval French Literature and Law.* Berkeley: University of California Press, 1977.

Bolton, Brenda M. "Mulieres Sanctae." In *Sanctity and Secularity: The Church and the World,* edited by Derek Baker, 77–95. Studies in Church History 10. New York: Barnes and Noble, 1973.

Bonnes, J. P. "Un des plus grands prédicateurs du XIIᵉ siècle, Geoffroy du Loroux dit Geoffroy Babion." *Revue Bénédictine* 56(1945–46): 174–215.

Bosl, Karl. "Der 'Adelsheilige.' Idealtypus und Wirklichkeit, Gesellschaft und Kultur im merowingerzeitlichen Bayern des 7. und 8. Jahrhunderts." In *Speculum historiale: Geschichte im Spiegel von Geschichtsschreibung und Geschichtsdeutung. Festschrift für Johannes Spörl*, edited by Clemens Bauer, 167–87. Freiburg/Munich: Alber, 1965.

Bosseboeuf, L. A. "Un missel de Marmoutier du XIᵉ s." *Revue de l'Art Chrétien,* n.s. 7(1889): 420–33.

Bouchard, Constance. "The Origins of the French Nobility: A Reassessment." *American Historical Review* 86(1981): 501–32.

_____. *Sword, Miter, and Cloister: Nobility and the Church in Burgundy, 980–1198.* Ithaca: Cornell University Press, 1987.

Boureau, Alain. "Les structures narratives de la *Legenda aurea:* De la variation au grand chant sacré." In *Legenda aurea: Sept siècles de diffusion,* edited by Brenda Dunn-Lardeau, 57–76. Montreal: Bellarmin, 1986.

Bournazel, Eric, "Suger and the Capetians." In *Abbot Suger and Saint Denis,* edited by Paula Lieber Gerson, 55–72. New York: Metropolitan Museum of Art, 1986.

Boussard, Jacques. "L'enclave royale de Saint-Martin de Tours." *Bulletin de la Société Nationale des Antiquaires de France,* 1985, 157–79.

_____. "Essai sur le peuplement de la Touraine du Iᵉʳ au VIIIᵉ siècle." *Moyen Age* 60(1954): 261–91.

_____. "Etude sur la ville de Tours du Iᵉʳ au IVᵉ siècle." *Revue des Etudes Anciennes* 50(1948): 313–29.

_____. "Les évêques de Neustrie avant la réforme grégorienne (950–1050 environ)." *Journal des Savants,* 1970, 161–96.

_____. "L'éviction des tenants de Thibaut de Blois par Geoffroy Martel, comte d'Anjou en 1044." *Moyen Age* 69(1963): 141–49.

_____. "La seigneurie de Bellême aux Xᵉ et XIᵉ siècles." In *Mélanges d'histoire du Moyen Age dédiés à la mémoire de Louis Halphen,* edited by Charles-Edmond Perrin, 43–54. Paris: Presses Universitaires de France, 1951.

_____. "Le trésorier de Saint-Martin de Tours." In *Mémorial de l'année martinienne M.DCCCC.LX–M.DCCCC.LXI,* 67–88. Paris: J. Vrin, 1962.

Branner, Robert. "Historical Aspects of the Reconstruction of Reims Cathedral, 1210–1241." *Speculum* 36(1961): 23–37.

Bredero, Adriaan H. "Cluny et le monachisme carolingien: Continuité et discontinuité." In *Benedictine Culture, 750–1050,* edited by W. Lourdaux and D. Verhelst, 50–75. Louvain: Leuven University Press, 1983.

Bréhier, Louis, and René Aigrain. *Grégoire le Grand, les états barbares et la conquête arabe (590–757).* In *Histoire de l'Eglise depuis les origines jusqu'à nos jours,* general editors Augustin Fliche and Victor Martin, volume 5. Paris: Bloud and Gay, 1938.

Brémond, Claude, Jean-Claude Schmitt, and Jacques Le Goff. *L'"Exemplum."* Typologie des sources du Moyen Age occidental 40. Turnhout: Brepols, 1982.

Brentano, Lujo. "Preliminary Essay on the History and Development of Gilds, and the Origin of Trade-Unions." In *English Gilds,* edited by Toulmin Smith, liii–cxciv. Early English Text Society 40. 1870. Reprint London: Oxford University Press, 1963.

Brooke, Rosalind. "The Lives of St. Francis of Assisi." In *Latin Biography,* edited by T. A. Dorey and Donald R. Dudley. New York: Basic Books, 1967.

Browe, Peter. *Die eucharistischen Wunder des Mittelalters.* Breslauer Studien zur historischen Theologie, n.s. 4. Breslau: Müller und Seiffert, 1938.

Brown, Elizabeth A. R. "La notion de la légitimité et la prophétie à la cour de Philippe Auguste." In *La France de Philippe Auguste: Le temps des mutations,* 77–110. Colloques internationaux du Centre National de la Recherche Scientifique 602. Paris: CNRS, 1982.

Brown, Peter. *The Cult of the Saints: Its Rise and Function in Latin Christianity.* Chicago: University of Chicago Press, 1981.

_____. "Eastern and Western Christendom in Late Antiquity: A Parting of the Ways." In *The Orthodox Churches and the West,* edited by Derek Baker. Studies in Church History 13. Oxford: Basil Blackwell, 1976.

_____. "Relics and Social Status in the Age of Gregory of Tours." In *Society and the Holy in Late Antiquity,* 222–50. Berkeley: University of California Press, 1982.

_____. "Society and the Supernatural: A Medieval Change." *Daedalus* 104(1975): 133–51.

Bur, Michel. *La formation du comté de Champagne, v. 950–v. 1150.* Mémoires des Annales de l'Est 54. Nancy: Publications de l'Université de Nancy II, 1977.

Bynum, Caroline Walker. *Holy Feast and Holy Fast: The Religious Significance of Food to Medieval Women.* Berkeley: University of California Press, 1987.

_____. "Introduction." In *Gender and Religion: Essays on the Complexity of Symbols,* edited by Caroline Walker Bynum, Stevan Harrell, and Paula Richman, 1–20. Boston: Beacon Press, 1986.

_____. *Jesus as Mother: Studies in the Spirituality of the High Middle Ages.* Berkeley: University of California Press, 1982.

_____. "Religious Women in the Later Middle Ages." In *Encyclopedia of World Spirituality,* 1, edited by Jill Raitt, 121–39. New York: Crossroad, 1988.

Cabrol, Fernand. "Litanies." In *Dictionnaire d'archéologie chrétienne et de liturgie,* edited by Fernand Cabrol and Henri Leclercq, 9:2:1540–71. 15 vols. Paris: Letouzey et Ané, 1907–53.

Calin, William. *The Old French Epic of Revolt: Raoul de Cambrai, Renaud de Montauban, Gormond et Isembar.* Geneva: E. Droz, 1962.

Canivez, J.-M. "Arnaud de Bonneval." In *Dictionnaire de spiritualité, ascetique et mystique,* 1:888–90. Paris: G. Beauchesne, 1932–.

Catalogue des manuscrits en écriture latine portant des indications de date, de lieu ou de copiste. Charles Samaran and Robert Marichal, general editors. Vols. 1–. Paris: Centre National de la Recherche Scientifique, 1959–.

Catalogue général des manuscrits des bibliothèques publiques de France, départements. Issued by Ministère de l'Education Nationale, Direction des Bibliothèques de France. Paris: Plon, Nourrit, 1885–.

Catalogus codicum hagiographicorum Bibliothecae regiae Bruxellensis. 2 vols. Edited by Society of Bollandists. Brussels: Polleunis, Ceuterick et Lefébure, 1886, 1889.

Catalogus codicum hagiographicorum Latinorum antiquiorum saeculo XVI qui asservantur in Bibliotheca nationali Parisiensi. Edited by Society of Bollandists. 3 vols. Brussels: Society of Bollandists, 1889–93.

Chambers, E. K. *The Mediaeval Stage.* 2 vols. Oxford: Oxford University Press, 1903.

Chartrou, Josèphe. *L'Anjou de 1109 à 1151.* Paris: Presses Universitaires de France, 1928.

Chélini, J. "Alcuin, Charlemagne et Saint-Martin de Tours." In *Mémorial de l'année martinienne M.DCCCC.LX–M.DCCCC.LXI,* 19–50. Paris: J. Vrin, 1962.

Cheney, C. R. *Episcopal Visitations of Monasteries in the Thirteenth Century.* 2d ed. rev. Philadelphia: Porcupine Press, 1983.

Chenu, M.-D. *Nature, Man, and Society in the Twelfth Century.* Translated by Jerome Taylor and Lester K. Little. Chicago: University of Chicago Press, 1968.

Chevalier, Bernard. "La cité de Tours et Châteauneuf du Xe au XIIIe siècle: Note sur l'échec du mouvement communal dans le centre de la France." *Cahiers d'Histoire* 17(1972): 237–47.

———. *Tours, ville royale, 1356–1520.* Louvain: Vander/Nauwelaerts, 1975.

Chevalier, Cyr Ulysse Joseph. *Repertorium hymnologicum.* 6 vols. Sudsidia Hagiographica 4. Louvain, etc.: Lefever, etc., 1892–1921.

Chibnall, Marjorie. *The World of Orderic Vitalis.* Oxford: Clarendon Press, 1984.

Clanchy, M. T. *From Memory to Written Record: England 1066–1307.* Cambridge: Harvard University Press, 1979.

Conant, Kenneth J. *Benedictine Contributions to Church Architecture.* Latrobe, Pa.: Archabbey Press, 1949.

Congar, Yves. "Modèle monastique et modèle sacerdotal en Occident de Grégoire VII (1073–1085) à Innocent III (1198)." In *Etudes de civilisation médiévale (IXe–XIIe siècles): Mélanges offerts à Edmond-Réné Labande,* 153–60. Poitiers: Centre d'Études Supérieures de Civilisation Médiévale, 1974.

Constable, Giles. *Cluniac Studies.* London: Variorum Reprints, 1980.

———. "The Monastic Policy of Peter the Venerable." In *Pierre Abélard-Pierre le Vénérable,* 119–38. Colloques Internationaux du Centre National de la Recherche Scientifique 546. Paris: CNRS, 1975. Reprinted in Constable, *Cluniac Studies.* London: Variorum Reprints, 1980.

———. *Monastic Tithes: From Their Origins to the Twelfth Century.* Cambridge: Cambridge University Press, 1964.

———. "Papal, Imperial and Monastic Propaganda in the Eleventh and Twelfth Centuries." In *Prédication et propagande au Moyen Age: Islam, Byzance, Occident,* 79–199. Penn-Paris-Dumbarton Oaks Colloquia 3. Organized by George Makdisi, Dominique Sourdel, and Janine Sourdel-Thomine. Paris: Presses Universitaires de France, 1983.

———. "Renewal and Reform in the Religious Life: Concepts and Realities." In *Renaissance and Renewal in the Twelfth Century,* edited by Giles Constable and Robert L. Benson, 37–67. Cambridge: Harvard University Press, 1982.

Constable, Giles, and Robert L. Benson. "Introduction." In *Renaissance and Renewal in the Twelfth Century,* edited by Giles Constable and Robert L. Benson, xvii–xxx. Cambridge: Harvard University Press, 1982.

Coornaert, E. "Les ghildes médiévales (Vᶜ–XIVᶜ siècles)." *Revue Historique* 199(1948): 22–55, 208–43.

Cousin, Patrice. *Abbon de Fleury-sur-Loire.* Paris: P. Lethiellaux, 1954.

Cowdrey, Herbert Edward John. *The Cluniacs and the Gregorian Reform.* Oxford: Clarendon Press, 1970.

Crozet, René. "Recherches sur la cathédrale et les évêques de Tours des origines à la fin du XIIᶜ s." *Bulletin Trimestriel de la Société Archéologique de Touraine* 34(1965): 187–95.

Curtius, Ernst Robert. *European Literature and the Latin Middle Ages.* Translated by Willard R. Trask. Princeton: Princeton University Press, 1973.

Danielou, Jean. *From Shadows to Reality: Studies in the Biblical Typology of the Fathers.* Translated by Dom Wulstan Hibberd. London: Burns and Oates, 1960.

Davis, Natalie Zemon. "The Sacred and the Body Social in Sixteenth-Century Lyon." *Past and Present* 90(1981): 40–70.

———. *Society and Culture in Early Modern France.* Stanford: Stanford University Press, 1975.

Delehaye, Hippolyte. "Guibert, Abbé de Florennes et de Gembloux." *Revue des Questions Historiques* 46(1889): 5–90.

———. "Saint Martin et Sulpice Sévère." *Analecta Bollandiana* 38(1920): 5–136.

Denton, Jeffrey Howard. *English Royal Free Chapels, 1100–1300: A Constitutional Study.* Manchester: Manchester University Press, 1970.

Dereine, Charles. "Chanoines." In *Dictionnaire d'histoire et de géographie écclesiastiques,* 12:353–405. Vols. 1–. Paris: Letouzey et Ané, 1912–.

Devailly, Guy. "Expansion et diversité du monachisme du XIᶜ au XIIᶜ siècle." In *Histoire religieuse de la Touraine,* edited by Guy-Marie Oury, 53–73. Chambray: C. L. D. Normand, 1975.

Dix, Gregory. *The Shape of the Liturgy.* London: Dacre Press, 1945.

Dorange, A. *Catalogue descriptif et raisonné des manuscrits de la bibliothèque de Tours.* Tours: Jules Bouserez, 1875.

Dubois, Jacques. *Un sanctuaire monastique au Moyen Age: Saint-Fiacre-en-Brie.* Paris: Champion, 1976.

————. "La vie des moines dans les prieurés du Moyen Age." *Lettre de Ligugé* 133(1969): 10–33. Reprinted in Dubois, *Histoire monastique en France au XIIe siècle*. London: Variorum Reprints, 1982.

Duby, Georges. "Le budget de l'abbaye de Cluny entre 1080 et 1155." *Annales: Economies, Sociétés, Civilisations* 7(1952): 155–77.

————. "Les chanoines réguliers et la vie économique des XIe et XIIe siècles." In *La vita comune del clero nei secoli XI e XII,* 72–81 Miscellanea del Centro di Studi Medioevali 3. Milan: Società Editrice Vita e Pensiero, 1962.

————. *The Chivalrous Society.* Translated by Cynthia Postan. Berkeley: University of California Press, 1980.

————. *The Early Growth of the European Economy: Warriors and Peasants from the Seventh to the Twelfth Century.* Translated by Howard B. Clarke. Ithaca: Cornell University Press, 1974.

————. *The Knight, the Lady and the Priest: The Making of Modern Marriage in Medieval France.* Translated by Barbara Bray. New York: Pantheon Books, 1983.

————. *Medieval Marriage: Two Models from Twelfth-Century France.* Translated by Elborg Forster. Baltimore: Johns Hopkins University Press, 1978.

————. *Rural Economy and Country Life in the Medieval West.* Translated by Cynthia Postan. Columbia: University of South Carolina Press, 1968.

————. *The Three Orders: Feudal Society Imagined.* Translated by Arthur Goldhammer. Chicago: University of Chicago Press, 1980.

Du Cange, Charles Du Fresne. *Glossarium mediae et infimae latinitatis.* New edition by Léopold Favre. 10 vols. Niort: L. Favre, 1883–87.

Duchesne, Louis. *Fastes épiscopaux de l'ancienne Gaule.* 3 vols. Paris: A. Fontemoing, 1907–15.

————. *Origines du culte chrétien: Etude sur la liturgie latine avant Charlemagne.* 5th ed., rev. and enl. Paris: Boccard, 1925.

Duggan, Lawrence. *Bishop and Chapter: The Governance of the Bishopric of Speyer to 1552.* New Brunswick, N.J.: Rutgers University Press, 1978.

Dumoutet, Edouard. *Corpus Domini: Aux sources de la piété eucharistique médiévale.* Paris: Beauchesne, 1942.

Dunbabin, Jean. *France in the Making, 843–1180.* New York: Oxford University Press, 1985.

Edwards, Kathleen. *The English Secular Cathedrals in the Middle Ages.* 2d ed. Manchester: Manchester University Press, 1967.

Erdmann, Carl. *The Origins of the Idea of Crusade.* Translated by Marshall Baldwin and Walter Goffart. Princeton: Princeton University Press, 1977.

Ewig, E. "Le culte de Saint Martin à l'époque franque." In *Mémorial de l'année martinienne M.DCCCC.LX–M.DCCCC.LXI,* 1–18. Paris: J. Vrin, 1962.

Farmer, Sharon. "Persuasive Voices: Clerical Images of Medieval Wives." *Speculum* 61(1986):517–43.

_____. "Saint Martin's Pentecost: Charisma and Authority in Twelfth-Century Hagiographical Literature." Paper presented at the Spring 1983 meeting of the American Catholic Historical Association.

_____. "Societal Change and Religious Expression: Saint Martin's Cult at Tours, 1050–1200." Ph.D. diss., Harvard University, 1983.

_____. "Softening the Hearts of Men: Women, Embodiment, and Persuasion in the Thirteenth Century." In *Embodied Love: Sensuality and Relationship as Feminist Values,* edited by Paula M. Cooey, Sharon A. Farmer, and Mary Ellen Ross, 115–33. San Francisco: Harper and Row, 1987.

Ferguson, Chris D. "Autobiography as Therapy: Guibert de Nogent, Peter Abelard, and the Making of Medieval Autobiography." *Journal of Medieval and Renaissance Studies* 13(1983): 187–212.

Fiske, Adele M. *Friends and Friendship in the Monastic Tradition.* Cuernavaca, Mexico: Centro Intercultural de Documentación, 1970.

Fliche, Augustin. *Le règne de Philippe Ier, roi de France, 1060–1108.* Paris: Société Française d'Imprimerie et de Librarie, 1912. Reprint Geneva: Slatkine-Megariotis Reprints, 1975.

Folz, Robert. "Pierre le Vénérable et la liturgie." In *Pierre Abélard–Pierre le Vénérable,* 143–61. Colloques Internationaux du Centre National de la Recherche Scientifique 546. Paris: CNRS, 1975.

Fontaine, Jacques. *Sulpice Sévère: Vie de Saint Martin.* 3 vols. Sources Chrétiennes 133–35. Paris: Cerf, 1967–69.

Frank, Roberta. "Viking Atrocity and Skaldic Verse: The Rite of the Blood-Eagle." *English Historical Review* 99(1984): 326–44.

Franz, Adolph. *Die kirchlichen Benediktionen im Mittelalter.* 2 vols. Freiburg-im-Breisgau: Herder, 1909.

Frappier, Jean. *Les chansons de geste du cycle de Guillaume d'Orange.* 2 vols. Paris: Société d'Edition d'Enseignement Supérieur, 1955, 1965.

Freed, John B. *The Counts of Falkenstein: Noble Self-Consciousness in Twelfth-Century Germany.* Transactions of the American Philosophical Society 74, part 6. Philadelphia: American Philosophical Society, 1984.

Fulton, Rachel. "The Liminal Status of the Excommunicated Monk." Unpublished paper.

Gaiffier, B. de. "Mentalité de l'hagiographie médiévale d'après quelques travaux recents." *Analecta Bollandiana* 86(1968): 391–99.

_____. "Le trinubium Annae: Haymon d'Halberstadt ou Haymon d'Auxerre?" *Analecta Bollandiana* 90(1972): 289–98.

Galbraith, V. H. "The Literacy of the Medieval English Kings." *Proceedings of the British Academy* 21(1937): 201–38.

Galinié, Henri. "La résidence des comtes d'Anjou à Tours." *Archéologie Médiévale* 7(1977): 95–107.

Galinié, Henri, and Bernard Randoin. *Les archives du sol à Tours: Survie et avenir de l'archéologie de la ville.* Tours: Société Archéologique de Touraine, 1979.

Gallia Christiana in provincias ecclesiasticas distributa. 3d ed. Edited by Denis de Sainte-Marthe, Benedictines of Saint Maur, and Barthélemy Hauréau. 16 vols. Paris, 1715–1865.

Gantier, Odile. "Recherches sur les possessions et les prieurés de l'abbaye de Marmoutier du Xᶜ au XIIᶜ siècle." *Revue Mabillon,* 3d ser., 53(1963): 93–110, 161–67; 54(1964): 15–24, 56–67, 125–35; 55(1965): 32–44, 65–79.

Gasnault, Pierre. "Etude sur les chartes de Saint-Martin de Tours des origines au milieu de XIIᶜ siècle." *Positions des Thèses, Ecole Nationale des Chartes,* 1953, 37–40.

————. "La 'Narratio in reversione beati Martini a Burgundia' du Pseudo-Eudes de Cluny: Sources et influence." *Studia Anselmiana* 46(1961): 159–74.

————. "La sainte ampoule de Marmoutier." *Analecta Bollandiana* 100(1982): 243–57.

————. "Le tombeau de Saint Martin et les invasions normandes dans l'histoire et dans la légende." In *Mémorial de l'année martinienne M.DCCCC.LX–M.DCC-CC.LXI,* 51–66. Paris: J. Vrin, 1962.

Gasté, Armand. "Les drames liturgiques de la cathédrale de Rouen." *Revue Catholique de Normandie,* 1893, 349–72, 477–500, 573–604.

Gautier, Léon. *La chevalerie.* New ed. Paris: C. Delagrave, 1890.

Geary, Patrick J. *Before France and Germany: The Creation and Transformation of Merovingian Gaul.* New York: Oxford University Press, 1988.

————. "La coercion des saints dans la pratique religieuse médiévale." In *La culture populaire au Moyen Age,* edited by Pierre Boglioni, 145–61. Montreal: Aurore, 1979.

————. *Furta Sacra: Thefts of Relics in the Central Middle Ages.* Princeton: Princeton University Press, 1978.

————. "Humiliation of Saints." In *Saints and Their Cults: Studies in Religious Sociology, Folklore and History,* edited by Stephen Wilson, 123–40. Cambridge: Cambridge University Press, 1983.

————. "The Ninth-Century Relic Trade: A Response to Popular Piety?" In *Religion and the People, 800–1700,* edited by James Obelkevich, 8–19. Chapel Hill: University of North Carolina Press, 1979.

Genicot, Léopold. *Les généalogies.* Typologie des Sources du Moyen Age Occidental 15. Turnhout: Brepols, 1975.

Giry, Arthur. *Les établissements de Rouen: Etudes sur l'histoire des institutions municipales.* 2 vols. Paris: F. Vieweg, 1883–85. Reprint Geneva: Slatkine, 1975.

————. *Manuel de diplomatique.* 2 vols. Paris: Félix Alcan, 1925.

Gold, Penny Schine. *The Lady and the Virgin: Image, Attitude, and Experience in Twelfth-Century France.* Chicago: University of Chicago Press, 1985.

Gougaud, Louis. *Anciennes coutumes claustrales.* Vienne, France: Abbaye Saint-Martin de Ligugé, 1930.

Graham, Rose. "An Appeal, about 1175 for the Building Fund of St. Paul's Cathedral Church." *Journal of the British Archaeological Association,* 3d ser. 10(1945–47): 73–76.

Grandmaison, Charles de. *Chronique de l'abbaye de Beaumont-lez-Tours.* Mémoires de la Société Archéologique de Touraine 26. Tours: Rouillé-Ladevèze, 1877.

———. *Tours archéologique, histoire et monuments.* Paris: H. Campion, 1874.

Griffe, Elie. *La Gaule chrétienne à l'époque romaine.* 3 vols. Paris: Letouzey et Ané, 1964–65.

Griffiths, Quentin. "The Capetian Kings and St. Martin of Tours." *Studies in Medieval and Renaissance History* [old series 19] 9(1987): 83–133.

Guenée, Bernard. *Histoire et culture historique dans l'Occident médiéval.* Paris: Aubier Montaigne, 1980.

Guillot, Olivier. *Le comte d'Anjou et son entourage au XIᵉ siècle.* 2 vols. Paris: A. et J. Picard, 1972.

Haenens, Albert d'. *Les invasions normandes en Belgique au IXᵉ siècle.* Recueil de Travaux d'Histoire et de Philologie, ser. 4, 38. Louvain: Publications Universitaires de Louvain, 1967.

———. *Les invasions normandes: Une catastrophe?* Paris: Flammarion, 1970.

Hallam, Elizabeth. *Capetian France, 987–1328.* London: Longman House, 1980.

Hallinger, Kassius. *Gorze-Kluny: Studien zu den monastischen Lebensformen und Gegensätzen im Hochmittelalter.* Studia Anselmiana 22–25. Rome: "Orbis Catholicus," Herder, 1950–51.

Halphen, Louis. *Le comté d'Anjou au XIᵉ siècle.* Paris: A. Picard, 1906. Reprint Geneva: Slatkine-Megariotis Reprints, 1974.

Hanning, Robert. *The Vision of History in Early Britain: From Gildas to Geoffrey of Monmouth.* New York: Columbia University Press, 1966.

Hautcoeur, Edouard. *Histoire de l'église collégiale et du chapitre de Saint-Pierre de Lille.* 3 vols. Société d'Études de la Province de Cambrai 4–6. Lille: L. Quarré; Paris: A. Picard, 1896–99.

Head, Thomas. "Andrew of Fleury and the Peace League of Bourges." In *Essays on the Peace of God: The Church and the People in Eleventh-Century France,* edited by Thomas Head and Richard Landes. *Historical Reflections/Réflexions Historiques* 14(1987): 513–29.

———. *Hagiography and the Cult of the Saints in the Diocese of Orléans, 800–1200.* Cambridge: Cambridge University Press. 1990.

Heath, Robert G. *Crux Imperatorum Philosophia: Imperial Horizons of the Cluniac Confraternitas, 964–1109.* Pittsburgh: Pickwick Press, 1976.

Heers, Jacques. *Fêtes, jeux et joutes dans les sociétés d'Occident à la fin du Moyen Age.* Paris: J. Vrin, 1971.

Heinzelmann, Martin. *Translationsberichte und andere Quellen des Reliquienkultes.* Typologie des Sources du Moyen Age Occidental 33. Turnhout: Brepols, 1979.

Herlihy, David. "Land, Family and Women in Continental Europe, 701–1200." In *Women in Medieval Society,* edited by Susan Mosher Stuard, 13–45. Philadelphia: University of Pennsylvania Press, 1976.

———. *Medieval Households.* Cambridge: Harvard University Press, 1985.

Herrmann-Mascard, Nicole. *Les reliques des saints: Formation coutumière d'un droit.* Paris: Klincksieck, 1975.

Histoire littéraire de la France. Edited by Benedictines of Saint-Maur and Members of Académie des Inscriptions et Belles-Lettres. 41 vols. Paris: Imprimerie Nationale, 1733–[1981].

Hobsbawm, Eric, and Terence Ranger, eds. *The Invention of Tradition.* Cambridge: Cambridge University Press, 1983.

Hourlier, Jacques. *L'âge classique, 1140–1378: Les religieux.* Histoire du Droit et des Institutions de l'Eglise en Occident 10. Paris: Cujas, 1974.

Hourlier, Jacques, and Maria Chiara Celleti. "Maiolo." In *Bibliotheca sanctorum,* 8:564–67. 13 vols. Rome: Istituto Giovanni XXIII della Pontificia Università Lateranense, 1961–69.

Hughes, Diane Owen. "From Brideprice to Dowry in Mediterranean Europe." *Journal of Family History* 3(1978): 262–96.

Huneycutt, Lois. "The Idea of the Perfect Princess: The Life of St. Margaret of Scotland in the Reign of Matilda II (1100–1118)." *Anglo-Norman Studies* 12 (1990), 81–97.

––––––. "Medieval Queenship." *History Today* 39(1989): 16–22.

Hunt, Noreen. *Cluny under Saint Hugh, 1049–1109.* London: E. Arnold, 1967.

Huyghebaert, Nicolas. *Les documents nécrologiques.* Typologie des Sources du Moyen Age Occidental 4. Turnhout: Brepols, 1972.

––––––. "Les femmes laïques dans la vie religieuse des XIᵉ et XIIᵉ siècles dans la province ecclésiastique de Reims." In *I laici nella societas christiana dei secoli XI et XII: Atti della terza Settimana internazionale di studio,* 346–89. Milan, 1968.

Hyde, J. K. "Medieval Descriptions of Cities." *Bulletin of the John Rylands Library* 48 (1965–66): 308–40.

––––––. *Society and Politics in Medieval Italy: The Evolution of the Civil Life, 1000–1350.* New York: St. Martin's Press, 1973.

Imbart de la Tour, Pierre. *Les élections épiscopales dans l'église de France du IXᵉ au XIIᵉ siècle.* Paris: Hachette, 1890. Reprint Geneva: Slatkine-Megariotis Reprints, 1974.

Jaeger, C. Stephen. *The Origins of Courtliness: Civilizing Trends and the Formation of Courtly Ideals, 939–1210.* Philadelphia: University of Pennsylvania Press, 1985.

James, Edwin Oliver. *Seasonal Feasts and Festivals.* London: Thames and Hudson, 1961.

Johnson, Penelope D. *Prayer, Patronage and Power: The Abbey of La Trinité, Vendôme, 1032–1187.* New York: New York University Press, 1981.

Jones, Charles W. *Saint Nicholas of Myra, Bari, and Manhattan: Biography of a Legend.* Chicago: University of Chicago Press, 1978.

Jordan, William Chester. *From Servitude to Freedom: Manumission in the Sénonais in the Thirteenth Century.* Philadelphia: University of Pennsylvania Press, 1986.

Kantorowicz, Ernst H. *Laudes Regiae: A Study in Liturgical Acclamations and Medieval Ruler Worship*. Berkeley: University of California Press, 1946.

Keane, Mary Michael. "Martin Hymns of the Middle Ages: A Collection and Analysis of Hymns in Honor of Saint Martin of Tours up to c. 1300." Ph.D. diss., Catholic University of America, 1968.

Kennedy, V. L. "The Moment of Consecration and Elevation of the Host." *Mediaeval Studies* 6(1944): 121–50.

King, Archdale A. *Liturgies of the Religious Orders*. London: Longmans, 1955.

Knowles, David. "The Reforming Decrees of Peter the Venerable." In *Petrus Venerabilis, 1156–1956*, edited by Giles Constable and James Kritzeck, 1–20. Studia Anselmiana 40. Rome: Herder, 1956.

Koehler, Erich. "Observations historiques et sociologiques sur la poésie des troubadours." *Cahiers de Civilisation Médiévale* 7(1964): 27–51.

Koziol, Geoffrey. "Pageants of Renewal: Translations of Saints in the Province of Reims (893–980)." Paper delivered at the December 1987 meeting of the American Historical Association.

Krappe, Alexander. "The Squire's Adventure in *Perlesvaus*." In *Balor with the Evil Eye: Studies in Celtic and French Literature*, 114–25. New York: Institut des Etudes Françaises, Columbia University, 1927.

Kretzenbacher, Leopold. *Santa Lucia und die Lutzelfrau: Volksglaube und Hochreligion in Spannungsfeld Mittel- und Südosteuropas*. Munich: R. Oldenbourg, 1959.

Lackner, Bede K. *The Eleventh-Century Background of Cîteaux*. Washington, D.C.: Cistercian Publications, 1972.

Landes, Richard. "The Dynamics of Heresy and Reform in Limoges: A Study of Popular Participation in the 'Peace of God' (994–1033)." In *Essays on the Peace of God: The Church and the People in Eleventh-Century France*, edited by Thomas Head and Richard Landes. *Historical Reflections/Réflexions Historiques* 14(1987): 467–511.

Latouche, Robert. *The Birth of Western Economy: Economic Aspects of the Dark Ages*. Translated by E. M. Wilkinson. New York: Harper Torchbooks, 1966.

Laurent, Jacques. "La prière pour les défunts et les obituaires dans l'ordre de Cîteaux." In *Mélanges Saint Bernard*, 383–96. XXIVᵉ Congrès de l'Association Bourguignonne de Sociétés Savantes. Dijon: Association des Amis de Saint Bernard, 1953.

Leclercq, Henri. "Chape de Saint Martin." In *Dictionnaire d'archéologie chrétienne et de liturgie*, 3:1:381–90. 15 vols. Paris: Letouzey et Ané, 1907–53.

———. "Marc (Procession de Saint)." Ibid. 10:2:1740–41.

———. "Quatre-temps." Ibid. 14:2:2014–17.

———. "Tours." Ibid. 15:2:2570–2677.

Leclercq, Jean. *Aux sources de la spiritualité occidentale: Étapes et constantes*. Paris: Cerf, 1964.

———. *Etudes sur le vocabulaire monastique du Moyen Age*. Studia Anselmiana 48. Rome: "Orbis Catholicus," Herder, 1961.

————. *The Love of Learning and the Desire for God: A Study of Monastic Culture*. Translated by Catherine Misrahi. Reprint New York: New American Library of Western Literature, 1962.

————. *Otia monastica: Etudes sur le vocabulaire de la contemplation au Moyen Age*. Studia Anselmiana 51. Rome: "Orbis Catholicus," Herder, 1963.

————. "Recherches sur d'anciens sermons monastiques." *Revue Mabillon*, 3d ser., 36(1946): 1–14.

————. "Solitude and Solidarity: Medieval Women Recluses." In *Medieval Religious Women II: Peaceweavers*, edited by Lillian Thomas and John A. Nichols, 67–83. Cistercian Studies 72. Kalamazoo, Mich.: Cistercian Publications, 1987.

————. "Un traité sur la 'profession des abbés' au XIIᵉ siècle." Studia Anselmiana 50.177–91. Rome: "Orbis Catholicus," Herder, 1962.

Lecoy de la Marche, Albert. *Saint Martin*. Tours: A. Mame, 1881.

Le Goff, Jacques. "L'apogée de la France urbaine médiévale." In *La ville médiévale*, edited by Jacques Le Goff, Jacques Rossiaud, and André Chédeville, 189–405. Histoire de la France Urbaine 2. Paris: Seuil, 1980.

————. *The Birth of Purgatory*. Translated by Arthur Goldhammer. Chicago: University of Chicago Press, 1984.

————. *Time, Work, and Culture in the Middle Ages*. Translated by Arthur Goldhammer. Chicago: University of Chicago Press, 1980.

Le Goff, Jacques, Jacques Rossiaud, and André Chédeville. *La ville médiévale des Carolingiens à la Renaissance*. Histoire de la France Urbaine 2. Paris: Seuil, 1980.

Lelong, Charles. *La basilique Saint-Martin de Tours*. Chambray: C. L. D. Normand, 1986.

————. "Etudes sur l'abbaye de Marmoutier." *Bulletin Trimestriel de la Société Archéologique de Touraine* 39(1980): 279–320.

————. "Observations et hypothèses sur l'église abbatiale gothique de Marmoutier." *Bulletin Monumental* 138(1980): 117–71.

————. "Recherches sur l'abbatiale de Marmoutier à l'époque romane." *Académie des Inscriptions et Belles-Lettres, Comptes Rendus des Séances*, 1976, 704–34.

Lemarignier, Jean François. *Etude sur les privilèges d'exemption et de juridiction ecclésiastique des abbayes normandes depuis les origines jusqu'en 1140*. Archives de la France Monastique 44. Paris: A. Picard, 1937.

————. "L'exemption monastique et les origines de la réforme grégorienne." In *A Cluny: Congrès scientifique. Fêtes et cérémonies liturgiques en honneur des saints abbés Odon et Odilon, 9–11 juillet 1949*, 288–340. Société des Amis de Cluny. Dijon: Bernigaud et Privat, 1951.

————. "Political and Monastic Structures in France at the End of the Tenth and the Beginning of the Eleventh Century." Translated by Fredric L. Cheyette. In *Lordship and Community in Medieval Europe, Selected Readings*, edited by Fredric L. Cheyette, 100–127. New York: Holt, Rinehart and Winston, 1968.

Leriget, Marthe. *Des lois et impôts somptuaires*. Montpellier: "Abeille," 1919.

Leroquais, Victor. *Les bréviaires manuscrits des bibliothèques publiques de France.* 5 vols. and volume of plates. Paris: Protat Frères, 1934.

_____. *Les sacramentaires et les missels manuscrits des bibliothèques publiques de France.* 3 vols. Paris, 1924.

Le Roy Ladurie, Emmanuel. *Montaillou: The Promised Land of Error.* Translated by Barbara Bray. New York: G. Braziller, 1978.

Lesne, Emile. "Les origines de la prébende." *Revue Historique de Droit Français et Etranger,* 4th ser. 8(1929): 242–90.

Lévêque, Pierre. "Histoire de l'abbaye de Marmoutier jusqu'au XIᵉ siècle." *Positions des thèses: Ecole National des Chartes,* 1901, 93–101.

_____. "Trois actes faux ou interpolés des comtes Eudes et Robert et du roi Raoul en faveur de l'abbaye de Marmoutier." *Bibliothèque de l'Ecole des Chartes* 64(1903): 54–82, 289–305.

Lewis, Andrew W. "Dynastic Structures and Capetian Throne-Right: The Views of Giles of Paris." *Traditio* 33(1977): 225–52.

_____. *Royal Succession in Capetian France: Studies on Familial Order and the State.* Harvard Historical Studies 100. Cambridge: Harvard University Press, 1981.

Lex, Léonce. "Eudes, Comte de Blois, de Tours, de Chartes de Troyes et de Meaux (995–1037) et Thibaud, son frère (995–1004)." *Mémoires de la Société Académique d'Agriculture, des Sciences, Arts et Belles-Lettres du Département de l'Aube,* 3d ser., 28(1891): 191–383.

Little, Lester K. *Religious Poverty and the Profit Economy in Medieval Europe.* Ithaca: Cornell University Press, 1978.

Lopez, Robert S. *The Commercial Revolution of the Middle Ages, 950–1350.* Englewood Cliffs, N.J.: Prentice-Hall, 1971.

Lot, Ferdinand. *The End of the Ancient World and the Beginning of the Middle Ages.* Translated by Philip and Mariette Leon. New York: Harper, 1961.

_____. *Etudes sur le règne de Hugues Capet et la fin du Xᵉ siècle.* Paris: E. Bouillon, 1903.

Mabille, Emile. *Les invasions normandes dans la Loire et les pérégrinations du corps de St. Martin.* Paris: Henaux, etc., 1869.

_____. "Notice sur les divisions territoriales et la topographie de l'ancienne province de Touraine." *Bibliothèque de l'Ecole des Chartes,* 6th ser. 27(1866): 335–83.

_____. *La pancarte noire de Saint-Martin de Tours brulée en 1793 et restituée d'après les textes imprimés et manuscrits.* Paris: Librairie de Henaux, 1866.

Mabillon, Jean. *Annales ordinis S. Benedicti.* 6 vols. Lucca: Typis L. Venturini, 1739–45.

McGuire, Brian Patrick. *Friendship and Community: The Monastic Experience, 350–1250.* Kalamazoo, Mich.: Cistercian Publications, 1988.

McLaughlin, Molly Megan. "Consorting with Saints: Prayer for the Dead in Early Medieval French Society." Ph.D. diss., Stanford University, 1985.

Marot, Pierre, and Jean-Loup Lemaître. *Répertoire des documents nécrologiques français*. 2 vols. Recueil des Historiens de la France. Paris: Imprimerie Nationale, 1980.

Martène, Edmond. *Histoire de l'abbaye de Marmoutier*. Annotated by C. Chevalier. 2 vols. Mémoires de la Société Archéologique de Touraine 24, 25. Tours: Guilland-Verger, 1874–75.

Martimort, Aimé Georges. *La documentation liturgique de Dom Edmond Martène*. Studi e Testi 279. Vatican: Biblioteca Apostolica Vaticana, 1978.

Martin, Henri. "Autour de Thomas Pacitius, prieur de la collégiale de Loches." *Bulletin Trimestriel de la Société Archéologique de Touraine* 41(1986): 389–95.

Mas-Latrie, Louis de. *Trésor de chronologie d'histoire et de géographie pour l'étude et l'emploi des documents du Moyen Age*. Paris: V. Palmé, 1889.

Meersseman, Gérard G. *Ordo fraternitatis: Confraternite e pietà dei laici nel medioevo*. 3 vols. Italia Sacra, Studi e Documenti di Storia Ecclesiastica 24–26. Rome: Herder, 1977.

Mesnard, P. "La collégiale de Saint-Martin à l'époque des Valois." In *Mémorial de l'année martinienne M.DCCCC. LX–M.DCCCCLXI*, 89–100. Paris: J. Vrin, 1962.

Mirot, Léon. *Manuel de géographie historique de la France*. 2d ed. Edited by Albert Mirot. 2 vols. Paris: A. et J. Picard, 1947–50.

Molinier, Auguste. *Les obituaires français au Moyen Age*. Paris: Imprimerie Nationale, 1890.

Moore, R. I. *The Formation of a Persecuting Society: Power and Deviance in Western Europe, 950–1250*. Oxford: Basil Blackwell, 1987.

Moorman, John. *A History of the Franciscan Order*. Oxford: Clarendon Press, 1968.

Morris, Colin. *The Discovery of the Individual, 1050–1200*. New York: Harper and Row, 1972.

Mostert, Marco. *The Political Theology of Abbo of Fleury: A Study of the Ideas about Society and Law of the Tenth-Century Monastic Reform Movement*. Hilversum: Verloren, 1987.

Muir, Edward. *Civic Ritual in Renaissance Venice*. Princeton: Princeton University Press, 1981.

Murphy, James. J. *Rhetoric in the Middle Ages: A History of Rhetorical Theory from Saint Augustine to the Renaissance*. Berkeley: University of California Press, 1974.

Murray, Alexander. *Reason and Society in the Middle Ages*. Oxford: Clarendon Press, 1978.

Mussat, André. *Le style gothique de l'ouest de la France, XIIe–XIIIe siècles*. Paris: A. et J. Picard, 1963.

Musset, Lucien. *Les invasions: Le second assaut contre l'Europe chrétienne (VIIe–XIe siècles)*. Paris: Presses Universitaires de France, 1965.

_____. "La renaissance urbaine des Xᵉ et XIᵉ siècles dans l'ouest de la France: Problèmes et hypothèses de travail." In *Etudes de civilisation médiévale, IXᵉ–XIIᵉ siècles: Mélanges offerts à Edmond-Réné Labande*, 2;563–75. 2 vols. Poitiers: Centre d'Etudes Supérierues de Civilisation Médiévale, 1974.

Neiske, Franz. "Vision und Totengedenken." *Frühmittelalterliche Studien: Jahrbuch des Instituts für Frühmittelalterforschung der Universität Münster* 20(1986): 138–85.

Newman, William Mendel. *Le domaine royal sous les premiers Capétians (987–1180)*. Paris: Librairie de Recueil Sirey, 1937.

Omont, Henri. "Deux incunables imprimés à Tours le 7 mai 1496." *Bok-Och Bibliotheks-historiska Studier tellägnade Isak Collijn*, 153–60. Uppsala: Almqvist och Wiksell, 1925.

Ong, Walter J. *The Presence of the Word: Some Prolegomena for Cultural and Religious History*. New Haven: Yale University Press, 1967.

Oury, Guy-Marie. "Culte et liturgie de St. Martin." *Ami du Clergé*, 8th ser. 44(November 2, 1961): 641–50.

_____. "L'érémitisme à Marmoutier aux XIᵉ et XIIᵉ siècles." *Bulletin Trimestriel de la Société Archéologique de Touraine* 33(1963): 319–33.

_____. "L'érémitisme dans l'ancien diocèse de Tours au XIIᵉ siècle." *Revue Mabillon* 60(1970): 43–92.

_____. "L'idéal monastique dans la vie canoniale: Le bienheureux Hervé de Tours (+1022)." *Revue Mabillon* 52(1962): 1–29.

_____. "Les messes de Saint Martin dans les sacramentaires Gallicans, Romano-Francs et Milanais." *Etudes Grégoriennes* 5(1962): 73–97.

_____. "La reconstruction monastique dans l'Ouest: L'abbé Gauzbert de St.-Julien de Tours (v. 990–1007)." *Revue Mabillon* 54(1964): 69–124.

_____. "Les sept dormants de Marmoutier: La vocation à la réclusion." *Analecta Bollandiana* 99(1981): 315–27.

Patin, J.-P. Valery, and Jacques Le Goff. "A propos de la typologie des miracles dans le *Liber de miraculis* de Pierre le Vénérable." In *Pierre Abélard–Pierre le Vénérable*, 181–87. Colloques Internationaux du Centre Nationale de la Recherche Scientifique 546. Paris: CNRS, 1975.

Penco, Gregorio. "Il tema dell'Esodo nella spiritualità monastica." In *Bibbia e spiritualità*, edited by C. Vagaggini, 337–77. Rome: Edizioni Paoline, 1967.

Petit-Dutaillis, Charles. *The French Communes in the Middle Ages*. Translated by Joan Vickers. Europe in the Middle Ages 6. Amsterdam: North-Holland, 1978.

_____. *La monarchie féodale en France et en Angleterre (Xᵉ–XIIIᵉ siècle)*. Evolution de l'Humanité 29. Paris: A. Michel, 1971.

Pietri, Luce. *La ville de Tours du IVᵉ au VIᵉ siècle: Naissance d'une cité chrétienne*. Rome: Ecole Française de Rome, 1983.

Plat, Gabriel. *L'art de bâtir en France des Romains à l'an 1100*. Paris: Editions d'Art et d'Histoire, 1939.

Poly, Jean-Pierre, and Eric Bournazel. "Couronne et mouvance: Institutions et représentations mentales." In *La France de Philippe-Auguste: Le temps des mutations*, 217–34. Paris: Centre National de la Recherche Scientifique, 1982.

Prévost, Arthur. "Arnaud, Arnold, et Ernaud de Bonneval." In *Dictionnaire d'Histoire et de Géographie Ecclésiastiques*, 4:421–23. Vols. 1–. Paris: Letouzey et Ané, 1912–.

Prinz, Friedrich. *Frühes Mönchtum im Frankenreich: Kulture und Gesellschaft in Gallien, den Rheinlanden und Bayern am Beispiel der monastischen Entwicklung (4. bis 8. Jahrhundert)*. Munich: R. Oldenbourg, 1965.

Pycke, Jacques. *Le chapitre cathédral Nôtre-Dame de Tournai de la fin du XIᵉ siècle à la fin du XIIIᵉ siècle: Son organisation, sa vie, ses membres*. Recueil de travaux d'histoire et de philologie; ser. 6, fasc. 30. Brussels: Nauwelaerts, 1986.

Rabory, J. *Histoire de Marmoutier*. Paris, 1911.

Radding, Charles M. "The Evolution of Medieval Mentalities: A Cognitive–Structural Approach." *American Historical Review* 83(1978): 577–97.

Rainey, Ronald E. "Sumptuary Legislation in Renaissance Florence." Ph.D. diss., Columbia University, 1985.

Ramackers, Johannes. "Analekten zur Geschichte des Reformpapsttums und der Cluniazenser." *Quellen und Forschungen aus Italienischen Archiven und Bibliotheken, Herausgegeben vom Preussischen Historischen Institut in Rom* 23(1931–32): 22–52.

Reames, Sherry. *The Legenda Aurea: A Reexamination of Its Paradoxical History*. Madison: University of Wisconsin Press, 1985.

———. "Saint Martin of Tours in the *Legenda Aurea* and Before." *Viator: Medieval and Renaissance Studies* 12(1981): 131–64.

Remensnyder, Amy. "Bernard of Angers and the *Liber Miraculorum Sancte Fidis*: Lay and Clerical Perceptions of Miracles." Paper delivered at the March 1987 meeting of the Medieval Association of the Pacific.

Reynolds, Susan. *Kingdoms and Communities in Western Europe, 900–1300*. Oxford: Clarendon Press, 1984.

Riché, Pierre. "Consequences des invasions normandes sur la culture monastique dans l'Occident franc." In *I Normanni e la loro espansione in Europa nell'alto medioevo*, 705–21. Settimane di Studio del Centro italiano di Studi Sull'alto Medioevo 16. Spoleto: Presso la Sede del Centro, 1969.

Robin, Françoise. "Les chapelles seigneuriales et royales françaises au temps de Louis XI." In *La France de la fin du XVᵉ siècle: Renouveau et apogée*, edited by Bernard Chevalier and Philippe Contamine, 237–52. Paris: Centre National de la Recherche Scientifique, 1985.

Robinet, André. "Un conflit entre pouvoir civil and pouvoir ecclésiastique: Voies de faits et voies de droit entre comtes de Blois et abbés de Marmoutier." *Bulletin Trimestriel de la Société Archéologique de Touraine* 39(1981): 781–809.

Romilly, Jacqueline de. *Magic and Rhetoric in Ancient Greece*. Cambridge: Harvard University Press, 1975.

Rosenwein, Barbara. *Rhinoceros Bound: Cluny in the Tenth Century.* Philadelphia: University of Pennsylvania Press, 1982.

———. "Rules and the 'Rule' at Tenth-Century Cluny." *Studia Monastica* 19(1977): 307–20.

Rosof, Patricia J. F. "The Anchoress in the Twelfth and Thirteenth Centuries." In *Medieval Religious Women II: Peaceweavers,* edited by Lillian Thomas and John A. Nichols, 123–43. Cistercian Studies 72. Kalamazoo, Mich.: Cistercian Publications, 1987.

Said, Edward. "On Repetition." In *The Literature of Fact: Selected Papers from the English Institute,* edited by Angus Fletcher, 135–58. New York: Columbia University Press, 1976.

Santifaller, Leo, ed. *Quellen und Forschungen zum Urkunden- und Kanzleiwesen Papst Gregors VII.* Studi e Testi 190. Vatican: Biblioteca Apostolica Vaticana, 1957–.

Saxer, Victor. *Le culte de Marie Madeleine en Occident: Des origines à la fin du Moyen Age.* 2 vols. Cahiers d'Archéologie et d'Histoire 3. Paris: Clavreuil, 1959.

Schmitt, Jean-Claude. *The Holy Greyhound.* Translated by Martin Thom. Cambridge: Cambridge University Press, 1983.

———. "Jeunes et danse de chevaux de bois: Le folklore méridional dans la littérature des exempla." *Cahiers de Fanjeaux* 11(1976): 127–58.

———. "Les revenants dans la société féodale." *Temps de la Réflexion* 3(1982): 285–306.

Schmitz, Philibert. "L'influence de Saint Benôit d'Aniane dans l'histoire de l'ordre de Saint-Benôit." In *Il monachesimo nell'alto medioevo e la formazione della civiltà occidentale,* 401–15. Settimane di Studio del Centro Italiano di Studi Sull'alto Medioevo 4. Spoleto: Presso la Sede del Centro, 1957.

———. "La liturgie de Cluny." In *Spiritualità Cluniacense,* 85–99. Convegni del Centro di Studi Sulla Spiritualità Medievale 2. Todi: Presso l'Accademia Tudertina, 1960.

Sébillot, Paul. *Le folk-lore de France.* 4 vols. Paris: Librairie Orientale et Américaine, 1904–7.

Semmler, Josef. "Benedictus II: Una regula—una consuetudo." In *Benedictine Culture, 750–1050,* edited by W. Lourdaux and D. Verhelst, 1–49. Louvain: Leuven University Press, 1983.

Semmler, Josef, and Heinrich Bacht. "Benedikt von Aniane." In *Lexikon des Mittelalters,* 1:1864–67. Munich: Artemis, 1980–.

Sigal, Pierre-André. "Un aspect du culte des saints: Le châtiment divin aux XIe et XIIe siècles d'après la littérature hagiographique du Midi de la France." *Cahiers de Fanjeaux* 11(1976): 39–59.

———. *L'homme et le miracle dans la France médiévale (XIe–XIIe siècle).* Paris: Cerf, 1985.

———. "Les voyages de reliques aux onzième et douzième siècles." In *Voyage, quête, pèlerinage dans la littérature et la civilisation médiévale.* Senefiance 2(1976): 75–104.

Silvestre, Hubert. "Le problème des faux au Moyen Age." *Moyen Age* 66(1960): 351–70.

Sot, Michel. *Gesta episcoporum, gesta abbatum.* Typologie des Sources du Moyen Age Occidental 37. Turnhout: Brepols, 1981.

―――. "Historiographie episcopale et modèle familial en Occident au IXᵉ siècle." *Annales: Economies, Sociétés, Civilisations* 33(1978): 433–49.

Southern, Sir Richard. "Aspects of the European Tradition of Historical Writing: 2. Hugh of St. Victor and the Idea of Historical Development." *Transactions of the Royal Historical Society,* 5th ser. 21(1971): 159–79.

―――. "Aspects of the European Tradition of Historical Writing: 4. The Sense of the Past." *Transactions of the Royal Historical Society,* 5th ser. 23(1973): 243–63.

―――. "Between Heaven and Hell." *Times Literary Supplement,* June 18, 1982, 651–52.

―――. *The Making of the Middle Ages.* New Haven: Yale University Press, 1953.

―――. *Saint Anselm and His Biographer: A Study of Monastic Life and Thought, 1059–c. 1130.* Cambridge: Cambridge University Press, 1963.

―――. *Western Society and the Church in the Middle Ages.* Harmondsworth, England: Penguin Books, 1970.

Spiegel, Gabrielle. *The Chronicle Tradition of Saint Denis: A Survey.* Brookline, Mass.: Classical Folia Editions, 1978.

―――. "The Cult of St. Denis and Capetian Kingship." *Journal of Medieval History* 1(1975): 43–69. Reprinted in *Saints and Their Cults: Studies in Religious Sociology, Folklore, and History,* edited by Stephen Wilson, 141–68. Cambridge: Cambridge University Press, 1983.

―――. "Genealogy: Form and Function in Medieval Historical Narrative." *History and Theory: Studies in the Philosophy of History* 22(1983): 43–53.

Stancliffe, Clare. *St. Martin and His Hagiographer: History and Miracle in Sulpicius Severus.* Oxford: Clarendon Press, 1983.

Stock, Brian. *The Implications of Literacy: Written Language and Models of Interpretation in the Eleventh and Twelfth Centuries.* Princeton: Princeton University Press, 1983.

―――. "Medieval Literacy, Linguistic Theory and Social Organization." *New Literary History* 16(1984): 13–29.

Strayer, Joseph. *On the Medieval Origins of the Modern State.* Princeton: Princeton University Press, 1970.

Talbot, C. H. "The Date and Author of the Riposte." In *Petrus Venerabilis, 1156–1956,* 72–80. Studia Anselmiana 40. Rome: "Orbis Catholicus," Herder, 1957.

Teetaert, Amédée. *La confession aux laïques dans l'église latine depuis le VIIIᵉ jusqu'au XIVᵉ siècle.* Paris: J. Gabalda, 1926.

Tentler, Thomas N. *Sin and Confession on the Eve of the Reformation.* Princeton: Princeton University Press, 1977.

Thompson, Stith. *Motif-Index of Folk Literature*. Rev. and enl. ed. 6 vols. Bloomington: Indiana University Press, 1955–58.

Tierney, Brian. *The Crisis of Church and State, 1050–1300*. Englewood Cliffs, N.J.: Prentice-Hall, 1964.

Trexler, Richard. *Public Life in Renaissance Florence*. New York: Academic Press, 1980.

Tricard, Jean. "La Touraine d'un Tourangeau au XIIᵉ siècle." In *Le métier d'historien au Moyen Age: Etudes sur l'historiographie médiévale*, edited by Bernard Guenée, 79–93. Paris: Université de Paris I, Panthéon-Sorbonne, Centre de Recherches sur l'Histoire de l'Occident Médiévale, 1977.

Tubach, Frederic C. *Index Exemplorum: A Handbook of Medieval Religious Tales*. FF Communications 204. Helsinki: Academia Scientiarum Fennica, 1969.

Turner, Victor. *The Forest of Symbols: Aspects of Ndembu Ritual*. Ithaca: Cornell University Press, 1967.

Van Dam, Raymond. *Leadership and Community in Late Antique Gaul*. Berkeley: University of California Press, 1985.

Van den Bosch, J. *Capa, basilica, monasterium et le culte de Saint Martin de Tours: Etude lexicologique et sémasiologique*. Nijmegen: Dekker en Van de Vegt, 1959.

Van der Straeten, Joseph. *Les manuscrits hagiographiques d'Orléans, Tours et Angers*. Subsidia Hagiographica 64. Brussels: Société des Bollandistes, 1982.

———. "Le recueil de miracles de S. Martin attribué à Herberne." *Analecta Bollandiana* 95(1977): 91–100.

———. "Le recueil de miracles de S. Martin dans le manuscrit 117 de Charleville." *Analecta Bollandiana* 94(1976): 83–94.

Van Dijk, S. A. "Historical Liturgy and Liturgical Studies." *Dominican Studies* 2(1949): 161–82.

Van Doren, Rombaut, and Angelo Maria Raggi. "Odilia." In *Bibliotheca sanctorum*, 9:1110–16. 13 vols. Rome: Istituto Giovanni XXIII della Pontificia Università Lateranense, 1961–69.

Van Engen, John. "The 'Crisis of Cenobitism' Reconsidered: Benedictine Monasticism in the Years 1050–1150." *Speculum* 61(1986): 269–304.

———. *Rupert of Deutz*. Berkeley: University of California Press, 1983.

Van Gennep, Arnold. *Manuel de folklore français*. 3 vols. in 7. Paris: A. et J. Picard, 1937–58.

Vaucelle, Edgar Raphaël. *La collégiale de Saint-Martin de Tours des origines à l'avènement des Valois (397–1328)*. Tours: L. Péricat, 1907.

Vidier, Alexandre Charles Philippe. *L'historiographie à Saint-Benoît-sur-Loire et les miracles de Saint Benoît*. Paris: A. et J. Picard, 1965.

Vieillard-Troiekouroff, May. *Les monuments religieux de la Gaule d'après les oeuvres de Grégoire de Tours*. Paris: H. Champion, 1976.

———. "Le tombeau de S. Martin retrouvé en 1860." In *Mémorial de l'année martinienne M.DCCCC.LX–M.DCCCC.LXI*, 151–83. Paris: J. Vrin, 1962.

Vivier, R., and E. Millet, *Pour comprendre et visiter Tours* (Tours, 1977).

Vodola, Elisabeth. *Excommunication in the Middle Ages*. Berkeley: University of California Press, 1986.

Vogel, Cyril. "La vie quotidienne du moine en Occident à l'époque de la floraison des messes privées." In *Liturgie, spiritualité, cultures,* edited by A. M. Triacca and A. Pistoia. Conférences Saint-Serge, XXIXᵉ semaine d'études liturgiques, June 29–July 2, 1982. Rome: C. L. V. Edizioni Liturgiche, 1983.

Voigt, Karl. *Die karolingische Klosterpolitik und der Niedergang des westfränkischen Königtums: Laienäbte und Klosterinhaber*. Kirchenrechtliche Abhandlungen 90–91. Stuttgart: F. Enke, 1917.

Wallace-Hadrill, J. *The Long-Haired Kings*. London: Methuen, 1962.

———. "The Vikings in Francia." In *Early Medieval History*, 217–36. Oxford: Basil Blackwell, 1975.

Ward, Benedicta. *Miracles and the Medieval Mind: Theory, Record, and Event, 1000–1215*. Philadelphia: University of Pennsylvania Press, 1982.

Warren, W. L. *The Governance of Norman and Angevin England, 1086–1272*. Stanford: Stanford University Press, 1987.

Weinstein, Donald, and Rudolph Bell. *Saints and Society: The Two Worlds of Western Christendom, 1000–1700*. Chicago: University of Chicago Press, 1982.

Weiser, Francis X. *Handbook of Christian Feasts and Customs*. New York: Harcourt, Brace, 1952.

Weissman, Ronald. *Ritual Brotherhood in Renaissance Florence*. New York: Academic Press, 1982.

Werner, Karl Ferdinand. *Les origines*. Histoire de France 1. General editor Jean Favier. Paris: Fayard, 1984.

———. "Untersuchungen zur Frühzeit des französischen Fürstentums." *Welt als Geschichte* 18(1958): 256–89.

White, Stephen D. *Custom, Kinship, and Gifts to Saints: The Laudatio Parentum in Western France, 1050–1150*. Chapel Hill: University of North Carolina Press, 1988.

Williams, George H. *Wilderness and Paradise in Christian Thought*. New York: Harper and Row, 1962.

Wilmart, André. "Une riposte de l'ancien monachisme au manifeste de Saint Bernard." *Révue Bénédictine* 46(1934): 296–344.

Wollasch, Joachim. "Ein cluniacensisches Totenbuch aus der Zeit Abt Hugos von Cluny." *Frühmittelalterliche Studien* 1(1967): 406–43.

———. *Synopse der cluniacensischen Necrologien*. 2 vols. Munich: Wilhelm Fink, 1982.

———. "Die Überlieferung cluniacensischen Totengedächtnisses." *Frühmittelalterliche Studien* 1(1967): 389–401.

Wood, Erika Laquer. "The Politics of Sanctity: The Thirteenth-Century Legal Dispute about St. Eloi's Relics." Ph.D. diss., University of Pennsylvania, 1979.

Young, Karl. *The Drama of the Medieval Church.* 2 vols. Oxford: Clarendon Press, 1933.

Index

Odo II, count of Blois, 19n, 20, 68–70, 97, 103
Omont, Henri, 301n
Ong, Walter, 146n, 181n
Oury, Guy-Marie, 31n, 40n, 68n, 76n, 101n, 124n, 125n, 153n, 166n, 171n, 172n, 191n, 193n, 226n, 247n, 274n, 310–13

paradise, image of, 185, 196–97, 221
Patin, J.-P. Valery, 124n
peace: monastic, 184–85; urban, 195–96, 276–78, 286
Péan Gatineau, 53n, 171n, 192n, 208n, 230n, 243n, 268, 271n, 279–84, 295, 315–17
Penco, Gregorio, 60n
Perpetuus, bishop of Tours, 22–24, 224
persuasion, interest in, 91–93, 101, 106, 109–13
Peter the Venerable, abbot of Cluny, 121–24, 128, 134n, 179n
Petit-Dutaillis, Charles, 266n
Philip and Renaud, dean and treasurer of Saint-Martin, letters about the cult of Saint Martin, 53, 195–97, 210, 223–24, 228–30, 232–34, 268, 270n, 272n, 274n, 285–86, 289n
Pietri, Luce, 22n, 23n, 24n
Plat, Gabriel, 314
Poly, Jean-Pierre, 1n
prebends, canonical, 191n, 202–3
Prévost, Arthur, 125n
Prinz, Friedrich, 16n, 24n, 29n
purgatory, purgatorial punishments, 105–9, 114–16, 135–36, 141, 147
Pycke, Jacques, 192n, 193n, 201n, 202n, 209n, 215n

Radbod, bishop of Utrecht, 31–34, 51, 80, 84, 208, 210
Radding, Charles M., 113n
Raggi, Angelo Maria, 293n
Rainey, Ronald E., 200n·
Ralph (I) of Langeais, archbishop of Tours, 43–47
Ralph (II) of Orléans, archbishop of Tours, 43, 47–49
Randoin, Bernard, 17–18, 19n
Ranger, Terence, 4n
Reames, Sherry, 241n
rebirth or renewal, images of, 174–79, 182, 287, 290–95
relics, disputes about, 12, 27–28, 58–60, 277
Remensnyder, Amy, 1n, 2n
residency, at Saint-Martin, 202–3

Restoration of Marmoutier, The. See Liber de restructione Majoris monasterii
Reynolds, Susan, 211n
Riché, Pierre, 20n
Robin, Françoise, 301n
Robinet, André, 67n, 216n, 302n
rogation processions, 52, 256
Rosenwein, Barbara, 36n, 68n, 71n, 81n, 119n
Rosof, Patricia J. F., 101n

Said, Edward, 152n
Saint-Cosme, house of regular canons near Tours, 193, 221, 245–53, 256–57
Saint-Julian, Benedictine abbey in Tours, 30, 31, 41, 48, 220n, 253n, 255–57
Saint-Martin, struggles with archbishop of Tours, 245, 247, 249–51. *See also* abbess; abbot; exemption, monastic
Saint Martin's Return from Burgundy. See De reversione beati Martini a Burgundia tractatus
Saint-Pierre-le-Puellier, house of canons in Tours, 245–47, 249–51, 256–57
Saint-Venant, house of canons in Tours, 245–52, 256–57
Saxer, Victor, 181n
Schmitt, Jean-Claude, 2n, 138n, 148n, 287n
Schmitz, Philibert, 119n, 120n
Semmler, Josef, 68n, 119n, 161n, 191n
sermons, from Marmoutier, 125–27, 173
Seven Sleepers of Marmoutier. See Historia septem dormientium (Majoris monasterii)
Sigal, Pierre-André, 1n, 271n, 273n, 274n, 275n, 283n
Silvestre, Hubert, 181n
Sot, Michel, 159n, 164n
Southern, Sir Richard, 4n, 67n, 71n, 76n, 85n, 88n, 104n, 105n, 113n, 115n, 132n, 152n, 166n, 181n, 182n, 283n
Spiegel, Gabrielle, 1n, 81n, 82n, 85n, 164n, 182n
Stancliffe, Clare, 14n, 16n, 19n, 21n, 22n, 24n
Stephen, count of Blois, 69, 100
Stock, Brian, 81n, 146n, 180n, 181n
Strayer, Joseph, 111n
Sulpicius Severus, 14n, 16n, 19, 21–22, 26–27, 142, 242, 288

Talbot, C. H., 121n
Teetaert, Amédée, 104n
Tentler, Thomas, 104n
Theban martyrs. *See* Maurice, Saint
Theotolus, archbishop of Tours, 30–31, 314

Library of Congress Cataloging-in-Publication Data

Farmer, Sharon A.
    Communities of Saint Martin : legend and ritual in medieval Tours
    / Sharon Farmer.
        p.   cm.
    Includes bibliographical references and index.
    ISBN 0-8014-2391-0 (alk. paper)
    1. Martin, Saint, Bishop of Tours, ca. 316-397—Cult—France—
Tours.   2. Basilique Saint-Martin de Tours—History.   3. Marmoutier
(Abbey : Tours, France)—History.   4. Tours (France)—Church
history.   I. Title.   II. Title: Communities of St. Martin.
BX1533.T69F37   1991
282'.44545'0902—dc20   90-43451